YO-AEE-825

THE BROKEN REBEL

THE BROKEN REBEL

A STUDY IN CULTURE, POLITICS, AND AUTHORITARIAN CHARACTER

Rupert Wilkinson

HARPER & ROW, PUBLISHERS

New York, Evanston, San Francisco, London

1817

THE BROKEN REBEL. Copyright © 1972 by Rupert Wilkinson. All rights reserved. Printed in the United States of America. No part of this book may be used or reproduced in any manner whatsoever without written permission except in the case of brief quotations embodied in critical articles and reviews. For information address Harper & Row, Publishers, Inc., 10 East 53rd Street, New York, N.Y. 10022. Published simultaneously in Canada by Fitzhenry & Whiteside Limited, Toronto.
FIRST EDITION
STANDARD BOOK NUMBER: 06-014660-5
LIBRARY OF CONGRESS CATALOG CARD NUMBER: 70-156557

Designed by Sidney Feinberg

CONTENTS

	Foreword	vii
1.	INTRODUCTION	1

PART I: AUTHORITARIAN CHARACTER

2.	PORTRAIT AND CONCEPT	15
3.	AN AUTHORITARIAN "SYNDROME"	20
4.	THE INNER STRUCTURE	30
5.	DEFINITION AND DETECTION: SOME PROBLEMS	39

PART II: CAUSES

6.	CHILDHOOD PRESSURES	51
7.	BEYOND THE FAMILY	63
8.	FLUX AND DISRUPTION	67
9.	PURITAN CREEDS	89
10.	A GENERAL THEORY OF CAUSE	103

PART III: CHARACTER TYPES AND POLITICAL APPEALS

11. RIGID REBELS AND THE "LIBERAL" AUTHORITARIAN — 115
12. POLITICAL APPEALS — 137

PART IV: NAZI GERMANY

13. THE FOLLOWERS — 151
14. THE EXECUTIVES — 163
15. ADOLF HITLER — 196
16. CULTURE, CHARACTER, AND POLITICS — 206

PART V: RECENT AMERICA

17. THE WHITE SOUTH — 225
18. OTHER SETTINGS — 241

EPILOGUE

AUTHORITARIANISM AND THE FUTURE — 270

APPENDIXES

APPENDIX A: CHARACTER AND CULTURAL CONFLICT: TWO COLLEGE STUDENTS — 295
APPENDIX B: LUTHER AND CROMWELL — 313

Notes — 321
Bibliography — 365
Index — 381

FOREWORD

This book has some hard things to say about the work from which it draws so much. It is doubly important therefore to acknowledge my immense debt to the many thoughts and findings embodied in *The Authoritarian Personality* by Theodore Adorno, Else Frenkel-Brunswik, Daniel Levinson, and Nevitt Sanford.[1] It must be said, however, that *The Authoritarian Personality* is not the only source of our notion of authoritarian character. Henry Fielding in 1747, both in his portrait of Deborah Wilkins and as a general phenomenon, described vividly the basic links between the authoritarian's submissiveness and wish to tyrannize. A century later, still well before Freud, Samuel Butler depicted much the same character in Theobald Pontifex. My own coming to the subject partly reflects a boyhood in British boarding schools, followed by RAF conscription. Long before reading any psychology—or even Fielding or Butler!—I had sensed a difference between the well-integrated "military man," who took orders happily and dished them out likewise, and a person whose more extreme need to submit demanded cruel and desperate compensations. In defining authoritarian character rather simply, in terms of feelings about *authority*, my model is thus "psychodynamic" but not very "psychoanalytic" in the full Freudian sense.[2]

Although my primary intent is to explore authoritarian character in relation to society, a recurring theme in the book, a sort of counterpoint to the main argument, is a concern about the use of psychological terms for covert moral and political ends, for both attack and defense beneath an umbrella of scholarly analysis (see especially the first and last chapters.) "Authoritarianism" is only one of many terms used in this manner and with varying degrees of glibness. I am not the first to point out this phenomenon, but I believe that its sources are more complex than past criticisms have indicated. It involves not only conceptions of psychopathology, illness, and weakness, but the sociology of professionalism and science and the nature of moral authority in its dependence on the nonexplicit. A short sequel to this book, exploring the subject more fully, is being planned.

The initial conception of this work owes much to Nevitt Sanford, and so does the basic description of authoritarian character. For various kinds of help I am grateful to Craig Comstock, Fred Greenstein, Marie Jahoda, and Bessie White. I am also grateful to Richard Christie for his generous comments and constructive criticisms.

RUPERT WILKINSON

January, 1971
Middletown, Connecticut

THE BROKEN REBEL

1 INTRODUCTION*

This book mixes old and new perspectives on the concept of authoritarian character. "Authoritarianism" is used here in a fairly narrow psychological sense. It denotes a particular ambivalence about authority, involving maladjustments within the personality and unconscious feelings of weakness. Authoritarian people have a strong desire both to submit and to attack, and they have a stifled rebelliousness which they have unconsciously diverted, expressing much of their hostility against people seen as deviants, inferiors, or weaklings.[1]

This book has two main purposes. First, to refocus attention on the inner workings of authoritarian character—on its *psychodynamic* core—and to do so in a language intelligible to the interested layman. By "psychodynamics" is here meant the largely unconscious, emotional forces of a person's character and the way he or she controls and channels them. The seminal work, *The Authoritarian Personality,* did not treat these aspects in a manner very accessible to lay readers, and few subsequent writings on authoritarianism have paid much attention to them.

The second, more important purpose is to relate these inner workings

---

* Notes of particular importance or general interest are marked with asterisks or other symbols and printed at the foot of text pages. The rest, mainly more technical qualifications or elaborations, are numbered and printed in a section of Notes, beginning on page 321. Fuller details of works briefly cited in all notes are in the Bibliography (p. 365).

of authoritarian character to social environment and political movements, and in doing so to illustrate the complex relationship between a man's character and the culture about him. By "culture" is simply meant those attitudes and procedures learned and shared through membership in a community. We all know that people tend to act differently in different societies—in part because of the situations they have to deal with and in part because of the cultural attitudes and ways of doing things that they learn. But what I would like to emphasize is the extent to which people act differently in different societies because of the way their societies and cultures induce them to regard and deal with *themselves*—in short, the social and cultural impress upon the individual fabrics of personality. As much as possible, therefore, we shall apply the authoritarian concept to *specific individuals in* varied but specific cultural and historical contexts. I do not believe that this twin focus—on the psychodynamic and on the cultural—has been used before in any detail to study authoritarian cases in a range of situations.[2]

Before we preview our theme at more length, some explanatory comments must be made on the book which stimulated this one. *The Authoritarian Personality* was published two decades ago. It was based on studies of strongly anti-Semitic Americans in the 1940s. From this material the authors produced the complex picture of a submissive-aggressive character type, a "pre-fascist" personality, predisposed to a whole roster of intolerant, punitive, and fearful attitudes. Perhaps the book's greatest contribution was to show how a person's general ideology, his attitudes and beliefs about all kinds of things, might reflect his *psychodynamics*—the largely unconscious, emotional forces of his character and the way he controls and channels them.

Within a short time *The Authoritarian Personality* had become one of the most referred-to books in American psychology. In the parlance of behavioral scientists and their student apprentices, "authoritarianism" acquired new connotations and a special importance. Psychology courses using the concept, often in the context of ethnic relations, proliferated. So did monographs and dissertations, most of them very technical works dealing with uses of the famous "F scale" questionnaire (F for "fascistic" character) designed by the authors of *The Authoritarian Personality* to measure their subjects' authoritarian tendencies. Some of these works were extremely critical of the authors' methods and biases, but their strictures, on balance, seemed to fan academic interest in the subject.

The remarkable thing in all this is that *The Authoritarian Personality* is hardly a book. Its 976 pages of text (in the hardcover edition) consist of a collection of papers bundled together in little apparent order. Among the many friends and colleagues whom I have heard refer to the book's ideas, I know few who have read it cover to cover.

Another point about the work is that the authors never really defined their subject. They did not always make it clear whether they meant by "authoritarianism" a type of outlook on others and the world, a personality structure of emotional needs and unconscious defenses, or a specific combination of the two.[3] Owing to their psychoanalytic position, the authors appeared to assume that almost any manifestation of authoritarian attitudes reflected authoritarianism in the deeper sense, an inner pathology of conflicts and complexes. The result was a smear effect, which, at least on the conversational plane, acquired some influence among behavioral scientists, including many who did not consider themselves friends of psychoanalysis. In some academic circles, to call a right-wing politician, or an autocratic school administrator, or an overpunctilious colleague an authoritarian was not simply to *say* that he was mean, but (more devastating) to *imply* that he was sick.

This raises further issues which must be dealt with in any proper consideration of *The Authoritarian Personality* and its legacy. Its smear potential did not just reside in verbal vagueness and intellectual ambiguity. The work itself was stimulated by political and moral animus. Started in World War II, it represented largely a Jewish liberal intellectual response to anti-Semitic Nazism ("it must not happen here"); it also represented an academic counterattack upon American bigotries and anti-intellectualism, and a left-wing antipathy (never closely argued) to the allegedly dehumanizing effects of capitalist values and industrial organization.* The tools of dissection thus concealed the weapons of defense and attack. From a scholar's standpoint it would be silly to say that this should never have happened; one cannot ignore the fact that moral animus may inspire insight and furnish intellectual energy. But it would be equally silly to ignore the political biases which

---

* With the exception of Sanford, Jewish scholars, including émigrés from Hitler's Germany, were largely responsible for the work, and it was sponsored by the American Jewish Committee. Psychoanalysis itself was banned as a "Jewish science" by the German Congress of Psychology in 1933; on the other side of the hill, the Allied Control commission used a psychoanalytic concept of authoritarianism for a brief spell after World War II to screen from public office Germans of "fascist temperament," whether or not they had been Nazis. The concept was developed and applied by British psychiatrists independently of Adorno *et al.*, but was much the same as the latter's. See Money-Kyrle, 1951, pp. 9-11.

have continued to affect application of the theory. Like many behavioral scientists, academic psychologists tend to espouse liberal, rationalist, and fairly egalitarian ideologies and they are often prepared to use their expert knowledge to discredit those values and styles which they happen to dislike. Thus, some investigators of authoritarianism—especially the more psychoanalytic—have regarded spontaneity and flexibility as both healthy and virtuous, and have deprecated "intolerance of ambiguity" in all individuals save those who reject ambiguity in holding leftish or liberal values. It is true that authoritarians do tend to be rigid and intolerant; but so do many others who in virtually no sense are greatly maladjusted and who are not particularly submissive-aggressive. Psychological writers, who sometimes equate asceticism with masochism and a cultural narrow-mindedness with anxious self-constriction, can underestimate the extent to which quite well-adjusted and secure persons may hold illiberal views because that was the morality they learned from authoritative sources and because it endorses social and economic interests.

More recently, too, among *sociological* critics of American culture, it has become fashionable to practice subtle denigration by attributing the anxieties of the conservative and the intolerances of the "hard hat" to an adamant denial of the individual's own doubts and a repressed envy, vehemently denied, of the supposedly spontaneous rebel. In some cases this *may* be true—especially when it is a person's own children who challenge his values—but evidence is seldom cited. Today's newish-left sociologist is often not above psychologizing, but he is above individual cases. It follows, then, that the authoritarian type can be made a psychiatric scapegoat for much more of man's cruelty and intolerance than in fact it is responsible for. I do not wish to add to this liability. Even among people whose hatreds reflect deep fears and frustrations, the authoritarian is but one of many kinds; and I, for one, am appalled by the amount of human destruction that has been caused by leaders and followers whose characters seem in no sense to be either barbarous or very sick.

While on one plane stimulating a psychological moralizing, *The Authoritarian Personality* on another plane stimulated research of a largely pedestrian sort. Systematic followup work on authoritarianism has shown two remarkable deficiencies. It has left out most of personality; and it has ignored discussion of society except in superficial terms. In saying that it "left out most of personality" I mean that it largely omitted deep emotional aspects of character—the psychodynamic.

Nearly all the research relied on attitude questionnaires; and unlike the original work reported in *The Authoritarian Personality* the questionnaire approach was rarely combined with depth interviews and tests designed to tap fantasy.[4] Although the research is supposed to be about people, it has seldom produced case studies of individual persons; but then even *The Authoritarian Personality* contains only one real case study of an individual deemed authoritarian.[5] The outcome is that psychologists writing on authoritarianism have increasingly defined it (when they bother to define it at all) in *cognitive* terms, as a certain way of consciously looking at oneself and the world. Perhaps this is partly because academics are themselves in the business of knowing and perceiving; presumably it is also because attitudes and ideology are easier to detect and measure in large numbers of people than are fine nuances of feeling and desire. In many writings, "authoritarianism" has become synonymous with dogmatism, prejudice, rigid conventionalism, and closed-mindedness about self; the idea of a punitive, submissive person who craves a scapegoat is sometimes mentioned but with less force and frequency. In the original work, it was postulated that all these traits went together, but the emphasis has now changed, and in changing, the concept of authoritarianism has lost depth and dimension—the notion of underlying pathology often remains, but it is not explored.*

The second great deficiency of the research is that it has virtually ignored the relationship between character and social environment. In *The Authoritarian Personality* the authors attributed the formation of character chiefly to patterns of child rearing, and in general terms they allowed that social and economic circumstances would in turn shape these patterns. They also argued that some political climates would be more encouraging than others to the overt *expression* of authoritarian attitudes. But these general statements did not lead to any specific investigation of social and historical factors. Within America, it is true, studies using the F scale questionnaire have established that people in certain social groups and sections of the country tend more to endorse "authoritarian" attitudes than people in other groups and sections. This is not a remarkable finding, and the same studies have never tried

---

* In applying the medical metaphor "pathology" to our authoritarian concept, I do so in a primarily *intrapsychic* sense. That is to say, I would consider authoritarianism pathological, or a disorder, because it involves (1) conflicts "within the soul" (dis-ease); (2) anxieties about self which are not simply the direct response to a continuing stressful situation but which have acquired a momentum of their own.

to investigate causes. If students in Houston tend to "score higher" than students in Bridgeport on a scale measuring authoritarian ideology, is this (1) because Houston society has indoctrinated *many* kinds of personality, including some of its most secure and well-integrated, with authoritarian attitudes; (2) because it has made authoritarian ideology respectable to those individuals who have emotional dispositions to it but might otherwise have remained "latent" authoritarians; (3) because it has created those very dispositions, by laying stresses and pressures upon the basic personality? Some of the F scale studies pay lip service to *some* of these distinctions, but none of them tries to meet the question by showing precisely how several or all of the factors may be combined.[6]

A PREVIEW

The first part of this book describes the authoritarian as a character type. It seeks to bring out the psychodynamic pith of the concept, without omitting those aspects of attitude and behavior which appear to go with the authoritarian's distinctive emotional structure. Throughout the book little use is made of studies employing the F scale and other questionnaires, for we seldom know how much they can detect psychodynamic traits as opposed to merely learned attitudes, or an outlook reflecting other types of personality. Although the first part of the book is not claimed to be greatly original, it reformulates and explores certain aspects of the "authoritarian" concept—for instance, the idea of vicious circles within personality, and various problems of definition and detection.[7]

The second part looks at the familial and social genesis of authoritarian character. First, it reformulates, qualifies, and adds to the notions about child rearing presented in *The Authoritarian Personality*. Then it considers some social circumstances and cultural traditions which appear to foment authoritarianism on many levels of character, in part by affecting the behavior of parents. The last chapter of this part binds these factors together in a general theory of cause. In many cases (by no means all), authoritarianism seems to be a reaction to social flux and disruption, in favor of represssive doctrines which offer themselves as an antidote to the specters of social chaos and threat. On unconscious levels, authoritarianism provides a way of squelching the sense of conflict caused by contradictory messages received from the surrounding society. When values of toughness and "control" clash with values of tenderness and sensual freedom, the authoritarian response is to make extreme alignment with the former against the latter. But this is only liable to happen when parents or other agencies make the individual feel weak and then encourage him to compensate through harsh identification with authority. According to this view of authoritarianism, physical needs, emotional forces, imitation of others, the learning of specific attitudes and roles, and the exigencies of the moment all affect each other and affect behavior. Likewise, individual psychodynamics both affect and reflect *culture,* though they also are shaped by the specific way in which parents and other agencies pass on cultural pressures to the individual.[8]

Part III of the book deals with the relationship between character types and the psychological appeals of political and social doctrines. At the outset a distinction is made between left-wing authoritarians and "rigid rebels." It is true that in many ways, emotional as well as ideological, the two can be alike; and this part describes some important personality combinations of authoritarian and anti-authoritarian, embracing the overtly liberal as well as the revolutionary. In general, though, I still contend that the distinction is crucial in considering the appeal of political doctrines to authoritarian character. I would suggest that many so-called "authoritarians of the left" are better described as rigid rebels, rigid *anti*-authoritarians, on a deep level of personality as well as in their overt ideology. The main argument here is a fairly old-fashioned one: that strongly right-wing doctrines, including "fascism," have more to offer authoritarians psychologically than other beliefs. This statement, however, cannot stand alone, even as a hypothesis. For one thing it requires a careful definition of "fascism," "right wing," and the "radical right." It also demands some thought about motifs common to these doctrines—"strength," "order," and "purity," for example—and the way in which these concerns seem to connect with each other and with character on more than one level. I do not thereby mean that all authoritarians are right wingers, or that the right-wing appeal to authoritarians is purely psychodynamic. It will be suggested that some of the cultural milieus which tend to produce authoritarian personalities also foster right-wing views in a *variety* of characters. Thus, by their very location in society, many authoritarians will be exposed to right-wing views presented authoritatively by others. They will be well placed for their authoritarian feelings to find expression in right-wing beliefs: this expression, therefore, will be the result of opportunity and exposure as well as emotional need.

In the fourth part of the book we apply these ideas to Nazi Germany. The resort to various concepts of authoritarian character as a way of understanding Nazi behavior is not new, yet to my knowledge only two pioneer works have related theories of authoritarianism to specific individuals.[9] Since that time new material on leading Nazis has been produced, and we are now in a position to explore further the complex relationship between Nazism, authoritarian character, and German society and culture. In Joseph Goebbels, for instance, we shall see how authoritarian psychodynamics provided a way of coping—albeit shakily—with conflicting values, and impelled him toward an infatuation with Hitler. We will also trace the workings of culture and emotion in some low-rung Nazi followers. The trick here is to focus on authoritarian character as a Nazi bastion while meticulously opposing the idea that Nazism simply sprang from personality needs and that it depended on just one type of individual.

In our study of Nazi leaders and executives we must take up issues that involve the very nature of evil. How do men bring themselves to carry out cold-blooded atrocities? What happens to them when they do it? Heinrich Himmler, Rudolph Hoess,[10] Hans Frank—men involved in the mass exterminations—were neither monsters nor brutalized automatons. In some spheres they were humane men. Complicated but not incomprehensible, they were conscientious executives of the state, timid yet ambitious, unknowingly propelled by reserves of savagery, yet revolted by what they "had" to do. In differing ways, their authoritarianism helped to bring them to their predicament; it then provided mechanisms for suppressing and diverting some of their doubts. To put these matters in proper perspective, we must consider the whole question of brutality versus scruple. As a set of psychological processes, authoritarianism of course represents but one of many ways in which a person's humane feeling may be prevented from curbing cruelty.

The case of Adolf Hitler raises its own issues. With regard to the mass exterminations, he was too entrenched in sadism and special hatreds to show much need to suppress qualms. Yet the concept of authoritarianism seems to apply to his case, too. He was not as free from submissiveness as may be supposed, and he was not beyond using fierce declarations of doctrine to divert some of his doubts. This perspective on Hitler stimulates questions about the historical influence of a powerful leader's personality. At what points and in what sense can one say that Hitler's temperament had a decisive effect on events, and how much of this can be attributed to authoritarian processes?

Firm answers to such questions we cannot give, but we can make a beginning, and in doing so, we can say something about the relation of personality factors to social factors in a train of history.

The last part of the book considers authoritarianism in American society and ways of limiting it in the future. We begin with the white South. It is the only section of the American people to provide evidence that authoritarianism (as defined here) has been an important factor in its social and political life. As in Germany, much of its authoritarianism has appeared to be the product of social creeds whose harsh requirements of the individual (white as well as black) reflected a moral insecurity, a contradiction by other values. The important clue lies not in racial prejudice per se, but in the defensive, even guilty nature of that prejudice, and its ties with sadism, sexual ambivalence, and brittle puritanism. In this study of the South, as in our general treatment of the authoritarian personality in America, we will not seek absolute topicality. Almost none of our material dates beyond the mid-1960s— we have no evidence that either Wallaceites or Black Power militants have tended to be authoritarian in the clinical sense used here. Looking back across recent decades in America, we will study some personal situations in which authoritarianism does seem to have emerged, and then relate these to our general theory of social and cultural causation. In the last chapter, we look to the future in Western society as a whole, paying particular attention to the authority of science and pseudo-science and the rise of new forms of covertly moralizing aggression. We end by considering a few ways in which social policy might reduce the pressures which seem to foment not only authoritarian but other psychopathologies.

Despite the use of case portraits, this work focuses upon an abstraction, not upon individuals but upon a *category* of individuals. The case studies are presented merely to show how the concept fits real people, and in what circumstances. The problems and biases involved in using "authoritarianism" this way, to denote a *type* of personality, are discussed in subsequent chapters; but something more general must be said here about the use and misuse of psychological concepts and categories when these are presented in the abstract. Like almost any theory about people, they can become a sort of intellectual game, generating their own logic and plausibility, supported by snippets from real lives, yet seldom applied to individuals whom the "player" knows well in the round (much less applied to himself.)[11] As it happens, my collection of case studies does include self-portraits in authoritarian terms; even so, as a way of learning about people, the approach taken in this book can only complement those novels, biographies, and clinical studies which focus directly and perceptively on individuals and their backgrounds, and are governed by no one concept or set of categories. It must be noted, however, that some portraiture of individuals can seem very fluid on the surface while covertly depending on a few rigid notions about human nature. In this work we at least have our categories out in the open; having stated them, we can then blur their edges by describing anomalies and borderline cases. But the main advantage of this approach—delineating a specific character type—is that it gives us a clearly defined psychological entity, a set of emotional processes, which we can systematically relate to social environment and modes of political expression. This searching for patterns and relationships is, of course, the scholar's function, the ordering of experience so that it is comprehensible; but again a warning must be sounded. In our craving for security, we academics, like other mortals, sometimes settle for spurious order; we file away experience in a neat row of pigeonholes; we entertain beautiful schemes to end all puzzlement. In this there is the scholar's aesthetic: the creative blended with the imperial, the wish to see patterns but also to impose them upon a universe. Insight and distortion may go together; indeed the shaft of a concept may penetrate by its own partiality.

All these considerations apply to the readers of theoretical works as well as their writers, for the play of ideas obviously depends on the way they are received no less than on the way they are presented. (The reader rewrites the book.) I mention these things not to dump my own responsibility for the truth, but to limit that responsibility by asking that the authoritarian concept be treated as a perspective rather than a giant and comforting explanation.

The sources used in this book are extremely varied. I have drawn from several kinds of psychological and anthropological studies, from biographies, and from other historical and political materials. Although a nucleus of the research consists of first-hand observation and an analysis of interview tapes, we shall consider at length many accounts by others which do not explicitly deal with authoritarian character. Marion Starkey on the Salem witch accusers, Davis and Dollard on New Orleans blacks, Robert Coles on Southern whites—these and other writers, journalists as well as psychologists, cannot be ignored if we are to find our subject and trace its social relations. One reason why this book is so long is my belief that a work of this sort must rest its arguments on a backbone of case studies, and these always take space. As it is, some critics will argue that a proper psychiatric report on a person requires more elbowroom for detail than can usually be provided here, in a review of many societies and individuals. But, even if we had more room for individual analysis and portraiture, by scientific standards many of the inferences made would be far short of conclusive. One difficulty, for instance, is the matter of deciding what different figures and alignments mean to the personality in question. Consider a hypothetical case—a young instructor who identifies vehemently with a group of militant students engaged in semiviolent attacks on their professors and administration. His identification *might* reflect a deep wish to side with rebels and the oppressed against authority; or it might reflect a more authoritarian wish to immerse himself in a new, strident power against "wishy-washy" liberal professors symbolizing a weakness and gentleness which he really despises. It might reflect neither of these things; or, on different levels of attitude and feeling, it might reflect both. A look at the instructor's attitudes in other spheres would perhaps help answer the question, but here too the same ambiguities could exist.

It will be seen from this that objective tests, such as questionnaires, or exercises performed by the subject under experimental conditions, are usually crude devices when it comes to detecting a complex and deeply laid pattern like authoritarianism. On the other hand, more sensitive tests—exhaustive interviews, examination of a person's fantasies, or close observation over time—may suffer from the investigator's bias, and suffer in ways which are hard to allow for. Intensive interview studies, moreover, seldom examine great numbers of people; the time and funds needed to study each person discourage it. As we move among the different studies, I will try to indicate how good I think the evidence is—whether it is fairly conclusive, merely suggestive, or something between.[12]

A special word is needed on the treatment of historical figures. Some scholars doubt that historical biographies can shed much light on a personality's unconscious processes. My answer is that it depends on the biography. Some accounts are revealing, especially when they include first-hand observations by contemporaries and are accompanied by the subject's own statements, diaries, and so forth. The deceased subject is no different from the living in that the inner workings of his personality—his emotional makeup—can only be inferred from what he has said and done. (After all, one cannot perceive emotions directly except in oneself.) This is not to claim that history provides conclusive evidence on character structure. One reason why I have used historical matter is to see what place authoritarianism may have had in past ages, and how it has been involved in social change.[13]

It must be stressed that this book is no comprehensive substitute for *The Authoritarian Personality*. That work, for example, makes many psychoanalytic inferences which we shall barely touch upon, in part because of the limitations of our material. As it is, some will say, no doubt, that the material is "overinterpreted"; but then others will say it is "underinterpreted." Nor should this simply mean that more Freudian categories should be added to our explanations. Transcending the orthodoxies of psychoanalysis, it seems to me that the human soul has a diversity to which human behavior is a bottleneck. The tendency of an individual action to reflect many motives within the individual, and the propensity of a form of behavior for expressing different motivations from different individuals, indicate a general poverty of social and behavioral forms compared with the richness—happy or unhappy—of the unconscious spirit, even including the much-repressed spirit of the archetype authoritarian. This is true perhaps in all societies. In part it may reflect the dependence of social cooperation on the limiting of behavioral alternatives and hence a fairly narrow overt channeling of desires. But it may also reflect the ease of unconscious or semiconscious feeling compared with its translation into highly individualized action, and the sheer convenience of letting one action or form of expression do more than one emotional job for the individual.

PART I

AUTHORITARIAN CHARACTER

2 PORTRAIT AND CONCEPT

> It might have been better if Theobald in his younger days had kicked more against his father; the fact that he had not done so encouraged him to expect the most implicit obedience from his own children.

So wrote Samuel Butler in his autobiographical novel, *The Way of All Flesh*, about the Reverend Theobald Pontifex. But then George Pontifex, Theobald's father, was not the easiest of men to kick against. He thrashed his children several times a week, a little oftener than his neighbors beat their children; nor was this his chief oppression. From yeoman origins George Pontifex had made himself a successful man of affairs, and he carried his wish to exploit and manipulate into his own home. He knew to a fine art how to get people to do what he wanted them to do, by developing their self-doubt. In the case of Theobald, the task was not difficult, for Theobald had an elder brother beside whom he felt incompetent and awkward. George Pontifex wanted his younger son to enter the church, and enter the church he did—although there was a short period when the young man resisted the plan, believing from a devious letter of his father's that he had been set free to make his own choice. A second letter from his "troubled" father, threatening to cut off his allowance, made matters plain.

After his ordination, so Butler tells us, Theobald led a rather restricted life as a college fellow. He disliked most of the arts, and he felt unsuccessful with the ladies at university parties. Yet he admired himself for his academic success, and for a certain pure virtue marred only by a fitful temper. His temper was not to be observed by such strong characters as the masculine Mrs. Cowey, wife of the eminent

Professor Cowey and an energetic college hostess. It was largely through Mrs. Cowey's managing and conniving that he met Christina Allaby, the daughter of a nearby vicar with a large family. For women as a whole Theobald felt dislike mixed with a fear, but after many months—and some thinly veiled pressure from the Reverend Allaby—Theobald tepidly proposed, and was accepted. It took time for Theobald's father to accept the engagement: the Allabys' poverty was an affront. George Pontifex wrote a courteously cruel letter to Theobald, a missive so denigrating that its recipient could not really think about it. Years afterward,

his sense of wrong was still inarticulate, felt as a dull, dead pressing weight over present day by day, and if he woke at night still continually present, but he hardly knew what it was. . . . He was by nature secretive, and had been repressed too much and too early to be capable of railing or blowing off steam where his father was concerned.

At the very start of their marriage, indeed the first evening, Theobald bullied his bride to do wifely chores; and when she complied, he felt great relief that he was not to be henpecked. After the honeymoon, the couple settled down to the routine of a parsonage. Theobald was a conscientious rector, but when he visited sick parishioners, he was too constricted to give much comfort. Toward his children he was a hard man, using the rod when they seemed slow to learn the Lord's Prayer or Confession. He was particularly bad-tempered on Sunday evenings, for of course the rector's duties did not sit easily upon him. It was on one such evening that a bewildered little Ernest was thrashed and sent to bed supperless: being "self-willed and naughty," he would persist in saying "tum" instead of "come." Later events suggested that Theobald did not love his children as much as he supposed he did, but then he did not really love himself. As it was, he believed he was in more danger of being overly indulgent to his children than excessively severe. The natural instincts of childhood stood for anarchy and competition.

He remained greatly in awe of his father; visits to the paternal home made him feel quite weak about the knees, although, once safely away from the scene, it was some compensation to talk of his father's distinguished acquaintances. And always there was the admiring Christina to convince him that he was master in his own home. Christina was also useful in making difficult confrontations. When the son, Ernest, was an adolescent, and the attractive little servant girl became pregnant, it was not surprising that both parents should suspect Ernest—quite wrongly as it turned out—or that Christina should be the one to try wheedling the truth out of him. But later on, when the subject of Ernest's career came up, it was Christina who sat him down on the couch and told him, hastily and vaguely, that before entering the Church he must understand the doubts and difficulties of a clergyman's life. Lip service thus paid to Theobald's own unhappiness, the matter was swiftly dropped.

When Ernest came back from the university, he was full of evangelicalism. His father, a very orthodox Anglican, appeared to enjoy squashing him.

Theobald hated the Church of Rome, but he hated [Protestant] dissenters too, for he found them as a general rule troublesome people to deal with; he always found people who did not agree with him troublesome to deal with; besides, they set up for knowing as much as he did.

Theobald's position did not simply reflect the ideas of Victorian upper-middle-class orthodoxy; they expressed an anxious intolerance and a vague sense of threat, both feelings deeply rooted in his character. Theobald's rigidity showed itself in sundry little ways besides religion. For much of his life he had a habit of whistling two tunes, the same two tunes, with the same notes left out. He also filled his speech with "tags," one of which was the comforting and mechanical "it will answer every purpose."

At the age of twenty-eight, Ernest suddenly returned home after a long estrangement; Christina was seriously ill. Theobald, expecting his son to be poor, was surprised and unsettled to behold a well-dressed young man with an air of prosperity. When Ernest explained that his aunt had left him a great inheritance, Theobald became jealous and excited. "I must know that this is all open and above board." Ernest turned on him for this, and Theobald immediately backed down, adopting a most conciliatory tone. At church the following Sunday, Ernest was surprised to discover that Theobald held a more ornate form of service than in former times. This, he subsequently learned, had been gradually and deviously foisted on Theobald by a neighboring clergyman, a strong-minded parishioner, Christina herself, and Charlotte, their daughter. After brief expostulations to his own family, Theobald had accepted the changes, but at heart he always deemed them a subversive Roman influence.

When Christina died, Theobald did not seem greatly grieved. Perhaps he kept it to himself; but he was a man in whom tender feeling and expression had long been stunted. During his last years, there was something of a rapprochement between father and son. The father would make brief visits to Ernest in London, bringing country vegetables wrapped in brown paper, though Ernest said repeatedly that he did not really want them. Theobald's letters to his son expressed—what did they express? Dependence? A muted, gruff affection? A widower's loneliness? It is very hard to say. When Theobald died, he was praised by many as a just and honorable man.

"AUTHORITARIANISM"

Being semi-fictional, Butler's portrait of Pontifex proves nothing; it is presented here mainly as an illustration.[1] The precise way in which it fits the concept of authoritarianism will become more apparent as we explore the concept in detail; it must, however, be stressed that authoritarian character can take many forms. The general type includes some of those executives described by David Ogilvy—"toadies who suck up to their bosses; they are generally the same people who bully their subordinates."[2] It explains Harold Lasswell's "Administrator H"—prudish, submissive, yet domineering.[3] It resembles the "Antisemite" described by Jean-Paul Sartre.[4] It is among the escapers from freedom described by Erich Fromm, Calvinists in a bygone age, fascists in ours.[5] And, of course, it is the central figure, dogmatic and intolerant, described in *The Authoritarian Personality*.[6] Not all of these variations are equally political. In Victorian England a man like Theobald Pontifex would have found little opportunity for political activism, and little inducement to it. But in other social settings it has been different. Many authoritarians seem to be conventional persons whose urge to punish and submit does not become very public until times of stress and fervor—the conditions of pre-fascist Germany, or the closed and fear-ridden life of Mississippi in the sixties—make hatred respectable.

In declaring that Pontifex, or any other character, was "authoritarian," I do not mean that authoritarianism explains all of his behavior. When we speak of an authoritarian *type,* we refer to a cluster of traits and attitudes shared by members of that type. These features are connected, but in no case does the type embrace the whole person, even on the level of basic temperament. Authoritarians, thus, differ in many qualities which have little to do with authoritarianism, and from some standpoints the differences may be as important as the likenesses. There are also degrees of authoritarianism; all of us, perhaps, have its fragments. The fawning of hero worship; ambivalence about power and weakness (both ours and others'); distrust of people who seem "different"; the castigation of scapegoats for varied emotional reasons—these are no monopoly of a special type. (Some of these elements, indeed, are a matter of biological instinct shared by the whole human species.) On the other hand, to say that everything is a matter of "more or less," that character differences can be reduced to a mere continuum, is itself a simplification. I shall later argue that authoritarianism is a matter of kind and not just degree, although the existence of borderline cases must be conceded. The shorthand "authoritarian" and "unauthoritarian" is valid providing one remembers that these terms cut across several diagnostic categories used by psychiatrists. For the moment we must discount the possibility that a student of authoritarianism may attribute his own traits and secret desires to his subject, thus exaggerating the difference between "authoritarians" and "us normal people," or in other ways describe the subject in an emotionally convenient fashion; but the thought should not be forgotten.

3 AN AUTHORITARIAN "SYNDROME"

In some of the earliest studies reported by *The Authoritarian Personality*, it appeared that extreme anti-Semites tended to hate not just Jews but all groups considered alien, deviant, or weak—from Mexican immigrants to the mentally ill.[1] It also appeared that a disproportionate number of anti-Semites shared a distinctive cluster of attitudes and traits. This cluster, which amounted to authoritarianism, included a fearful outlook, a marked concern with power, and repressed feelings of weakness. From psychoanalytic interviews and tests, and their own general thinking, the authors had come to believe that both the concern with power and the ethnic prejudice sprang from deep-seated conflicts and insecurities. Their conclusions thus gave some endorsement to Leo Lowenthal's memorable exaggeration: "Anti-semitism has nothing to do with Jews."[2]

The Authoritarian Personality depicted a syndrome, that is, a group of attributes that tend to go together in certain individuals. These attributes are submissiveness; punitive aggressiveness, hostility, and cynicism; extreme concern with strength; distrust of tender feelings and broad imaginings; superstitition; an outlook that sees the world in black-and-white categories; a rigid, moralistic, yet superficial conventionalism; morbid fascination with sex; and an aptitude for investing the world with evil threats.[3] As already said, it is clear from their own material that the authors exaggerated the emotional needs of their subjects, and there has been debate as to how far these attributes hang together as a character type in different populations. Nevertheless, they do seem to in some groups, and the psychodynamic theory explaining this received a measure of corroboration from a study of German POWs, done quite separately from the *Authoritarian Personality* research.[4] It has also received limited support from experimental test situations in which some individuals more than others respond with "authoritarian" types of hostility.[5]

The following dissection presents the authoritarian in extreme archetype form. The portrait has a right-wing bias, since the components are taken from the original studies by Adorno *et al.*, which focused on authoritarians showing racial prejudice. This bias, however, is largely confined to idiom. In differing forms, many if not all the nine attributes seem to apply generally to authoritarians, whether or not they hold right-wing beliefs.

SUBMISSIVENESS

Authoritarians exhibit a deep wish to yield to strong authority, especially the authority of an "in-group," be it family or nation, church or fraternity. Some authoritarians submit to human leaders; others, finding mortal man too fallible or personal subservience unacceptable in their milieu, defer mainly to doctrines and magic institutions. Above all, the authoritarian craves moral commandments that proceed very visibly and directly from an external source.

PUNITIVE AGGRESSIVENESS

Aggressiveness and hostility are not always the same thing; the former can be a relatively amicable assertion. But, for the authoritarian, aggressive feelings tend to be particularly hostile and punitive, and to explain this we must say something about how the personality is shaped— a subject dealt with more properly later. At a formative time in his life—often childhood—the authoritarian has had to make extreme submission to a domineering authority. Authoritarian aggressiveness is often an imitation of that authority, but it also offers a way of compensating for the sense of weakness engendered. And it likewise provides a way of making those assertions which the individual really wanted to make against authority. His hostility is now concentrated on anyone who can be castigated for traits he really resents in authority and for tendencies which he fears or despises in himself.

For all its ambivalence, this submissive-aggressive posture often becomes a fairly rigid pattern, a characteristic way of relating to others. As a result, the authoritarian will make sharp distinctions between people he considers part of his own group and those he calls outsiders. In his own group he seeks a father-figure authority to which he can unequivocably submit; overt hostility is turned upon those beyond the pale. To be an outsider is, by his definition, to be morally inferior. By the same token, members of his own chosen in-group—be they fellow Americans, fellow Aryans, or just fellow members of a "nice neighborhood"—are admired with anxious pride as a moral elect.

An important subcategory of authoritarian aggression is *cynicism and general hostility*. When public opinion and other circumstances deter the authoritarian from attacking specific scapegoats, he often becomes the cynic who murmurs jaundiced words about humanity in general, however smiling his everyday face. Perhaps by ascribing his own destructive urges to everyone else, the authoritarian cynic gives himself a good excuse for outright aggression when conditions permit it.

And yet, for all the aggressiveness, the authoritarian continues to feel unconscious resentment at authority itself. Since the resentment cannot be admitted, it is most often expressed in self-pity, a vague sense of victimization. When the authoritarian does attack his leaders, he often makes the assault in the name of another, more repressive authority; the attacked leaders are called traitors or interlopers. By this means he can express underlying resentments against authority, while preserving his essential submissiveness. He is also likely to attack leaders who seem "flabby" or do not command high prestige in his own milieu. In both cases, he can enjoy the kicks of rebellion without its dangers, although it must be added that authoritarians are not the only ones to make this kind of psychic deal.

POWER AND TOUGHNESS

At first sight the authoritarian's great assertion of strength looks like a cloak—a device for hiding his real sense of weakness from others and from himself. As far as it goes, this explanation is correct; but it is not the whole story. By connecting with the two other attributes of submission and aggression, the authoritarian's concern with power epitomizes his ambivalence. On the one hand, and on the deeper level, he wants to yield to external power; on the other, he longs to hold power himself and assert it aggressively against others.

These two sides of power-mindedness were demonstrated well by a rich California suburbanite whom Nevitt Sanford tells of visiting.[6] For the first part of the visit the host did not know that his guest was a psychologist. He rattled away like an archetype authoritarian, criticizing "those wooly-minded, softy professors" and getting in a few thinly-veiled barbs at Jews. But, when he learned his guest's occupation, his tone became deferent and modest, and he back-pedaled on his views ingratiatingly—more, it seemed, than party manners required. Yet the shift was not wholly insincere. It turned out that he classed psychologists along with psychiatrists as powerful healers rather than mere do-nothing intellectuals. Doctors of the mind fascinated him, as magicians fascinate small boys.

In many cases, the authoritarian shows his ambivalence toward power by identifying vicariously with powerful figures, or by getting close to them in the unconscious hope that some of their magic will rub off on him. Covert stratagems like these indulge the authoritarian's wish to submit, yet at the same time help him to avoid the conscious feeling of weakness which submission often brings. Instead of obviously kowtowing to power, he can tell himself that he is a part of power, as indeed he may be. Under such conditions, his submissiveness will not always be very visible.

With authoritarian women, on the other hand, it is often the power attribute which is muted, or rather disguised. In America, as in many other societies, customary standards of womanliness deter the female authoritarian from asserting herself or her views in the tough-guy way permitted men (authoritarians are often very deferent to orthodox opinion). As a consequence, authoritarian women may be apt to express their power urge more by sweet submission to authority and by identification with power than by overt aggression. Like male authoritarians they have felt compelled to repress all rebelliousness; again like the men they convert much of their repressed hostilities into aggressive feelings against outsiders; but many of them do not make this conversion to the same extent. The result is that women authoritarians may be specially marked by strong resentments and hatred which have not found any permanent target. When safe avenues for these feelings do appear, their hatreds can be released with volcanic fury.

SELF-CENSORSHIP[7]

Many authoritarians keep a tight rein on emotional and intellectual expression. They distrust spontaneity and fantasy; they tend to shun a wide exercise of aesthetic, humane, and sensual feeling; they generally dislike abstract theory and sustained intellectual questioning. This applies even to the college educated. Although some authoritarians are attracted to romantic ideas and philosophical doctrines, their attraction is usually narrow and submissive, uncomplicated by independent speculation.

Like other attributes, disinterest in "soft feelings and fancy ideas" does not by itself signify authoritarianism. For some people it may simply express a hard-headed impatience with whatever seems impractical. In the authoritarian case, however, this attitude reflects an intense need for self-censorship, which in turn is connected with submission. As we have already seen, the authoritarian often submits by repressing desire for self-assertion against authority. Self-censorship aids the process: by blocking out fantasies and speculations it helps to keep subversive thoughts below the level of consciousness. Since the individual is often attuned to a puritanical power—the kind of authority which helped shape his character in the first place—censorship may proscribe a wide range of sensual and spontaneous feeling which, if expressed, might incur that authority's wrath. Censorship also proscribes self-analysis, for this might uncover the authoritarian's sense of weakness and the loss of self-respect exacted by extreme submission.

SUPERSTITION

Despite its general ban on fantasy, the authoritarian's self-censorship mechanism does let through certain superstitions. These, in fact, assist self-censorship by removing many of the individual's circumstances from the domain of intelligent, probing thought. Through superstition, the authoritarian can blame his own shortcomings and inadequacies on primitive forces beyond his control. But this makes him all the more inclined to fear the outer world as a hostile, encircling net—or a ring of unknown giants which may yet crash everything to apocalyptic doom.

About such specters the authoritarian is ambivalent. If his superstitiousness includes fear, it also contains submission, for fate represents power. At the same time, superstition can help him to weave a mystique of his own strength and a cult of hatred for outsiders. As the race theories of Hitler demonstrated, mystic superstition and aggressive prejudice are easily entwined.

STEREOTYPES

Most authoritarians grossly oversimplify. We have already seen that they divide people into crude categories: for example, categories of power (the strong versus the weak) and categories of virtue (in-group versus deviants). The same basic tendency marks their whole outlook. Even where moral principles are not at stake, the authoritarian detests ambiguity and uncertainty; he prefers work that is sharply defined and clearly organized;[8] he craves simple solutions and obvious results. In his personal life there are few neutrals: people and causes are to him either black or white.

His longing for the definite is a direct response to feelings of weakness. He cannot stand uncertainty or complexity in the world because he is uncertain about himself. If he did not find definite things to hang on to, he would feel lost, powerless, naked. In part, then, the authoritarian's dependence on clearcut stereotypes of the world is a variation of his dependence on external power and authority. To this extent, it is merely the extreme form of a universal longing: the search of man for security, meaning, and identity.

But the authoritarian's use of stereotypes connects with weakness in a more indirect fashion, too. Like superstition, reliance on stereotypes both supports and results from the censored mind. A person who cannot permit himself fine intellectual distinctions, who unconsciously shuns sophisticated questioning lest it upset his own inner balance, will necessarily think in oversimplified categories—just as he will often resort to superstitions, mythical explanations. In fact his very use of stereotypes is frequently bound up with superstition. The most obvious example of this is authoritarian racism, in which superstitious fantasy attaches all sorts of evils and threats to a despised, stereotyped group.

These tendencies, of course, have different effects on different minds. In general, the erection of rigid stereotypes impairs the imagination, inhibits interest in new ideas, and deprives the mind of mental exercise; but it does not always clog the intelligence in every area of thought. On matters that do not seem to involve basic outlook and beliefs, authoritarians may be no less adroit intellectually than others. Even where basic beliefs are involved, some authoritarians develop a talent for nimble argument in defense of their crude premises. As for the general correlation between authoritarianism and stereotyped outlooks, this may be reduced by the fact that some kinds of anti-authoritarians, "rigid liberals," are also prone to dogmatic oversimplifying.

RIGID CONVENTIONALISM

Throughout the authoritarian's aggressiveness and hostility there runs a central streak of moralism. The morality is often what Western people think of as conventional, middle-class values—cleanliness, hard work and thrift, honesty and devout respectability. It is a conventionalism which suits the authoritarian, for it approves of self-censorship and its criterion of strength is apt to be red-blooded masculinity, not artistic refinement. Yet, unlike many "middle-class" consciences, the morality of the authoritarian is rigid rather than deep. It is "conventional" in the most literal sense of the word, for it puts minor rules and social respectability above deeply-held principles. Social orthodoxy represents a power to which the authoritarian often defers.

Even criminal offenders can show a rigid conventionalism. A San Quentin prison study, reported in *The Authoritarian Personality*, showed this well. Inmates who seemed authoritarian tended to agree strongly with such questionnaire statements as

Young people sometimes get rebellious ideas, but as they grow up they ought to get over them and settle down.
Obedience and respect for authority are the most important virtues children should learn.[9]

Other studies, too, of criminal offenders in America and Britain have noted an element of conventionalism; and among the San Quentin inmates just mentioned, many people seemed to combine a record of sudden impulsive outbreaks with an ethos of emotional repression.

Here lies one important reason why authoritarian conventionalism is so rigid. As we shall see more fully in the next chapter, the authoritarian's morality is weakly integrated with the rest of his makeup. Lacking deep roots within the personality it demands constant reinforcement from external moral authority. The result is that the authoritarian hangs on tightly to the brittle shell of his conventionalism. Any sign, either in himself or in others, that the rules are being relaxed produces unconscious fear lest the whole framework collapse, leaving him defenseless before his own impulses and isolated from his fellow men. Small wonder that he censors thoughts and feelings which might strain his fragile morality; that he attacks others for the laxness he dare not permit in himself; and that his conventionalism mixes self-censorship with cast-iron intolerant stereotypes crudely dividing mankind into the virtuous and the wicked.

The same urge, to vanquish anything which may compromise his morals, frequently causes an obsession with the conventional bourgeois values of neatness and hard work. To the authoritarian even more than to most people, neatness symbolizes order, control, discipline, a bulwark against lapses born of weakness. Hard work likewise means discipline; it also takes one's mind away from "subversive" introspection. This is not to say that conventional middle-class values are basically authoritarian; merely, that in exaggerated form they answer, without always resolving, authoritarian needs.

MORBID FASCINATION WITH SEX

Authoritarians are inclined to paint lurid but disapproving pictures of sexual goings-on, especially among despised minority groups. Repressing their own exotic desires, they may project them instead onto other people. By so doing they can enjoy sex vicariously and at the same time find in moralizing an outlet for aggression.

There are several reasons for the authoritarian's repression and projection of sexual desires. One is a lack of self-confidence that he, or she, can handle a close relationship. In many cases, particularly with male authoritarians, sexual inhibition is more easily dispelled when the relationship is purely physical and the partner is considered weak or inferior. This attitude, of course, is by no means a monopoly of authoritarians.

Sexual feeling may also be an element which the authoritarian felt he had to suppress when he first submitted to super-strict authority. On an unconscious plane, some authoritarians continue to feel that emotional spontaneity will invoke wrath from a jealous father figure. They also fear that it will shatter their precarious morality. In this, emotional inhibition merges with self-censorship and rigid conventionalism; and so the uncontrolled eruptions they fear in themselves are attributed to others.

THE THREAT COMPLEX[10]

Authoritarians tend to people their environment with all manner of threats, from dirt and disease to armed conspiracy. Some are real dangers exaggerated; others are imagined. Behind this characteristic there often seems to lie the process of *projection,* a mechanism which we have already observed in other attributes. Traits which he dislikes or fears in himself, from dirtiness and weakness to sensuality and rebelliousness, the authoritarian may project onto others. Where this happens, projection is partner to repression and self-censorship in keeping unwanted feelings away from consciousness.[11]

The link between projection and a threat complex can be seen in authoritarian fears about secret plots. The authoritarian may openly worship power and toughness without admitting all that his worship entails. The desire to exploit and the very craving for power itself are features which he would sometimes rather pin on other people. Conspiracy theories enable him to do this; they also give him a way to express his nagging sense of victimization. The idea that "unscrupulous men are out to get us" is an attractive notion to the self-pitying.

The same basic attitudes mark much of the whole authoritarian outlook. Most authoritarians view the "world as a jungle," and an unfair and victimizing environment.[12] Yet this view is partly of their own making, if only because they project onto mankind those destructive urges which they cannot or dare not express in personal aggression. The threat complex links directly with cynicism, the authoritarian's distrust of human nature. It also involves superstitious stereotypes, irrational generalizations about "evil" outsiders.

None of these attributes is the special badge of one character type. Even in combination they may reflect and serve temperaments which are not really authoritarian—for example, the type of "boy scout" personality which, for many possible reasons, craves clear-cut authority and routine, revels in aggressive, manly missions, and may even have a certain moral intolerance, without a great need to punish or tyrannize. We must also recognize that there are rigid and punishing people who show many of the attributes just listed and whose craving for order and dominance may well reflect deep as well as "situational" insecurities, without suffering the compounding effect of the authoritarian's broken revolt, his extreme submissiveness. In their wish to find anti-Semites not just wrong but pathologically weak, the authors of *The Authoritarian Personality* tended to conclude that bigots who were not *obviously* submissive were either *covertly* submissive or else had come to grovel before ideologies rather than Fuehrers. Certainly this pattern exists but we should not exaggerate its extent.

On the other side of the coin, we must recognize that even those who are fully authoritarian, in the submissive-aggressive sense, do not necessarily show all nine attributes of behavior listed above. Self-censorship is a good case in point. Some authoritarians can repress their basic fears and hostilities without laying a general embargo on the imagination. We must make here the psychologist's distinction between *suppression,* the conscious or half-conscious avoidance of thoughts and feelings, and *repression,* a much deeper unconscious mechanism by which the personality keeps feelings hidden from the rational self. While suppression often bolsters repression, it is the latter which is most directly involved in the "censored mind" attribute. Thus, an authoritarian may unconsciously repress his feelings of weakness and anger at authority, and yet, on more conscious planes, have ideas and fantasies about many subjects.

4   THE INNER STRUCTURE

In his study of Chinese "thought reform," Robert Lifton tried to find out what made some Westerners more susceptible than others to Communist conversion. The crucial fact, he concluded, was not so much the individual's previous beliefs or specific qualities of behavior as the degree of balance and integration in his personality, "not so much who one is as how well one is put together." The most vulnerable were those who were poorly integrated, whose sense of identity "could be undermined through the self-deprecating effects of guilt and shame." Such people tended to seek new identity in total alignment with the new power, and for that very reason—among others—their number included an authoritarian type.[1]

This underscores the point that authoritarianism, as we defined it, must be described on two levels. The last chapter described it primarily on the level of outlook and behavior (a recurring behavior pattern) although we paid some attention to underlying feelings. We turn now more exclusively to the underlying part, the basic disposition. This includes not simply deep-seated and characteristic feelings and values, but the unconscious ways in which these feelings are regularly managed, controlled, channeled. Disposition also includes the unconscious and semi-conscious bases of reason—the ways in which a person thinks, and his capacities and propensities for reasoning, perceiving, and knowing. The interrelationship of all these elements is sometimes called personality *organization*. The disposition, then, may be thought of as an "inner structure" of personality comprising both a form of organization and substantive traits, the two being very much interdependent. As before, the account that follows concentrates on an archetype, while indicating some variations.

In describing the basic structure of a personality, we shall assume the existence of three major elements: impulses, conscience, and ego. Whether they actually exist is impossible to prove since they cannot be physically measured. But people behave as if they do exist, and they provide clear explanations of much that has been discovered about human character.[2]

"Impulses," or "impulse," corresponds very roughly to what the classic political philosophers called "desires" or "desire." They are the basic emotional drives, seeking among other things to maximize pleasure and minimize pain. Largely though not wholly unconscious, impulses are basically the most asocial part of man, and to some extent—exactly how much we do not know—their root is physiological and their strength and proportions inherited. Within the web of impulse are the opposite drives of dependency—including the wish to be nurtured—and the desire for autonomy. The latter provides a very basic and general source of rebelliousness and of self-assertion.

Conscience is the moral representative of external authority and society within a person's character. It is a watchdog over the impulses, sanctioning some and opposing others, meting out both punishment and reward. When it punishes, it may induce guilt or shame or fear of punishment from without. It rewards by creating a sense of safety or achievement or virtue. The little girl who does a kind deed and then feels "all warm inside" is being rewarded by her conscience. Since these punishments and rewards are feelings, the conscience seems to draw its emotional energy from the source of impulses themselves, although the process is not necessarily one of depletion. (Emotional energy should not be thought of as a fixed volume upon which impulses and conscience make competing demands.)[3]

In describing different sorts of conscience, we must distinguish between two extreme types: the conscience which is relatively autonomous, whose sanctions are highly *internalized*; and the conscience which depends largely and directly on external authority, a conscience whose actions follow in the immediate wake of outside commands and precepts. The first type of conscience punishes chiefly by guilt; the second type, by fear and shame. (The operation of fear alone may not be so much a matter of conscience as of direct impulse, a wish to avoid harm.) Yet these types are only relative, for nearly all consciences possess some internal force of their own, and practically all are subject to a modicum of influence from outside sources. The purest example of a weakly internalized conscience is to be found in a small child. In most homes, the child makes many of his parents' moral values his own by imitating and identifying with his parents, even though he may also rebel against them. But before the values *are* made his own—before, in other words, they are internalized—the child's "conscience" depends almost entirely on authority. At an early age, conscience may involve guilt but even this will depend on frequent cues from authority; there are no clear lines between the instinct of imitation, the desire to please parents or "keep out of trouble," and the gradual development of a deeper morality. That is why a part of the child really likes firm adult rule, a bulwark against his own impulses. To be at the mercy of uncontrolled impulse is not a pleasant situation, as children unconsciously know.

Consciences also enlist the force of habit, and in varying degree they may represent tradition and custom. We often think of a custom-bound conscience as a weakly internalized mechanism, dependent on the rules of a highly traditional or conventional society, and more prone to the sanction of shame than of guilt. This is frequently so but not always. During the past century, for instance, the archetype of a British "public" schoolboy has been a person who internalized the custom and etiquette of his traditional school community. When he went abroad in the service of Empire, he carried a force of the community about him; the specifics of "good form" became, in his eyes, a universal "good taste."[4]

Between conscience and impulse there functions a broker—the ego. A person's ego includes his reason but it embraces unconscious mechanisms as well. The role of broker arises from the fact that, in their pure state, impulses are asocial and impatient, each seeking immediate gratification. The ego adjusts impulses to reality. It actually promotes their gratification, for it sets priorities among them, thereby preventing conflict; it also modulates the impulses and controls their timing, so that they can get as much as possible without painful rebuff from outside forces or the person's own conscience. On the impulse to power, for example, most egos have a tempering effect; brute assertion becomes a desire to lead, control, influence.

In a well-integrated personality, ego tempers conscience, too, not necessarily the most basic moral values but the harshness and rigidity with which these values confront the impulses and external situations. This function emerges as the personality develops. A child's conscience is weakly integrated with its ego, and hence with its impulses. By contrast, the mature personality joins conscience and ego so closely that the two can no longer be thought of as separate entities. A person's ethics may still be rooted in feeling, but the application and development of those ethics will be informed by reason, and even the ethical feeling itself will be a blend of conscience and ego.[5]

Another function of the ego is to provide a focus point for self-esteem. Like conscience, the ego draws its energy from the impulse side of character; it also absorbs whole impulses. One such impulse is narcissism, which the ego can expand from the purely sensual into a wider self-love, a self-confidence and hence a self-reliance. Within the personality this appears to strengthen the ego, enhancing its capacity to integrate conscience with impulses.

Let us now contrast this picture with the personality organization of the archetype authoritarian.[6] Here the ego is weak in several respects. It has not developed under a regime, parental or other, that has given it great responsibility in managing self. As a result it is a poor broker between conscience and impulses, not good at tempering and harmonizing either. In other ways, too, it is weak. It has not been permitted or encouraged to build on primitive narcissism a greater self-love, and it has not developed a sure, stable, and yet flexible sense of identity—in part because the personality is not well integrated. Across a gulf, as it were, the ego faces a rigid and punitive conscience. These qualities of conscience derive in part directly from the moral content of the regime under which the authoritarian personality has developed, and in part from the ego's weakness at tempering and guiding conscience. The conscience is not well internalized; it is brittle; it depends on frequent cues from forces felt to be an external authority.[7] When these are not forthcoming, the authoritarian conscience will often "create" an external authority, imagining, say, a punishing and avenging God. This means, however, that the authoritarian's conscience is not wholly dependent on real external authority; it does have internalized elements, implanted values, for the authoritarian has not been so treated by life that he or she has had *no* effectively loving and fortifying inducements to identify with others and thereby learn social morality. In this, if only in degree, the authoritarian differs from the true psychopath, who may conform at times to "get along," but who is deeply amoral and asocial, and has a stunted capacity to make identification with his fellows. The authoritarian, however, often has a conscience which is divided against itself—with warfare between "control" values of orderliness and uncompromising strength, and a humane tenderness which draws both from learned humane traditions (content of conscience) and impulses of affiliation. The authoritarian's solution is to deny the tenderness from consciousness or to restrict it to narrow areas of scope and legitimacy. This brings us back to the operations of the ego.

Because of its weakness at tempering and harmonizing impulses and conscience, and because the individual's formative experience with authority has been threatening, the authoritarian's ego is especially concerned that impulses will get out of line and cause trouble—an internal chaos making the whole character feel it is falling apart, with retribution from puritanical authority and its intolerant viceroy, conscience. In dealing with impulse, and particularly rebellious impulse, the ego relies heavily on the crude, simple weapon of *repression*, and the partner weapons of *displacement* and/or *projection*. Feelings unwanted in self are turned (displaced) against scapegoat targets, or attributed to (projected onto) these targets. Displacement and projection can work together: the ego might, for example, project sensual feeling onto a scapegoat and then displace rebelliousness onto that scapegoat in the form of castigating him for his sensual immorality.[8] Authoritarians —and others—may also use repression against their own consciences, although repressed guilt feelings are apt to come back in the form of fantasies, phobias, or nightmares; and displacement too may be used in turning the punitive demands of conscience outward, against others.

With regard to sensuality, "disorderly and subversive" spontaneity, the authoritarian's use of projection produces a basic contradiction within his character. On the one hand, he derives unconscious, vicarious pleasure from the license ascribed to others; but then he envies them for doing what he really wants to do. He is like the small girl who scolds her doll for all kinds of imaginary naughtiness; but underneath there is much more self-pity in his castigation. Vicarious pleasures can be sweet; jealousy is always misery.

In addition to this, repression and projection create vicious circles within the authoritarian personality. There are two connected types. In the first, repression of assertiveness against authority, combined with the ego's rejection of self-love, adds to the authoritarian's general feelings of weakness. The weaker the authoritarian feels, the more he wants to submit, to lose himself in strong authority; and the more he wants to submit, the more he must shun rebelliousness and also self-love, which, as we have already seen, stands in the way of extreme submission. The circle thus created can be called "vicious" for two reasons. First, society, especially modern society, seldom provides an opportunity for the ultra-submission that an authoritarian really craves. Second, the circle reinforces a basic contradiction within the personality. Extreme submissiveness, and the emotional sacrifice it entails, heightens the authoritarian's sense of inadequacy and damages still further his self-respect. These negative feelings are, of course, repressed —partly in defense against conscience, which deprecates weakness and self-doubt—but often they are compensated for by a superficial web of self-glorification. Although the web is based on narcissist impulse, it is sanctioned and used by the ego, and deployed in a way that will not offend authority. Even so, the sheer act of self-praise runs counter to the ego's rejection of self-love and, in some cases perhaps, its displacement of some hostility onto self. The poor ego is thus involved in two contradictory operations. On the one hand, it propitiates authority by promoting self-dislike; on the other, it uses a conscious self-glorification to help repress self-dislike.

As long as it can keep the two feelings on different levels of consciousness the ego can maintain a precarious balance, relieved somewhat by the projection of unfavorable traits onto others. Unfortunately, repressed self-dislike sometimes floods into overt form, especially when the individual is suddenly made to believe that he has failed authority and his conscience. Once the ego's repressive mechanism has cracked, it is powerless to prevent a general backfiring of aggressive hostility, directed by conscience onto self. The authoritarian's preceding tendency to glorify himself only adds to the shock, and in dire circumstances the final result may conceivably be suicide.[9]

The second vicious circle within authoritarian character involves the strength of the ego itself. An ego acquires strength by exercise in difficult tasks and by the absorption of different feelings. It follows that repression, a simple device which blocks out feeling, will stunt the ego if it is used too extensively. The weaker the ego, however, the more it relies on repression; and so the vicious circle is set up. Nor is this all. By concentrating and thus intensifying impulse within a few narrow forms, repression "frightens" conscience into greater rigidity, as a defense against the fierceness of impulse. The result is a personality which is much harder for ego to integrate.[10]

Since repression is a mechanism operated by ego, we again find ego in a position where it is forced to act against itself. One facet of this is the way in which authoritarian repressing obstructs the development of reason. The blocking-out of feeling narrows a person's awareness and starves his imagination; for the perception of new relationships depends on an easy crossfeeding between intuition, which is partly based on impulse, and logical thought. Like the whole ego, reason grows with exercise, and the less it is exercised upon the self, the more it remains incapable of meeting and resolving a person's fears and resentments. Of course there are so many exceptions that, taken in their variety, they may conceivably outnumber cases of the archetype portrayed above. For example, the authoritarian who permits himself large areas of fantasy, while still repressing or suppressing certain impulses, in a sense mans his defenses "further in" to himself. There are also authoritarians such as "Pat," the college girl portrayed by Nevitt Sanford, who are spontaneous in many spheres of impulse, but who crave strong (male) authority to "step on" them and keep them in line.[11] Another variation is a "stop-go" pattern, in which submissiveness and prudery alternate with sudden impulsive action, breaking through the person's brittle controls but bringing punishment from conscience in its train. The authors of *The Authoritarian Personality* found that some prison inmates, especially sex offenders, seemed to show this pattern, castigating other deviants for their own tendencies.

It remains, however, that the stunting of ego by repression tends to freeze the personality at a primitive stage in its development. The poor integration of conscience with impulse, the dependence of conscience and ego on external authority, and the weakness of ego as a broker are essential features of a small child's personality. Certainly there are differences: most children do not make rigidly authoritarian uses of repression and displacement; but the weak integration is the same. It is notable that Bruno Bettelheim, in his account of authoritarianism induced among concentration-camp prisoners whose egos had been weakened by terror, restriction, and humiliation, should emphasize their "regression into infantile behavior—sudden and short lived quarrels, extravagant boasting, and a limited capacity to plan ahead or consider problems with an objective mind.*

---

* Bettelheim, 1943. The comparison with small children is complicated and depends much, of course, on the age. Despite psychoanalytic views of early "oral sadism" it is my impression that hostility is far less basic to the infant than fear and the aggressive drive (including the powerful motives of curiosity, acquisitiveness, and the drive for mastery, all included in the infant's drive to *incorporate*). Early hostility arises from aggression thwarted or the self re-

SUMMARY

It is on the level of personality organization that authoritarianism becomes a matter of kind and not just degree, that one can speak most accurately of authoritarian, as opposed to non-authoritarian, formation. The main distinguishing features of an authoritarian organization can now be summarized:

—A rigid and punitive conscience, largely dependent on external authority or an image of that authority. The conscience is punitive both in the stance it adopts toward the personality's own impulses, especially rebelliousness and "tender feeling," and in its condonement of hostility toward external objects.

—A general weakness of the ego, reflected by low self-esteem and by the ego's limited ability as internal coordinator. The result is a poor integration of conscience, ego, and impulses. To control the impulses —especially impulses of aggression—the authoritarian's ego relies heavily on repression, and on displacement, projection, or both.

—Impulses which are either released quite untamed or else throttled and diverted, rather than tempered. In either case, they generally retain a basic fierceness. This produces a constant state of threatened warfare between impulses and conscience. At some level of consciousness/unconsciousness, the authoritarian is always afraid that his impulses get out of hand.

Each of these features, to be sure, is a matter of "more or less" when considered by itself. As we have already noted, all consciences have some dependence on external authority; and nearly all contain a punitive element. Likewise, virtually all egos repress, and many displace and project. The weakness of the authoritarian's ego is no less relative

---

jected or threatened. At the same time I would accept the point made by Spock and others that one-to-two-year-old infants seem to displace rage from their parents (whom they wish to please) by hitting safe, often inanimate objects. And this may be reflected in jealous attacks on a younger brother or sister (when the self really *does* feel rejected or threatened).

With regard to authoritarianism, it is often said that children, too, have a stereotyped "we-they" view of the world and a dependence on the status quo that can be quite rigid. In some ways, and at some ages, this may be true; but I am struck by the flexibility of the pre-verbal infant, who has not learned the verbal categories of adults and therefore does not assume that certain objects, feelings, and responses (e.g., crying and laughter) are "not supposed" to go together. It is more than simply being *labile*. In general, then, it is unfair to equate authoritarianism with "infantile regression"; it may, however, be seen as a primitive pattern readily but ephemerally adopted by many slightly older children as a response to the very chaos and insecurity of their infant beings.

than the fierceness and threat of his impulses, and on some impulses even the ego of an authoritarian has a tempering, rather than merely repressive, effect. It is only the combination of all these features that makes the authoritarian's inner structure different in kind and not simply in degree—though the existence of borderline cases must be conceded. True, the features may be highly interrelated, but no one feature leads inevitably to the others. Thus, some non-authoritarians have punitive consciences without being very repressed; some have strong impulses without particularly rigid consciences, and so on.[12]

Even within the three categories of conscience, ego, and impulses, there are important, if more relative, differences of combination. Many non-authoritarians, for instance, have egos which are weak in some respects but not particularly repressive; others repress their rebellion and aggressive impulses to a great extent without needing to displace or project them. Similarly, some non-authoritarians have consciences which are internally very rigid and punitive, ever ready to inflict guilt, but which are deeply and consistently humanitarian. This difference may seem to hinge more on a substantive quality of character—humanitarianism—than on the way the character is organized, but the difference really involves both.

5   DEFINITION AND DETECTION: SOME PROBLEMS

Our tidy archetypes must now be complicated. In the first place, differences *between* authoritarians can extend to deep levels of character. Take, for instance, the targets of authoritarian hostility. The precise and complex meaning of these targets, their psychological significance to the individual, will vary somewhat, depending on the authoritarian individual concerned. One should not even assume that all authoritarians turn their hostility on targets which symbolize their own shunned or feared traits. Some may primarily attack "safe" targets, unthreatening figures, as a substitute for confronting the authoritative. These different types of motivation may often go together, but we have no evidence that they always do so.

Another complication involves the differences and likenesses between authoritarian and unauthoritarian. So far we have emphasized the differences. It must be stressed, therefore, that authoritarians do not always act in an "authoritarian" way. For one thing the authoritarian's characteristic pattern of impulse control does not necessarily apply to all his impulses and relationships with others. He may, for example, show a deeply tender affection for women and children while tending in general to avoid the claims of tenderness. Again, there are some people whose authoritarian dispositions are expressed very little in behavior, but rather in dreams or private fantasies (conscious or semiconscious). Through these means a person may unwittingly express submissive-aggressive urges, though the idiom may be highly symbolic and therefore disguised. But in none of these cases can one say for sure that there is *no* expression in behavior. In virtually all societies normal behavior, whether authoritarian or not, includes an element of submission and domination, however mild and indirect. Through such behavior the largely-latent authoritarian may express some of his disposition, even if the expression is impossible to detect.

Henceforward, when we use the term "authoritarian" without qualifying it, we shall refer to a disposition which is perceptibly expressed in behavior. This does not invariably involve "abnormal" or "deviant" behavior; it will not, at least, in a group or society dominated by authoritarians. Another point to bear in mind is that behavior can affect disposition as well as vice versa. We have already seen that, early in the formation of authoritarianism, extreme submission may stunt self-esteem and magnify feelings of weakness. If the submission includes stark behavior and not simply a repression of rebelliousness it may be that much more degrading, as with the prisoners described by Bettelheim. At a later stage, similarly, specific actions may weaken self-esteem and/or produce conflicts with conscience. Alternatively, they may exercise and strengthen the ego: for example, a person invested with new responsibility may be induced to act in a way that strengthens his self-reliance generally and extends his mental horizons.

DEFINITIONS AND FUTURE RESEARCH

For further research on authoritarianism, our definition will produce practical difficulties. Even the short definition set forth in Chapter 1 includes unconscious processes—most specifically, a pattern of repressed rebellion. The occurrence of this process can seldom be established in a way which will predictably command agreement among scholars. Yet, without some agreement, studies seeking to show prevalence of authoritarianism in different groups, and the relation of authoritarianism to social factors, will not be persuasive.

To identify submissive individuals who wish to align themselves with punitive power against symbols of weakness, rebellion, or inferiority—this is *relatively* easy. It is rather harder, but not much more so, to detect in some of these people a medley of conflicts and anxieties including a fear of weakness. One may, furthermore, sense that the submissive-aggressive tendencies are in some way related to the conflicts and anxieties. By scientific standards, even these things are not provable, but they stand a chance of being widely accepted—at least among those who agree that unconscious dispositions affect behavior.

When, however, one seeks to identify precise mechanisms that link the submissive-aggressive tendencies with the fear of weakness and other anxieties, and when one includes these mechanisms in a definition of authoritarianism, then the problems really begin.

Our detailed description of authoritarianism has so far stressed two main links between the fear of weakness and the desire to be aligned with punitive power. The simpler one—simpler because the linkage is more direct—is the process of compensation and denial. The authoritarian feels weak, so he denies and hides his feeling of weakness by identifying with power. He dissociates himself from symbols of weakness as much as possible by attacking them as alien and deviant. He may likewise dissociate himself from symbols of feminine tenderness and of social inferiority, in part because both to him mean weakness.

Combining as it does simplicity with common-sense reason, the idea of a linkage based on compensation and denial may be relatively acceptable. In practice too, even the observer untrained in psychology may often sense that a person's extreme alignment with power serves to cover up fears and insecurities.

The second reinforcing kind of link is more difficult to establish because it is more indirect. This is the process in which rebelliousness is repressed, and some of it turned onto symbols of weakness and inferiority, thereby facilitating extreme identification with power. In a phrase, a process of diversion whether by displacement, projection, or both. Now in some rare cases in everyday life one can observe behavior which suggests very forcibly this process—the subordinate, for example, who is humiliated by his superior and, rather than defending himself, walks off and bawls out an underling or kicks the office cat.[1] But in most cases of authoritarianism the process is more obscure. Even the fantasy tests revealing a large amount of stifled revenge feelings against parents—even these do not actually demonstrate that the hostility is diverted against other objects. Still less do they prove that feelings of weakness or rebellion are projected.[*]

Admittedly, we have already noted experimental-situation tests, in

---

[*] Some psychiatrists appear to assume that almost any exaggeration by an individual of "bad" traits in others means that he is projecting his own unadmissible feelings. But all of us, to a varying degree, judge others by ourselves; thus the unusually hostile man who always suspects the hostility of others does not necessarily do so in order to deny or repress his own hostility. Nor is the exaggeration of badness in others in order to have an excuse to blame them the same as projection. The best test of projection is by Sears, 1936, in which he used an ingenious combination of questionnaires and controls, although his account is not clear at all points.

some of which authoritarian displacement of aggression does seem to have been elicited. But these tests involve unpleasant and improper uses of deception and/or harassment (for all the support of some of them by Federal health agencies!) and on these grounds alone further refinements of them are to be seriously questioned.[2]

It is true that the first process mentioned—compensation for and denial of weakness—may often involve the second (diversion of rebelliousness). This is particularly so when authoritarianism is engendered in childhood and when it takes the form of extreme identification with paternal power against feminine softness and tenderness. As the next chapter will explain, this pattern involves the repression of "Oedipal rebellion." But in other cases, we do not know whether the first process necessarily entails the second. It is conceivable that a person may deal with anxieties about weakness in a submissive-aggressive way, aligning himself with a punitive, anti-weak authority, and yet not harbor a great deal of repressed rebelliousness—still less divert it against the hated symbols of weakness. He may express his rebellion against other authorities.[3]

To clarify matters, it may help in the future to have two brief definitions of authoritarianism—a broad definition and the narrower one used in this book. Both would embrace disposition (inner structure) as well as behavior, but the broad definition would be less specific about the disposition. According to the broad definition, "authoritarianism" would mean a submissive-aggressive tendency to align oneself with power against symbols of weakness and inferiority, in response to deep conflicts and anxieties. The narrow definition would be the same but it would also emphasize a particular ambivalence about authority involving the repression of rebelliousness and its diversion against scapegoats. Whether the rebelliousness is turned against symbols of weakness and not just against other scapegoat authorities or against the self, is too abstruse and mechanistic a point to settle in the definition. Indeed, it may make better psychological sense to think of repressed rebellion as adding to a general fund of hostility, some of which is turned against symbols of weakness, inferiority, or rebellion.[4]

Since "authoritarianism" under the broad definition is easier to identify, that definition may be preferred by researchers seeking to detect authoritarianism (so-called) in large populations or from historical evidence. On the other hand, its very breadth gives it a social bias. Virtually by definition the broad type must correlate with the strains of social mobility, for it would include any emotionally insecure, upwardly mobile person of the sort who dissociates himself from the lowly and aligns himself with superior classes. The narrow definition requires a more rigorous appraisal of emotional processes and should be considered where intensive depth studies of individuals are to be made. In the following pages we shall continue to focus on the narrow definition, despite our use of historical portraits, where much inference must be made about the inner processes. But one may hope that, in time, other "narrow" delineations will be developed within the broad definition.

TRADITIONAL ATTITUDES AND BASIC DISPOSITIONS

In many cultures, standard conventional behavior involves a marked suspicion of outsiders, deference to an ascetic authority, and other authoritarian-like attitudes, without necessarily reflecting authoritarian pathology. This highlights the advantage of defining authoritarianism according to inner structure as well as behavior. In such communities the cruder manifestations of authoritarianism would be masked by customary behavior patterns, although nuances of personal style might still show up the most authoritarian.[5]

These problems of distinction, however, may not always be confined to the level of behavior. It has been suggested that, in some pre-modern cultures marked by rigorous demands for obedience, traditional hostility against outsiders and witches may provide channels for displacing rebellious and other aggressive impulses. The specific antagonism may be a learned attitude, but one reinforced and partially maintained by the service it performs for personality. On somewhat similar lines, applied more universally, George Herbert Mead argued that moral indignation against criminals helped law-abiding citizens to affirm their solidarity with convention and "inhibit" their own delinquent feelings.* Again, in everyday relationships, it is conceivable that much aggressiveness is swiveled away from boss figures. On the playground most children refrain from attacking bigger children—if only out of physical prudence—but they can attack or order about children of their own size or smaller. And so it is with adults. This general phenomenon, the "pecking order," may well rest on processes of displacement as well as imitation and compensation.

---

* Mead, 1918. Strictly speaking, the antagonism against criminals which provides a symbolic way of battening down one's own delinquency is not necessarily or entirely the same as displacing or projecting delinquent feeling, but the one may very often involve the other.

But, even if these things are true, they do not by themselves signify authoritarian pathology. For one thing, they do not invariably reflect profound feelings of weaknesses and personal inadequacy. Thus, a diversion of rebelliousness onto deviants or juniors is not always accompanied by the authoritarian's need to cover up and compensate for a sense of past failure at self-assertion.* In the second place, diverted rebelliousness does not always entail much inner conflict. Here we must emphasize the difference between emotional conflict and stable repression. Feelings which oppose other feelings may be effectively repressed and channeled in other directions and disguised forms so that they do not threaten to produce that clash of emotion, unconscious but nearer the "surface"—insecurely unconscious—which deserves the term "conflict." "Conflict," in short, is no synonym for "opposition," and one can think of people who in many areas of feelings are repressed yet are inwardly well adjusted. All of this applies to feelings about authorities including parents. A person who overtly but nonetheless deeply reveres an authority may repress a simultaneous antagonism to that authority, and may do so quite stably, perhaps displacing the emotion. At a very deep level of unconsciousness he is ambivalent to authority but not in the sense of that brittleness and tension which characterize the more authoritarian.[6]

There are other points, too, at which it is important to distinguish the authoritarian's special makeup from more universal patterns of emotion and behavior. Consider, for example, the authoritarian's vicarious enjoyment of forbidden desires. By no means is this the preserve of one type of personality. The modern liberal author or film producer who attacks tyranny and violence through its vivid portrayal may often be drawing upon his "normal" reserves of sadism; but this does not necessarily mean that his humane motives are not equally strong, or that he feels a need to stamp on these motives. For the audiences likewise: violent films have replaced public executions and other live spectacles as outlets for very basic fascinations with conflict, and films in general, like other media, provide channels of displacement and projection for all sorts of "bad" urges; but this does not mean that most filmgoers are authoritarian. It must also be noted here that mixed feelings about the unknown and potentially threatening are

---

* On the other hand, if Mead is right, the ordinary blaming of criminals mentioned above *might* involve some process of moral compensation: striking at other delinquents to deny one's own delinquency could amount to a shoring-up of one's own sense of goodness at the expense of the deviant.

well-nigh universal. The authoritarian's attack on forces which both attract and repel him is in part a product of his particular experience, but it has a biological basis in opposite drives, both necessary to survival. One sees this in an infant's reaction to strangers and sudden new noises: he is alarmed or distrustful, and yet fascinated; the one reflects the drive of apprehension, caution, self-custody; the other the drive of curiosity, exploration, mastery of the environment.

DEGREE AND DIMENSION

From all that has so far been said, it follows that a degree of authoritarianism cannot fully be measured along any one dimension. This holds even when one is just comparing people who can be diagnosed as "authoritarian"—that is, people for whom authoritarian feelings are an important determinant of behavior. The statement that X is "very authoritarian" can mean, first of all, that he shows a marked pattern of authoritarian behavior. This criterion breaks down into several "subdimensions": for example, when compared over time with authoritarian Y, X may or may not show more submissive behavior, punitive behavior, and so on. Despite these complications, the criterion of behavior pattern is the simplest one to use, since it is from behavior that we largely gauge personality needs. The criterion works best, however, when the compared individuals have the same social background and setting, for it does not distinguish between personality needs and the social opportunity for their expression. Although social factors affect the basic disposition (as we shall see), a person with a "given" level of authoritarian needs will be encouraged to show clear authoritarian behavior much more in some social settings than in others. (This is quite aside from the fact already noted that, in some societies more than others, roles and institutions requiring submissive-aggressive behavior may conceal much authoritarianism from detection.)

A deeper dimension of authoritarianism is the extent of internal maladjustment giving rise to authoritarian inclinations. This in turn breaks down into the various subdimensions of personality organization described in the last chapter—harshness and rigidity of conscience, weakness of integration, brittleness of impulse control (felt or real), and irrational feelings of weakness. Although these elements are largely gauged from behavior, they may also be revealed to some extent through fantasy, as shown in psychological tests and accounts by the individual. Using this dimension, however roughly, one can try to allow for the fact that two people, say, even two people in the same social setting, may show about the same degree of authoritarian behavior without having the same level of authoritarian need and inner maladjustment.

Because of these complexities, it is wise not to think of some authoritarian individuals being "more so" *in toto*, than other authoritarian people. It is more precise to speak of marked authoritarian *behavior*, and of extreme authoritarian needs and maladjustments; but even these distinctions are complicated by different *forms* of authoritarian behavior and needs.

"SITUATIONAL AUTHORITARIANISM"

Yet another complication must be allowed for. Some people may react to specific stressful situations in an authoritarian way without showing any sign of a basic authoritarian structure. Personality structure may in a general and negative way be responsible, by permitting such a reaction, but this does not mean that on a deep level the individuals have an authoritarian makeup. The situation may suggest authoritarian behavior so forcibly that specific personality dispositions have relatively little to do with it, in the sense of positively promoting it.[7]

An acquaintance who underwent basic training as an Ulster Irish paratrooper has described what seemed to be this kind of process. One purpose of the training was to demoralize and humiliate the individual, and then build him up again as a disciplined soldier, skilled, but completely prepared to carry out any order under fire.[8] During the first phase, the period of humiliation, the trainees were particularly apt to vent on each other the rage and tension caused by their bullying, snarling sergeant. This appeared to be a clear case of rebellion displaced onto weaker targets, in part to reassert one's own stature. To explain such a phenomenon is the concept of an authoritarian disposition invariably needed? I doubt it. One distinctive feature here is that the aggression was displaced onto weaker targets primarily because they were safe (and readily accessible) for attack, and not necessarily because they symbolized weakness or other qualities which the attacker shunned in himself.[9] But even situational authoritarianism may conceivably include hostility directed at symbolic targets. A few years ago I interviewed the lawyer-secretary of an American beer wholesalers' association. I asked him his views on drunkenness and alcoholism, and on the way they related to his section of the alcohol trade. He at once gave a liquor-industry cliché—that alcoholism "is in the man, not the drink." And anyway, he asserted, "it's not beer those Skid Row *bums* drink." He said the word "bums" with absolute contempt. Whether he was deeply and more generally authoritarian I cannot say; certainly he was a "tough guy"; the point is that his business situation alone could have elicited such a response, given a personality that was not strongly opposed to it. It is three decades since Prohibition but many alcohol businessmen in the United States still feel that theirs is a stigmatized occupation. They are also subject to the general uncertainties in America about drinking and how drinking problems should be dealt with. At the same time they want to be 100 percent respectable and a part of the mainstream of American business. Given these circumstances, our beer representative may well have blasted the Skid Row "bum" not only to dissociate himself from drunks and shore up a precarious status, but to quell doubts about the professional group to which he owed allegiance. The quelling would be done by a process of displacement.

The concept of "situational authoritarianism" is more hypothetical than that of deep authoritarianism.[10] I mention it only to acknowledge that authoritarian processes may be resorted to but temporarily or marginally—marginally, that is, to the individual's main pattern of emotion and behavior. Situational authoritarianism may involve unconscious conflicts, fears, a sense of inadequacy, but these will have shallower roots than in authoritarianism (they will tend to be suppressed rather than repressed) and they will relate more specifically to a given situation—even though some of the fears may distort reality and in this sense be irrational.

However, from the standpoint of further research, there are several reasons why situational and deep authoritarianism will be hard to distinguish in practice (assuming that the former does occur). In the first place, one detects an authoritarian disposition very largely by observing patterns of behavior in several areas—several spheres of activity and self-expression. Yet a person with a deeply authoritarian disposition may show overt authoritarian behavior in but one or two spheres. Conversely, a person without an authoritarian structure may conceivably encounter, and encounter recurringly, a situation which urges an authoritarian response. The training camp N.C.O. who docilely takes a reprimand from his officer and then with special vehemence bawls out his recruits on some unrelated matter—is this man a situational authoritarian, or did a more basic authoritarianism attract him to military hierarchy in the first place? To find out one would have to know the different facets of his personal life, but even if he was only punitive toward his recruits, could it be that barrack room and drill square were the only situations that had (as yet) elicited overt behavior from an authoritarian disposition?[11]

Another contingency is that the situation which at first produces situational authoritarianism may ultimately help forge an authoritarian disposition. To be precise, both the situation and the situational behavior may have this effect. The sheer fact of behaving in a particular way in one situation may "suggest" that the person act in the same way in other situations. Thus, a general disposition to a specific pattern of behavior in different situations is built up. The original behavior, specific only to one situation, can lead to a general way of coping with stress and insecurity—perhaps with insecurity on a much deeper level than in the initial situation.

But, as already said, it is not just the situational *behavior* which may produce a more general authoritarianism. The specific situation itself may affect the disposition: for example, by weakening self-esteem. Take a person plunged into a situation where his professional or social status is at once important and precarious. A new job, say, which is really more than he can handle. Suppose that he already has fairly marked feelings of personal inadequacy, but that these feelings have not hitherto been coped with in a predominantly authoritarian way, even on the level of basic personality structure and disguised fantasy. Imagine further that the new situation elicits authoritarian behavior. In the new job, for example, it may appear that he can only hold his own by identifying uncritically with unpleasant superiors and colleagues, and the situation may also make it easy for him to attack scapegoats. The office, perchance, will have a secretary or two incompetent enough to seem legitimate targets for ire—including the added ire of his pent-up resentments and fear. At first, his response to these circumstances will reflect little more than situational authoritarianism. After a time, however, the effect on him may become deeper and more general. Not only may his basic sense of inadequacy, his pre-existing feelings, be increased, but these feelings will make him more insecure in the specific situation, the new job. And this is not all. At an unconscious level, his basic sense of inadequacy may be largely expressed in anxiety over the new job and his authoritarian response to it. A bridge is thereby created between anxieties deep within the personality structure (the general disposition) and situational authoritarianism. The authoritarianism ceases to be merely situational, for it now reflects a deeper need.

PART II

CAUSES

6   CHILDHOOD PRESSURES

In 1954 a British boy scout, sixteen years of age, stabbed and killed a woman of seventy-two. He had been afraid she would discover his forgery of some scout certificates; but this hardly explained why he stabbed her twenty-nine times. His mother's description of his childhood suggested some answers. Apparently, he was toilet trained by the age of nine months: his father, an ex-army officer, made him sit on the pot if necessary for hours. By nine months, too, he had been taught to put every toy away. His father apparently "kept on at the boy," who nonetheless seemed to worship him. As a child he was shy and timid. The sight of a broken toy made him cry with fright, and when he was older he disliked horror films. The mother also said she sometimes beat him. When angry, he would "just go white, clench his hands and say nothing, and in a moment it was all over." The boy himself said that he had a temper, but that he had always controlled it and could put anything unpleasant "completely out of his mind."

A psychiatrist called in on the case believed that "his repressive upbringing had aroused resentment to which he had blinded himself, and that aggressive impulses, which he had long repressed, suddenly broke through."[1]

This combination of all-or-nothing control with the apparent worship of a punitive father suggests an authoritarian pattern—utter submission followed by violent displacement against a person who may have symbolized reproving authority but also was an easier, weaker person

51

to attack than the father. Before the murder the aggressive side of his authoritarianism was only latent, and it must be a qualification that we do not know how central to his disposition the displacement process was either before or after the killing. Nevertheless the case demonstrates with unusual directness the way in which a harsh upbringing may induce an authoritarian response. It says nothing, of course, about the prevalence of such backgrounds among authoritarians: there may or may not be other important childhood patterns that produce authoritarianism. It might also be claimed that the background of a killer sheds little light on the backgrounds of less violent authoritarians. As it turns out, however, other childhood studies of authoritarianism have emphasized some of the same factors, if in less cruel form.

About five years after World War II, Else Frenkel-Brunswik, an author of *The Authoritarian Personality*, made a study of fifteen hundred children between eleven and fifteen years old in the San Francisco Bay area. She believed that of those who showed most contempt for minority groups—blacks, Mexicans, Chinese, Japanese, and Jews— a very great proportion were already exhibiting authoritarian tendencies. What is more, an interviewer who visited forty-three of the children's homes discovered distinctive features in the family background of the most racially prejudiced. Their parents, for example, were demanding more than loving; they set a high premium on submission, and they required "stereotyped behavior" governed by a "set of conventional and rigid rules." Although the *less*-racist children conformed more to their parents, the racist ones submitted fearfully, albeit inconsistently.[2]

Frenkel-Brunswik's report was devoted mainly to a portrait of Karl, an eleven-year-old boy who showed most of the traits found "statistically to be prevalent" among the more racially prejudiced children. Highly authoritarian, Karl was an extreme archetype of the "prejudiced" group, though he was most representative of the lower-class "prejudiced."[3] His parents, too, felt strong dislike for Jews, Negroes, and Orientals, but there were other points of interest about them. Both had come from broken homes, and both told proudly of their strict upbringing. The father described his own father as a deranged drunkard, who deserted the family; he praised, by contrast, his grandfather, who had raised him: "He was really strict. He had thirteen children, and even when they were grown up there wasn't one of them that would talk back to him. . . . He could handle any of them." By becoming a simple mechanic, Karl's father had not lived up to his grandfather's expectations, but he believed that someday he would accomplish great things through an invention.

Karl's mother, too, enjoyed fantasies of grandeur, in a way that combined self-importance with fatalist superstition. Her hopes were partly pinned on Bill, Karl's elder brother and like him very much an authoritarian. Bill, she reported, was born under the sign of the Twins. "He is a dreamer of far places. He will go far and wide. The stars show that." To the interviewer it seemed, in fact, that the boys were "overtrained," that they welcomed their father's strictness to an unusual degree. The father held very conventional views about the proper behavior expected of boys as opposed to girls ("boys shouldn't work in the home" was a *fiat*).

Karl's grandparents, on both sides of the family, were foreign born, and this may have caused a fear of being lumped with underprivileged minorities. It is notable that far more of the "prejudiced" children than of the others had foreign-born grandparents. As Frenkel-Brunswik saw it, the rigid discipline imposed on Karl and his brother by their parents was all part of an anxious drive to be accepted as respectable middle-class Americans. To some extent Karl's racial attitudes were simply a carryover of his parents' views, but they also expressed the deep authoritarianism in him engendered, at least partly, by their behavior.

Frenkel-Brunswik's report did not pretend to cover a cross-section of authoritarians: it concentrated in the first instance on the racially prejudiced, not on authoritarians per se, and it was confined to the San Francisco Bay area. It said, moreover, very little about the exact way in which authoritarianism was inculcated within the person. Yet it was a rare work. No other study, to my knowledge, has made so direct an investigation of authoritarian childhood.[4] Other, more detailed findings, reported in *The Authoritarian Personality* and other works since, are based almost entirely on what authoritarians themselves say. According to some critics, this perspective is useless since authoritarians may be inclined to distort in a uniform way their early experiences. Such criticism makes an important point but I think it is overstated. True, Henry Dicks in his study of German POWs concluded that the most authoritarian individuals were inclined to exaggerate the harshness of authorities, including their fathers: they seemed to project some of their aggressive impulses onto authority without attaching any blame thereby. But on the same deep level of analysis Dicks also found a pattern of submission and repression, suggesting a relationship with an oppressive and debilitating authority, whether in the home, in school, or in the culture at large.[5]

Against this, admittedly, one might argue that a hard childhood authority has nothing to do with the actual genesis of authoritarianism: that a variety of circumstances, social and personal, create feelings of weakness, conflict and anxiety; and that the person then finds, or imagines, a strong authority to which he can submit in an authoritarian way. But why should he take the path of authoritarianism? There are many ways of responding to insecurity. And why in particular should he feel so strong a need to stifle rebellious and other impulses? The most reasonable, if not proven, answer is that a certain kind of authority encouraged him to do these things in the first place.

In the original interviews reported by *The Authoritarian Personality*, people scoring very high on the F scale questionnaire described some distinctive tendencies in the way they had been brought up.[6] For example, they commonly told of a discipline which seemed to stress fear rather than love; was unpredictable and inconsistent; and attached great importance to a detailed respectability. At the same time, the high F scorers were apt to glorify their parents, leaving criticism to the oblique comment, vague resentments, and disguised fantasies of revenge. They were also apt to express a strong dependence on their parents, but as a source of "goodies" rather than of love.[7]

From these studies and impressions, and from other biographical matter (to be seen in later chapters), we can picture an archetype authoritarian childhood. Let us first consider this pattern and then take in some variations and other patterns which modify the main thesis of *The Authoritarian Personality*.

In the archetype case, the father dominates the home and rules intolerantly; the mother is submissive to him, though submission can make her the harsh executive of her husband's regime. If the child is a boy, he represses his Oedipal feelings to an unusual extent. On one level he respects his mother as part of parental power; on another, he feels her to be a symbol of weakness. He is too afraid of the father to picture himself the champion of his mother against him; instead he identifies as much as possible with parental authority. Deprived of that love which fortifies, the child dissociates himself from tender feelings which remind him of womanly weakness, and from any impulses which might cause friction with his father. The tenderness he does show he will somewhat concentrate on figures of male authority. Yet alignment with his father does not really gain him strength. On a very deep level, the situation produces fears about his masculinity: he feels unconsciously "ashamed" of failing to be his mother's champion, of repressing sexual tenderness and of making himself love his father in a forced and exaggerated way.* Submission to power alleviates his most conscious feelings of weakness, but it only does so by driving them underground at the price of basic self-respect. His submission does not even produce a contented relationship between father and son, for the rejection of Oedipal feelings means that they linger on below the surface of consciousness. Whereas most boys express and then resolve their Oedipal feelings, the authoritarian male continues to be plagued by vague resentments against his father and a throttled yearning to be close to his mother. Because it *is* throttled, his basic fondness for her never develops past the small boy's feeling of dependence, and this, added to the degradation of extreme submission, makes him all the more anxious to assert his strength.

With female authoritarians the pattern may be a little different. For one thing, there is often greater emulation of the mother, as well as admiration of the father. More than in the case of a son; the mother's example also tells the daughter how convention expects her to behave. To an authoritarian girl, therefore, her mother has special cause to represent power and authority. And yet, on another level, she too despises her mother for the weakness her sex seems to represent. As in the boy's case, extreme submission to her parents makes her long unconsciously for the strength of her father at the same time that it creates unadmitted resentments against him.

Some authoritarian girls meet these feelings by unmistakable ag-

---

* The word "ashamed" is in quotation marks because it is more like guilt than shame, as we used these words in chap. 3, and yet it is hard to tell how much it is even guilt. Both guilt and shame are emissions of conscience, or *superego*, and in the archetype case described above the authoritarian superego is formed largely by identification with hard paternal authority. Since the ashamed feeling is *against* this authority, how can it too be part of the superego? One explanation might be that this shows the divided nature of the authoritarian superego itself: that the authoritarian retains from very early childhood, and from his relation then with his mother, an element of conscience that endorses Oedipal feeling— reinforced by humane traditions of a democratic culture. This element of conscience, like the Oedipal feeling itself, could be repressed in deference to the predominant, authoritarian element of his conscience. Also, there is submerged conflict even between the authoritarian part of conscience and the repression of Oedipal feeling, insofar as the authoritarian conscience endorses the value of masculine strength. This value is really the opposite of the weakness implied in yielding to paternal authority. Both factors—the desertion of Oedipal feeling and the failure to uphold masculine autonomy—may lead to unconscious self-contempt.

gressiveness, acting in a way that seems to be telling men, "See? I can be like that too." Many more, however, at least in American society, identify with power by overt submission. Parents in the kind of authoritarian-producing home we have just described may well insist that their daughters display a sweet, conventional femininity. The result could be the kind of woman who is extremely gentle, if a little tense, with her friends—and who raves for a General MacArthur. In personal life her aggressiveness is largely confined to gossip; her main urge to dominate is projected onto father figures, heroes, political causes. But her political persuasion is not bound to be radically right; in the 1953 presidential elections, such a woman might conceivably have identified with General Eisenhower, the great sweeper who would replace the "mess in Washington" with a clean and ordered household.[8]

It can now be seen that even in similar homes the stresses producing authoritarian dispositions in girls are not all the same as the stresses upon boys. In both cases, extreme submission damages self-respect; in both, the child reacts by seeking strength through alignment with power. Beyond this, there are differences. By the same token that Western cultures, like so many others, expect a certain submissiveness from girls, they demand a greater show of assertion from boys. As a result the extreme submission and the throttling of Oedipal feelings are more likely to make a boy feel he has lost sexuality than they are a girl. An authoritarian girl may also repress an "Oedipal" (Electral!) jealousy of her mother, and her sexual confidence may be shaky, but she would feel not so much that she has failed her sex as that her sex is weak. Exceptions there are, of course, but in general I would guess that authoritarian boys want to prove themselves males, whereas authoritarian girls really want to get away from their sex—or from that part of their sex which spells softness and weakness.

In most cases, a boy's basic disposition is probably more vulnerable to authoritarianism, since he must contend with particular conflict between feelings of weakness (feelings shared by all humans to an extent) and the toughness and autonomy demanded of males. This is reflected in the social roles of male and female. The transition from little girl to housewife is, in a sense, smoother than the transition from small boy to breadwinner competing outside the home. With the growing exception, perhaps, of career women, society's demands on the modern male are more liable than its demands on the modern female to create or reinforce a complex about strength. On the other hand, those females who do acquire authoritarian dispositions are subject to peculiar tensions of their own. Where society and parents demand feminine sweetness, the authoritarian girl must stage a double reaction to her insecurities—first, a straight authoritarian reaction, and second, a counterreaction against the more directly aggressive aspects of authoritarianism.

The early submission and fear of "womanly" weakness wrought in so many authoritarians produces what psychoanalysts call "anal" concerns. On an unconscious plane, the anus can be a symbol of vulnerability and defilement; it may also be seen as a testing point of self-control. From an authoritarian standpoint the connection is vital: strong people must show self-control, must always be on guard lest they fall helplessly into the tides of filth within them. These fears, which of course are very unconscious, blend fear of weakness and dirt with a basic self-loathing and concern about controlling impulse. One would expect status-minded parents, who insist very rigidly that their children be clean and proper, to produce just such anxieties.[9] (The same insistence will tend to suppress curiosity—"Keep out of that, Johnny, it's *dirty*"—and it should not be assumed that this sort of properness is concentrated just among middle-class parents.)

The early pressures on boys which help create authoritarianism can likewise lead to strong homosexual tendencies. In these cases, extreme yielding to strong male authority takes sexual form; the authoritarian's repression of real fondness for his mother creates a general aversion to relations with women; and the authoritarian's Oedipal feelings, being repressed, are not extended in the normal way from his mother to other women as he grows up. This is one reason why so many authoritarians, and not just the particularly homosexual ones, see women through two lenses, each focusing on part of a maternal image. Through the first lens they see a weak and basically contemptible womanhood; through the second they see "The Noble Provider," hailed rather than loved, a representative of childhood authority. Their attitudes to women, in short, remain partly fixed at a mother-son level.

Most American authoritarians are probably not overt homosexuals. Where strong homosexual tendencies exist, the most expected authoritarian response would be to repress them lest they affront conventional, moral authority. Among the first high F scorers interviewed, there was a policeman who walked with a heavy swagger, yet who spoke to his interviewer, a man, in a voice of exaggerated deference, soft, almost effeminate, a sidling tone. From time to time he would swivel his body, self-consciously exposing his revolver—the mannerism seemed to epitomize masculine parade blended with a flirtatious yielding.[10] In America particularly, the inducements to an authoritarian of *conscious* homosexuality must be weak, since most conventions abhor homosexuality as the very opposite of red-blooded toughness. But, even when the homosexual feelings are repressed, they may still affect overt attitudes. Thus, in the authoritarian's threat complex there is sometimes an imagery of penetration—imagined poison plots, or allusions to burrowing vermin—which can reflect both anal and homosexual concerns. The individual fears anal penetration, but the concern is ambivalent—he fears the *wanting* of anal penetration. These feelings are not confined to authoritarians; in some people they are turned very little against personified symbols of threat; in others they may even be turned against immediate authority. But in the case of authoritarians especially, concerns about anal penetration may be traced to an inverted Oedipal situation which made the individual feel emasculated and made him want to—but also *not* want to—merge his sexual identity with an overwhelming father. Essentially, he has wooed his father rather than his mother; and he has had a masochistic urge to expose himself to his father before he could be taken forcibly and punished.

Whether female authoritarians tend to be strongly homosexual, overtly or otherwise, is a matter of which we have no knowledge. In some circumstances, one can imagine the wish to dissociate from feminine "weakness" leading to an aggressive lesbian assumption of male sexuality; and authoritarian submission to the mother might work against an extension of fondness for the father into more developed forms of heterosexuality. But these things are hypothetical. Girls induced at an early age to view sex as a dirty assault by the strong upon the weak can have rape fears which, in many ways, resemble the male concern about penetration and defilement. But, again, we do not know how far the parallel goes, at least not in the case of authoritarians.

So far we have only mentioned one pattern of authoritarian childhood. Some of the sexual conflict described in authoritarian men and women can be traced to other patterns as well. Among these other variations, at least four patterns are discernible. They have many points in common, and many childhoods may show elements of more than one pattern as defined here.

In the first, the mother dies when the child is young; the father is, perhaps, remote or does not give much affection.[11] As the child grows up, he or she expresses a nostalgic self-pity over the lost mother, but he also feels vague contempt for the picture of weakness she portrayed. If he remembers her when she was ailing, his contempt may be all the greater; he may also despise and resent her "desertion." One response to these feelings is to seek strength through extreme identification with the father. The child with but one parent can feel particular guilt about rebelliousness against that parent.

In the second pattern, the parents are not unkind but they do little to develop the child's self-confidence. Between them, the parents make the child feel that he or she cannot "match up," yet cannot safely rebel. There may be a tension between the parents, linking the father with a potentially annihilating force. If the parents fail to sow deeply humane values, then the child may resort to punitive displacement of his fears. On the face of it, the regime may not be very harsh, and in this respect it departs from the sort of child rearing highlighted in *The Authoritarian Personality*. It must be stressed that the father who seems vaguely threatening without using physical force may cause all the greater anxieties about annihilation and castration because the threat *is* so vague—its boundaries have not been tested.[12] And the non-physical element may threaten a *psychic* annihilation, a taking-away of some inner self-esteem, which a more physical oppression may not emphasize to the same degree.

In the third pattern, the child consciously hates a father who is oppressive to the point of cruelty. Despite this hatred, the child feels weakened at being forced to hide his or her real feelings and submit. If the child is a boy and sees the father maltreating his mother, his sense of failure can be all the more acute. When he reaches adolescence he may finally rebel and leave the home, but even then he will often follow an authoritarian course, identifying with a harsh authority which bears some resemblance to his father. This kind of authoritarian may be found in criminal gangs.[13] The revolt against the father is, in the first instance, an *evasive* revolt very often; and without his realizing it, a part of the person is reacting to his own past submissiveness. But in this and all the patterns so far mentioned, an important element may be the learning of values which associate feminine tenderness with weakness.

Fourth, there is a pattern in which the mother, not the father, dominates the home. Some mothers are possessive, demanding, and yet, in terms of real love, rejecting. The effect on a child can be an intense conflict between dependence on the mother and a wish to get away from her, to deny the weakness that dependence signifies. Such feelings may lead to authoritarianism, especially if the father is absent, weak, or not particularly pleasant, so that there is no benign male authority for the child to emulate. As we shall see much later, this pattern has occurred among black Americans (especially, perhaps, among girls). It also seems to have appeared in a study of Irish American schizophrenic men. We might dwell on this briefly as a way of illustrating a clear deviation from *The Authoritarian Personality* model with its emphasis on the hard father.

Many of the patients described mothers of the sort to whom all sons were "forever boys and burdens"; the father was often a "weak and shadowy figure."[14] These portraits jibe with other accounts of Irish peasant and working-class Irish American families.[15] In the schizophrenics' case, their reaction was a repressed complex about their mothers in particular, and women in general. To both they showed much hostility. One man, for example, cursed his mother, blaming her for the gory death of his father on the road in front of their home, whereas the father had actually died in a hospital at a ripe old age. Yet, with many of the group, fear of the mother, and presumably the absence of a strong father figure, had made them insecure as men. As adults they were guilty about sex and extremely compliant toward authority; a large proportion, indeed, felt afraid of doing anything which might separate them from the hospital.

Anxious, withdrawn, and generally repressed, they tended toward a passive type of authoritarianism. Apart from hostile remarks about women, their aggressiveness came out mainly in the form of general resentment and delusions of persecution or of having remarkable powers. By contrast, a group of Italian American schizophrenics in the same study were much more violent; they felt open rebellion toward their fathers or brothers, and they acted out their impulse rather than repressing and projecting it into fantasy and delusions. In a majority of both groups, there was some homosexuality, but only among the Italians was it overt.[16] For all their aggressiveness, it is plain that the Italians were not predominantly authoritarian; as a whole they had not taken the course of extreme submission adopted by the Irishmen. In the latter case, ambivalence about parental authority was more obvious than it is among most authoritarians—for the fact that the authority was female allowed it to become in time openly acceptable to them as a target of hate. But overt hostility to the mother after they grew up did not prevent them from becoming dependent on other authorities, nor did it cut away a strong, basic yielding to the mother. The result seems to have been a large amount of repressed and then projected rebelliousness. In their general hostility toward women they struck indirectly at the dominance of their mothers, but they also seemed to be striking at their own feminine and "soft" identity.[17]

None of these authoritarian-producing patterns can be described in a wholly comprehensive way. Children with intolerant fathers and mothers do not always become authoritarian; they may acquire other anxieties instead, or unknown influences—from school, perhaps, or friends—may counter the cowing effect of their parents. Another factor may be the relationship with brothers and sisters. In Britain I know of a Victorian-Edwardian family where one of the daughters—who never married—became almost savagely prudish and demanding, much more so than her sisters and brothers. Her parents had been meticulously demanding themselves, but they had also left her in the charge of an older sister who bossed and bullied her. And then, much later, a younger sister was born, to be greatly babied by the rest of the family. Partly as a result, it seemed, her strait-laced morality became edged with feelings of rejection and a wish for revenge—desires turned mainly upon young people and servants.

But, in most cases, the influence of brothers and sisters is less dramatic and harder to analyze. There are other uncertainties too. It is my guess—I cannot prove it—that inborn neurological and other traits make children more or less susceptible to authoritarian submission. Such elements may form a necessary, though surely not sufficient, condition.[18]

Even confining ourselves to parental behavior, we do not know all the precise qualities which contribute to authoritarianism. Certainly a parent can keep strict discipline without denying a child love or stunting self-respect. What counts is the spirit behind the discipline. Many homes which foster authoritarianism do so not just by weakening the child but by passing on certain values that encourage authoritarian behavior. Quite obviously, the more the individual identifies with his parents' power, the more he will take over their values, including the very values that oppressed him. One may even conjecture that authoritarians are just the sort of people to make authoritarians of their children; but in any case, the parents are most likely to make authoritarians of their children when their values combine a repressive morality with craving for power and position. Transmitted to the children, such values not only encourage authoritarian behavior but influence the basic disposition, the inner structure of personality. They affect, in other words, the way the child deals with himself as well as the way he relates to others. So, if it is true to say that an authoritarian's inner structure conditions his moral beliefs, it is also true to say that those beliefs sanction and reinforce the inner structure. Thus, the values of an authoritarian's parents can affect his inner structure in two ways: first, by working on the parents' behavior toward him, sanctioning intolerance and oppressiveness; and second, by becoming part of his own morality.

A POSTSCRIPT ON SEXUALITY

This chapter has placed some emphasis on sexual factors, for where authoritarianism can be traced back to childhood it is often difficult to separate Oedipal and other sexual concerns from feelings about authority, strength, and tenderness. In chapters to come, we give less attention to the sexual, while recognizing that we may be underestimating it. There are two reasons for this. First, we have defined authoritarianism as a certain kind of relationship to authority and symbols of inferiority and weakness. Sexual makeup is not part of the definition. From a psychoanalytic viewpoint, indeed, our definition is extremely simple. Within the authoritarian category—and even within the category of "inverted Oedipus"—there may be a variety of sexual patterns, each involving processes that we have barely hinted at. Nevertheless it is possible to detect and discuss the basic features of authoritarianism without always knowing these intricacies; and one can envisage authoritarian responses to a repressive power, be it parental power or otherwise, that barely involve sexual feelings at all.

But second, even when the authoritarian pattern clearly involves sexual concerns, the *causal* importance of these concerns is often obscure. In some individual cases, a "sidling up" to masculine strength and a contempt for feminine "weakness" may conceivably reflect and express, rather than have caused, a more general concern with strength and weakness. So when one knows little about an authoritarian's childhood—and one seldom knows a great deal—it is prudent to avoid bold inferences about sexual factors.

7 BEYOND THE FAMILY

It is obvious, perhaps, that in some social situations and cultures families are more likely than in others to transmit the beliefs and pressures that foment authoritarianism—although much may depend on the particular experiences of the family concerned, and on the physiological basis of the parents' temperament.

This does not mean that social factors can only shape authoritarianism via the family or other childhood agencies. In adulthood, too, social "climate" may elicit a punitive and censorious behavior from characters whose authoritarianism might otherwise have remained largely a matter of disposition, a web of feelings rather than action. Consider the following statement, a letter written to the *New York Times,* in the shock of the first riot of the 1960s but somewhat before ensuing riots had enflamed the public concern about "law-and-order."

I have been in favor of the Civil Rights bill from its beginnings until now.

It has become apparent that it has arrived too soon. In this most ambitious attempt to grant the Negro the rights of full citizenship the Harlem Negroes have reacted like a pack of wild animals.

Perhaps they need another 50 years to prove their claim to membership in the fraternity of rational human beings. Do the leaders of the various Negro movements expect full privileges in the face of this behavior.[1]

This letter does not prove the writer an authoritarian. Nevertheless it is just the kind an authoritarian might write. Coming from a civil-rights proponent (if such he ever was), it ignores remarkably the black condition—and the white one. The whole tone of harsh elitism and crude, moral dichotomy gives an impression of long-held feelings now brought to the surface.

As a practical matter, it is often impossible to distinguish a society's *eliciting* effect on behavior from deeper effects on dispositions. The social stresses, beliefs, and opportunities which encourage authoritarian behavior may, by the same process, develop authoritarian patterns of feeling. For example, cultures which endorse moral militance, extreme worship of power, and anxiety about subversion might encourage insecure persons to displace or project their fears onto symbols of decadence and revolt rather than wrapping up their anxieties in other types of emotion: direct rebelliousness, say, or passive depression, or strong identification with many types of underdogs.[2] On a deeper plane, social climate and conditions may sow the kind of inner turmoil and sense of weakness which induces the individual in the first place to adopt unconsciously the "blunt instruments" of authoritarian repression, displacement, and projection—especially when these instruments are "suggested" to him by the tone of his environment.

Despite these possibilities, we do not know whether adult experiences can often produce authoritarianism *irrespective of childhood background*. The most plausible account of such a process is based on an extreme situation, the life in concentration camps described by Bruno Bettelheim, who spent a year in Dachau and Buchenwald in the late 1930s.[3] Although he does not use the term "authoritarian," his account is really a study in the making of that character. Tortured, terrorized, starved, and humiliated, those prisoners who survived finally responded to their utter helplessness by identifying with the guards. In true authoritarian fashion, they tried to be like the power which had forced their submission; resentment at their ill-treatment was converted into brutality against newcomers and those classified by the Gestapo as "unfit."

Both forms of behavior, aggression as well as submission, went much further than physical safety demanded. It is true that, from an "old prisoner's" standpoint, newcomers and "weaklings" added to the dangers of camp life by their inability to adjust and their tendency to complain. "Bad" behavior in the labor gang invited reprisals against the whole group. As a result, old prisoners sometimes took the initiative in killing the ailing and unfit, most of whom were likely to die anyway within the first few weeks. But, when they killed their fellow prisoners, they did not do so quickly and efficiently, although that would have served their self-protection as well as any other method. Instead they imitated the Gestapo, torturing their victims for days and then slowly killing them.

The old prisoners' identification with their guards went to incredible lengths. Even though it was a punishable offense, they would scavenge for pieces of Gestapo uniform and change their own dress so that they looked more like the guards. They used aggressive words taken over from Gestapo speech; they also copied their guards' leisure activities:

> One of the games played by the guards was to find out who could stand to be hit longest without uttering a complaint. This game was copied by the old prisoners, as though they had not been hit often and long enough without needing to repeat this experience as a game.[4]

Old prisoners prided themselves desperately on being tough like the Gestapo; but their submission to the guards' values exceeded mere praise of physical strength and brutality. Before entering the camp very few had espoused Nazi racism; after several years' imprisonment most believed that the Germans were a master race, although the Gestapo made no attempt to propagate Nazi doctrine within the camp.

On minor precepts, too, old prisoners identified vehemently with their captor.

> Often the Gestapo would enforce nonsensical rules, originating in the whims of one of the guards, but there were always some old prisoners who would continue to follow these rules and try to enforce them on others long after the Gestapo had forgotten about them. . . . These prisoners firmly believed that the rules set down by the Gestapo were desirable standards of human behavior, at least in the camp situation.[5]

Bettelheim is here describing a pure case of rigid, authoritarian-type conventionalism. To old prisoners the most superficial rules represented power, security, and moral force. They wanted so much to submit that they even created benign father figures among the Gestapo—a pathetic fiction which held that certain officers were friendly and kind.

According to Bettelheim arrest and imprisonment *changed* people in these directions, whether or not they were so disposed in the first place. At times, it is true, prisoners who identified with the guards showed great courage in disobeying them. But this does not contradict the idea of authoritarian submission, which, being fraught with underlying resentment, is less complete than the individual would, on one level, like it to be. For many people, perhaps, new resentments against authority are not repressed as easily in adulthood as they are in childhood, when ego and self-awareness are particularly undeveloped.[6]

From Bettelheim's concentration camp we turn to larger social units and more insidious pressures. The next three chapters explore features of social environment which seem to promote authoritarianism. The first chapter focuses on authoritarianism as a response to various kinds of "flux and disruption"—real or threatened social disorganization, the pressures of social mobility, conflict in cultural values. Then, we consider the influence of puritan creeds, with special reference to evangelical Protestantism. Finally we try to connect these elements, tracing a complex triangular relationship between social flux and threat, repressive doctrines, and personality. For reasons already given we will not be able to distinguish clearly and constantly between social effects on behavior and effects on disposition, but we will concentrate on those factors which seem likely to involve both.

8   FLUX AND DISRUPTION

AN ALLEGORY

William Golding's novel *The Lord of the Flies* has many levels of meaning, but in one sense it can be read as a historical account of authoritarianism, a sequence portrayed in telescoped, allegorical form.[1] The collapse of adult values among castaway schoolboys may be seen as the breakdown of an old, once-magic social authority. The boys do *not* react to their new freedom by perpetrating out-and-out anarchy; the group does not dissolve into ultra-individualism, the rampagings of myriad, rival warriors; at no time does the island become a Hobbesian jungle in which all the strong creatures bully all the little ones. Instead the boys seek a new authority to replace the commands of adult civilization now remote beyond the water. At first they turn to Ralph, who with his brain truster, Piggy, most nearly represents grown-up reason, the authority they have known. But Ralph is too moderate and rationalist to strike the emotional chords which the castaways, in their nakedness and confusion, crave unknowingly to hear. The turning point comes in one of the last "assemblies" held by all the boys. Ralph tries to reason away their fears of the unknown, but this approach is so abstract that it does not hold them. Gradually he loses influence to the fierce Jack, who by then has taken on the role of chief hunter. Jack calls them "cry-babies and sissies"; he derides their terror, yet he encourages them to point it at a specific target; he really teaches them to hide their fears in sadism. The meeting ends tumultuously with Jack's cry, "We're strong—we hunt! If there's a beast, we'll hunt it down! We'll close in and beat and beat and beat—!"

Jack is a sort of proto-fascist. Early in the story he catches a wild pig, but humane repugnance—the vestige of an older conscience left him by adult civilization—stays his hand and the pig escapes. He is desperately ashamed of what he considers to be weakness and from that moment on his desire to hunt and kill becomes an obsession. Goaded by a continuing aversion to blood, he takes his own band of special followers after the pigs and away from the signal fire they had promised to guard. The choice is symbolic, for the fire was Ralph's idea and their only way of contacting adult authority. As the fire goes out, a ship appears on the far horizon and then, like the old world itself, recedes from sight.

The first violence, apart from hunting, occurs when Jack strikes Piggy. By himself he dares not fight Ralph, but Piggy is simply a "fat slug," to be reviled in much the same way that the Nazi reviled the bourgeois Jew. Intellectual, asthmatic, a symbol of softness, Piggy it is who repeatedly receives the main brunt of Jack's aggression. But, behind the aggression, Jack himself feels weak, hiding "shame and self-consciousness" beneath a face mask of war paint. He also feels a love for Ralph, a denied feeling which sharpens their rivalry.

Jack depends for strength on his disciples. From traditional society, the well-ordered routinized world of an English preparatory school, he inherits an obedient organization—the choir![2] He speedily converts this to a military machine. Black caps and cloaks, the choirboys' churchly garb, surrender to war paint made of charcoal and clay. Jack is touchy about his battalion; he prides himself immensely on commanding a hunters' elite. Gradually he acquires the human trappings of a potentate—a small chorus to say, "The Chief has spoken"; subordinates who bring him drink when he commands it. The hunters, for their part, accept a cruel regime. From the very beginning Jack cuts away the traditional restraints which bind an English school monitor. He makes his choirboys stand at attention in a broiling sun until one of them, by fainting, becomes the butt for Jack's derision. Much later in the tragic tale, his subordinates punish an "offender" with great excitement and no comprehension, dumbly acting upon Jack's orders. The victim is tied up, left for hours in the hot sun, and then beaten.

Their response to fear and frailty might be seen as an authoritarian

sado-masochism; masochist, by trying to lose themselves in a punitive group discipline; sadistic, by having uncontrolled orgies of slaughter.*
The rituals begin when they cook their first pig. "*Kill the pig. Cut her throat. Spill her blood.*" Their chant becomes a custom, to be repeated in successive rites; the "pig" becomes a human, first a mock target from among their own ranks, and then in hysterical earnest a boy from the others, a sickly and pitiful outsider who crawls in from the forest.[3] Near the end of the story, when Ralph is isolated from his fellows, the chant is heard again. "*Kill the pig. Cut her throat. Spill her blood.*" This time the pig is meant to be Ralph, the self-exile, the deviant, the emblem of an old, fading authority which may yet spoil the new. Submissive as ever to Jack's paranoid hate, the boys go hunting for Ralph.

Once their fears have found new targets, Jack's followers can do homage to the island's "beast." The boys' superstitiousness has potential for both aggression and submission. At first it takes the path of aggression: Jack's cry "If there's a beast we'll hunt it down," answers every half-formed fear of the unknown. But later the boys propitiate the beast by mystically offering it the head of a pig. The beast now represents an awesome power to which all, including Jack, can submit.

"ALONENESS," MOBILITY, AND STATUS CONCERN

In *Escape from Freedom*, Erich Fromm anticipated Golding's theme.[4] He depicted a type of person who felt afraid and alone in a very profound sense—isolated, without purpose, without meaning. Fromm argued that such people often sought security and relatedness in an authoritarian "sado-masochism." He blamed much of this state on a Protestantism whose God demanded a self-denigrating submission unalleviated by easy atonement, but as part of this argument he emphasized the assault by capitalism and mass-industrial organization on those traditional ties which gave men the spiritual union and security that they craved.[5]

On a more scientific plane, the closest thing to a study of aloneness and authoritarianism is the work done by Herbert McCloskey and John Schaar. They found that Americans scoring high on tests measur-

* It is the unstable, uncontrolled nature of the sadism, plus the savagery of the group discipline, which distinguishes this from less pathological forms of submission-aggression. In many societies, ritual controls aggression by its formality; on the island, however, ritual meant an emotional orgy, the loss of control in mass hysteria.

ing "anomie"—the feeling of being alone and adrift in a chaotic and morally deteriorating world—were apt to show many of the most distinctive attributes of the authoritarian character.[6] In their responses to various questionnaires, anomic people tended more than others to be hostile, disapproving of weakness and softness, and suspicious. They tended to be highly conventional, rigid, and superstitious; to like matters clear-cut and certain; and to place an "obsessive" value on hard work and persistence. They were apt to shield their thoughts and wishes from disclosure; to be anxious, guilty, and lacking in social self-confidence. In belief, they tended to be undemocratic, racially prejudiced, and generally intolerant; to hold either extreme left-wing or right-wing views; and, in line with Fromm's theory, to espouse the values of Calvinism and the "Protestant ethic" (although it must be noted that the phrasing of the anomie test questionnaire had a vaguely right-wing slant). On many of these points, a clear majority of those who scored high in the particular trait scored high in anomie; and the correlations between all traits and anomie remained "strong and significant" when "response set" (a person's tendency to agree or disagree with questionnaire statements per se) and various background attributes were allowed for.[7]

Unfortunately, the research does not show whether these apparently authoritarian tendencies were a response to feelings of anomie, let alone to any real circumstances of aloneness and social insecurity. McCloskey and Schaar themselves argued that the character traits produced an anomic outlook on the world rather than vice versa; but both may have intensified each other. It is also possible that a "left behind" or isolated social condition may produce both the character traits and the anomic outlook; in America, rural inhabitants, blacks, and the socially declining, the aged, the widowed, the foreign-born, the poorest, and the least educated score particularly high on the tests measuring anomic outlook.[8]

Social theorists have often connected the alleged isolation of the individual in industrial society with rapid movement between classes. Even apart from this, there are various reasons for supposing that class mobility—either a loss of status or a rapid rise—can promote authoritarian behavior, given other facilitating circumstances. There is, however, no evidence on the matter, so the hypothetical reasons need not here be enumerated.

We do, on the other hand, have some slight evidence that social mobility and concerns about mobility among *parents* can in certain circumstances help to foster authoritarianism. In the original F scale studies the investigators became convinced that parental concern about status and "appearances" was a factor in authoritarian conformity; and they adduced statistical evidence in support of their case.[9] They did not show that social mobility itself was to blame; but in subsequent pages we will catch fleeting glimpses of the strains which "mobility values" can place upon the young. In the pathology of authoritarianism, so it seems, there is sometimes a case history of parental pressures to "match up" and improve the family position. These pressures foment the young person's worries about prowess, self-worth, and identity, while forcing his submission to a commanding father or other *testing* authority.*

The strain of aloneness and the pressures of mobility come together in the life of Martin Luther, whose personality showed much of the authoritarian, for all his spirit of revolt. Luther's father was a driving, manipulative, self-made man, and the demands he made upon his son were the product of a newly competitive world. It was the world described by Fromm and caricatured by Golding, in which the decline of old authorities led the fearful to seek harsh new ones. When temporal authorities, based on custom and coercion, seem ineffectual and yet irreplaceable—when the individual is no longer sure of his worldly place but cannot envisage a new worldly order—then he is likely to turn from the secular to the spiritual, to the clear, uncompromising commands of God or morality. Without belittling the humane side and genius of Luther, we may see in these factors one aspect of his break with Rome and his subsequent hatreds and submissions.[10]

PRE-INDUSTRIAL SOCIETIES

Everything which has been said so far points to modern industrial societies as the most nourishing environment of authoritarianism. In line with this, one might argue that anomie and status fears are bound

---

* See Appendix A, pp. 295–309: the case of "Roger Stanton." In some other cases recounted below—Hung Siu-tshuen, Goebbels, Hitler—there is the catalyzing effect of failure at tests and exams, which to some extent are institutions of mobility and the pressure to achieve.

Some of these notions may help to explain the authoritarianism described by Samuel Butler. For all the apparent stability of Victorian England, there was increasing class mobility and pressure to *win* success while being "respectable." This might produce a manipulative man like the father of Theobald Pontifex—driving ambition squeezed into genteel manners. Consider also the powerful yet difficult position of the governess in many Victorian upper-middle-class homes.

to correlate with cultural change and modern types of social mobility. Yet one must still ask whether pre-industrial societies may not have their own tendencies promoting authoritarianism among some personalities. As much as possible we must guard against the bias of our own cultural position. Among Western scholars it is quite fashionable to attribute all manner of psychic woe to modern flux and disruption, and to look longingly at cultures which seem snugly knit. Other fields do look greener, and embedded within such longings there may be a liberal intellectual version of popular American concerns with law-and-order. A fascinated worry about anarchy and aggression sharpens the academic interest in social stability and cohesion.

In the absence of systematic research comparing a substantial number of different societies, one must concede that pre-industrial groups as a whole may have their own route to authoritarianism. The most plausible influence here would be the sheer weight of tradition and religious awe. Where family and social authorities are tightly meshed and mystically sanctioned, the individual is likely to repress all thought of rebellion and turn his aggressiveness on others. We have already noted that this does not necessarily entail authoritarian maladjustment, but it might be argued that those few in the society who are particularly insecure and unhappy with themselves will be pushed by the culture toward an authoritarian formation—especially when orthodox beliefs permit the scapegoating of witches and outsiders. Even the pressure to prove oneself and show prowess is by no means always absent in a pre-industrial society. There may also be persons upon whom traditional authority places a particularly oppressive burden and whose only aggressive outlet is to abuse others in their predicament who are younger or weaker than they. Consider in this regard the gentry families of Imperial China, whose exploited and subjugated women folk sometimes turned to suicide, but sometimes also became clan martinets enforcing the regime on younger women.[11] However, even *if* this sequence did at times involve authoritarianism, it must be noted that the Chinese examination system and other influences levied upon the gentry family an intense pressure for social advancement of a sort most commonly found in modern societies. In subtle ways, this pressure may have added to the emotional burden placed on the women.

In considering both pre-industrial and modern societies, I would argue that authoritarianism is likely to occur where the environment includes both a commanding traditional authority and social flux or disruption. The latter element may involve (1) changes, contradictions, or ambiguities in values and social understandings; (2) a high rate of personal movement, between classes or geographically; or (3) a combination of these elements.[12] The idea in brief is that a person may become authoritarian when social stresses and uncertainties impel him to cling fiercely to a traditional or part-traditional authority, and yet make it more probable that he will be ambivalent about the values represented by that authority. (It is this aspect—cultural and personal value conflict—which Erich Fromm's thesis leaves out. Of course the *content* of the traditional moral teachings will be important too, but we will defer that aspect as much as possible to the next two chapters.)

I do not wish to imply that this is the only type of environment likely to produce authoritarianism. It must also be admitted that the term "flux and disruption" embraces a number of things which do not always go together in the same society. In practice, however, it is often difficult to distinguish the psychological effect of mobility from the influence, say, of shifting norms in the community as a whole. Such combinations are not necessarily modern; ancient metropolitan civilizations sometimes combined cultural clashes with high mobility rates, at least of a geographical sort: consider the teeming, eclectic cities of Asia Minor and the eastern Mediterranean. It should also be said that a low degree of cultural integration—a separation in spirit of the principles underlying different social activities—does not always mean cultural conflict in the sense of principles which clash and contradict each other. But both are most commonly found—though not invariably —where foreign influences have affected the culture.[13]

Among pre-industrial societies which are fairly untouched by modern contacts, I know of just two cases where research has indicated widespread authoritarianism. Both, in different ways, give a tentative support to my thesis. One is the study of Alor, an East Indian island, by Cora DuBois and associates in the late 1930s. Among the Alorese there seemed to be a two-way relationship between authoritarian tendencies and a fluid, uncohesive social organization. Acutely but passively ambivalent to their authorities, the men in particular seemed to displace their antagonisms in teasing contempt for the awkward young. Ties between people were informal and loose; child rearing was inconsistent; social bonds were weakened by a competitive business materialism. There was much about the Alorese which was very "modern." Yet values were also traditionalist: some customs held important sway, and the people deferred to traditional authorities.[14]

The second of the two studies focused on male character in Sidi Khaled, an Algerian oasis community. As described by an anthropologist and psychologist, family life in the oasis was tinged with deception and intrigue.[15] Young people often saw their fathers as suspicious, threatening figures. Children avoided conscious feelings of rebelliousness against their elders, and boys frequently submitted to older males in a homosexual way. Since passive submission was considered feminine, this produced conflict and anxiety. With the men, concern over impotence was common, all the more since the culture laid great value on virile male prowess. Men blamed sexual failure on their wives, who, like children, were fair game for aggressive rage. To a great extent, people distrusted each other and a large number of men felt a personal threat complex, in unconscious sexual terms as well as in conscious superstitious fear.

In an immediate sense, the authoritarianism could be attributed partly to cultural conflict—inducements to homosexuality, for example, clashing with learned conceptions of strength. Cultural conflict, in other words, helped to make authoritarianism a recurring phenomenon in successive generations. On the other hand, these conflicting values and expectations were themselves, it seems, very largely the expression of authoritarian characters. As with the Alorese, cultural pattern and character disposition helped to maintain each other, and we do not know if one historically came first. It is interesting, however, that *added* cultural conflict seemed to increase in some ways the authoritarian disposition. The observers of Sidi Khaled also studied men who had migrated from the oasis to Algiers, where they were very much exposed to the "whole complex of French urban lfe." According to varied psychological tests, the migrants were prone to more authoritarian feelings and tensions than oasis residents of similar family and class background. (There is little reason to suppose that the most authoritarian people had tended to migrate in the first place.)[16]

SOCIAL CHANGE AND CULTURAL INVASION

In thinking about character and cultural dislocation, some reference must be made to Japan. Masao Maruyamah has written about the effects of Japanese industrialization much as Erich Fromm did about Western Europe's transition from a feudal to a capitalist order. Maruyamah argued that dramatically rapid social change disrupted communal ties and estranged the individual from traditional precepts;

and that it produced some "atomized" people, anxious and frustrated, who felt alone yet depended heavily on others for moral direction.

> The atomized individual is usually apathetic to public affairs, but sometimes this very apathy will turn abruptly into fanatic participation in politics. . . . He is inclined to identify himself totally with authoritarian leadership or to submerge himself into the mystical "whole" expressed in such ideas as national community, eternal racial culture, and so on.[17]

Maruyamah discerned this type among socialist agitators of the early twentieth century, déclassé white-collar workers in the 1930s, and other people. The type was prominent among right-wing terror groups, whose members often combined fanatic patriotism with dependence on father-figure gang leaders. In their patriotism they reverted to the old traditions of *ronin*: unemployed warriors who mixed lawlessness with militarism. (Under the previous Tokugawa state, the warrior class had the theoretical right of *kirusute*, to "cut down and leave" a disrespectful commoner on the spot.) But, despite the shared traditions and common cause, there were frequent clashes between these groups, suggesting the impact of rigid, generally hostile, and power-thirsty feelings. Fear and hatred seemed to be aggravated by economic distress. On all of these points, the Japanese terrorists were remarkably like the Ku Klux Klan.

Robert Lifton has also described what may be an authoritarian type in postwar Japan. Among Japanese youth and young adults, he found a keen "sense of historical dislocation," a feeling that traditional links with the past had been broken.[18] One response to this feeling was a "mode of restoration," an urge to return to the past, to "draw upon great and ennobling symbols of Japanese history." Many right-wing university students fell into this category, including at its most extreme end the fanatic who was ready to assassinate and die for his beliefs. The intensely personal form that restorationism could take was shown in the words of a religious youth group leader. He told Lifton of visiting the sacred shrine of Japan's legendary first Emperor, and of how, after the visit, "I felt the Emperor Jimmu alive inside me . . . and the blood of Japanese history running through my veins." Yet the same people often felt an "ambivalent attraction" to modern intellectual figures—Freud, Einstein, even Marx. They were fascinated by the power of these thinkers at the same time that they were denouncing their influence and the change they helped bring about. Purity against alien, corrupting influence was a strong motif. The religious group leader already quoted also told Lifton:

There is a prophecy of a time of purification for removing the filth from us. . . . We have to undergo this birth pain, which is the coming of the third world war. . . . Then, after that, there can be a world state, having the whole world as one family with the Emperor of Japan at its center.

Views of the future were both utopian and anxious, and the anxiety was increasing as the "impurities" became more embedded around them. In response, the restorationists were apt to "vent anxious . . . hostility" on left-wing student intellectuals, seeing them as "threatening embodiments of evil."[19]

These Japanese perspectives are largely free of the chicken-and-egg problems which we encountered in the case of Alor and Sidi Khaled. It is clear that Japan's social flux was not primarily a reflection of divisive personalities, however much those personalities added to the turmoil. On the other hand, neither Lifton's report nor Maruyamah's says as much about the precise mechanisms of personality as do the Alorese and Algerian studies. To combine some of the advantages of both types of study we shall now focus at length on one man, a historic leader whose personality made a vivid response to a tumult of circumstances.

HUNG SIU-TSHUEN AND THE TAIPING REBELLION[20]

The rebellion led by Hung Siu-tshuen ravaged southern China for more than fifteen years and evidently killed about twenty million people, nearly the number killed in World War I. The story of Hung shows in very personal terms an effect of cultural disruption, combined with social mobility and traditional ethnic hatreds, and operating in an environment where obedience ("filial piety") was immensely stressed. We must look at Hung's character over a lifetime. Feelings of failure; resentments at authority obliquely expressed; alignment with punitive gods representing a blend of old and new; a puritanical, sadistic, but fragile morality—these elements gradually revealed themselves before Hung's final disaster.

Hung Siu-tshuen was born in 1814, of a poor peasant family near Canton.[21] His parents belonged to the Hakka ethnic group, whose villages dotted Kwangtung province. "Hakka" means "Guest" or "Sojourner," and from the third century B.C. the group had been intermittently harassed by their neighbors. Persecution had driven them from the highlands of northern China to the south—to Kwangtung and the

Kwangsi mountains. A proud and vigorous people, the Hakkas retained their own distinctive customs and dialect, a form of ancient Mandarin. In later years, when the Western trading powers had made their impact on Kwangtung, many Hakkas even spoke to other Chinese in Pidgin English! Both sides considered themselves the real natives, the others foreigners. Vehement nationalists, they had fought valiantly against China's Mongol and Manchu conquerors, and at the time of Hung's boyhood they still bitterly resented the Manchu Imperial regime. As a schoolboy, Hung was bright, ambitious, a bully. After he left school, his relatives combined resources to prepare him for the Chinese civil service exams. If he passed the bachelor's degree exam he and his family would automatically become part of the scholar-gentry elite, enjoying specific legal privileges, and if he passed further exams, he might obtain a much-coveted post in the Chinese bureaucracy.

In his early twenties, Hung journeyed twice to Canton to take the annual bachelor's exam; in both years he failed. This in itself was not unusual: many educated Chinese went on trying and failing examinations into old age. But on his second failure Hung reacted differently. He appears to have undergone a rather dramatic nervous breakdown. Following the news of the exam results, he became deeply depressed and felt physically ill. Despite his slender means, he hired a sedan chair and was carried to his father's house, where he is said to have fainted on arrival, lain prostrate for hours, and developed a high fever. He then went into what seemed to be a trance, during which he dreamed that a great throng of people were bidding him welcome to their ranks. On waking, he called his family and apologized for his failures: "My days are counted, and my life will soon be closed. O my parents! How badly have I returned the favor of your love to me! I shall never retain a name that may reflect its lustre upon you."[22]

Again he fainted, and it was during this spell that he had his great vision. He dreamed that he was carried on a sedan chair to a fashionable place where multitudes honored him but an old woman appeared and called him dirty. She washed him and took him among some elders, who cut out his heart and other organs and replaced them with new red ones. Hung was then taken before an old man with a golden beard, a godlike figure, who declared that men, instead of worshiping him, were serving demons. He instructed Hung to slay the demons and recall the people of the world to their duty. The dream then displayed to him some of the world's depravities.

When he awoke, Hung immediately told his father of his commission. For the next few days he was extremely keyed up, and continued to have vivid dreams or hallucinations. In one, he saw Confucius being scolded for faithlessness, and repenting. In another, a middle-aged man taught him how to slay demons; and he repeatedly had visions of the demons themselves, which he tried to kill. Hung's relatives, who after one of his earlier fainting spells had taken him for dead, now thought him mad and confined him to his room. The anthropologist Anthony Wallace has described this "hyperactive" period, following the trance and main vision, as a "paranoid" stage, and he argues that some other prophet-leaders of social "revitalization" movements underwent the same sequence of phases.[23]

Hung recovered from his illness, and to his family and friends he seemed a greatly changed person—physically heavier, but also more dignified and imposing. He turned to schoolteaching and became noted for his severity and his efforts to reform the "vicious." Goaded by poverty, he decided to compete once more in the government examinations. He traveled to Canton in 1843 at the age of thirty-one, and again failed the exam, owing possibly to the corruption of his examiners.[24] This time his reaction was more explosive. When he heard that he had failed, he flung his books on the floor, shouting, "Wait till we examine scholars of the Empire ourselves." Hung was now determined to lead a revolt against the Manchu government; already, it seems, he identified the Manchus with demons.

The previous year China had signed a treaty with Britain, opening several ports to British trade and residence. Westerners and their books had acquired some prestige and in 1843, not long after he failed the examination, Hung turned again to some Christian tracts which a Western missionary had given him at the time of his first examination failure. They consisted of sermons, essays, and some very poor Chinese translations of Bible passages, but in comparison with the New Testament they stressed the destruction of idols and tortures in hell.[25] The work inspired Hung. He interpreted the Kingdom of Heaven as China, *the* China, morally reformed and freed of the Manchus. At some point, either then or later, Hung apparently came to believe that the old man of his dreams was God, and that the middle-aged man, who taught him about demons, was Jesus.

With a close school friend, one of his earliest converts, Hung began preaching a version of Christianity. Their duties, as they saw them, included the destruction of Catholic images and Confucian tablets.

This, predictably, lost Hung his job as schoolteacher, and the two then traveled to Kwangsi, where they made more than a hundred converts. In 1843, after some months of writing and tutoring at home, Hung again visited Canton. He spent two months studying with the Reverend Issachar J. Roberts, a Southern Baptist missionary from Tennessee, and he then continued to live in the city, very poor, writing his doctrine of revolution. His old school friend, Feng Yun-shan, was in the meantime working as a laborer in Kwangsi and building an army of converts, mainly Hakkas. In the summer of 1847, Hung joined Feng and his followers at "Thislemont" (Tzu-chin-shan in Kwangsi province). The Association of God-Worshipers was organized; it numbered more than three thousand men, and Hung became their leader. This marked the beginning of the Taiping Rebellion.

At the time of the rebellion, southern China was in turmoil. To famine and depression was added an alien government which combined oppressiveness with weakness. Through heavy taxation and other devices, the corrupt Manchus abused Chinese of all classes; and at the same time, administrative services were deteriorating, especially in remote areas like Kwangsi. Riots and uprisings were a feature of the day. In Kwangsi, strife between the Hakkas and their neighbors was increasing, and at one point, indeed, the Taiping forces received a horde of Hakka peasants who had been dispossessed from their land.

Another source of turmoil was the Opium War of 1839-42, provoked by the British in order to win trading facilities along the Chinese coast. Britain's easy victory accelerated the decline of Manchu influence and prestige, and the war itself, coupled with the growing presence of Westerners after the war, inflamed the Chinese national consciousness. This was particularly true among the Hakkas, who provided Western merchants with much of their coolie labor in Canton. The "red-haired devils" were respected for their knowledge and skills but resented for their arrogant, alien ways. To make matters worse, the opening of other ports to Western trade caused a sharp downturn in the Cantonese economy. Hung's God Worshipers attracted a number of unemployed coolies from Canton, as well as some pirates whose lives had been interrupted by the British navy.

Economic distress, political oppression, war, the decline of order, the decay of old authority, and (yet) the inflaming of patriotism—these made the Taiping movement attractive. In the early years particularly, the Taipings were a fanatic religious sect. The religion was based on Hung's writings, and it contained elements of Christianity,

Confucianism, and Taoism. Its ethics were severely puritan and stressed a Communist fellowship.

> In the world there are many men, all brothers; in the world there are many women, all sisters. For the sons and daughters of Heaven, the men have men's quarters and the women have women's quarters; they are not allowed to intermix. Men or women who commit adultery or who are licentious are considered monsters; this is the greatest possible transgression of the Heavenly Commandments. The casting of amorous glances, the harboring of lustful imaginings about others, the smoking of opium, and the singing of libidinous songs are all offenses against the Heavenly Commandments.[26]

Hung's doctrine inveighed against aggression between individuals, against killing, robbing, and injuring; it also enjoined respect for parents and praise of one God; but beyond this it attached no real importance to Christian love and humility.[27]

The Taiping rebels created their own theocracy. Hung was the Celestial King, considered to be the Younger Brother of Jesus. "Taiping" meant "Great Peace," a period of perfect order idealized in classical Chinese thought. The regime's official name was the Heavenly Kingdom of the Great Peace, and so it combined traditional ideals with new and partly alien programs. It preached, and in some areas implemented, a system of public land ownership, yielding wealth to each adult in equal shares. Small wonder that the Taiping movement has attracted the attention of historians, as a precursor of Chinese Communism. The position of women was greatly enhanced. They held equal civil and military positions with men; polygamy and forced marriages were discouraged; and foot binding was banned. Equality was accompanied by strict enforcement of morals. A number of followers, convicted of idolatry and of smoking opium, were publicly executed.

In its early years the Taiping army won dramatic success. It swept through southeast China and made its headquarters in Nanking. Foreign observers were impressed by its discipline and morale, and the friendship within its ranks. But after 1856 its fortunes declined. With the help of Western forces, reorganized government troops finally crushed the rebellion amid appalling slaughter. A month before the end, Hung lost hope and took poison. His body, clad in imperial yellow, was found in a sewer beneath his Nanking palace.

One reason for the failure was the moral collapse of the Taiping leadership. As another writer puts it, Hung's "whole personality disintegrated" after he took Nanking.[28] He withdrew from active command into his palace, where he violated Taiping codes by keeping a virtual harem. Despite the new uplifting of women, Hung was said to have been brutal to female retainers until complaints made him modify his behavior.[29] Extravagance and indolence marked his new life, and several of his top subordinates—the five Kings—followed his example.[30] Each acquired the lavish ways of an old-style emperor. Power struggles broke out between them, and Hung's position was so threatened that he had two of his Kings assassinated. But the corruption spread to other leaders in the movement. Hung's old school friend, the dedicated Feng Yun-shan, had fallen in battle before the occupation of Nanking, and Hung came to trust nobody but his relatives and his Cantonese guards. Relations deteriorated between Hung and two of his ablest generals, who completely failed to cooperate with each other. And yet, among many of the rank-and-file, religious dedication remained to the end. The last one hundred thousand defenders of Nanking burned themselves to death *en masse* rather than surrender.

To what extent others in the revolution shared Hung's character traits it is difficult to say.

Two of his five Kings claimed, like Hung, to receive direct revelations from God. One of them, Yang Hsiu-ching, the Eastern King, combined arrogance and intelligence with an almost sheeplike deference to the advice of the Northern King, who used him to intrigue against Hung.[31] Yang was also capable of using the whip to administer punishments ordered by his God.

But we have more to go on when we turn to Hung's own personality. How did his authoritarianism show itself? In what sense and to what extent was it the product of social flux and cultural conflict? We simply do not know how much of Hung's authoritarian disposition was formed before his first attempt at the Canton examination. His domineering behavior as a schoolboy suggests that some elements, at least, had appeared by adolescence. Be that as it may, Hung's experiences with the examiners created, or at least magnified, a sense of failure and frustration, and to understand this one must appreciate the cultural circumstances in which Hung went to Canton.

First, China was a mobile class society. Among the different careers, government posts held overwhelming prestige and they were filled very largely by competitive examinations. Through this system a humbly born Chinese could climb to the top of the civil service. In fact, however, wealth and high birth conferred immense advantages. Money could help provide the scholarly background needed to pass the examinations, and when government standards declined, as they did in the 1800s, family means could even buy a government post or bribe the examiners. The stakes were high because a family's fortunes rode with each candidate. If it did not have a member among the literati elite—that happy elect of baccalaureates—a family could not for very long hold gentry status. It was better still if a member passed several examinations and won a government post, for this was a family's best protection against arbitrary imperial power—sudden conscription, demands for corvée labor, or plundering by government troops. All these conditions put enormous pressure on the promising student. Officially, the examinations were supposed to be a fair test of merit, yet if the candidate was poor, the dice were loaded against him. Small wonder that the system made people feel failures for reverses that they could not help. The examinations became focal points of "anxiety, tension and social strain,"[32] and the candidate's response sometimes took the form of an almost craven dependence. In 1768, decades after he had passed the highest examination, a scholar addressed a poem to his revered examiner:

> What agony it was thirty years ago
> At Peking, waiting for the lists to appear . . . !
> I met someone who told me I had passed;
> I was bowled over by this thunderclap of joy and surprise,
> I thought it was a mistake, thought it was only a dream;
> I was in a sorry state of doubt and dread.
> Yet it was true; that staunch master Tang . . . ,
> Had written that my name was to figure on the list,
> Had rescued me out of my dark abyss. . . .
> Parents, however much they love a child,
> Have not the power to place him among the chosen few,
> Only the examiner can bring the youth to notice,
> And out of darkness carry them up to Heaven.[33]

No such rapture came to Hung, at least not until his vision. Poverty reduced his chances of passing the examinations, yet his family continued to pin their hopes on his efforts. This brings us to another circumstance of Hung's failure—his Hakka identity.

We can only speculate about the part this factor played, but judging by what is known about the Hakkas, it cannot be ignored. I suggest that being a Hakka intensified Hung's social ambition and his shame, or guilt, at failure. There is no evidence that Hakka membership gave people a sense of cultural inferiority—far from it—but it did place them in an anomalous situation. For one thing, there was an imbalance between their ethnic pride and the contempt shown them by other Chinese, particularly by the more ignorant. For another, the Hakkas' claim to be a part of old China permitted them to compete within the traditional examination system at the same time that they hated the alien Manchu regime—a special historic hate. Both imbalances would intensify the Hakkas' drive to succeed, to uphold the honor of their group, to "beat the system" and "show them" (the Hakkas indeed produced many noted scholars). The position of the Hakkas may also have increased the pressures levied by the family on its more promising members. This would add to the burden of "filial piety" felt by virtually all Chinese, and certainly felt by Hung, as his words to his father after the second failure showed.

These two circumstances, the Chinese class system and Hakka membership, may have helped shape Hung's authoritarian disposition as well as simply eliciting more noticeable authoritarian behavior. The dreams themselves indicate that pressure to achieve and the fear of social failure fostered at some level a concern with strength and weakness; and the rebellious Hakka tradition may well have encouraged an aggressive response to insecurity. If the tradition was felt deeply enough, if the young Hung absorbed at an especially formative age some of the violence and resentments that occurred between Hakkas and their neighbors, these influences would encourage the basic personality structure to evolve aggressive mechanisms for coping with stress. And anyway the Hakka tradition must certainly have encouraged aggressive *behavior,* given a basic authoritarian disposition.

Another circumstance was the general lawlessness and weak government of the late Manchu era. When government was strong and the Empire well ordered, nearly all candidates who failed the examinations reacted in one of two traditional ways. Either they took up teaching and continued to prepare for the exams (or pretend they were preparing) or else they retreated, becoming hermits or monks. In times of unrest, however, failed candidates were occasionally bold enough to take the path of rebellion. For Hung, as for others before him, decline of civic order not only provided political opportunities for aggressive behavior in response to failure; it also made it easier for him to *think* of rebellion in some forms. At the same time, however, the growing acceptance around him of rebelliousness was in conflict with traditional deference to authority. "Authority," for its part, included officialdom, whose majesty the ritual of the examination system affirmed. If this cultural conflict had become an inner conflict deep within the individual, it would by definition have affected Hung's basic personality structure.

The mixture of rebellious urge and traditional awe at authority can be seen in a poem attributed to Hung. According to a cousin, he wrote this after he had failed the examinations for the second time.

> The dragon hiding in a sea corner fears to disturb the sky.
> He is waiting for the gathering of the wind and clouds
> Before he flies to all directions of the sky and sets the universe in order.

Historians are not sure if the poem really was written at this time, but Hung's illness, which followed soon afterward, expressed the same theme. His very homecoming, crowned by apologies to his parents for failing them, mixed filial submission with a grandiose self-pity. The illness provided a way of vengeful self-assertion—through the dreams —without directly assailing authority in real life. The emotional overtones to Hung's illness suggested that it expressed impulses which he could not gratify more directly (both psychosomatic disorders and conversion hysteria may perform this function).[34] Like the poem, Hung's dreams provided a way of projecting aggression into fantasy; and after the illness his schoolteaching role enabled him to express aggression against "bad" pupils. Whether or not he was here re-enacting the system's rejection of himself, the record of his life suggests that, in direct personal confrontations, both character and situation made it easier for him to attack the wayward and weak rather than strong male figures.

Note also that after his illness Hung again attempted the government examinations. Economic need helped provoke this, but it does show that Hung only became an active rebel after he had repeatedly failed to win status within the traditional system. In a sense, social mobility can corrupt the rebellious, enticing them to seek power within the system they hate, and making their attitude toward authority more ambivalent. It is all the harder to rebel when the system combines enticements of mobility with awe-inspiring tradition and ritual.

Hung's visions showed his dependence on stern authority figures. In the name of new authorities, the old power, Confucius, with its stress on moderation, could be attacked as a degenerate betrayer. One historian has argued that the god with a golden beard in Hung's dreams was the Western missionary, also bearded, who had given

Hung his Christian tracts; and that the middle-aged man who taught Hung about demons was the missionary's Chinese interpreter, who had also apparently been middle-aged.[35] Both this account and Hung's own interpretation may be true. In other words, the two figures in the dream may have represented, or come later to represent, God and Jesus, but they were closely associated with the missionary and his interpreter. Hung's concept of Jesus as his elder brother enabled him to feel a part of supreme power at the same time he was submitting.

His submission to the two figures showed a strong sado-masochist tone. To get close to authority in his dreams, his dirtiness had first to be exposed, his inner being purified and made strong. The old woman who washed him like a baby, the elders who destroyed part of him and then gave him clean new organs—these authorities demanded the utmost in submission, a return to infantile dependence and more. Having submitted, he could then attack the defilement of the world, but he could only do so as part of authority, closely instructed and supported by a divine elder brother.

The beginning of Hung's first dream was a dramatic reversal of his real fortunes. Lording it over reverent multitudes in a sedan chair seemed a clear compensation for the honor he did not receive at the hands of the examiners. But fantasies of glory were not enough, hence the appearance of the old woman who called him dirty and washed him. Only through submission could he rid himself of defilement and failure. He could then switch targets, from his own felt flaws to the demons and depravities of the world.[36]

To what extent Hung's "identity crisis" affected his basic structure it is impossible to say. Judging by his heightened severity and moralism after the dreams, they at least marked a point at which his behavior became more actively authoritarian. His subsequent, and last, failure in the examinations probably heightened his resentments still further and intensified his wish for a strong new authority. Hence the turning to Protestant doctrines and his destructive attack, mounted in their name, upon Confucian and Catholic ornaments. The historian Ssu-Yu Teng claims that Hung saw political advantages in Christianity. The Opium War had just ended, and Hung could sense that the creed of the victors would make an impressive revolutionary doctrine. According to this argument, Hung was a shrewd propagandist who knew how to advance his political fortunes through religious superstition. This interpretation, however, does not contradict the idea of authoritarianism. Mass leaders are often able to exploit their own fanaticism, to sound chords in other people which echo their own characters. With some this process is more intuitive than explicitly self-aware.

One must also recognize that identifying with the aggressor can be very attractive to authoritarians, particularly when the symbols of native authority spell irredeemable weakness, or when the aggressor's creed can somewhat be aligned with a drive to restore "old virtues." Hung's religion, indeed, combined new and old, alien and native. It reflected in part the uncomfortable position of the Hakkas, fiercely Chinese yet harried by Chinese neighbors and exposed to Western influences. For Hung himself and other Taiping leaders, the religion did not provide a well-implanted morality; this was amply demonstrated by their subsequent lapses from Taiping principles. It is here that cultural conflict had its clearest effect on Hung's basic structure. The decline of Confucian orthodoxy and the rise of new doctrines enabled Hung to rebel against the old—first in fantasy, then in action—and to establish his own religion. The establishment was a brave work, but its roots in the Chinese soil were too shallow to survive prolonged stress. Hung was a man plunged between cultural traditions. Consciously or unconsciously he tried to fuse them, but the result for his own character was a brittle morality, fierce rather than deep. The morality, in short, of an authoritarian conscience. For others in turn, his new creed's strictness and messianic fervor had great appeal in a time of uncertainty and flux. Thus, cultural disruption not only fostered Hung's authoritarian morality but gave it political influence.

The Taiping religion gives an insight into Hung's conscience and personality because it was based so largely on his own writings and because it matched so well the domineering moralism he had already shown. Although it drew from existing theologies, the selections and omissions were very much his. We must contrast his doctrine's stress against sexual "license"—even in thought—with the facts of his later life. In view of his continuing earnestness, his keeping of a virtual harem when he was still leader of the faith suggests an all-or-nothing control and a projection of desire into severe laws. True, his lapses can also be seen as a reversion from Christian puritanism to Chinese imperial corruption, but this again shows that Hung's morality was not well integrated with impulse.

In many respects, admittedly, Taiping doctrines were genuinely aimed to raise up the oppressed masses. The Hakka spirit of independence was a vital force behind the revolt, and its influence could be seen vividly in the improved status given women. Unlike other

Chinese groups, traditional Hakka culture shunned foot binding, the bone-breaking and stunting device by which women were made daintily helpless. In banning the practice, therefore, Hung was true to his forebears, and his whole revolutionary zeal may well have contained humane elements. But the humanity did not seem to go very far in his own personal dealings, nor for that matter did egalitarianism.

With the collapse of Hung's puritan morality, his authoritarianism became more obvious. His conscience (or crude superego) retained a rigid dependence on external images of authority, for all his newfound sensual freedom. Not long before the Taipings' final defeat, a loyal and competent general pointed out to Hung that Nanking, his capital, was in dire military danger, and that the headquarters should retreat south. Hung said that God would protect and provide for them, and he insisted on remaining. Indolence and the vanity of power came together with submissive fatalism—a disastrous mixture. In the last part of his life his character was described as being stubborn, irritable, and violent—indeed he likened himself to fire—and his mixture of passive sloth and rigid fanaticism boxed him into some upsetting relationships (now submissive, now dominating) with rivalrous subordinates. At his suicide, before drinking the poison, he cried out, "It is not the Heavenly Father who has failed me, but I who have failed the Heavenly Father."[37] He repeated this over and over again as if to deny and turn onto himself the angry rebellion he really felt.

It is clear, anyway, that even toward the end Hung's preachments about God were not mere propaganda. They seemed deeply involved with personality. This was shown in Hung's relations with Yang Hsiu-ching, the Eastern King. During the early days of the movement, Yang had made the same spiritual claim as Hung: that God entered his body to give orders. Despite the potential threat to his authority, Hung accepted Yang's claim and with his own hand he wrote a note in the Taiping Bible, declaring that Yang was a beloved son of God and that Yang and he were born of the same sage mother. At the time, Hung had political incentive for making the concession. Both he and his chief coordinates were far from the region where Yang claimed his power, and the zeal of Taiping disciples in that area was waning. The place had a tradition of similar claims by its leaders.

And now to summarize. The disruption of traditional Chinese culture contributed to Hung's authoritarianism in three main ways. First, it encouraged aggressive behavior, and it may even have fostered vehicles for hostility within Hung's basic disposition. Second, magic symbols of authority continued to demand submissive behavior; this encouraged the rebel to stake his revolt in authoritarian form, in the name of a harshly dominating power over him. Again, conflict may have been fostered in the basic personality structure, a clash of submissiveness and rebelliousness. In the third place, competition between old and new doctrines led to a fused morality which, lacking deep roots in Hung's cultural background, lacked deep roots in his own personality. Evolved not until the middle of his life, the final Taiping synthesis could do nothing to foster a well-implanted morality. And before that Hung had been exposed to a moral climate in which new values of science and Christianity, too alien to sink in far, had even so weakened old values. Traditional authority retained some magic, but the ethics on which the magic ultimately depended were fading. All of this surely affected Hung's basic structure. His conscience was relatively superficial; hence it was all the more dependent on external authority, or harsh images thereof, to keep his destructive impulses in some sort of order. Small wonder that he turned to a puritan creed and that his main religious mentor was a Southern Baptist. The full significance of this will become apparent in the next chapter.

9 PURITAN CREEDS

Many readers will have heard the kind of fundamentalist preacher whose castigation of sinners seems to be answering more general hatred within him; who dwells with salacious moralism on the excesses of high society, builds a black gulf between the elect and the damned, and rejoices in portraits of an apocalypse; whose God is a jealous God, punishing rather than forgiving, less a spiritual force than a feared dictator. In such cases, it may be argued that puritanism provides a mere channel for authoritarian behavior and that it cannot be cited as a cause. I contend, however, that some of the harsher Protestantisms have indeed fomented authoritarianism, not simply by encouraging authoritarian behavior but by reaching into the very structure of personality. At its most restrictive, evangelical Protestantism promotes a vivid sense of original sin, a guilty, repressive attitude toward sensual impulse, and a moralizing intolerance toward others.

When the Puritan or the modern Christian finds that his right hand offends him he not only cuts it off but sends an executioner with a chopper all down the street, chopping off the hands of all the men, women and children in the town. Then he has the curious feeling of comradeship and of everybody being comfortable together.

This comment of G. K. Chesterton's is itself indiscriminate but it scores a point.[1] Some puritan faiths seem to develop within a person the mechanisms of displacement and projection by encouraging him to attack in others what he hates in himself.

Consult the spiritual interest of your neighborhood as well as the temporal. Be concerned lest the deceitfulness of sin undo any of the neighbors. If there be any idle persons among them, I beseech you, cure them of their idleness.... If any in the neighborhood are taking to bad courses—lovingly and faithfully admonish them.

The spirit in which Cotton Mather wrote these words was too charitable to be called authoritarian; the same tract indeed exhorts the reader to help the poor, care for the sick, and comfort the bereaved. But, in the execution of his commands, tenderness sometimes fell by the wayside, leaving an aggressive moralism of the most intolerant kind.[2]

As several writers have pointed out, Protestant churches do not have an equivalent of the confessional through which the worshiper may unload some of his guilt.[3] In the confessional, moreover, the Catholic may express some of the irksome feeling that his duties to God can create. The devout puritan, by contrast, must carry full responsibility for any champing at religious discipline. This perhaps is one reason why the early New England puritans so often kept voluminous diaries, castigating themselves for letting their minds wander from religious study and for other acts of disloyalty which to us may seem small. The diaries were a substitute for the confessional, without offering anything like the same mechanism for draining off guilt and potential rebellion; the principle of an intensely direct and constant responsibility to God remained. Hence an added attraction of the moral crusade, alleviating guilt generally, and in some cases, it seems, denying and diverting more serious doubts about God's demands.

In much of this the authoritarian potential is plain. When instilled at an early age, puritan teaching is all the more likely to affect the basic character structure; and when parents are anyway tyrannical, it may encourage them to be more so. Nor need the Protestant ethic of self-criticism prevent the individual from taking a typically authoritarian view of himself. The literature of English and American puritanism is full of self-rebuke; yet, once the individual felt that God was going to save him, his very humility could carry overtones of elitism and boastfulness. "O God, I am your own sinner sent to save others" has been the virtual motto of many a radical Protestant. On some level he would still fear a fall from grace, but the flagellation of his character often took a stereotyped course, as if he were attacking not just himself but the sorry nature of all mankind. And, indeed, the belief that earthly fortune was a sign of grace gave religious sanction to a material-minded snobbery.

So much for the general argument that puritanism can help to shape authoritarian character. Before looking to concrete examples we should recognize that authoritarian character is only one of several prominent forms of personality found among puritan Protestants. For many puritans, their religion really has meant a brave autonomy of spirit. Their earnest loyalty to God, their ability to declare dependence on divine spiritual strength, seems to have affirmed a sense of identity and strengthened a basic self-esteem, for all the talk of original sin. What is more, among the earliest American puritans, as among their friends left behind in Britain, many combined a rigid sense of duty with considerable enjoyment of the senses and great tenderness to loved ones. Excess in physical pleasure, not physical pleasure itself, was abhorrent. And even the most repressed and guilty ones did not all release their feelings in predominantly authoritarian ways: some displaced their energies in deeply humane crusades for the oppressed and afflicted. Puritan teaching was, perhaps, least likely to produce authoritarianism where parents and teachers balanced the dogmas of hellfire and sin with a fortifying love and they emphasized the Christian precept of humanity. It was when this balance was lacking that puritanism would "suggest" most forcibly to a young disposition the authoritarian mechanisms for dealing with feelings of weakness—the displacement and projection of impulse in punitive desires.

The following accounts are taken from American history, for it is here that the potential links between puritan creed and authoritarian character have been very apparent.[4]

The most somber side of puritanism was seen in Salem, Massachusetts, in 1692. That year a group of young Salem girls fell into a series of hysterical fits. During these spells they accused various citizens of witchcraft. The accused were brought to trial, where the judges accepted most of the "evidence" against them. To the bewilderment of themselves and their families, twenty people were executed. Today, at such distance in time, no one can explain it all with certainty; nevertheless the events seem to indicate a rampant authoritarianism, at least among the leading accusers. It is true that witchcraft beliefs and witchcraft trials have an ancient and "respectable" history, and they were part of Massachusetts culture. The experience of Salem was unusual less in kind than in magnitude—the accusation and conviction of witches became an epidemic which reached a point of threatening the whole community. The roots of this epidemic lay deep in the puritan potential, and for this it deserves an extended discussion.

Of the girls who first broke into fits, the natural leader was Ann Putnam, an ailing, highly-strung, and precociously well-read twelve-year-old. Like her mother she had devoured such literature as the Book of Revelation and Wigglesworth's savage poem *The Day of Doom*. Desperately earnest, she spoke and acted with the fierce sense of a merciless God. To the weight of her Calvinist beliefs was added the influence of a bitter, self-pitying, and neurotically suspicious mother, her confidante from an early age, who made her an authority on the misdoings of her neighbors and every rumored scandal of the past twenty years. As for her father, he seemed a tolerant and affectionate husband—to the point, once, of savagely persecuting a clergyman who had resisted his wife's prying.[5]

Two of the other girls were the cousins Abigail Williams and Betty Parris, both friends of Ann Putnam. Abigail lived with Betty, whose father was Salem's minister.[6] Not much is known about Betty except that she seemed a quiet, submissive little person, ever ready to follow Abigail's lead. Abigail, for her part, was a smug, malicious eleven-year-old, the kind of puritan who seemed to enjoy lurid stories of the devil and who assumed (in one part of her mind) that children of the elect would inherit salvation. Yet both girls had been taught that a newborn babe which died unbaptized went straight to hell (if the "easiest room" in it). What chance, then, for a sinning child? As in the case of Ann Putnam, family tensions compounded these burdens. The Reverend Samuel Parris had been an unsuccessful businessman; as a minister he was hard, resentful, tyrannical. Mrs. Parris is an obscure figure: self-effacing, it seems, but active in numerous good works.

The girls' hysteria suggests authoritarianism in several ways. First, the initial accusations of witchcraft struck an enjoyed but forbidden fruit. The Parrises owned a West Indian slave, named Tituba. When the parents were out of the kitchen, Tituba would instruct Abigail and Betty in the secrets of black magic. Their number was soon joined by three fascinated teenagers who lived nearby. All of them knew that what they were doing was very wrong and expressly banned by the church. It is not surprising, really, that the first "witch" to be accused was Tituba.

By this point, however, the girls' hysteria had been under way for some time. Beginning with Betty, the fits had spread like contagion to other girls in the village. Girl after girl fell to writhing and screaming as if afflicted by hell's torment itself. With Betty, at least, guilt was clearly involved, for after one fit she cried out that she was damned.

One senses that the fits contained a strong element of self-hate, but this is only a hunch. What is more apparent is that at some stage the fits offered an unconscious formula for enjoying and yet attacking the forbidden. The adults of Salem quickly assumed that the girls were hapless victims of witchcraft. If the idea had not already occurred to some of the girls, it soon did. They were encouraged to identify their tormentors, and several names were suggested to them, including that of Tituba. The girls now had sanction to act like witches, the very objects they were attacking. Thus Abigail at one point attempted to fly up the chimney, having first tried to fight off the black influence assailing her. Even before the witchcraft notion became explicit, the fits seemed to express an urge to get away from conscience, indeed from self. Betty in a fit once hurled a Bible from her; and Abigail barked on all fours like an animal, and would shout and cover her ears to blot out the sound of holy words. Like the rebellious dreams in Hung Siu-tshuen's trance, the fits enabled people to express revolt that they dared not show in ordinary behavior. The fits also provided fantasies by which the girls could project sensual feelings entwined with fears of threat. At least two of their number reported seeing a woman of the village (an accused witch) suckling a strange creature. In one case the alleged creature was a yellow bird; in the other, a snake.

In her review of the Salem events, Marion Starkey emphasizes the "repressed vitality" of the many teenage girls living in the village. This, she suggests, coupled with the strong anxiety about sin that was dinned into them, sought release in the witchcraft delusion.[7] In many children of the time, puritan teaching produced a sense of sin that was inseparable from outright terror of hell. The combination often led them into a forced religious precocity. Thus, Samuel Sewall, one of the Salem judges, used to find his little daughter weeping at the thought that she would not find God but would go to hell.[8]

Marion Starkey also suggests that the fits gave the girls a much-craved-for status and attention, not to speak of diversion from the winter's drudgery. "Hitherto snubbed and disregarded, they were now cossetted and made much of."[9] In some girls, surely, the exhibitionist element was much stronger than in others; but it was not generally so conscious as to make the whole affair a farce. As in much authoritarianism, the behavior gave opportunities for self-pity ("those poor afflicted girls"), and if there was opportunism, it seemed to be intuitive rather than coldly premeditated.

Starkey does claim that the fits expressed rebellion—against temporal figures of authority as well as religious inhibitions. Before the attacks, the girls "lived at the mercy of smug matrons and dowagers, and how some of them resented those dowagers and matrons."[10] Although the first three accused witches were not "respectable" people, later victims included solid citizens of the community. But even here the girls' behavior did not stray from an authoritarian pattern. They accused their victims in the name of the religious authority that had so dominated their childhood; they did not confront them as brave individualists, as persons responsible for their own actions. If something happened to jolt them out of their hysteria, they could be very submissive to their elders. When several girls started making their scenes in church, their parents abruptly hushed them—and hush they did. A more notable incident occurred at nearby Andover, where another circle of hysterical accusers had formed after visits from the Salem girls. An accused businessman threatened to initiate a "one thousand pound action of defamation" against the adolescents. He heard no more about it, and the mass panic at Andover subsided shortly thereafter.*

But what of the adults who followed the young girls' lead, accepting their pronouncements as religious truth? Here some of the same mechanisms seemed to be at work. Just as "young girls lived in dread of a spectral rape by the incubus," so—to quote Marion Starkey—"young men and older were haunted by the spectres of not unshapely matrons who at midnight hopped over the windowsill or dropped down from a beam and got into bed with them." Increasingly, these "shapes" adopted the trim form of Suzanna Martin, a saucy young woman long suspected as a witch; or else wore the flashy red bodice of Bridget Bishop. Bridget ran a couple of taverns, and neighbors had often complained that she let young customers make an uproar playing "shovel-board" at ungodly hours. Married men now said that she was trying to bewitch them at night, and that she sometimes hid her shape in monstrous animal forms. When they repelled her advances, several of their children fell ill and died. "She was not enchantress only, but murderess."[11]

These responses did not necessarily involve the full authoritarian

---

* Such slander suits were not new in Massachusetts, but this is a most revealing incident. The trouble with Salem was that its social control system worked *too* well. All the agencies for controlling behavior—family, church, the law—meshed together tightly; there were no nooks between them for delinquency. By the same token, when part of the social control system became destructively *out of control,* there was no separate agency of control to prevent its running riot through the whole system and taking it over. In the short run, at least, it required the prosaic defense of our stalwart businessman to short-circuit the system by "fusing" the mumbo-jumbo with a threatened suit of cold cash.

pattern. But, at the very least, they reflected a repressive climate conducive to authoritarian behavior. Nor was religion the only stimulant. According to several writers, the major witchcraft persecutions in history have tended to occur in times of social unrest or sudden hardship—again, a scapegoating response. This pattern did, at least, seem to apply to medieval Catholic persecutions, and it was not confined to witches. For example the Flagellant sect, though later proclaimed a heresy, practiced its extreme physical forms of submission-aggression and anti-Semitism during the Black Death. Salem, too, would seem to fall into this pattern. The winter of 1691-92 had been particularly unpleasant—Indian raids, smallpox, and rising concern over London's withdrawal of the Massachusetts charter. Both individual land rights and the theocracy itself had legal basis in the charter; both were now politically threatened. But, to many people, the loss of the charter meant that God had turned from them. Cries were heard that Doomsday was imminent; the devout examined the conduct of others as well as their own hearts, to find out what had gone wrong. In this fashion, religious belief compounded social anxiety and endorsed an aggressive response.

Given these circumstances, other elements in puritan tradition could encourage authoritarian behavior and give it social influence. One such element could be seen in the popularity of Michael Wigglesworth's bestseller, *The Day of Doom*. With remorseless logic it tells its readers that those admired ones who go to heaven must be impervious to the cries of those (formerly) loved ones who do not. The blessed mother must sing praises to the jealous God who plucks the cursed wight from her breast. Fleetingly the poet recognizes human tenderness for the cursed, but only that the tenderness may be struck down. This suggests an authoritarian paradox: that men may be cruelest not when they are stony through and through (are they ever?) but when they feel they must strike at their very tenderness—and when, in sado-masochist fashion, they enjoy the striking. Puritanism could well foster this situation, for its leaders were mostly aware that compassion was a Christian virtue. By retaining this ethic, while still stressing original sin and cruel notions of hell, puritanism harbored a conflict conducive to authoritarianism. In Catholic dogma, by contrast, the notion of a purgatory between heaven and hell has softened the conflict.*

Another dangerous element in the culture was the development of

---

* We may note here in passing that Calvin stressed both predestination and personal culpability for sin, and he sought to combine these opposites with a cruel tortuousness that bordered on sophistry.

both practical scientific and intensely religious interests that sometimes permitted superstition to masquerade in the language of scientific proof. In the determination of witchcraft the Salem judges accepted various criteria, including "spectral evidence"—an assertion by the accuser that the "shape" of the alleged witch had appeared to him. The subjective nature of such evidence suited the subjective temper of puritanism, its respect for intense personal experience. At the same time, the judges thought they were being legally scientific about the whole matter of evidence. With fantasy and reality blurred into one, religious specters could be all the more easily identified with "ordinary" people. In a curious way, Salem culture could promote a large-scale witch-hunt because the society had not made it a fully organized institution with strong circumscribing rules. The absence of criteria limiting the number of those who could be called witches, or confining the term to those clearly beyond the social pale, meant that aggressive and paranoid behavior could reign relatively unchecked. It likewise meant that action against scapegoats could cut across social relationships, generating more tension and fear.

But why Salem, more than other communities of Massachusetts puritanism? Salem had been an unusually bad-tempered community before this—hectoring its ministers and letting quarrels harden into feuds. Witchcraft beliefs catered to spite, for at the Salem trials the judges decided that any "mischief" following a quarrel—a broken cartwheel, perhaps, or the sickening of a hog—could be grounds for suspicion of witchcraft practice. The dehumanizing effect of this (everyday adversary a monstrous tormentor) and the "paranoid climate" that ensued may be imagined; but the start of the chain of destruction in Salem specifically can only be attributed to the convergence there of key personalities. To the authoritarianism of the young accusers was added the unusually cruel outlook of Samuel Parris, the minister, and William Stoughton, the presiding judge. Of the two men, Parris seemed the more like an archetype authoritarian, but even that is unclear. It is, however, evident that the accusers' authoritarianism gained currency by sounding a chord in the whole culture. Because the authoritarian's essential fears and hates both reflected and resembled a puritan imagery, he or she could cow other puritans whose basic character structure was not the same. All the more could he obtain a following from many whose characters possibly *were* authoritarian.*

---

* In his study of the Plymouth colony's family life, Demos (1970a) argues that curbs on aggression in the home were more extreme than curbs on sexuality,

Despite these forces for authoritarianism, large numbers of Salem folk may well have had other kinds of temperament. Throughout the proceedings many people—especially in the rural lower classes, so Starkey suggests—remained skeptical about the accusations. Even those who supported the girls included individuals without obvious authoritarian tendencies. Samuel Sewall, one of the judges, was a kind and generally realistic man; his actions seemed largely motivated by concern for the afflicted maidens. To do his painful duty as he saw it, he appeared to suppress his doubts, but this was not necessarily an authoritarian response.[12] Other humane people were swayed more or less reluctantly by superstitious belief. In the end, community sentiment at Salem did swing against the witchcraft accusations, and some compensation was paid the victims' families and the few survivors. By itself this says little about authoritarian dispositions: it might simply mean that the community could no longer tolerate a form of social control which had become *out of* control and degenerated into wanton killing. But among the remorseful were those who had always been uneasy about the accusations yet had felt too ignorant to challenge the judges' learning.

In America's Calvinist revival of the 1730s and '40s we return to further strong hints of a puritan-authoritarian bridge. In New England at least, the movement involved reaction against secular and sensual enjoyments brought by prosperity. Jonathan Edwards, in his famous Enfield sermon of July 8, 1741, castigated the congregation for what he considered an irreverent dress and manner, and he persuaded a large number of them that only God's whim stood between them and eternal agony.

The God that holds you over the pit of hell, much as one holds a spider, or some loathsome insect over the fire, is dreadfully provoked; you are ten

---

and through displacement may have contributed to the large amount of quarreling between neighbors. Anger and willfulness, indeed, were so tabooed that one can imagine the pressure to cloak these feelings in religious and legalistic demands. Demos' more recent work on New England witch accusers reached me too late to be used fully here. Among his more convincing points, he suggests that many young witch accusers displaced aggression from restrictive maternal regimes onto "witches" who were often social deviants (eccentrics, etc.) but who also symbolized female authority. Accusations that the witch was attacking the accuser may also have reflected projection of (tightly curbed) aggressiveness, and the whole procedure provided a way of "making trouble" without seeing it as this and getting blamed for it. On these points, and some interesting uses of cross-cultural data, see Demos, 1970b. The processes depicted by Demos would seem to fall at the borderline, or point of overlap, between authoritarianism and anti-authoritarianism.

thousand times more abominable in his eyes, than the most hateful venomous serpent in ours; yet it is nothing but his hand that holds you from falling into the fire every moment; since you have sat here in the house of God, provoking his pure eyes by your sinful manner of attending his solemn worship....

If, when once the day of mercy is past, you cry to God to pity you, he will be so far from pitying you, that he will only tread you under foot; he will crush out your blood, and make it fly, and it shall be sprinkled on his garments.[13]

By the time Edwards was finished with them, people in the church were hysterically moaning and crying. The sermon was extreme even for Edwards, but he had already terrified other congregations. In his own parish of Northampton there was a wave of religious melancholia; a leading citizen, mortified by guilt, cut his throat. Edwards himself had expressed more than once an almost suicidal wish to submit. "If only I might be rapt up to Him in Heaven, and swallowed up in Him for ever!" he cried upon his "conversion"; the same theme was repeated in later life.[14]

Edwards' behavior showed much that seemed authoritarian. His sermons suggested an element of sado-masochism, and his fascination with hellfire was all the more remarkable because he refused to make fear of hell a requirement for conversion. He loved nature, yet as a precocious twelve-year-old he wrote a study of spiders which ended on a morbid imagining, that their chief faculty was to sail out to sea and destroy themselves. At first he resisted his father's Calvinist theology of predestination, and he was appalled that God should let little children suffer from diphtheria; but when he accepted the doctrine, he became an intolerant enemy of religious liberalism, and he saw men as puppets in God's works. Was this in part a reaction against humane doubts? He sacrificed pastoral visiting for labors in his study, and his congregation came to resent his Olympian reserve and unbending contempt for frivolity. Yet in other ways—in his fondness of children, for example—he seemed sweet and kind.[15] By the time his congregation finally turned against him, he had perhaps mellowed: he was magnanimous in defeat and ready to debate on equal terms with laymen, for all his tendency to intellectual arrogance. He studied his dreams, and his introspection went further than the righteous breast beating of many puritans; though he too tended to substitute lists of sins for analysis.[16] In outright behavior his aggressiveness was largely confined to religious expression, but even here, as we have already seen, his terrorizing of people could be brutal. The humane intellectual in him simply points up more forcibly the link between puritan creed and authoritarianism. Despite his humanity, he could not—a part of him *would* not—resist the harshest concept of God. One wonders if his response to feelings of weakness and guilt would have been so authoritarian if Calvinism had not been so ripe in the culture, if an authoritarian response had not been so vividly suggested to him.

Beyond these ifs, it is clear that the revival helped lead attracted ministers who were more repressive than he.

The old New England of beer-drinking and barn-raisings died away.... His more distant disciples were intolerant fanatics who hated nature and spontaneous impulse; a new refusal to look realities in the face became the mark of the Puritan.[17]

The religious revival of the 1830s again produced behavior which looked very like authoritarianism. One preacher harangued his audience:

Hell is paved with the skulls of infants one span long, and their parents look down from Heaven, praising God for the justice of their damnation.[18]

The speaker was more extreme than most revivalists, but this suggests that his words were not simply a ritual expression of doctrine. The movement attracted and encouraged people who seemed to enjoy the full implications of "original sin." One possible response to the concept was a squelching of all doubts about its justice by a vigorous alignment with God and the saved. The statement just quoted seems to fall into this category. Instead of accepting uncertainty, that "God moves in mysterious ways," or elaborating a complicated argument that jibes "original sin" with humane values, the preacher appears to attack all humane considerations. Parents must not simply accept the justice of separation from their condemned offspring; they must revel in it.*

And yet the 1830s revival also stimulated a surge of humanitarian activities, including movements for prison reform, women's rights, world peace, education of the blind, deaf, and dumb, and most famously, the emancipation of Negro slaves. Such leaders in these as Theodore Weld and Arthur Tappan were clearly not authoritarian

---

* It is logical, of course, for a Christian believing in hell to deny the continuation of earthly loves between those sent to hell and those who go to Paradise. For how can those in Paradise be perfectly happy if they are distressed at the thought of loved ones tormented in hell's spiritual flames? But there is a difference between the person who tries to approach the problem humanely, as he would the problem of pain and God's love on earth, and him whose style and tone denote a *reveling* in cruel logic.

(we know less about the minor figures). As in earlier times, a religious "forcing" of children sometimes made them into priggish and hostile Paul Prys,[19] but puritanism per se was not a *sufficient cause* of authoritarianism. This comes out strikingly in the memoirs of John Muir, the Scots-American naturalist and inventor. Muir's father was a hellfire puritan. His outlook was rigidly ascetic and restrictive, and to his children his regime seemed at times unjustly oppressive. Yet it is hard to imagine anyone less authoritarian than John Muir. His mother, strong and gentle, seems to have provided an offsetting influence. Perhaps, also, his father's rule was more physically restricting than inwardly degrading; perhaps, again, the labor of wresting a new family home from the Wisconsin wilderness developed self-reliance in the lad. And who knows how much of his curiosity and awareness and adventurous spirit was inborn? The fact is, according to his memoirs, at an early age he could take a doughty attitude to the frights of hell.

I was so proud of my skill as a climber that when I first heard of hell from a servant girl who loved to tell of its horrors and warn us that if we did anything wrong we would be cast into it, I always insisted I could climb out of it. I imagined it was only a sooty pit with stone walls like those of the castle, and I felt sure there must be chinks and cracks in the masonry for fingers and toes. Anyhow the terrors of the horrible place seldom lasted beyond the telling; for natural faith casts out fear.*

But if other factors had stunted his "natural faith," how easily puritan "fear" might have swept all before it in an authoritarian formation.

CATHOLIC REACTION

Having focused so much on Protestantism, it would be unfair to overlook the possible links between authoritarian character and Catholic strains. I suggest that the Roman church is likely to foster authoritarianism when two conditions obtain: first, a type of parent who, being oppressive, accentuates the intolerant aspect of Catholic dogma, which in turn then seems to sanction a fettering regime;[20] second, a prevailing Catholic tradition which has "hardened," whether in response to an unfriendly environment or because of other, more obscure factors.

---

* Muir, 1965, p. 16. This charming book has other accounts of how the young dealt with puritanism. In his native Scotland, a little boy was helping his sister drive home the cows when he said a forbidden word. "I'll have to tell fayther on ye," she cried. "Weel," said the boy, "I couldna help the word comin into me, and it's na waur to speak it oot than to let it rin through ye." *Ibid.*, pp. 105-106.

In an earlier chapter we cited a comparison of Irish and Italian American schizophrenics. This and other studies suggest a characteristic Irish childhood that could be very conducive to authoritarianism. The emphasis was on relationships with the mother, but there was also a generally repressive upbringing.[21] In this the teachings of Irish Catholicism were very probably a factor; several writers have remarked on the "puritanism" and censorship of the Irish and Irish American church, compared with the more relaxed attitudes taken by the French, Spanish, and Italian clergy.[22] Seymour Lipset has argued that the Irish and French Canadian churches are more intolerant than those in the European Latin countries because "they have been affected by Protestant values, or perhaps more accurately by the need to preserve the church in a hostile Protestant environment."* Even in Ireland, Catholicism had to face the influence of a powerful and often hostile Protestant neighbor and ruler. As we argued in the last chapter, the kind of authority most likely to produce authoritarianism is one which is repressive yet not quite master in its own house, so that the individual is subject to contrary tugs. How well this fits much in Irish American Catholicism, particularly where the old tenets are fiercest. Protestantism is not all that is ranged against it. Protestantism shades into secularism, scientific questioning, and the new permissiveness of a consumer culture. Democracy itself is alien to the principles of Catholic hierarchy and obedience. Under these conditions one can visualize some devout Catholic parents reacting against irreligious pressures and making their regime the more repressive. Yet they can hardly insulate their children from a "teenage culture" and other elements of the main society. On the contrary, immigrants and recent immigrants often express a great need to be ultra-American, to identify with the larger society. In some spheres, and for some people, the tradition can be satisfactorily fused: for example, Irish Catholic asceticism over sex and so on can join fundamentalist Protestant asceticism. Even so, the potential remains for great ambivalence toward authority

---

* But also Diana Barringer has suggested to me that in Spain and Italy close ties with the upper classes made the church more worldly and therefore less repressive of sensual life. For the "defensiveness" thesis, see Lipset, 1964, pp. 355 n.-356 n. In part, he attributed the political intolerance of Irish Americans to a sexual repression and hostility to deviants promoted by Irish Catholic teaching. I do not know, however, of any study showing that Irish Americans have been more intolerant politically than Italian Americans; indeed some survey data presented by Lipset makes a tentative challenge to this (*ibid.*, p. 406). Perhaps it could be argued that the predominance of Irish priests in the American Catholic church has affected Italian Catholics too, but this is all debatable.

—especially parents and church. This in fact can characterize both parents and children, and the famous Irish qualities of warmth and humor are not always enough to prevent it from taking a form very like authoritarianism. A Boston probation officer told me of a poor Irish family which griped at the heavy church dues it had to pay, yet felt bitter toward one of the children who left the church in his first year of high school. The probation officer sensed some envy in the bitterness —a grudging "he got out"—and he thought the pattern was not unusual. He also agreed that Italians and Italian Americans tended to be less oppressed by their religion: the Italian "Viva Papa" to the Pope reflected a special feeling of relaxed warmth.

None of this "evidence" is conclusive, and it is not suggested that most Irish American Catholics are authoritarian. What we would expect to find is that Irish Catholicism helps to produce more authoritarians than most other churches, both by seeming to endorse authoritarian behavior, and in some family patterns by helping to forge an authoritarian disposition. This is not to discount varieties of religious tradition, some more conducive than others to authoritarianism, even among Irish Catholics. Nor should it be implied that only *Irish* Catholicism is likely to produce authoritarian character; one wonders if the same pattern might not be found in Quebec, where Catholicism has encouraged many kinds of narrow defensiveness.[23]

10 A GENERAL THEORY OF CAUSE

The last three chapters have described three factors in the genesis of authoritarianism: the behavior of parents; social flux and cultural disruption; and repressive cultural orthodoxies (traditional ideologies). Not every case of authoritarianism can be traced to all three factors: some combinations of inborn qualities and parental treatment may conceivably be enough; some mixtures of parental character and social stress, and so on. But, in many cases, as we have already seen, the factors cannot easily be separated, and indeed they act upon each other. The behavior of parents, for example, obviously reflects the influence of cultural values; it may also bear the scars of social stress. Likewise, cultural orthodoxies can become more rigid and repressive in reaction to social forces which threaten to disrupt traditional ways and challenge moral assumptions. This was suggested in the case of Irish Catholicism, the Salem witch trials, and the "Great Awakening" led by Jonathan Edwards.

On the basis of these observations we can arrive at a composite theory of authoritarian cause, describing a society and culture prone to produce authoritarianism. The following diagrams illustrate a sort of hydraulic pattern, a triangle of forces playing upon each other and upon the individual, who responds in a characteristic way.

In the first diagram, parental influence has not been portrayed. The influences lettered a and c may be thought of as partly passing through the parents: see Diagram II.

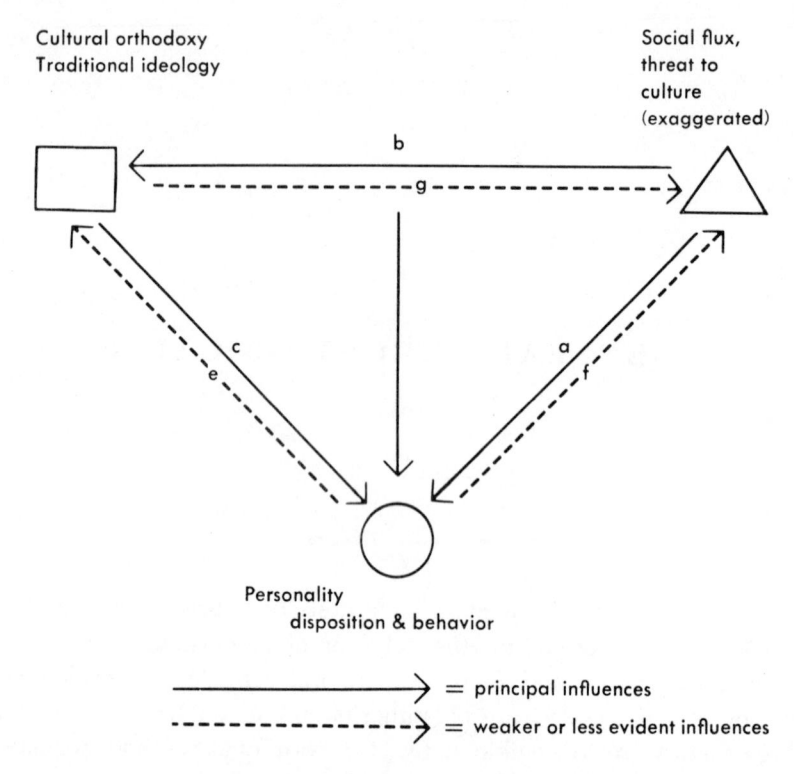

```
Cultural orthodoxy                                    Social flux,
Traditional ideology                                  threat to
                                                      culture
                                                      (exaggerated)

                           ────────b────────
           □ ←────────────────g───────────────→ △


                    c                   a
                      e               f


                            ○
                       Personality
                       disposition & behavior


        ──────────────────→  = principal influences
        ─ ─ ─ ─ ─ ─ ─ ─ ─→   = weaker or less evident influences
```

Influences a = Social stresses building up frustration and leading to fears and doubts about self, and thereby contributing to the formation of authoritarian character.

Influences b = Social threats which help to make the cultural orthodoxy more rigidly traditionalist, defensively patriotic, intolerant, punitive, repressive, and narrow in moral outlook. Since the orthodoxy is a collective expression of individuals (*see below*), it is through individuals that social threats will affect the orthodoxy. In disrupting circumstances, people may stiffen their moral attitudes for varied reasons, ranging from a genuine desire to protect a cultural heritage to personal insecurity and uncertainty. These motives are not confined to authoritarians.

Influences c = Harshness of orthodoxy, which stunts self-esteem yet, ironically, offers the individual symbols of strength and aggression to identify with. Cultural values endorse and encourage the formation of an authoritarian disposition—e.g., a punitive conscience, submissive repression, aggressive displacement and projection. The orthodoxy likewise encourages authoritarian behavior.

All three types of influence (a, b, and c) depend partly on qualities of cultural tradition and the personality produced by factors other than social stress. Hence some orthodoxies do not respond to new threats in a predominantly rejecting way, and many individuals do not become authoritarians, however much they are buffeted by social stress and a repressive culture. But these conditions make them more *likely* to become authoritarian.

Influences d = Disruption of cultural values, or perceived threats to same, promoting conflicts within the individual—e.g., between "new temptations" and traditional morality. Also, general feelings of insecurity when traditional guidelines seem challenged.

Influences e and f = Compounding effect of authoritarian behavior on the rigidity and narrowness of the cultural orthodoxy, and on social flux and stress—the latter effect due to authoritarian traits of suspicion, resentment, and exploitativeness. Both effects are only worth noting where authoritarians are evident in some numbers or otherwise wield influence.

Influence g = Cultural orthodoxy's contribution to social divisiveness: especially noticeable where traditions themselves sanction social and personal relationships which clash and cause psychological conflict—e.g., the Algerian oasis culture described in Chapter 8.

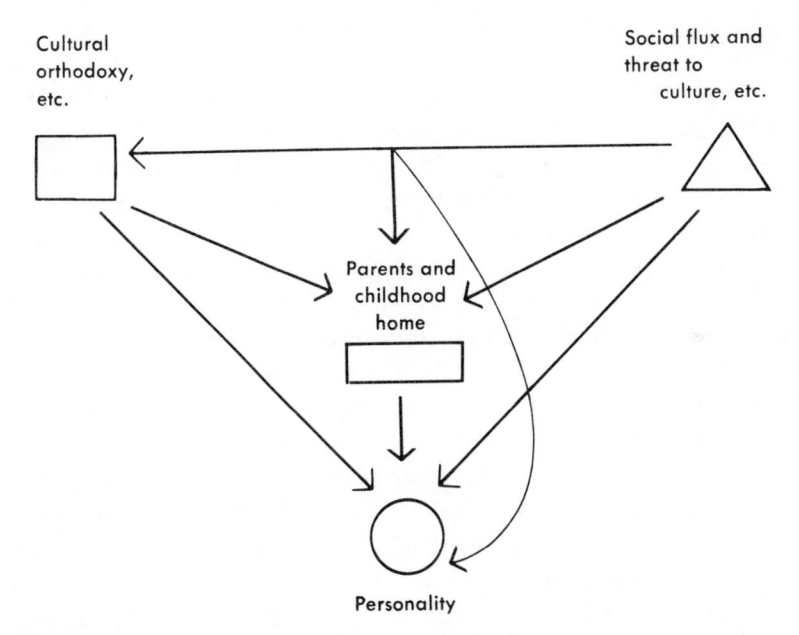

This design recognizes that much of the influence from cultural orthodoxy and social stresses is received by the individual via parents or guardians and the home environment. The kinds of social and cultural factors portrayed here are likely to help make homes more "authoritarian producing," with an atmosphere both tense and repressive and dominated by values that suit the authoritarian's inner management. The arrows in the diagram showing direct lines of influence from cultural orthodoxy and social flux to personality may also be thought of as passing through various agents—face-to-face groups like school and work mates, and more remote agents such as media and community leaders. Like the parents and home environment, each of these agents may to some extent modify (not necessarily *moderate*!) the influence of social stresses and the cultural orthodoxy. Cultural orthodoxies are only rough common denominators of the ideologies of individuals and recognized spokesmen; they represent what people as a whole *consider* to be convention; and even in a tight society there may be individual differences in what people view as conventional.

Unlike other groups, however, parents and the family may also pass on certain hereditary traits (biochemical, neurological, and so on) which predispose the personality to a submissive-aggressive pattern. Some of these traits, on the other hand, may conceivably be inborn but not hereditary; they may also be affected by stresses on the individual both within the home and without. Very little is known about such matters.

The kinds of cultural situation described by these two diagrams are more varied than at first they may appear. Some defensive orthodoxies, for example, mix new mystiques and values with traditionalist appeals; and the threats to a cultural orthodoxy can range from outright disruption of traditional ways to a challenge by new ways and values which in general have not gone much past the stage of "knocking at the door." The point at which new forces are perceived as threats depends on a mixture of three things—the nature of the new forces, the orthodoxy's vulnerability to these forces, and the pre-existing characters of the people and their leaders. Authoritarians may comprise but a fraction of the whole; I would still contend that this type of cultural situation produces a greater proportion of authoritarians than most other situations. Because the hardening of the orthodoxy is expressed and reflected in individual attitudes, the behavior of many basically unauthoritarian people will look superficially like authoritarianism. In other words, on the plane of social attitudes, many people will become more intolerant, rigid, hostile to alien influences and reverent to traditional authority, without necessarily becoming more authoritarian in terms of inner personality structure. The combination of social stresses and hardened cultural orthodoxy must surely produce other salient personality structures besides the authoritarian one.

Despite these complications, the authoritarian personality may be seen as a microcosm of the cultural situation. The tension between a rigid, punitive conscience and impulses which seem on the point of causing chaos is analogous to the tension between the rigid cultural orthodoxy and social forces threatening disruption. It is more than just analogous, of course, because the individual tension reflects in part the larger, social tension. The two tensions are particularly alike when the disruptive social forces include inducements to a way of life more sensual and permissive than the traditional orthodoxy condones. The stage is then set for a cultural conflict between moral tradition and subversive temptations—a conflict very similar to the authoritarian's inner opposition between ascetic conscience and brittly controlled impulse. Again, the conflicts are not just similar: the one reflects, in part, the other. The authoritarian's conscience will tend to represent the cultural orthodoxy, but his control over "immoral" urges will tend to be weakened by new temptations and values. His conscience itself may be divided between a stoutly-proclaimed loyalty to tradition and suppressed doubts about it. These things are especially likely to happen when home influences have fostered a keen but ambivalent identification with authority rather than strong ego controls and deeply implanted values.[1]

In the cultural situation just described, authoritarians who hang desperately on to the traditional orthodoxy may find themselves commanding a certain political high ground. Changes in what is considered moral orthodoxy tend to lag behind changes in actual practice. When times are uncertain and social ways shifting, the relatively flexible person who seeks to absorb rather than reject new influences may still vaguely feel that those who champion the old morality are the better men. Not only is tradition apt to have a powerful mystique, but in times of flux there do not always arise prophets who can articulate new moralities as clearly as the old. Under these conditions one would expect to see authoritarians holding a "cultural initiative" and hence a *moral* initiative—out of all proportion to their numbers.* In the forces of political reaction they may seldom be rational, flexible, and autonomous enough to retain top leadership positions, but one would expect to find them overrepresented as minor chieftains and dedicated followers. During times of acute social stress and equally acute cultural reaction, authoritarians may well reach the top positions too, especially when there is a "leadership vacuum" among more rational men, and splintered or weak political institutions which give the virulent demagogue a stage.[2]

* The concept of "cultural initiative" and minority power need not, of course, be confined to authoritarians. See its application to Japanese militarists (Wilkinson, 1964, p. 211) and to the drys in modern American liquor politics (Wilkinson, 1970).

A comparison of two North American religious sects, the Doukhobors and the Hutterites, first suggested to me the full triangular relationship set forth in the diagrams above. Both peoples emigrated from Russia to western North America in the late nineteenth century. Both have been pacifists and religious ascetics (the Doukhobors, of Mennonite tradition; the Hutterites, Anabaptist), and both were persecuted in Russia for refusing to do military service. In North America as in Russia, they established systems of collective farming and communist living; and they have struggled to preserve distinctive, highly traditional ways of life against the influences of an advanced capitalist society. Here the main similarities end. Unlike many Hutterite groups, the Doukhobors did not keep together in self-contained economic units: collectivism broke down. In other ways too they lost cohesion over the years. Major conflicts within the sect seem to have begun in Russia at about the time that they came into contact with large numbers of other people and acquired sharp differences of individual wealth (this was before they collectivized).[3]

Many groups among the Doukhobors have adjusted peaceably to the larger social system that surrounds them, while retaining their own civic and religious bodies. One group, however, the Sons of Freedom in British Columbia, have remained angrily traditionalist; and they have attracted a variety of hostile, submissive, and withdrawn adults. Again and again Sons of Freedom have burned or dynamited Canadian public property, the homesteads of the Doukhobors, and, significantly, their own houses and monuments. They have also mounted aggressive nudist parades, confronting outsiders with the symbol of their (unclad) asceticism. Canadian officials, for their part, have treated Doukhobors with a variety of policies ranging from hospitality to crude intolerance.

From Russian times Doukhobor history has been marked by a succession of priestly leaders, fanatic yet almost whimsically exploitative. The Sons of Freedom have accepted these authorities with extreme docility, but not without a great deal of tension and misunderstanding among themselves. Their religious leaders and teachings have encouraged a displacement of hostility against outsiders, not only Canadian officials (whose very real persecutions have been greatly exaggerated in the telling), but other Doukhobors alleged to be apostates. There is no clear evidence that Sons of Freedom have shown marked authoritarian dislike of weaklings and social underdogs per se, for much of their hostility has focused on public authorities, and their tradition bids them avoid personal violence, be good neighbors and fond parents. But some of the most fanatic Sons of Freedom have turned at least verbal aggression against their children, and the spontaneity of house burning suggests that much frustration and anger has been vented on "safe" objects. In addition, the behavior of arsonists and those watching the fires has shown an emotional intensity with strong sexual overtones—the fire has provided symbolic outlet for a people who are apt to be sexually repressed and generally self-censored. For the child of parents who suddenly burn their home, the experience can be extremely upsetting; observers have seen such children bewildered and then glum, bottling up their hurt feelings.[4]

Taken as a whole, the predicament of the individual Son of Freedom has not promoted an integrated personality. Religion has taught him to eschew material goods and sensual pleasures; but the breakdown of collectivism has exposed him to a more materialist, modern culture (many Sons of Freedom work for non-Doukhobors). This has added to the conflict between impulse and a puritanical conscience, producing much guilt about desires. One observer of child-rearing among the Sons of Freedom has reported an early sex training which makes for furtive playing rather than stable repression, and a reliance on pacifiers and bottles—sometimes well past infancy—which helps perpetuate a very materialist sort of dependency. This was particularly pronounced in the more militant families whose fathers were often away in jail. There was the harried mother, tempted to take out her frustrations on the children, sometimes quite harshly demanding that the children bother her. On the other hand, those Sons of Freedom children raised in more supportive homes have had to undergo the stress of transition from a well-knit family group to an adult society fraught with suspicion and dominated by harsh leaders. And, like other Doukhobor children, they have often been despised and abused by their non-Doukhobor fellows at school.

These stresses, then, come from both inside and outside the community. The matter can be summarized by saying that Sons of Freedom have shown various mixtures of the rebellious and submissive-aggressive, and that these traits stem from an interaction between social instability and a repressive, defensive orthodoxy. In the past a type of leader emerged, who intensified and maintained (if he did not initiate) the vicious circle. In response both to external cultural threats and to his own drive for power, he emphasized the messianic demands of a religious tradition which tended anyway, perhaps, to put more store by subjective intensity than by a clear allocation of rights, roles, and obligations. Hostile and rigid, the leaders helped to make collectivism impossible, yet they continued to demand it. The result of such imbalances was a jarred and brittle way of life.[5]

Hutterite culture, by contrast, has not been dislocated in the same way.[6] Many of its communities have held together, on prosperous collective farms. As groups rather than individuals, they have made gradual concessions to modernity, but not at the price of cohesion, and peace. Life on the collective farms combines a strict (rather than punitive) social discipline with strong ties of affection between individuals. People who leave the collective communities are not rejected as traitors, and there has been virtually no aggression against outsiders. This, despite the antagonism of some non-Hutterite neighbors in the past, and the Hutterites' great pride in their culture. Much rebelliousness is suppressed or *re*pressed, and psychological tests have indicated some submerged hostility against parents, expressed in fantasies. But there are no indications that this rebelliousness is displaced or projected onto other people. Where acute maladjustment does occur, it usually takes the form of depression—a turning of hostility onto self, or a projection of hostility or guilt onto God, who is then seen as rightfully threatening. By comparison, Doukhobors have tended both to depression and to forms of paranoia involving suspicion of others besides their own moral authorities. All in all, the organization of Sons of Freedom personalities has tended to be much closer than that of Hutterites to the archetype authoritarian.

Again, this is not to deny a two-way link between culture and personality. To an extent, Hutterite communities hold together because individuals make them work! On the other hand, the sheer fact that the communities have resisted culture disruption has reduced conflict within the individual and moral incitements to authoritarian behavior. The society's cohesion probably stems from a medley of factors—in personality, in the Hutterites' religious and social tradition, and in their North American environment—but this does not remove the element of social cohesion itself in preventing or reducing authoritarianism.

I do not suggest that authoritarians have represented *the* central Sons of Freedom type, but rather that the social and cultural circumstances of this group have been conducive to authoritarianism among other patterns. The apparent fact that many of its leaders were not authoritarian, as defined in these pages, means that one can think of the orthodoxy becoming defensive and intolerant not simply because authoritarians made it so. Somewhat the same thinking can be applied to Irish American experience: we have already shown how defensive religion may reach through the family to produce authoritarianism where parents were anyway oppressive. Historically, too, the Irish American home has conveyed the strains of social flux and mobility. Under economic stress, Irish immigrant family structure has in the past tended to weaken; although an imbalance between family discipline and a boisterous male peer group had long been a feature of Irish life. With high rates of unemployment and of drunkenness among the men, the father often seemed a weak figure, whereas the mother, traditionally strong in the home, would react by trying to bind the children possessively to her. The result, I suggest, was sometimes the kind of mother-focused authoritarianism described earlier.*

But the triangular model (defensive orthodoxy, social pressure, authoritarian personality) would seem most applicable where the orthodoxy has explicitly endorsed contempt for softness and "inferiors." From this aspect, the Christian pacifism of the Doukhobors and their "underdog" political position may be deemed a tempering factor. When we come to the subject of Nazi Germany, we will see how very applicable the triangular model is. The theory will also help us to understand some of the harsh-tender conflicts in white American Southerners. Conversely it provides some of the reasons why black Americans, for all the cowing force of their past treatment, have not shown more authoritarianism in their history. Black traditions and white expectations have not *usually* encouraged a repressive morality among blacks; their cultural and psychological response to stress has *tended* to take a different course from that of reactive asceticism.

* On social and family stresses among the Irish and Irish Americans, cf. Bales, 1946; Warner and Srole, 1945; Glazer and Moynihan, 1964. Note particularly the sharp distinction made in the past between "shanty" and "lace-curtain" Irish on both sides of the Atlantic, and the alternations between wildness and conformity. More speculatively, one may ask if there is not a character element in the dependence on City Hall (sometimes an addiction) so vividly described by O'Connor in *The Last Hurrah*. Glazer and Moynihan observed that autonomous businessmen formed a much larger proportion of New York's Italians than of the Irish.

PART III

CHARACTER TYPES AND POLITICAL APPEALS

11 RIGID REBELS AND THE "LIBERAL" AUTHORITARIAN

Henry Simpson lives by himself on the outskirts of a small Western town. He is a bachelor, retired from the carpentry trade five years ago—a vigorous, warm-hearted man, quite well known in his neighborhood for holding strong opinions and being ready to defend them at length. In many respects he corresponds to what used to be "the village atheist," except that he is not one. He does not go to church because "people just go there to be looked at and, anyway, you don't have to go to church to worship God." He has a profound distrust of all organized authority, a distrust bestowed evenly on unions and big business, to say nothing of politicians and the local school board. His neighbors like him, rather gingerly because with Henry Simpson there is no neutral ground—people are either his friends or he does not want to know them. But he is a generous, sensitive man, quick-tempered and obstinate yet at once humorous and courtly. As the local editor well knows, he is forever taking up cudgels on behalf of some humane cause. Racial discrimination in a local hotel; the poverty of the Indians; the cruelty done to animals in the interests of research—all claim his attention. Henry Simpson has always made deep identification with the underdogs of this world, and he usually attributes their plight to the machinations of selfish power groups, be it a cabal of local politicians or the medical profession. Nor is his concern purely of the armchair variety: he can usually be counted on to assist in local fund drives, and he is currently helping to establish a sanctuary for wild life, away from the reach of trappers and hunters.

Henry Simpson does not exist as such. The account given above is based on the experiences and common traits of several persons whom I know, of both sexes. All of these people are somewhat solitary in their pursuits. They have direct and compassionate relationships with people they know, but being basically quite rigid, they avoid many of the compromises and submissions which a more close-knit social life would require. In most things, great and small, they are rebels, yet each has some respect for forces of mystery. For one it is a fundamentalist belief in a God who is at once an egalitarian and Superman: "He made us all equal. . . . He has complete power—why, he could move an elephant into the ark, just like that." Others are agnostic, but are variously interested in astrology, spiritualism, and extrasensory phenomena.

Such people represent just one kind of rigid *anti*-authoritarian (rigid rebel). I contend that, for all their similarities, authoritarians can be distinguished from rigid rebels on a deep level of disposition. We will begin the comparison with a more detailed case study: the character of a man who, while ostensibly taking the underdog side in many matters, *was* very authoritarian.*

A MAN FOR THE WORKERS

We first met "Peter Scheewin" in the early 1960s, when he was the boy friend of a schoolteacher, Susan Hart, a divorcée with two small girls.[1] My first impression of Scheewin was of a quiet, obliging person with an indefinable quality—something listless, even absent. He was always very friendly to us, and in his quiet way was often eager to talk about politics and books. He called himself a strong labor man, and in a few general terms was inclined to berate the one-time business oppression of workers. The advance of unions since that time was a source of great satisfaction. In connection with social reform, he asked us if we had read Shaw, Upton Sinclair, and H. G. Wells.

---

* It must be repeated that not all deep "complexes" and ambivalence about authority can be classified as authoritarian, rigid anti-authoritarian, or a borderline mixture of the two. Feelings about authority and "underdog" symbols represent but one of many ways of classifying personality, and a way that applies more to some individuals than to others.

Deep differences between "authoritarian and anti-authoritarian personalities" have also been suggested by Bay, 1965, chaps 4 and 5.

He repeatedly extolled these authors, but as another acquaintance pointed out, it was always the same few authors and he never really said much about them. Despite his abstract concern for the "working man," he wanted to be an intellectual; and yet other people reported that he could scoff at "useless professors." He was rigidly anti-Republican, with an oft-repeated trick of saying "that Dixon." When corrected with "Nixon, you mean," he would add, "Well, Dixon, Nixon or whatever." When a pro-Goldwater friend of Susan's came to stay during the 1964 election, he argued heatedly with her; but her husband, equally pro-Goldwater, could not believe her when she told him this. Peter and he had discussed politics by themselves, and he had shown no antipathy to Goldwater. Susan, indeed, had overheard their discussion and had been amazed at the turnabout; among other things she had heard him declare, "It's time America stood up for her rights." Yet, talking with Susan on other occasions, he was no America Firster: he had been born in Canada, and he constantly criticized the United States. Susan said that he disliked arguing with men; he agreed with them much more than he did with women.

He was a great Anglophile. His mother was British-born and he fondly used the old-fashioned term "Blighty." He said he had a good time there in the war (he was a merchant seaman), but his feelings were also wrapped up with his intellectualism. He raved about the BBC and was rather uneasy when we criticized one program, even though we agreed with him about the BBC generally. His opinion of Churchill was equally lavish—but the reverse. "There's not a thing he did for the British people," he said at Churchill's death.

Peter's authoritarianism showed itself most plainly in relations with women and children. He had a "thing" about the need for men to keep the upper hand over their womenfolk. It took time for us to realize this because he usually went on about it in a sly, bantering way. Peter had a dry and funny turn of wit, but he used it to make guarded, oblique attacks, and Susan admitted that he loved to stir up arguments between others. Beneath the humor it basically irritated him to see me working with my wife in the kitchen. "Don't do it," he would say with a chuckle. "That's woman's work." Once we discussed it. "A woman's place is in the home," he said. "If you don't show them who's boss, they'll lord it over you." It was pointed out that if both husband and wife had careers but only the wife did the housework, she would have to do more than the husband. "That's how it should be," he declared. "And they *like* it." At this point his humor wore thin; he looked a little tense and heated. He himself never helped in Susan's house, though Susan had a full-time job. He would even bring her dirty clothes to wash. In various ways, he had a habit of pushing women, half in fun but half seriously, to see how far he could manipulate them. Going out with Susan, they would agree to eat Dutch, and then, at the table, he would ask her to pay for the whole meal. Once, when she had commented on how nice the waitress was, he stealthily tried to reduce Susan's tip at the end of the meal. Playfully. But seriously too. "She didn't deserve more," he said afterward.

Toward men Peter's attitude was quite the reverse. When he was sharing a house with some others, he let them cheat him and break up his car; and later, when he rented out part of a house to a family, he did nothing for months while the father of the family virtually refused to pay rent. Finally the tenant, a heavy drinker, went too far; he abused Peter, who lost his temper and practically knocked the man out. Peter had been in several fights, apparently, but only after taking more than most would put up with. By contrast, he could be quick to condemn aggressive women. According to Susan, the only time he expressed anti-Semitism was when a Jewish friend of Susan's, a very dynamic but not offensive woman, had been visiting. After she left he observed quietly that he didn't care for Jews.

Peter's treatment of Susan's young daughters was really quite unstable. At the time of our observations they were aged about four and six. On occasion Susan would send a child to her room for "bad" behavior, but usually she was a very permissive mother and this riled Peter. He would go on and on about how children needed discipline and had to be "shown who's boss." In the case of Susan's children he may have had some reason on his side, but there was also a note of irrational vengeance. Once, when the quieter, less "naughty" of the girls was sent to her room for fighting, he said, "There's a naturally *bad* kid." When the girls were watching TV, and one of the grownups wanted to see something else, he was all for clearing them out or abruptly changing the program without the least courtesy. At times he would play affectionately with the girls, but there were sudden spurts of jealousy. Once or twice we saw him roughly push aside one of the girls when she was holding on to her mother.

Occasionally—increasingly seldom—Susan left the girls in the charge of Peter when she had to be at a late evening class. In getting them to bed, he was inclined to choose the rough way. For example, when the youngest fell asleep in front of the TV, he started pulling off her pants, muttering that it was long past her bedtime. Not surprisingly there were squalls of surprised anger from the little girl. Susan and others found that giving firm but polite orders got them to bed with much less fuss. As she later admitted, "what he calls weakness we call intelligence." Peter was also apt to goad the girls behind a cloak of humor. Once when the youngest ran into the living room stark naked, he made playful passes at her; and when the girls and he were out in the garden together, there were often sudden cries of rage at him from one of them.

In view of the way he treated the girls, Peter's comments on his own childhood were particularly interesting. Either his father or grandfather had immigrated to Western Canada from Germany. His father had disliked the Nazis, but had shown pride at Germany's war successes and resented the anti-German tone of Canadian newscasters. From various accounts Peter gave Susan, his father had been a tyrant, his mother submissive. Peter told us that at meals he and his brothers and sisters (there were five or six of them) were not allowed to talk; "only Mother and Father could." Peter thought this right: "There's a time and place for kids." He admitted there could have been more love in his home, but in general he thought his upbringing was good in that it "forced me to conform." "It kept me out of trouble later with the police and authority." The underlying assumption, that one might easily get out of hand, was probably the result of a brittle training and an unconscious concern about impulses. It is not surprising that Peter had a passive, drained quality; he gave the impression that he was holding down huge reserves of aggressiveness.

In politics, Peter attributed his "liberal views" to travels as a merchant seaman. Yet they also seemed to perform what one might call "secondary rebellion," expressing against remote authorities ("big business," "the U.S.," "Republicans") what he dared not express against the more closely-felt authorities in his life (father, aggressive men, even the police). In this way he differed from many rigid *anti*-authoritarians, whose rebellion against remote political authorities can be an extension of, not substitute for, their private revolts. We shall consider this in more detail shortly. Peter's case was also unlike that of many "right-wing" authoritarians whose identification with power extends more plainly to the political sphere. But this difference is primarily one of idiom—a difference in the specific authorities that evoke submission and rebellion—for right-wing authoritarians, too, often express "secondary rebellion" against authority symbols: plots in high places, "wicked" officials, alien might, and so on. The difference between Peter and the deeply anti-authoritarian is more primarily one of basic structure. Unlike the loyalties of most anti-authoritarians, Peter's identification with the "working man" left little place for tenderness; instead it permitted an alignment with masculine authority *against* women and children.

COMPARISONS

It is now obvious that authoritarians and rigid rebels are not always easy to distinguish. Rigid rebels can be hostile, abrasive, even autocratic, putting "principle" or self-assertion above compromise. They tend to have a plot complex, investing power groups with sinister designs; this provides a rationale for rebellious expression, and in some cases, where the rebel has more hostility than he can directly show, it may involve projection. The rigid rebel tends likewise to intolerance and a stereotyped outlook.[2] "He goes to *military* school," wailed a rigid underdog defender that I knew, the trigger phrase "military school" automatically dismissing all such establishments and all parents who could send their sons to these places.

The matter is further complicated by the fact that authoritarians can be rebellious (the "secondary rebellion" already mentioned) and rigid rebels can fanatically revere their own authority symbols. Psychological rebels often want a cause to fight for; and anyone struggling against great opposition finds it heartening to cite a moral authority, be it God or political doctrine. But it is not only a question of *needing* a cause, for the moral authority may genuinely have instilled values which encourage rebellion. Thus, at an early age some rigid rebels may have identified with religious, humane, and reform-minded parents; subsequent stresses and frustrations may goad them to action, but their loyalties will not necessarily have the authoritarian kind of ambivalence.[3] With other rigid rebels, underdog crusades are partly the extension of revolt against one or both parents. I am reminded here of the middle-aged lady who has been rebelling for most of her life, in fact ever since she broke with an oppressive, cantankerous father who made it plain that he preferred sons to daughters. Her rebellion is not complete, for in some ways she resembles him—tempestuous, dominating, very much a "character"—but she reserves extra vehemence for "boorish" men, and she shows a warm and special affection for those of either sex who are gentler than she. Even if these feelings represent a "reaction formation" against their opposites, they appear to have other deep sources in her personality. Her mother was a sweet-natured and passive person; it is highly conceivable that the daughter both absorbed compassionate values from the mother and reacted against the father in her mother's "defense." (More about "reaction formation" will be said later.)

Another example is William Lloyd Garrison, the abolitionist. A biographer has argued quite persuasively that he was always "fighting" his father.[4] In this case, dislike of authority, greed for status, and espousal of causes in the abstract were more obvious than small-scale humanity to individuals: still, there is no evidence that Garrison was authoritarian. There are destructive rebels with even less tenderness than Garrison had who still do not have an authoritarian complex about authority. In practice, however, people like Garrison are not always easy to distinguish from the kind of authoritarian who kowtows to liberal crusades. I remember the secretary of a college department who accepted her professors' liberal political views to the point of saying, "I just love Negroes," with all the stereotype this statement implies. Yet under stress a more hostile ethnic prejudice could break through. Criticizing the "dirty" habits of one foreign-born professor (he didn't return his library book on time), she once blurted, "Is that what they do in *his* country?" Away from the requirements of ideology, her personal relationships reflected considerable authoritarianism. To her professional equals and superiors she showed great friendliness, of a rather tense and simpering kind; she was sometimes very pleasant to those under her too, but was apt to harry them, give them extra work which should really have been hers, and overorganize the accounts and files in petty ways without providing the most efficient basic system. She spoke in especially honeyed tones to a woman academic whom she really resented for giving her extra work at little notice.

Another confusing point is that both authoritarians and rigid rebels, needing scapegoats for their wrath, may attack the same targets, though not for entirely the same emotional reasons. A good example was the son of a rabbi whose rebellion against his father was deeply connected with his rebellion against traditional Judaism. A successful American professional man, he disliked the immigrants from European Jewish ghettoes, not primarily because they were poor and "inferior"—symbols of weakness—but because they represented a restrictive childhood discipline. In some ways a "difficult" man, he was not essentially authoritarian.

The basic distinction between authoritarians and rigid rebels is that they have a different "thing" about authority. Where the difference can be described in terms of childhood or adolescent relationships, the authoritarian personality has an "inverted Oedipal" formation, a forced but brittle and ambivalent identification with father figures; whereas a rigid rebel's personality is often fixed at a directly Oedipal stage. Corollaries of this anti-father pattern are strongly overt feelings of tenderness and even identification with feminine figures; but these corollaries do not always follow. As we have already seen, an anti-father rebel is not necessarily very tender, at least on an overt level. Like an authoritarian, he may repress much of his personal tenderness in order to overcome a sense of insecurity and make himself or herself feel strong. (This is most likely, perhaps, in the case of men.) But, whereas the authoritarian represses rebelliousness against authority, the anti-father rebel is apt to repress the exact opposite: his feelings of dependence on authority. The rabbi's son described above loved his father but could not admit it. The fact that authoritarians may deny their submissiveness and wrap it in harsh alignments with authority does not alter the basic contrast, for such denial and concealment are far from overt rebelliousness. Yet even the overt Oedipal rebel cannot help but learn some of the traits and values of his father.

Again one must emphasize the variety of types and geneses. One kind of rigid rebel may be the sort of person who has felt shame and irritation at a *weak* father, or frustration at generally permissive parents. His parents may be so forbearing that he guiltily suppresses his irritation, while, like other rebels, still longing for a harder authority to strike at and define himself against. At the same time, however, there is often a special identification with an influential mother. Among rebels as a whole, there seems to be a modern Western tendency to this general type, itself a highly varied phenomenon.*

Perhaps the pattern most like authoritarianism is found in the person who has unstably repressed hostility for his or her parents and largely displaced it onto other authority figures. Such people, of course,

---

* On related aspects of rigid rebelliousness, cf. T. W. Adorno on the "'Protesting' Low Scorer" in *The Authoritarian Personality*, 1950, pp. 774-76.

Since writing the above, I have read Keniston's analysis (1968) of eleven male student radicals, which stresses an exceptional tie with a strong, humane mother, ambivalence toward a father felt to be both strong and weak, identification with humane parental values, and great emotional spontaneity. Keniston relates their values and activism to new historical factors, but I would add that both new and old rebels have sometimes shown a martyr complex, including a wish to be persecuted and to exaggerate persecution.

should only be considered authoritarian, and then only in disposition, if they have a strong urge to assert themselves against symbols of weakness or tenderness as well as symbols of authority and power. In overt behavior they may never express these urges; instead, they may even counter the urges by "reaction formation" of a relatively superficial kind.* But one should also accept the possibility of rigid rebels who are very near a borderline between authoritarianism and anti-authoritarianism. Under stress their inner structures, their basic emotional organization, may change so that they cross the line or stay right on the border. In other words, the prime targets of their displaced rebellion may move from symbols of authority and power to symbols of softness and inferiority; it may come to include both classes of symbol about equally; or the principal scapegoats attacked may symbolize neither authority nor underdogs. The actual targets may not even change, but the symbolic reason for the attack, the targets' psychological meaning to the attacker, may shift or widen. It must be stressed, however, that even among clear-cut authoritarians, the targets for attack have varied psychological meanings: the labels I have so far used—"underdog," "weakling," "inferior," "rebel"—are quite crude categories.[5]

A person at the borderline between authoritarianism and anti-authoritarianism is sometimes, or in some areas of behavior, an overt rebel, in others, an authoritarian, with both modes having roughly equal bases in his personality structure. With such an individual it is unreal to talk of "secondary rebellion"; he is primarily both rebellious and submissive-aggressive, though consciously he may view himself as a rebel, a guardian of order, or what have you. I suggest very tentatively that Andrew Johnson was this kind of amalgam, at least under the stresses of his presidency. Again, I do not wish to imply that all psychopathology can be explained in terms of authority relations; nevertheless, in a complex and divided culture, where several authorities can press roughly equal claims on the individual's emotions, it may be easier to become both rebel and authoritarian, now rebel against one, now submissive to the other, and then vice versa.[6] Some

---

* Reaction formation, the development of feelings and behavior patterns which oppose and help repress unconscious opposites, may vary in its deepness within personality structure and in its integration with other facts of personality—traits, impulses, basic values. With some people, reaction formation on the side of tenderness may be the expansion of quite strong and deep tender feelings; with authoritarians it may be more like a mezzanine, fitting over the authoritarian structure. But these distinctions are relative.

of these elements appear in William Blanchard's trenchant and detailed account of Rousseau.[7] Blanchard describes a convergence of childhood experiences and associations which gave Rousseau a masochist desire to be taken by punishing authority; in aligning himself with underdogs everywhere against the chains of society he sought to hold at bay his own submissiveness. Yet his ideals of social authority, and the blueprint for training children—unnecessarily cruel even within its manipulative emphases; entirely deceitful despite his value on candor—reflected in part an oblique desire to join or replace a dominating and punishing authority. He feared many of his own impulses, his squeamishness and femininity, and he had repressed much hostility for a father whose ardent embraces had been vaguely threatening. A great deal of his antagonism was directed or projected onto other symbols of authority; in many spheres Rousseau *was* a tender-hearted rebel. He did try to confront himself; he clearly sensed his dependence on others and his vulnerability to social influence. But the wish to turn on those weaker than himself was not recognized.[8]

A PURITAN REFORMER

Let us now look in more detail at some historical personalities. During the nineteenth and early twentieth centuries, among the moral reform movements of America, there was a personality type which resembled the authoritarian on many points without being quite the same thing. Like the authoritarian, this type had a precariously integrated character, a fierce conscience, anxiety over sensual impulse, much guilt as a result, and a repressive ego which projected lurid fantasies onto enemy targets. Such people often expressed an almost groveling dependence on God. But they had a deeper, less ambivalent conscience than authoritarians; there was not, apparently, a great deal of repressed resentment against godly authority; the image of God was benign as well as strict; and there was little identification with toughness against softness.[9]

Such a person, it seems, was Anthony Comstock, the crusader against vice and pornography. We know little of his father, for Comstock did not often mention him; he was a frugal puritan but a man of some substance, owning two lumber mills and 160 acres in Connecticut. Comstock was devoted to his mother, who treated the children strictly but enthralled them with stories of "moral heroism." She died when Comstock was ten; he idealized her all his life. Fifty years after her death he told an interviewer that the purpose of his life had been to honor her. It may be connected that he married a woman ten years older than he, the daughter of a Presbyterian elder, who had a mind of her own but was very quiet and dressed somberly.

Comstock was raised in a strict faith, taken to church several times a day on Sunday, and often whipped. This was probably not unusual for the time and place; what he remembered more keenly was the humiliation of one occasion, when he was sent to sit with the girls in a sunbonnet.

At the age of eighteen, Comstock broke into a tavern one night, turned on the faucets, and let the liquor run out of the barrels onto the ground. The tavern was being run without a license and Comstock had tried in vain to get action from the sheriff. Later, as a soldier in the Civil War, Comstock used to pour away his whiskey ration; but as an older man he enjoyed the odd bottle of beer, brandy, or wine. Like many a dry, however, he edged his puritanism with nativism. Attacking the Shaw play *Mrs. Warren's Profession,* he referred to its author as "that Irish smut-dealer"; and his disgust at imported French paintings and drawings—much but not all of it less than good art— carried anti-foreign overtones.[10]

Throughout much of his life, Comstock evinced a strong feeling of dependence on God. In his sixties he told a friend,

You are in the surging billows, and all you've got to hold on to is a little thread, anchoring you to the pier; and it's very frail, and you're afraid it will break. And then it *does* break—it is Self—and you're about to go down. Just then you hear, "Fear not, for I am with thee, be not dismayed, for I am thy God"; and you see a strong cable thrown out, and you lay hold on it, and feel safe again. And when your hands grow numb, and you fear that you'll have to let go, you find that someone has put it under your arms and around your body, and you *cannot* sink.[11]

As a Civil War soldier he suffered terribly from the blaspheming he heard about him; and his diary for that time is full of self-reproaches for "wanderings of thought and sinfulness of head"—the "surging billows," perhaps, that he described as an old man. In his censorship crusades, the "appeal to passion" was an oft-cited reason for attacking certain works and despite his efforts to draw an honest line between beauty and pornography, his anxiety about impulse seemed to involve beauty itself. One of his diary's few descriptions of nature is a short paragraph from Florida, describing oceans and shore in moonlight. After admiring what he sees, the writer warns that the Devil may be on the other side of the moon, and the silvery sheen might be emitted from the very pit of hell. Not content with this corrective, he adds a postscript: "What glory for earth but it is not to be compared to that which is to be revealed in the last days...."[12] Comstock saw his life as a personal fight with the Devil, and one may suppose that he projected onto the Devil the sensual or wildly romantic impulse that the moonlit scene encouraged.

Comstock's words about womanhood give weight to this supposition. Setting womanhood on a pedestal, he was immensely concerned with purity and chastity; he spoke and wrote often about them.

> There is nothing on earth more chaste or beautiful than a modest and chaste woman, unless it be that of innocent childhood, and *that chastity every chivalrous man ought to defend and protect.* [His emphasis.] The nude in art is a menace upon this chastity. The youth of this country today are being cursed by the dissemination of pictures where woman is exposed to vulgar gaze.... There is nothing more repulsive than an unchaste woman; there is nothing more seductive than a beautiful woman.[13]

Through the act of chivalrous protection Comstock appeared to enjoy the sensuality that he attacked. The propagandist's pen gave him a certain license; so did the New England puritan's intellectualism, a tradition of mind that sought to analyze sin. He quoted the writer Sidney Lanier:

> Let any sculptor hew us out the most ravishing combination of tender curves and spheric softness that ever stood for woman; yet if the lip have a certain fullness that hints of the flesh, if the brow be insincere, if in the minutest particular the physical beauty suggest a moral ugliness, that sculptor—unless he be portraying a moral ugliness for a moral purpose—may as well give over his marble for paving stone.[14]

Ascribed to others, the idea of fleshly assault upon fair womanhood came easily to him—again the hint of projection. His diary of 1873 included this:

> Took the 6.12 am train at Manchester for New York. A young lady, Miss Miller, of Philadelphia came down with me. She occupied a seat with me and I treated her as I would like to have my wife or sister treated. She went to her uncle's 36 West 18th Street. She seemed a very simple-minded, pure, sweet girl and I was glad she had no villain to deal with. How can men be so base and low as to impose upon the young and pure?[15]

In part, Comstock was reacting against the corruption and turmoil of the post–Civil War period. It was very much a small-town puritan's reaction. But wrapped up in this was a paranoid exaggeration of threat. Consider this imagery:

[The sale of erotic literature] is a deadly poison, cast into the fountain of moral purity. This business and intemperance are twins; but they are twin devils. Intemperance strikes down the flower of the land, openly and publicly. . . . This cursed business of obscene literature works beneath the surface, and like a canker worm, secretly eats out the moral life and purity of our youth, and they droop and fade before our eyes. . . . It breeds lust. Lust defiles the body, debauches the imagination, corrupts the mind, deadens the will, destroys the memory, sears the conscience, hardens the heart, and damns the soul. It unnerves the arm, and steals away the elastic step. It robs the soul of manly virtues, and imprints upon the mind of the youth, visions that throughout life curse the man or woman. Like a panorama, the imagination seems to keep the hated thing before the mind, until it wears its way deeper and deeper, plunging the victim into practises that he loathes.[16]

Much of this suggests fear of weakness, the specter of an enfeebling threat; yet in Comstock's case the fear did not apparently become a general aversion to tenderness. Here, for all that we have cited, there seemed to be an essential difference between his character and that of authoritarians. True, Comstock was a man of narrowly and fiercely channeled energies. He was very much for the strict enforcement of law and order; and though he could recognize and discuss opposing points of view, to many opponents he was a bigot. He clearly depended on ascetic authority to keep his own impulses in order. But his actions as well as his words bespoke a deep sympathy for the weak, the distressed, and the afflicted. Because of this his crusading was psychologically *anti*-authoritarian.

Comstock was exceptionally tender to children. He had a habit of carrying cheap rubber toys in his pocket, and when he saw a child crying on the street, he would stop to comfort it, fumbling in his pocket for a toy to give. A man who worked with Comstock in his latter years said that, every so often, adults would come in and thank him for advice or encouragement given them as children. Nor was Comstock's sympathy confined stiltedly to his "own sort." In the course of some welfare mission, he visited a rundown tenement near Chinatown, New York, where he found a newborn baby girl whose mother was dying. The Comstocks' own daughter, Lillie, had died not long before, in her first year, and they adopted the baby.

Much earlier, during army days, Comstock recorded in his diary that he was teaching six Negro soldiers to spell: "Their perseverance and patience far surpasses many white people." He also sat up one night with a person who had delirium tremens. His temperance enthusiasm did not, evidently, involve personal rejection of the drunkard.

Even his censorship campaigns were tempered with mercy. As an agent of the U.S. Post Office, he arrested a young woman for distributing nude drawings on behalf of the Art Students' League; but when the material was seized and destroyed, Comstock got the charge against her dismissed, considering that the real culprits were hiding "behind this young woman's skirts." On another occasion he virtually reversed his tack against a Bowery art dealer who was selling "objectionable" foreign pictures. The man's daughter came and pleaded to Comstock that her father had only been in the country a short time and hadn't realized the illegality of his actions. A lawyer, apparently, had offered to defend him for $250. Comstock advised the dealer to plead guilty, and he himself explained the extenuating circumstances in court. The dealer got a relatively light fine and had to pay no lawyer's fees. There was at least one other such occasion of Comstock's responding to extenuating circumstances, explained to him by a defendant's daughter. And, when New York's corrupt Boss Tweed was finally jailed for felony, Comstock was very concerned that his son and relatives should suffer no more than could be helped. He got to know them that summer, and about Tweed himself he wrote, "The way of the transgressor is hard. Who makes me to differ. My temptations were not equal to this poor man's."[17]

The role of young women in these sympathies makes a point about the womanhood-chastity-purity concern. For Comstock women were largely underdog symbols, objects of tender feelings and compassion; and yet they can also be worshiped by authoritarians as impersonally pure "Roman matrons." On the plane of abstract imagery, the notion of chaste womanhood has a two-way potential. This is not to deny that the woman on a pedestal answers some of the same emotional needs in both authoritarian and rigid rebel—for instance, a repressed sexuality. But *all* of the needs answered are not the same, and it does not reinforce entirely the same kind of feelings about others. To be sure, Comstock, like an archetype authoritarian, despised the "unchaste woman"; but he made much less of this than of humble innocence. His main hostility seemed to be directed not at "corrupted" women, but at their "corrupters"—commercial art and book dealers, and the officials who tolerated them. These people he attacked as authority.

We have observed, it is true, a note of projection in Comstock's concern about sex and exploitation. His puritanical conscience, and the image of godly authority it represented, may have compelled him to project many impulses he dared not express directly. But this does not mean that, to any great degree, they included feelings of frustrated rebellion, magnifying submerged resentment at authority. And, even if they did, there is no evidence that they were primarily displaced or projected onto people representing weakness and tenderness. If anything, he displaced rebelliousness onto figures felt very deeply to be authority symbols. That, at least, is the more likely, from the way he wrote, spoke, and acted. Comstock, indeed, seems to have made a deep and yet overt identification with his mother; he may have displaced rebelliousness against his father onto other authority figures. In this case, his submission to God would not necessarily be very ambivalent, for religious faith was strongly implanted in him by his mother as well as his father.*

THE COMPROMISED REBEL

The unhappy life of Tom Watson, the Georgia Populist, shows how very close to each other authoritarianism and rigid rebellion can be. At his distance in history it is impossible to say for sure what Tom Watson became, but there is some evidence that he underwent a shift in basic personality. In a sense, the change can be described as a short step but one involving some major rearrangements of character.

During his early life anti-authoritarianism seemed deep in his emotions. As a schoolboy he challenged bullies—once in defense of a cripple, another time for a black. As a family man, he could be kind and affectionate. His book *The Story of France* was a passionate attack on tyrants. He fought against the exploiters of convict labor. He championed the poor farmer, and he continued to do so when he became a rich landlord. He romanticized Southern institutions, yet he opposed dueling, and he helped forge that most revolutionary alliance—a party uniting poor whites and blacks. The move was conceived for political advantage, but it required an independent mind and readiness to work with black speakers and organizers. In his mid-twenties, Watson had also shown he could criticize himself and his parents:

I have imagined enemies where there were none; been tortured by indignities which were the creatures of my own fancy, and have magnified the gloom of every reverse. . . . Had I been firmly governed and not with fitful

---

* This treatment of Comstock shows the psychological limits of cases taken from history, despite the relatively full records of his actions and words. It is conceivable that in fantasies he was more punitive toward weak outsiders; that he was authoritarian in disposition; and that his conscious tenderness for the underdog was unconsciously magnified as a check against underlying sadism. This last aspect may have some truth, but it does not necessarily entail an authoritarian type of submission. A harsher mix of anti-rebellion and humane militance can be seen in the life of Carry Nation, who broke up rum shops with a hatchet: see Nation, 1905; Sinclair, 1962, pp. 54-57.

harshness: had I not been abused, mocked and scorned there would be sunshine where now is shadow.[18]

But the enemies and indignities were not all the creatures of his fancy. Tom Watson's life is the story of a passionate, talented man whom political forces frustrated and blistered. In electoral campaigns his name was vilified, his life repeatedly threatened. Fraud deprived him of a congressional seat. As vice-presidential candidate on the Democratic-Populist "fusion" ticket, he was ignored by the presidential candidate, Bryan, to the point of insult. These and other blows were deeply felt. Whether or not because of them, his dictatorial streak, exhibited clearly in his personal life, became steadily more rampant. From his childhood, Watson had shown an explosive, demanding temper when even little things thwarted him. He also displayed a strong tendency to hero worship. In conjunction with these elements, frustration produced a gradual change in Watson's basic behavior.

An early sign of the change was Watson's sequel to *The Story of France*, a life of Napoleon, whom the author hailed as a champion of the people against "feudalism, castes, divine rights and hereditary imposture." In fact the book has much more praise of Napoleon than defense of liberty and the common man. C. Vann Woodward puts the matter shrewdly:

It is true that Watson readily admits that the Corsican was a "colossal mixture of the good and the bad," that a "more contradictory mortal never lived" and that Napoleon's treatment of Poland presents "a story picture." "The anti-Bonaparte biographers," however, provoke in him wrath and heated retorts. For an outstanding opponent of American militarians and materialism he seems strangely serene in the presence of "bleaching bones on battlefields" and strangely jubilant over the onward march of Napoleon's eagles. As an outstanding advocate of initiative, referendum, recall, and popular election of all officers, he seems reconciled with remarkable ease to the collapse of a republic, and the rise of an emperor—"the necessary man without whom they might relapse into chaotic conditions." While he gazes, transfixed by the splendor of Napoleon, the money-changers creep into the temple of French democracy, unchallenged, indeed unobserved, by Watson. One has the feeling upon closing the book that an author who can use the term, "the great Democratic despot," without consciousness of paradox is reconciled to a union of Caesarism and democracy.[19]

In the years following the book's publication, he became a more ardent Southern patriot, his words increasingly a Confederate tough-talk. In like spirit, his white following served its black ties. Electorally, the black alliance had become a handicap to the white farmers' movement, but there were personal repercussions; as time went by, Watson became more and more vituperative toward the blacks. True, the blacks shared this position with many other targets: Watson described new immigrants as "the scum of creation" and political opponents were frequently accused of lurid sexual doings. Watson's anti-Catholicism, another latter-day phenomenon, painted a picture of autocrats and exploiters, but he also attacked Catholics as dirty, deviant, alien, and soft—"chemise-wearing bachelors," "shad-bellies," "foot-kissers." "Jimmy Cheesey," the Pope, was a "fat old dago" who lived with "voluptuous women."

Once, Watson tried to pick a fight with a man whom he had suddenly recognized as a Knight of Columbus. "The sight of him was good to my eyes—as that of a red rag to a maddened bull," he later explained. In Woodward's view, however, a "peculiar malignity" distinguished his attacks on the black. "A friend betrayed is the enemy most despised."[20]

A further sign of change was the cracking of his moral integrity—an important sign because Watson had always appeared to view himself as a man of frankness and principle. In 1907 he turned against his ally Governor Hoke Smith of Georgia, and as a powerful boss, threw his support to Smith's opponent, Joseph Brown, who subsequently won the governorship in 1908. Brown was a big businessman, the son of a railroad millionaire, and a bitter foe of organized labor. As such, he stood for much that Watson abhorred and continued to abhor to the end. Smith, by contrast, was a Progressive reform Governor whose program had conformed with Watson's ideology. The manifest reason for Watson's shift was the case of Arthur Glover. A factory foreman with a violent record, Glover had been convicted of murdering a woman mill worker. The evidence against him was overwhelming, he was sentenced to death, and Governor Smith refused to commute the sentence. The previous decade, Glover had been a Watson lieutenant in a labor fight. Before he was executed, he wrote several letters to Watson, beseeching him for his support. Watson felt sure that Glover was being victimized: all the more so as Glover's prosecutor had been a political foe. Glover's cause became a crusade, and after the execution Watson detested Smith. Up to this point it could be said that he was acting out of conscience, and on behalf of an underdog. But to support Brown and attack Smith's political record, he had to distort truth and tread on his own convictions. When the election was over, he justified the results cockily and unrealistically—in terms of Populist strength.

"We hold the balance of power in the country counties, and the country counties rule the state." He wrote a letter to his wife, a soothing letter as if to comfort himself:

We cannot expect so very many years of health and strength and we must make the most of the Indian Summer. We have lost far too much already. . . . In other words, I am going to live more for you, and less "for the people." We will be happy, perfectly happy, and no cloud shall come into the sky for us any more.[21]

Two years later Watson practiced a more clear-cut dishonesty. In his periodical, *Watson's Jeffersonian Magazine,* he challenged some Marxian Socialists to a public debate in print. Pugnaciously, he offered to publish their writing, but he retreated when Daniel De Leon, editor of the *Daily People,* sent him a batch of his articles and in an open letter challenged him to publish them. In his own paper, De Leon had already printed a series of witty and blistering attacks on Watson's agrarian individualism; Watson now evaded debate by claiming that De Leon did not represent "true Socialist doctrine." (The *Daily People* was an official publication of the Socialist Labor party.) When Watson reprinted his challenge to a public debate, he again included De Leon's name among those challenged—as if De Leon had not taken it up. Conceivably this may have been a clerical mistake, but no such reason can be given for the way he first deflected De Leon's offer.

Just before the outbreak of World War I, Watson became involved in the famous Leo Frank case. Frank was a Northerner and a Jew, the superintendent of an Atlanta pencil factory. He was accused of murdering a fourteen-year-old employee, Mary Phagan, whose body was found in the factory basement. Anti-Semitism became rampant in the city, so much so that a later suspect, much more incriminated and a black to boot, was virtually ignored.[22] Frank's trial lasted a month, and in an ugly mob atmosphere the "Jew pervert" was convicted. His attorneys appealed the case to higher courts, but their case was in the end unsuccessful, and while they fought their battles, feeling in Georgia against Frank became more and more frenzied.

For nearly a year following Frank's arrest, Watson made no public comment on the case. Privately, he said that Frank could not have had a fair trial in Atlanta. Yet, months later, when he did take up a public position, it was to attack the Atlanta *Journal* for demanding a new trial. In his magazine, he then began a series of diatribes against Frank and all he allegedly stood for. On the face of it his campaign was largely anti-authoritarian. Behind Frank he saw a conspiracy of rich Jews, determined that one of their own should not die because of a simple "factory girl." Frank was "the Sodomite who took her sweet life." The crumpled white form, the torn garment "spotted with virginal blood," testified to the grotesque exploitation of a helpless and innocent creature. And so on. But there were also passages that reveled in authority and in-group power. Leo Frank was

> the typical young libertine Jew who is dreaded and detested by the city authorities of the North for the very reason that Jews of this type have an utter contempt for law, and a ravenous appetite for the forbidden fruit—a lustful eagerness enhanced by the racial novelty of the girl of the uncircumcised.[23]

One could see from his face—"those bulging satyr eyes . . . the protruding fearfully sensual lips; and also the animal jaw"—that Frank had perpetrated the very crime which had made the Almighty blast Sodom and Gomorrah. Despite Watson's portrait of the lawless Jew, he made increasingly obvious hints that the "people of Georgia" should look to lynch law—an institution he had already praised as a way of controlling blacks.

On the last day of his term, Governor John Slaton commuted Frank's death sentence. The next issue of Watson's *Jeffersonian* declared:

> Our grand old Empire State HAS BEEN RAPED!
> We have been violated, AND WE ARE ASHAMED!
> . . . We have been betrayed! the breath of some leprous monster has passed over us, and we feel like crying out, in horror and despair, "Unclean! UNCLEAN!"[24]

In defense of Atlanta mobs which had threatened Slaton's house, Watson harked back to the American Revolution. "The 'mobs' were Liberty Boys in those days—the old days before we become lollypops, vegetarians, grape-juicers, and sissy-boys."

On August 16, 1915, twenty-five armed men entered the state prison, took Frank away by automobile, and hanged him. Watson's magazine endorsed the event with an eight-page defense of lynching and a simple text:

> "THE VOICE OF THE PEOPLE IS THE VOICE OF GOD."

On the Frank case, Watson seems to have identified with symbols of cruelty and power much more than he consciously realized. As with his treatment of Napoleon, the identification came upon him in disguise, for both Napoleon and "the people" could be seen as standing against established authority. In this way Watson retained his underdog doctrines while satisfying a growing urge to dominate and punish. A dirt-and-threat complex blended with a punitive patriotism, so that the abuse of a pure girl became the "rape" of Georgia, and a cruel mob became historic folk heroes—Liberty Boys—ranged against modern-day softies.

At several points Watson gave the impression of a man shouting to drown his conscience. C. Vann Woodward hints at this in discussing his changing treatment of blacks, but it also seemed evident in the Frank case. He wrote a medical friend, at the time,

> A baffling nervous trouble returns on me about once a month and for several days I am so despondent and distressed, *about nothing,* that it is difficult to live.[25]

Intense depression without recognized cause often stems from unadmitted guilt feelings, or from aggressive impulse displaced inward. During the Frank case, Watson did things which his conscience—or the humane side of a conscience much divided—could not have approved of. We have already noted that he vehemently opposed any retrial of Frank, though he privately recognized that the trial had been unfair. Likewise, after Slaton commuted the sentence, Watson accused the Governor, without any evidence, of having a financial stake in Frank's defense. As an intelligent lawyer himself, and a lifelong champion of "justice," he could not easily have accepted his own demagoguery.[26]

It would seem, then, that Watson made extreme but ambivalent identification with mob authority; that this superficially assuaged his feelings of frustration, of relative powerlessness, while adding to self-contempt on a deeper plane; and that he displaced guilt feelings and rebellious doubts about lynch-mob rule onto outsiders and the mob's victims. Beyond the state of Georgia he continued to champion the underdog: he opposed big business at home, "militarism" abroad, and a wartime government's inroads upon civil liberties. These actions paid homage to lifelong beliefs and expressed "secondary rebellion"; they did not belie the apparent fact that he had trampled on his own humanity and substantially altered the way in which he managed his aggressive drives. Angry he had always been, and beleaguered by exaggerated threats; and perhaps in his romantic hero-worshiping there had long been a deep desire to submit. If so, his former self had largely resisted this desire by identifying with the rebel and the oppressed, and by emphasizing the genuinely humane side of his nature, though also by a belligerent, autocratic behavior. But now, it seems, he centrally capitulated to the submissive urge, and in so doing he turned against tenderness.

THE DIVIDED LIBERAL

We end this chapter with a contemporary portrait drawn from an autobiographical study. Here again we have an account which seems to complicate the notion of authoritarianism. Certainly it challenges the idea that authoritarianism is inevitably a "right-wing" phenomenon. The subject and author of the original account is a young professional man who is familiar with psychology and has looked at himself in the light of authoritarian psychodynamics. His study, which is only summarized here, does not purport to be a full self-analysis, but I think it both qualifies and develops the ideas about personality presented so far. It portrays a character whose authoritarianism, on the aggressive/hostile side, is almost entirely held from behavior by deeply entrenched humane values and perhaps also by a certain capacity for self-examination.

"James Thomas"[27] come from a well-to-do business and professional family, which respected both "ideas" and success at running organizations. Liberal values were inculcated and some guilt about social inequality felt at an early age. Quite recently he detected in himself a fearful contempt of people who reminded him of his own "fecklessness" and dependency. But the objects of his irritation were not obviously underdog types—the poor, the ailing—for if they were, the contempt would affront his liberal values and self-image.

He now connected his feelings of weakness with tacit family, school, and elitist pressures to succeed, be articulate, show leadership—especially a feeling that he had failed to emulate his father. The father was a masterful, dynamic, successful man with immense range of judgment and "flair," a well-integrated fusion of toughness and tender-minded tolerance, a loving and generous man but one who always seemed "larger than life" to his son—the more so as he was frequently away from home on business. While not admitting it in his youth, James really had more of a relationship with his mother and older sister, both of whom were warm, demonstrative, and "strong characters," if somewhat overprotective.

James noted in himself an "almost simpering submissiveness" in the presence of strong male figures, followed by resentments when he was out of their presence. His very perceptions would shift, so that behavior by a strong person which seemed fair at the time would seem unfair later. He usually felt more confident in the company of women. He reported various fantasies which appeared to reflect homosexual and castration fears involving other male figures.

Even in his youth James felt overt resentments against his father. They did have their quarrels, but James said he felt increasingly that he had stifled rebelliousness in his father's presence. "At the time he always seemed right." Today, he could not "get away from" a sense that he had failed to assert himself as he should. This had led to conflict between his own intellectualism and a feeling that he should be more "incisive" in affairs involving practical leadership. James also suggested that he made a two-way displacement of rebelliousness against his father:

1. Moral pique was channeled "upward," against symbols of authority and injustice, against various bosses for whom he worked (in fact kindly men for the most part) and an uncle who showed much of his father's charm and command.

2. The wish to do violence was largely channeled "downward," against people and objects whom he could imagine hurting without fear of counterviolence. Obsessional fantasies recurred, in which he dropped a cat or baby from a great height. There was "nothing personal" about it, no conscious or semi-conscious feeling of irritation with the victim. On the contrary, the imagined victim was often treasured and beloved. Some childhood episodes indicated a self-destructive element, including the wish to have over and done with the facts of a frail existence. But the main point was that the displacement separated, or tried to, the hostile from the physically aggressive. (It would seem too pat to say that the physically aggressive fantasies reflected a repressed sadism, but a thorough-going psychoanalyst might not agree.)

It is true that James also reported resentments against figures of passivity, softness, excessive gentility, but he read this more as a compensation for, and projection of, weakness feelings than displaced aggression. He suggested that if humane and liberal values had been less entrenched—by his father and others—and if the main women in his childhood had been weaker-seeming people, he might well have been more authoritarian in outright behavior. He suspected that "neurologically" he was "good material" for authoritarianism: the right mixture of timidity and nervous aggression. In reviewing this material, it is not clear how much his relative openness about himself has limited his authoritarianism, but his case indicates that authoritarian processes are compatible with more self-insight than the F scale archetype implies.[28]

12   POLITICAL APPEALS

It is often assumed—quite wrongly, I think—that deep emotional factors are only important in those political beliefs which seem nasty, foolish, or "far out," and that personality only affects political belief when it is neurotic. We saw in the last chapter that authoritarian dynamics, both latent and overt, can go with a wide range of ideologies; and apart from the case of German Nazism, there have been no studies directly indicating that authoritarians are more likely than other people to be right-wing "extremists." Despite these perplexities, I would argue that, where right-wing doctrines exist, authoritarians will *tend* to espouse them—insofar as their characteristic dispositions are expressed in any political stance. But I would also suggest that the problems involved in arguing this, even hypothetically, are more complicated than may be thought.[1]

We start with the premise that a person's political beliefs are often colored by character structure—not simply values and loyalties themselves, but the way the emotional ingredients of personality are put together. After all, the expression of political beliefs is but a form of behavior, and it has already been shown how behavior can be affected by unconscious processes. But the importance of this factor in a person's politics does not seem to be the same for all individuals. For Mr. "Smith" (a conscientious businessman), political attitudes have some limited roots in basic personality structure but chiefly as they represent values, loyalties, and learned notions of economic self-interest—in other words, represent a part of conscience and the cognitive and calculative

137

parts of ego. To harmonize political beliefs and self-interest with moral values requires some unconscious rationalizing of motive and suppression of thoughts, but Mr. Smith's personality structure does not depend on politics to any great extent. On the other hand, for Mr. "Jones" (a "middle-road" lawyer), political attitudes not only reflect moral values and self-interest but provide a way of extending deep emotional drives involving power, identity, and sexuality. These lead him to enjoy the charisma of young, handsome politicians and to identify himself with "can-do" Federal programs. Mr. "Green," a diehard liberal, finds in political issues a channel for rebelliousness and other feelings shaped and directed by the way his ego manages his impulses: in his case, political expression provides an outlet denied or not sought in personal life. On the whole, the political attitudes of Jones and Green both serve and reflect more of the basic personality than the politics of Smith. What causes such a difference is not altogether known, but some milieus and experiences must suggest more forcibly than others the uses of political belief as an emotional vehicle.[2]

It is partly because of this that the political ideologies of authoritarians will reflect their *authoritarianism* to a varying extent. But there is also another reason. Even among those whose political attitudes have broad and deep roots in personality, some people's political attitudes will be more central to their authoritarianism than will those of others. As explained already, an authoritarian disposition—that particular interaction of conscience, ego, and certain impulses—does not embrace all of inner personality, any more than it accounts for all of the individual's behavior. Thus, an authoritarian's political beliefs may have deep roots in personality without being very involved in his authoritarianism. He may, for example, subscribe to political ideals of humanity and tolerance, not because he is a hypocrite but because his urge to punish and eschew tenderness has not squelched humane feelings in all relationships.

These complications explain why, ideally, we should restrict the "right-wing hypothesis" to those authoritarians whose dispositions are considerably reflected in political beliefs. The restriction, granted, is as vague as it is difficult to work with. At what point should we decide that a person's political beliefs reflect, to a major extent, a specific personality pattern? There is no simple line between reflecting it and not reflecting it; and the few statistical studies which compare the political leanings of authoritarians and non-authoritarians do not allow for this factor. Nevertheless, the point is important. Of those whose authoritarianism is not greatly expressed in political ideology, a large number may espouse whatever groups hold governing power, wield social influence, and seem generally respectable. A priori one may infer this from the authoritarian's tendency to rigid conventionalism and his need to align himself with power. Therefore, when strongly right-wing groups do not hold much power—and still more when, in many milieus, they seem "far out"—the tendency of some authoritarians to support the governing groups may "cancel out" the tendency of other authoritarians to support right-wing groups for more specifically ideological reasons.

We suggest, however, that of those people who support nonrightist governing groups the authoritarian element will include a disproportionate number of latent right-wingers, people who would find their support for the country's governance become more enthusiastic if it moved right. We saw a hint of this with the authoritarian college secretary described in the preceding chapter. Overtly espousing "liberal" views, she seemed to do so more because her immediate authorities and the conventions of her milieu endorsed them than because her view jibed with an emotional structure. True, they had some roots in basic personality: they reinforced the self-image of a kindly, caretaking person, which in many ways, and on some levels, she was. Her political beliefs may also have connected with her authoritarianism as a counterforce or "reaction formation," a way of controlling hostile impulses. She gave an impression of this in the sugary way she said,—"I just *love* Negroes." The point remains that her liberal views did not centrally and directly reflect her authoritarianism. And, in a moment of wrath, as when she denounced the foreign professor's "dirty" habits, she showed a strident nationalism far more in keeping with the right wing. If our hypothesis is correct and such a person is not unusual among "liberal to moderate" authoritarians, then the study of overt political beliefs among authoritarians will often underestimate their particular right-wing potential. It will do so, at least, in liberal democratic countries.[3]

FASCISM

The defining tenets of fascist doctrine may be listed as three points. First, respect for a monolithic and unparliamentary state power, exerting great control over the individual. Second, a fierce nationalism, with an emphasis on military power and glory. Third and more generally, the mystique of an in-group—especially nation and race—which must be vigilant against outsiders and traitors. Although fascist programs have had a mass appeal, promising spiritual and economic uplift to the common man, they have always been elitist as well. Within the national or racial in-group, special bands of honor—officer corps, party elect, and so forth—have had their place in the sun. Official power has been strictly hierarchical, with a charismatic leader at the apex.[4]

The appeal to authoritarians is easily envisaged. Fascism provides opportunities for extreme submission; for postures of strength and alignment with absolutist power; and for moralizing attacks on weaklings and outsiders. It offers endorsement for conspiracy theories—the threat complex. It indulges narcissism and self-pity in its call to heroic, romantic self-sacrifice. It suggests scapegoats for displaced or projected hostility. And by proffering an alliance with strength—a mighty in-group—it may help the individual submerge his feelings of weakness. These are only a few, hypothetical examples: we shall note more specific connections when we came to the subject of German Nazism.

THE RADICAL RIGHT

As most Americans surely know, to be radically right does not necessarily entail "statism"—support for a strong and binding national government—except in matters military. Yet one can define the "radical right" so as to include both fascism and certain non-"statist" doctrines. Defined thus, radical-right doctrines may be said to idealize a national past and its traditions; espouse a harsh, "get tough" elitism; and, to bring these ends about, support radical changes in social structure and public policy. The hailed traditions may happen to include "freedom"; and the kingpin of the should-be elite may sometimes be "the common man"; but in the matter of beliefs, the radical right stands for censorship. Idealism precedes tolerance, and the ethic of strength and struggle becomes a crusade.[5]

The hypothetical appeals of the radical right to authoritarians may be considered in two main parts. First, there are radical-right values which merely intensify similar values held by moderate or Burkian conservatives—most "moderate Republicans," for example, and most British Tories. Among these are an acceptance of inequality (whether or not one praises the self-made man); keen patriotism; reverence for traditional authorities and conventional morality; and a concern for order that emphasizes the anarchic potential of man and the frailty of civilization's fabric.[6] The authoritarian attraction of most of these is obvious; only the last point needs further mention. On the plane of sheer imagery, there is a strong parallel between conservative concerns with order and anarchism and the more unconscious, authoritarian concern with controlling fierce impulse. To the extent, therefore, that the authoritarian expresses this concern in political beliefs, one would expect him to show a conservative or ultra-conservative concern with anarchy. Through this attitude he can project a sense of inner chaos onto the environment, and displace outward his anxiety about control. Also, and more simply, one may expect a person who fears his own impulse to assume, unconsciously, that society is peopled with individuals like him—fragile containers of rebelliousness. This motive for "law-and-order" must surely extend far beyond authoritarians.

The second class of appeal involves a more fundamental difference between radical right and moderate conservative. It is the difference between demanding a social restoration and accepting gradual evolution. The radical right longs for a past elysium—a vision which blends historical reality with romantic myth. For the sake of power it may revel in modern techniques and weapons, but its intent—or part of it—is to restore "old virtues" and a simple purity. For decades, and in countries as far removed as the United States and Japan, these longings have been a prime feature of radical-right movements. By contrast, moderate conservatives accept a status quo; they revere traditional institutions but tolerate their gradual change. Some would slow down that change to a virtual standstill; other, more "progressive" conservatives have a marked sense of history as an evolution, continuing from past to present and on into the future. They prefer to see change as continuity, not as a radical break.

Acceptance of evolution demands a certain pragmatism and flexibility. By contrast, political nostalgia and restorationism go well with a simplified, clear-cut dogma, for putting the historical clock back is an unrealistic business requiring much faith. The Nazi use of race doctrines and a Wagnerian mystique; the Japanese welding of Shinto with a new theory of state service; the abstractions about man in the books of Barry Goldwater and Ayn Rand—all these phenomena, diverse as they are, show a striving for ideologies which combine simple truths with the force of elaborate science. The results are unscientific, in part because the present and past are so superficially combined. Thus, the most fervent supporters of Goldwater craved an old "American Way of Life," simple, rugged, lean with frontier virtue, yet possessing all the power and comfort of modern technology and cradled in the midst of a lush capitalist order. At dawn on Senator Goldwater's estate, the natural light of the Arizona morning would strike a photoelectric mechanism connected to the flagpole, and Old Glory would slide to the top. The combination has its poetry, but the metaphor cannot be fulfilled by political programs.

Among radical-right dogmas a common element is the emphasis on purification—the need to purge society of modern corruptions and go back to old certitudes. Another frequently found element is the conspiracy theory: the notion that subversives and cabals are responsible for much of the society's ills. In this the radical right has some similarity with radical leftist groups, though the power rings identified are not entirely the same. The potential appeal to authoritarians is plain. The radical right endorses dogmatism and simplification; it offers scapegoats for aggression and a collective form of self-pity; it provides a way of displacing onto the political arena the authoritarian's concerns about dirt and danger.

But the radical right has two aspects which may not, at first, seem very compatible with authoritarianism. The first is the tendency to oppose great aggregates of established power—unions, big business, and governing institutions—when these are not dominated by the right wing. This aspect applies most to American radical-right groups, with their laissez-faire traditionalism and hatred of big government and Eastern vested interests. However, as Poujade of France showed us, a "common man" opposition to established power is by no means confined to the Americans, even if the "common man" in question is more typically a small businessman or farmer than a manual laborer.[7] The question remains: can political groups which tend to oppose established power offer much for the submissive-aggressive needs of authoritarians? The answer is that radical-right groups do not oppose *all* power; far from it. With ardent patriotism there usually goes an admiration of the military machine; and on the domestic front, even when a big national government is opposed, the radical right tends to support such things as restrictive liquor laws, curbs on student politics, book banning, and relatively unbridled police powers. Behind much of the American radical right's "freedom" ideology lies a wish that external authority could be, not weaker *in toto*, but more personal—closer to the individual, more binding upon him. Thus the radical right is often in a good position to express personal ambivalences about authority and indulge "secondary rebellion." It provides repressive authorities to identify with, and remoter authorities—weak betrayers of the national heritage—to rebel against. This imagery can be seen not only in America but in French right-wing distinctions between "real" France and "legal" France—and before that, in Nazi attitudes to the Weimar Republic. Being basically inegalitarian, the radical right's outlook on power expresses envy of that power more easily than an underdog dislike of organized power per se.

The second aspect which may seem incompatible with authoritarianism is the radical right's very radicalism. To a basically insecure person, with a rigid makeup and weak ego, the thought of major change can be particularly threatening. One would therefore expect many authoritarians to hang on to the status quo rather than follow the gospel of the radical right. But, in times of great flux, it is not always easy to locate a fixed and certain status quo. Whichever way he turns, the authoritarian may be faced with change, and modern bureaucratic institutions may seem too formless and colorless to offer the magic control he craves. Under these circumstances one can expect the radical right to be very appealing: it offers escape from complexity to a clear-cut moral order. Furthermore, not even the radical right is wholly radical and restorationist, for much of its moral tradition may be part of the contemporary culture, albeit a part that is on the defensive against other cultural forces. Hence, for all its revolutionary goals, the radical-right appeal can include a status quo appeal, declaring in effect: "*This* is the nation's essence. Stand here with us."[8] And when it holds political power—the Klan in Mississippi, the fascists in prewar Europe and Japan—the status quo appeal can be all the greater.

These points jibe with our hypothesis: if they are not right wingers authoritarians tend to be *latent* right wingers, that is, people especially quick to join the right when it gains social influence. Also, the idea of a radical-right appeal amid social flux corresponds to an argument already put: the notion of a hardened, defensive culture which not only foments authoritarian behavior but marshals it in political movements.

WEBS OF IDEOLOGY

It is now plain that the values and concerns which comprise a political doctrine reinforce each other on more than one level. Take, for instance, the right-wing notions of order, elitism, nationalism, and martial strength. On an ideological plane, these ideas are *logically* compatible, in large measure because of their *historical* associations. Nationalism has been historically defined in largely military terms. National leaders have historically tended to come from elites holding military as well as economic power. An orderly society has tended to mean a society in which people accept firm governance and "know their place," in a neat hierarchy of classes, roles, and traditional obligations. And so on, with some variations between national cultures and subcultures. But we have also seen that right-wing values on order, elitism, nationalism, and martial strength can represent emotional concerns which link up on the level of a character's organization. We have traced that, at least, in the case of authoritarianism; there is no need here to repeat the ways in which authoritarian concerns about order, in-groups, and power reinforce each other and stem from common needs.

These two levels of interrelationship may in turn be more connected than we often realize. *One* reason why fairly discrete, ideological traditions can be identified, transcending individual lives and generations, may be that certain ideologies appeal to certain kinds of character; they are evolved and maintained in part by deep personality needs, though these needs are partly shaped by social circumstance. In the case of the radical right, there are others besides authoritarians whose characters are deeply attracted to it. But there are also people whose dispositions are not intrinsically right-wing-prone, but who are plunged into specific stresses which, allied with appropriate traditions and institutions, make the radical right emotionally attractive.

THE CONCERN WITH CLEANLINESS

Right-wing imagery of cleanliness and dirt illustrates very well the complicated relationship between values and between *levels* of values. The importance of this imagery in authoritarianism makes the subject worth a special examination.

On an ideological plane, the ethic of cleanliness has tended to be an ally of elitism and "propriety." It is not surprising that in order to be clean and healthy (the two conditions obviously have a medical connection) many people have wanted to dissociate themselves from the relative squalor of poverty. Nor is it surprising that, in justification of social inequality, people have seen lower-class squalor not as the infliction of an oppressive environment but as a moral weakness to be overcome by individual effort. Public-health democracy has made inroads on this kind of thinking, but in the West at least, it is still too much a part of the "Protestant ethic" to be confined to the radical right. It is, rather, a generally conservative attitude which often takes strong form in extreme right-wing circles. The point is that one does not have to go to psychoanalysis to find some connection between attitudes that value cleanliness, stigmatize the poor, and equate dirtiness with moral weakness. Nor is this all. In the case of the radical right, there are sociological reasons for the concern about cleanliness and dirt. Many radical-right movements have drawn disproportionate support from small towns or country, and in their attacks on big-city influences they have not been inaccurate in calling the big city "dirty." "Dirtiness" is a relative and subjective word, but one usually considers a thing the more dirty as it is (1) corroding, corrupting, or unhealthy, *and* (2) alien or waste.* These two conditions are very much interconnected, but the big industrial city fulfills them both (the "alien" condition being fulfilled by immigrants and foreign ways). Logically, the symbol of "dirt" is also useful to the radical right because it implies inferiority (dirt despised and underfoot). This suits the radical-right view of enemy out-groups.

Despite all these considerations, it is hard to say where historical ideology ends and deep character traits begin. As already suggested, the difficulty of defining "dirt" indicates that it is intrinsically bound up with attitude, hence amenable to varying psychological uses. In the case of the authoritarian we have already argued that "cleanliness versus dirt" is a symbolic as well as physical concern that connects unconsciously with a strength-and-weakness complex. But we have also argued that authoritarians are only peculiar in a combination of traits; that in individual traits they differ from other people in degree rather than in kind. This is certainly true of the authoritarian's cleanliness concern. One need not take an out-and-out psychoanalytic position to recognize that feces and the anus play some part in general ideas of cleanliness and dirtiness, and that in our own culture, as in others, these bodily elements have been given an emotional loading—as shown by lavatory humor and the common usage of "shit." Given these factors, is it reasonable to suppose that deep psychological concerns are irrelevant to right-wing imagery of dirt and cleanliness? Leaving the right wing out of it for the moment, why are "dirt," "dirty," and kindred words so often used to describe whatever mankind dislikes or fears? In answer, one might lay emphasis on physical factors—the association of dirt with germs and disease, with all the threats of man's

---

* Thus, soil in the backyard where it belongs is not usually considered as dirty as when it is brought into the house. The inadequacy of dictionaries on the matter shows how very subjective it all is. The Concise Oxford Dictionary's definition of "dirt" begins with the tautology "unclean matter that soils," goes on to the objective but limited "wet mud," and thence to "anything worthless" (1946 edition). Webster's Collegiate Dictionary is more helpful: "dirt" is, first, "any foul substance, as excrement, mud, dust etc." (1947 edition). The primacy of "excrement" as an example supports a point we take up below. By "foul" Webster's means either "filthy" or "offensive to the senses." The second is of some help, but for every sense there are offensive things which are not counted dirty, e.g., pain, certain loud noises, and ugly but clean buildings.

natural environment, and hence with survival. But can these associations be separated from the deeply psychological, including exaggerated fears about oneself? If dirt is associated with ill-health, debilitation and a "dragging down," if cleanliness is associated with strength and vitality, the way is left clear for an association between dirt and those fears which combine the psychological and physiological—fears, for example, about sexual vitality. Furthermore, it has been observed that some forms of paranoia include the fear of taking in unclean and alien substances. Authoritarians may tend to have this anxiety, but it is not confined to them, and there is no hard and fast line between such paranoid feelings and "ordinary" concerns about health.*

In short, the cleanliness concern tends to be associated with feelings about strength and vitality, and with fears of threat, *both* on the level of conservative ideology and on the plane of personality structure. On neither level is this tendency confined to authoritarians. Yet it would be a remarkable coincidence if the two levels of association were not connected. I would suggest four rather complex connections between these levels. First, the psychological connotations of cleanliness-dirt make it a pungent *metaphor* on the political plane. Thus, men who are genuinely concerned about national honor and strength will unconsciously find it cogent and vivid to associate these things with "purity." Second, those political movements most concerned about strength, weakness, and threat will tend more than others to draw the metaphors of cleanliness and dirt from the personality plane, because the metaphor is so suitable to these concerns. Third, they will likewise tend to recruit authoritarian and other personalities whose emotional association of cleanliness with strength is pronounced. These individuals will intensify the political movements' usage of the metaphors. However, for them more than for most other recruits, the political uses of "purity" will go beyond the metaphoric, that is, beyond mere emotive and literary color. It will serve the specific function of projecting personal anxieties about dirtiness, weakness, and threat into the political arena.†

---

* Against some of the above it might be noted that young children are not naturally repelled by dirt. But, even if dirt concerns are greatly stressed and molded by social training, this training is in part a response to natural instincts for survival and vitality, however much the response has become rationalized and elaborated. That there is a biological element can be seen in the way carnivorous animals clean their lairs, themselves, and their young.

† There is no clear-cut line between the metaphoric and the projective, for much of the "ordinary" interest in cleanliness imagery (that is, relatively unauthoritarian and unparanoid interest) may reflect some anxieties about it. But

Fourth, those dislocated or unsettled cultures which nourish defensive, repressive orthodoxies will tend to produce both personalities and political movements that, on the respective levels, have marked concern about strength, threat, and hence cleanliness or purity. Character and political movement will then act upon each other, in the ways already described.[9]

A NOTE ON COMMUNISM

From fictional studies of the Stalin purges, we have the portrait of the frightened party hardliner who grovels to his bosses and takes out his fears on alleged deviationists and subordinates, who in turn pursue others. One may wonder if the Czechoslovakian crisis of the sixties did not bring out similar strains in some personalities. But, even if it did, was the effect directly attributable to communist doctrine, or merely to a potential residing in any totalitarian regime backed by terror, whatever its specific ideological component? Let us focus, therefore, on the basic elements of communist doctrine: how hospitable to authoritarianism may we expect them to be? Hypothetically, certain things can be said, allowing, of course, for national and other variations in what the official ideology stresses. In general the following attractions suggest themselves: first, a monolithic party to which the authoritarian can submit and thereby feel one of a moral elect; second, a historical dogma following iron laws—this may appeal to authoritarian fatalism, and the wish for simple rules and stereotypes; third, a conformist evangelism, placing the needs of the social edifice far above the value of individual variation for its own sake; fourth, in the purest forms of communism, a doctrine of violent, moralizing aggression, and ruthlessness about means. Partly as a result of these factors, *state* communist movements have tended to oppose sensual display and aesthetic variation—anything which smacks of capitalist decadence and lauds private concerns over public. The most recent example, at the time of writing, has been the puritanism of China's Red Guards, with their castigation of courting couples, love letters, bourgeois luxury, and "outlandish" customs. But Russia and other communist nations have also had their waves of organized prudery; it is not so true of minority communism in Western Europe and America.

---

in this case the anxieties may give emotional charge to the imagery without being so strong that the individual unconsciously feels he has to use the imagery to get rid of the anxieties.

A disadvantage of communism for the archetype authoritarian is its official support of the weak and oppressed everywhere. In communist doctrine, strength and power are not the *prime* values—ends as opposed to means—that they are in fascism. A corollary is that modern communist propaganda has not reveled in images of dirt versus cleanliness to anything like the same extent as Nazi and other radical-right propaganda. Communist movements can hardly blame the urban worker for his grimy circumstances, any more than they can castigate the alien for "racial impurity" and "degeneracy." True, they have portrayed their political enemies as swinish and decadent; but beyond that, the propaganda epithets have been largely and drearily abstract ("deviationist," "enemy of the people," "revisionist," and so on). Contrast these with such fascist expressions as the Norwegian Nazi pamphlet, *Fakta* (Facts), whose text and photographs portrayed various ethnic specimens of filthy and subhuman mien. A further corollary is that right-wing power, more concerned with subversion from below, from within the country, is better placed to express personality concerns about inner menaces. Left-wing power is more apt to take a stance against enemies "above or outside," although exceptions to this have already been noted.

In some circumstances, however, the egalitarian component of communism may present no great stumbling block to the authoritarian. One may conceive of this particularly when the communism is entwined with a militant nationalism or when it harasses subversives, Jews, and alcoholics, as it has done in Russia and elsewhere. Whenever, in short, communism helps establish an out-group which can be despised as deviant. The matter also may depend on the kind of authoritarian. Some persons may be able to lose themselves in Oppressed Mankind and the socialist cause, while not caring much for the "lower-case" individuals that make up Mankind. Communist dogmas may well facilitate this by depersonalizing the class struggle, seeming to lay more stress on problems of organization and long-term historical forces than on the individual.

In countries like Britain and America, most authoritarians would have to be very alienated from traditionally patriotic symbols for communist ideology to command them. Otherwise, they would be repelled by the British or American Communist party's alien connections and deviant image. In some milieus, however, the party may provide authoritarians with just the right means for "secondary rebellion" coupled with a more primary surrender to power and dogma.[10]

PART IV

NAZI GERMANY

13   THE FOLLOWERS

Junior Lieutenant W., German Army Signals Corps, was captured in Tunisia, in 1943. After passing through American and French hands, he was sent to a British internment camp. He was twenty-one at the time, and single, a small bespectacled man with watchful eyes and a tight mouth. At his interview with a British psychiatrist, and in other encounters with Britons, he was extremely polite and respectful, combining admiration with envy. Complaints about his captors were reserved for the Americans and French.[1]

W.'s father had been a businessman in Belgium but had transferred to a German state service. As a result, W.'s home had moved several times during his childhood. Evidently a strong Nazi, his father had sent him first to a National Socialist Political Training College and then to a private boarding school. W. failed to get into a university and joined the army.

In talking about his parents, W. showed no particular attachment to either, and gave but the dimmest picture of the kind of people they were. He expressed a much more intense loyalty to the Nazi state; it appeared, indeed, that political symbols had largely replaced his father as the authority with which he overtly identified. Insisting that his father was always head of the household—that it would never do for a husband to be henpecked—he likened this pattern to the proper, autocratic state, of which the family was a prototype. His mother was a staunch Lutheran Protestant, but her husband apparently had not let her interfere when W. wanted to leave the church on grounds of National Socialist ideology. W. did leave the church, but he continued to believe in a higher "Direction" of the world.

W. took a strong position against softness and femininity. The only trace of tenderness he showed was in some diary entries, sentimental but ambivalent, about a young fellow prisoner. He had a sister whom he regarded somewhat as a little toy, and he was at pains to emphasize that his Nazi school tolerated no such feminine nonsense as house matrons. True to official doctrine, he affirmed that his mother was the "Mittelpunkt" (center) of the family, but he otherwise said little about her.

His diary described a succession of girl friends, in a vein of exploitative eroticism, and he reveled in the role of tough, heart-breaking roué ("When the woman weeps and implores me I have to laugh"). He was engaged to a much-idealized girl, but he viewed his adventures as part of the life due a German gentleman. A prison acquaintance of W.'s said that he delighted to tell of schoolday episodes when he had bullied people weaker than himself. His suspicions of other prisoners ranged from charges of petty pilfering to accusations of disloyalty to Nazism. He saw himself as a watchdog of German honor, and he once wrote a rather tattletale letter to another POW, a superior German officer, alleging disorderly behavior on the part of some other party. He remarked that other officers in the camp were not comradely toward him, but he could not see why.

In the interview, when not nervously deferential he was apt to boast. Outside the interview he fairly glowed when he considered that the British were treating him with due respect. He was most concerned with maintaining face as an officer, and he declared great satisfaction that in military rank he had redeemed the shame of failing to get into a university. More unconsciously, he seemed to compensate for inferiority feelings by making himself an aggressive, military paragon of correctness.

W. was exceptionally restless, and he had a dread of flying. There were also tentative signs that he suffered from repressed guilt. Throughout the interview he felt he had to justify his exploitativeness—for example, by referring to "Darwinian" Nazi paganism. Likewise, when describing his sexual adventures, he would add postscripts like "Am I really a heel?" (And in his diary: "a whoremonger, after all!") Granted, these expressions may have been "pseudo-remorse" rather than real guilt, but in either case W. showed that the new, hard values on extreme power did not totally command his behavior. In W.'s background and environment, there were still humane values, and their survival was a potential source of moral conflict.[2]

That W. *learned* his Nazism, acquiring it in the first instance from father and schooling, is obvious. But it seemed to go further than this. The interviewing psychiatrist believed that his character depended on the Nazi faith to hold it together. There was a desperate intensity about the way in which he affirmed that might was right; that Christianity was soft, un-German, and "unbiological"; and that Jews were a major source of Germany's woes and must be treated mercilessly. Yet even his attitude to Germany contained aggression: he once declared that the country was so immature it must be bullied into a sense of unity.

With the portrait of W., we move to a harsher pattern than has generally been described so far. We find a climate in which aggressive authoritarian behavior received out-and-out political endorsement. W.'s case is taken from a study of German POWs, conducted by Henry Dicks. With his "rabid, compulsive quality," W. was typical of the salient personality type found among the more committed Nazis—although his manifestation of the basic traits was extreme when compared with others of the same type. The type itself amounted to authoritarianism, as Dicks acknowledged later when *The Authoritarian Personality* was published.[3]

In the Dicks study, POWs were divided into two groups. The first consisted of fanatic Nazis, and also committed believers (not all party members) who expressed some reservations about the regime, usually on grounds of efficiency rather than ethics. (The qualified believers were on the whole more educated than the fanatics.) The second group were the non-Nazis, representing many attitudes to National Socialism: passive acceptance, ambivalence, disillusionment, convinced opposition. In a sampling of 1,000 POWs, 36 percent were classed in the first, pro-Nazi group. The detailed study, however, focused on a much smaller sample, 138 men. It was drawn from both groups, in roughly equal proportions. Most of the sample were not officers, but a majority had received higher education, either technical college or university. The pro-Nazi and non-Nazi groups were not selected so that they were of the same social and family background: the implications of this are discussed later.

Dicks found that the following traits were shown in acute form by the pro-Nazis significantly more often than by the non-Nazi group.

154 THE BROKEN REBEL

1. Unquestioning identification with the father. As part of this, though more interpretatively, Dicks believed that impulsive aggression was displaced against the "greediness," "dirtiness," and "secret plotting" of Jews, Russians, liberal Germans, and Allied leaders. Dicks also implied that residual feelings of rebellion were expressed by identifying with Hitler as a father figure, but also an elder-brother figure, against the "bad" Ally leaders.

2. Homosexuality, usually covert, and intense male alignment. This category overlapped with (1) above and with other traits. One person exemplifying the trait had had a passive homosexual relationship with another prisoner. He said that he was "terribly fond of young people," that all his feelings were in "the comradeship of the Unit and of Hitler Youth," and that the place of women was "in the kitchen!" A fighter pilot talked of how "beautiful" it was to "educate young men"; likewise, "a father must train his son to his own liking and rescue him from his mother's apron strings." Another officer romanticized the love and trust of young men—but "only in the living emotional comradeship of the Hitler Youth or the Service." He praised his father for pulling him out of a "bad state" of pampering due to childhood illness. "My father shaped my education. I have to thank his firmness."[4]

3. Rejection of feminine ties; general "tenderness taboo." The portrait of W. has already given examples of these twin traits. It also shows their connection with a split attitude to women—on the one hand, an impersonal idealization; on the other, exploitative sexuality mixed with contempt. As Dicks saw it, "softness was equated with impotence, surrender and femininity," and the individual felt he must identify with "a punitive father-image." The tenderness taboo was interpreted in part as an abhorrence of "treason against the father and [of] a preference for the mother"—although Dick's reported material did not directly demonstrate these things.

4. Sadism, brutality, and violent aggressiveness. This trait appeared in several major variants. There was, for example, the tense, thrusting bomber pilot who said, biting his nails: "When we have liquidated Russia—then mercy on this Island! . . . Coventry will be child's play." He thumped his fist on the table as he talked vengefully of the French. Later on he expressed delight at the fate of the Jews, and spoke of "draconic hardness." He poured out streams of bitter words as if to lash with a whip. He also gave an impression of aggressive masochism, picking at spots on his face and declaring, "I won't let them heal." Another variant showed a more granite control: "The German *must*—

Frederick the Great's 'damned duty and obligation' rules everything. . . . Those who differ are outsiders and do not count." A third variant was brutal chiefly in a passive, depersonalized way: for example, the midshipman who described the drowning of his shipmates, a few days earlier, without the least note of concern. And the U-boat rating who calmly told how he had got a girl in trouble, and said approvingly that he had watched his mother being "sat on" by Father. He also said, "Can't help what the S.S. do—not my affair."

5. Projection. There was a great exaggeration of what the Allies would do to them if Germany was overrun; the specter included images of annihilation and castration. In identifying this trait, Dicks said that "an attempt was always made to allow for social stereotypes and recent experiences." In other words, he tried to distinguish between two sources of fears about external threats—an inner need to project aggressive and other feelings, and such external sources as indoctrination and actual, threatening experiences. In practice, of course, the two sources cannot easily be separated, as projected feelings latch onto and magnify received beliefs. One case of marked suspicion was shown by an engineer who felt certain the British were bent on annihilating the German people. He had had an episode of acute terror when he felt that British secret rays were inducing him to become a traitor. As a boy it appeared that he had always been shy, had felt overpowered by his father, and had thought that others were laughing at him. Another example was a lieutenant of propaganda who scented plots and dissension everywhere. In fact he was a great intriguer himself. He felt that other German officers had envied him his post, and because of "the way they have treated me" he was prepared to assist British propaganda efforts. He believed inaccurately that there was a "spirit of revolution abroad" among the German people—this was interpreted by Dicks as a projection of (unadmitted) "renegade" feelings.[5]

6. Symptoms of neurotic anxiety (excluding expressions portrayed above). In their reactions to captivity, members of the pro-Nazi group showed far more symptoms of neurotic disturbance. They reported, in particular, a great number of nervous and psychosomatic ailments. This was all the more striking as the non-Nazis had, by and large, undergone just as much external stress from warfare and capture. Indeed, at the start of their confinement, the Nazis had seemed the more physically fit. Dicks attributed the pro-Nazi rate of neurosis to (1) shame and guilt at being caught, and at being plunged into a powerless position from the supporting environment of one's fighting

unit; (2) conflict between paranoid fear of the captor and a desire to yield to him. From our standpoint the first part of (1)—shame and guilt at being caught—does not necessarily imply an authoritarian makeup, for one would expect the most ideologically committed militarists to be most upset at capture. But (2) suggests authoritarianism quite specifically. Before capture, the German authoritarian could express "secondary rebellion" against the British as a remote power; but with his capture, the remote power suddenly became a more intimate authority. The urge to submit to it increased, but how could one submit to it without perpetrating a betrayal, losing self-respect, and feeling the more vulnerable by "opening" oneself to an officially-hated power? One way of dealing with these feelings was to submit overtly, repressing the guilt but punishing oneself in physical ailments.[6]

It may be added, in the context of general anxiety symptoms, that the pro-Nazi group did not show more inferiority feelings than the non-Nazi group. There were signs, however, that the non-Nazis tended to express self-doubts more openly—though often in a "humble-pie-eating" form, with such plaintive remarks as "Who am I to judge such things? I am only a little man." The pro-Nazis seemed more apt to hide doubts about worth and potency behind brittle boasting, status claims, and alignments with power.

The Dicks report did not show how often the above mentioned traits went together in the same person. So we cannot say with any exactitude how many of the Nazis might be considered authoritarian. It is conceivable that some Nazis may have identified strongly with their fathers and had brutal attitudes toward out-groups without, say, feeling a "tenderness taboo" or projecting rebelliousness onto scapegoats. All this having been said, there remain two reasons for supposing that authoritarianism characterized many of the pro-Nazis—a good half at the very least. In the first place, clear majorities of the Nazi group showed in acute form each of the traits listed above, and for most traits it was an overwhelming majority. There must, therefore, have been a considerable amount of overlap between these majorities.[7] In the second place, where certain traits did characterize the same person—harsh opposition to feminine tenderness, submissive alignment with masculine power, symptoms of inner conflict, and general suspicion—it is reasonable to infer an authoritarian pattern of unstably repressed rebelliousness. And when we add what is known about child rearing and the organization of youth in prewar Germany, it may persuasively be argued that an "inverted Oedipal" situation was often involved—that is to say, an extreme denial of the wish to champion and compete for one's mother against a dominating father.

Dicks and others have made just this argument about patterns of upbringing in prewar Germany.[8] While of course there were variations, one salient pattern for boys seemed to be as follows:[9] At an early stage, the child felt compelled to identify totally with a harsh image of paternal power. His mother was indulgent and overprotective to him in infancy, yet, as Dicks put it, she connived at his "masculine build-up." Although she offered "no adequate counter-weight to the father," she increased her son's guilt and confusion over dependency by giving furtive rewards behind the father's back. In many cases, the son responded by repressing his desire for deep maternal and feminine ties, and by a homosexual alignment with masculine power. A very ambivalent relationship with his father was set up, in which affection was emphasized and hatred repressed. As he acquired political beliefs, feelings of weakness were projected onto Jews and others. He expressed sado-masochist longings in the idealization of *Truee,* a concept of conformist loyalty with an image of the obstinate, unruly boy hammered into dogged virility by paternal discipline (e.g., military induction). For allegedly weak authority, such as the corrupt, Christian-bourgeois rule of "arterio-sclerotic" elders, he would feel contempt.

To these last two points, we may add more speculative suggestions, Through the image of the unruly boy, the individual could project onto his former self a rebellion not actually shown. Second, the image of strong young authority triumphing over weak elders might with some people express a desperate desire to see masculine strength vanquish one's own projected impotence.

Despite these additions, the analysis so far contains little that has not been said or implied about authoritarianism in earlier chapters. There were also, however, some points made which suggest further possibilities within the general range of authoritarianism. For one thing, Dicks believed that the individual projected some of his repressed aggression onto his immediate authority, though not at all in a derogatory way. As a result, the authority often seemed tougher than it actually was. In the second place, even when the father seemed indulgent, and perhaps was indulgent, the individual found other, harsher symbols of authority to identify with—teachers, youth groups, political and military leadership. In W.'s case, for example, his father seemed in many ways to have been permissive; yet W. made extreme identification with male power. Granted, we do not know much about the behavior of W.'s parents: the same father may be in various ways demanding, indulgent, and debilitating. Be that as it may, it did seem that the ties of affection between W. and his parents were not great. Building on Dicks's theory, I would suggest the following: That, in many prewar German milieus, there were strong cultural pressures on a boy to align himself with hard male authority. That these demands were often poorly integrated with a semi-secret indulgence by the mother. And that authoritarianism was a likely outcome when the parents did not give much real affection, whether or not the father was directly oppressive.

These effects would not necessarily be incompatible with a form of adolescent revolt. Many Nazis and others were "Wanderbirds" in their youth, joining various romantic organizations. Some of these groups were homosexual; others intensely chauvinist. They were often organized around mystic symbols, such as "Nature," "Fatherland," "Art," or even "Essence." Members of these groups frequently expressed overt rebellion against their fathers, even declaring them to be mortal foes. Yet the revolt was not a revolt against oppression, and in many cases it was not really opposed to their fathers' values. As both Dicks and Erik Erikson have pointed out, the fathers often condoned their sons' activities, knowing they would resume their allegiance later.[10] Dicks also argued that the revolt entailed evasion of the parents, rather than a showdown with them. Then again, membership in the youth groups represented no diminishing of authority and male alignment. In their collective identity and their mystic symbols, the groups offered surrogate fathers; but the youthfulness of their leaders also suggested an elder-brother imagery, a clean young strength asserted against the impotence of older generations. At the same time, alignment with elder-brother figures could indulge the urge to submit more covertly than life in a father-dominated home. But, well before adolescence, there would have been time for acute authoritarian submission to the father to take place.

The last point in this analysis is perhaps the most speculative; it involves "secondary rebellion." Dicks argued that, as a corollary of authoritarian submission, many Germans projected desires for freedom onto the nation, declaring that it must be untrammeled. In another work, Dicks and colleagues maintained that one outlet for repressed resentments against the father was "romantic revolt"—enthrallment with the idea of a hero (Hitler) rescuing a people (the Germans and their German-speaking neighbors).[11] Through this attitude Oedipal feelings could be projected onto the political universe, thus releasing some of the tension caused by an "inverted Oedipal" relationship at home. It is true that German nationalism included strong father-figure symbols (e.g., "Fatherland"), but it also involved protective praise of German motherhood—"Roman matron" ideal. By subscribing to this ideal, the authoritarian could express Oedipal feelings without "surrendering" to feminine intimacy. The "Roman matron" image was almost masculine in the qualities it portrayed, and it was sufficiently abstract to permit a subordination of most women in actual fact—a subordination which, for authoritarians at least, amounted to contempt.[12]

The Dicks study, it must be remembered, offers no statistical proof that Nazi ideology attracted authoritarians, if by "attract" we mean initial recruitment. In the first instance, Nazi views and authoritarian traits may have been co-products of certain family and social milieus (a subject we will come to later). Thus, one would expect strongly pro-Nazi parents to have imbued their offspring with staunch National Socialist beliefs; and, quite apart from this, they might also have tended to be the kind of parents who engendered authoritarianism in the young. On the other hand, the Dicks material does show that submissive-aggressive feelings found a most accommodating channel in Nazi beliefs, however the individual first came to those beliefs. From the nuances given by Dicks it is clear that, in many cases, sadomasochist needs helped to maintain ideological commitment, and quite possibly drove the individual to a more extreme fascist position.

Besides the Dicks study there has been, to my knowledge, no systematic comparison of character in sizable Nazi and non-Nazi groups. Some mention, however, should be made of the journalistic study of nine anonymous Germans by Louis Hagen, a writer who lived in Germany until 1936.[13]

Hagen knew the nine as personal acquaintances before the war, and he went back and interviewed them afterward, on two occasions each. Two of his cases are specially instructive for our study—a Nazi girl who seemed very authoritarian, and a sailor who likewise was a Nazi member but in other ways was a very different person.[14]

"Hildegard Trutz," a tall blonde girl, had been one of the *Bund Deutscher Mädchen* (B.D.M.), the female equivalent of Hitler Youth.[15] Subsequently she married an S.S. man. She was full of self-pity and resentment, especially loathing other girls, whom she suspected of bitter envy. Quick to resent snobbery in the wives of her husband's superiors, she was equally quick to notice "common" traits or "racial inferiority" in less well-placed women. Toward male authority she was very submissive. She accepted without complaint everyone she worked for, and her adoration of Hitler had overtones of sexual yielding. More generally, she seemed to concentrate a great deal of her affection upon abstract and highly romanticized political symbols. When things went wrong for Trutz, as they increasingly did amid the travails of war, she readily found scapegoats, from Jews and traitors to her absent husband. She did not, apparently, blame German war policies, either during the war or after it.

A corollary trait was her callousness. She told of an East Prussian winter, toward the end of the war, when she was part of a refugee trek. There was a peasant woman in a cart in front. The woman was shrieking with labor pains, and subsequently she died. But while she lived, said Trutz, the cries helped her keep on the road in the thick blizzard. She mentioned this as if it were her first reaction to the pregnant woman's agony. In several contexts, likewise, she was apt to dehumanize personal relationships. When her father's boss, a Jewish baker, was sent to a "re-education camp" for making subversive remarks about the regime, his wife was told she could keep the bakery if she divorced him. Trutz considered her "stupid" for refusing to.

She seemed equally callous toward herself. She told of her part in the "Nordification" of Germany, when she was mated with an S.S. man of "good stock" for the sole purpose of giving a child to the state. (This was before her marriage.) Although she made various comments on the experience, she expressed no regrets at having to give her baby up after the first fortnight. As far as possible, her personality seemed to suit this extreme in totalitarian demands. On a smaller thing, however, she allowed herself to express more conflict. As a bride, she was forbidden by her husband to use makeup; such things were fit only for degenerate Negroid Frenchwomen, not for a German mother. Trutz said she agreed with him—but when she went out alone, she sometimes put on a little, because "there's no getting away from it, it is smart."

During much of the war, her husband, Ernst, was away a great deal on active duty. She resented this and constantly imagined that he was having a more comfortable time than she. During the early stages of Allied occupation, when Germany was in chaos, she heard that he was in a prison camp, and she then wanted to divorce him, reckoning that his S.S. affiliations would be "a millstone round my neck." By then, too, she was supporting her children and her father by taking a series of lovers, first from the Russians, then the Americans. At one point she even had a Jewish lover, though elsewhere in the interviews she emphasized that Jewish looks revolted her. The only boy friend she said she really respected was "Bill," a black G.I. who was "good and gentle and really kind." Physically, he was a big and powerful man, and this attracted her, though his being a black "took a bit of getting used to." But unlike the others, she said, he didn't boast and he didn't make her feel that he was just using her. Here, in perhaps the most unlikely quarter for a Nazi authoritarian, Hilde Trutz showed that not all humane affection had been squeezed out of her. There was something about Bill, a kind, unthreatening strength, which got through to Trutz. And perhaps the fact that he was so far from any status race in her eyes enabled her to like him in a purely private and genuine way.

Trutz's father, Herr "Troch," was a Nazi. According to his daughter, he resented being a weekly wage earner at the bakery and found it hard to make ends meet. It was through his efforts that the Jewish owner was sent to a "re-education camp"; the bakery ended up in Troch's hands. Hilde identified with her father against her mother, who was an invalid and a devout Christian. She vehemently opposed Hilde's entry into the B.D.M., the Nazi girls' group, and when her daughter did join up, "she just lay around being terribly tearful and sentimental." Trutz described some persecuted Jewish schoolmates in much the same way, as blubbering, cowardly, and trying to get sympathy for themselves. From quite early in her life Trutz took the side of male authority against softness. She thrilled to the martial life of the B.D.M. and the praise therein given her Germanic looks. During her teens, she had two great idols—Hitler and a legendary figure who showed how nearly a girl could become a man, the "Black Huntswoman Joanna," who had disguised herself as a soldier to fight against Napoleon. As with other Nazis, new allegiances came to replace affection for her father. When Hagen first knew her, as a young adolescent, he noticed that father and daughter seemed very proud of each other. But, by the end of the war, Herr Troch was a bewildered and pathetic person whose daughter not only despised him but feared that his Nazi connections would get her into trouble. Privately, she retained her Nazi beliefs.[16]

Let us turn to the case of "Fritz Muehlebach." His attraction to

Nazism, too, seems to have been much connected with submission-aggression, but his story shows that these traits do not invariably add up to authoritarianism.

Muehlebach was a merchant sailor who joined the Nazi S.A. He was out of work at the time, so that in giving him a job and a uniform the National Socialists provided both economic security and an initial boost to his self-esteem—the two were much entwined. Muehlebach had a quality of childlike dependence, and he seemed to believe practically everything that the Nazi propagandists told him. When he observed corruption among junior government officials, he lodged complaints; but his faith in Hitler and other high-ups was totally uncritical. As a result, he suppressed the few objections he had to particular policies, and was constantly finding scapegoats for German failures.

Yet the displacement, such as it was, did not concentrate on symbols of weakness and inferiority per se. He had a lot of aggressiveness, which he expressed in brawling and in parrot statements against aliens, and he once blurted out a remark which suggested concern about controlling rebelliousness.[17] But his aggressions showed no punitive tinge. He remained friendly and loyal to Jewish acquaintances, and though in general anti-Semitic, he thought that some policies against the Jews were "cruel" and had gone too far. In his personal life, there seemed no great emotional need to stamp on tenderness. After the war, he held on to his Nazi beliefs, but these had always included an "economic welfare" strain, a trust in his National Socialist masters for the common man's well-being.[18]

14   THE EXECUTIVES

It may well be that authoritarians tend to be unsuited to reaching the high command of political organizations. We have already considered reasons why they would tend to be ill suited for this, at least amid circumstances of change.[1] In the case of China's Taiping Rebellion, an authoritarian did lead an immense and powerful movement, including an army and a rebel state; his personality met a people's messianic needs, although it subsequently contributed to a breakdown of the movement and a betrayal of the people's trust.[2]

If the Taiping Rebellion was an exception, so too was Nazism, for at least several of the top Nazi leaders seem to have been authoritarian. Whether Hitler himself was authoritarian is more problematic than at first it may seem; we will begin, therefore, by looking at some of his executives.

First, a general impression. G. M. Gilbert, a psychologist who studied many of the leaders, some at first hand in Nuremberg prison, distinguished between Hitler's "club" or Old Fighters and a group of realist "diplomats."[3] According to Gilbert, many of the Old Fighters had been attracted to Nazism through feelings of frustration, aggression, and paranoia, and emotional needs for "ascendancy." The "diplomats" were those representatives of established political and financial interests who followed Hitler in part to maintain their own status and power, but whose underlying motivation was less "pathological" from a psychiatrist's viewpoint. They were often autocratic, but in a traditional German sense. (One might add that many old-guard army officers could be included in this group.) It has also been noted that at divers levels, both high and low, Nazi organization was riddled with corruption and bullying gangster practices. High Nazi officials tended to distrust each other, and the S.S. particularly was marked by internecine power struggles. On a personal plane, money-making exploitativeness often seemed to go with submissive adulation of the Fuehrer. Despite fierce declarations of Nazi belief—including contempt for "bourgeois values" and praise of sacrifice—the morality was thin enough to accept profiteering; nor was it only the Jew's money, or the anti-Nazi's, that was taken.[4]

As far as they go, these impressions hint at widespread authoritarian behavior among Nazi leaders as well as rank-and-file. Such evidence, of course, should only be admitted in conjunction with studies of individuals. To these we now turn.

HEINRICH HIMMLER AND THE PROBLEM OF QUALMS

Himmler joined the Nazis in their early years and played a minor part in the abortive *Putsch* of 1923. By the 1940s he was commander of a vast police network, including the S.S. The concentration camps were in his directorate, and he was responsible for carrying out the programs of mass extermination. As much as anyone portrayed in this book, he showed the "classic" model of authoritarian behavior.

He was born in 1900, in Munich. His father, Gebhard, was a language teacher whose hobby was numismatics. He taught Heinrich a great deal of history and he also fired his interest with the stirring adventures of Heinrich's grandfather, a soldier of fortune in several armies. There is no evidence that Gebhard was oppressive to his son, but very little is known about their relationship. The same is true of Heinrich's mother, who was the daughter of a rich merchant. We do know that she was a devout Catholic and that many years later, when she became anxious about what the S.S. was doing, Heinrich gently tried to allay her fears.[5]

Gebhard became headmaster of a high school, where Heinrich and his elder brother were subsequently enrolled. Heinrich was unpopular with his classmates; he had the reputation of telling tales to his father. At games he was hampered by a small, dumpy physique and bad eyesight. This frustrated him, although success and enthusiasm in his history lessons were some compensation. His father, who kept a diary, made him start one also and initially supervised it. Diary keeping was not common among boys of the time and place, but Heinrich maintained it punctiliously. Much of it is mundane detail, a time table of personal hygiene, but at the start of the 1914-18 war it breaks into martial enthusiasm. The Russian prisoners "multiply like vermin," he exults; and he scorns the "silly old women and petty bourgeois" of Landshut (his home town) who fear the Cossacks will "tear them limb from limb." Later entries again attack the "Landshuters"—for being "stupid and chicken-hearted" and for objecting when his parents gave bread and water to wounded French prisoners. The war sharpened his sense of physical handicap; his diary constantly mentions fevers and stomach upsets. "I use dumb-bells every day now so as to *get more strength*," he records, and referring to an army exercise nearby, he declares he "would have loved to join in."[6]

In the third year of the war he became an army ensign, but to his disappointment the war ended shortly afterward. He began working on a farm; this too was curtailed, by a bout of paratyphoid fever. Morose at these setbacks but keen to learn agriculture, he returned to Munich, where he enrolled in the university's Technical High School.

Himmler, the student, was a rather pathetic figure. He wanted to be gay and sociable—but beer disagreed with his stomach, and his fellows teased him for his solemn diligence. He tried hard at gymnastics and sport, but was hopelessly unsuccessful; he wrote his parents with deferent affection, but it was a worry that he had to ask them for aid. He was not without humanity: he visited sick and elderly people, and he once took the side of a young girl (a beauty) against her restrictive parents. On the other hand, he was decidedly straitlaced: he did not approve of the parents who let their three-year-old daughter "hop around in the nude" before his very eyes; and his diary carries vivid warnings about the danger of losing sexual self-control. He criticizes himself for being too warm-hearted, talking too much, and lacking self-control and a "gentlemanly assurance of manner." He admits that he despises women, except those who can be loved as children or honored as a pure wife and companion. In this period, as later, he finds solace in work, but has not yet fully justified it: "I am not quite sure what I am working for, not at the moment at any rate. I work because it is my duty. I work because I find peace of mind in working . . . and overcome my indecision."[7] About the same time as this, he declares that he looks forward to "wearing uniforms again." A few years later he has joined a minor Nazi group, and found his purpose.

Let us now take a longer view of Himmler's life, and the type of character that unfolded. The following traits stand out: a diffuse anxiety and insecurity; intense personal submissiveness; a crank "scientism"; and a mixture of tender-heartedness with power thirst and sadism. First, the insecurity.[8] Throughout his career he gave an impression of loneliness. At the height of his power he still seemed to some both pedantic and vacillating, but every so often a new project or policy would occur to him, and he would impulsively issue grand orders. Usually, however, he immersed himself in petty detail, staying in his office till the small hours. He suffered much from headaches and stomach cramps; toward the end of the war he was having his stomach massaged several hours a day. His pains were at least partly due to stress, for they were worst when he had to make difficult decisions, and they were particularly bad when his lieutenant, Reinhard Heydrich, seemed to be starting an S.S. faction against him.[9]

The second important trait was his submissiveness. Several people who met him during his years of power said that he was ingratiating, obsequious, as if afraid to offend. Likewise, his subservience to Hitler was extreme—even allowing for the fact that Hitler's magnetism had a peculiar hold over many kinds of people. In his early days as a party worker, he was once seen in front of a picture of Hitler, rehearsing how he would act when he first met the great man. His admiration continued at about that pitch nearly all his life. Although he may have tried to insure his political position against the possible downfall of Hitler's regime, his adulation did not waver until Hitler had virtually lost control of the war and was issuing increasingly irrational commands.

At that point he tried secretly to negotiate with the Allies through the Swedes, but he only did so under the influence of Felix Kersten, his doctor and masseur, who half convinced him that Hitler was a sick man. Himmler was divided between the harsh authority of Hitler and the humane influence of "my good Dr. Kersten," on whom he depended psychologically as well as medically. In fact his feelings about Hitler were inconsistent and none too peaceful. Speaking privately on one occasion he described his chief as a messiah who would be "born anew" whenever men lost respect for "law and truth." On another occasion he said that he himself was the "intellectual force" which would make the name of Adolf Hitler the greatest in German history. At other times he vaguely fused these two interpretations by seeing himself as a messianic prince vitally serving his lord. But on more mundane levels he found his encounters with Hitler upsetting. He once came to Kersten overjoyed because the Fuehrer had really listened to him; usually, Himmler said, he had a habit of interrupting, "which completely destroys one's train of thought." Kersten also reports that Himmler suffered acute stomach pains whenever a plan of his received the slightest criticism from his chief.[10]

As Alan Bullock puts it, Himmler was a man of essentially "subordinate virtues."[11] Throughout his career he was greatly drawn to and influenced by a succession of men more incisive than he. Among them was the handsome and cruel Heydrich; and after Heydrich's assassination in Czechoslovakia (for which Himmler exacted a terrible revenge[12]) there was the youngest of his S.S. generals, Walter Schellenberg. Even his racial "science" was stimulated by star-struck respect for such men as the racist theoretician Alfred Rosenberg, and the agricultural expert Walter Darré. It was Darré who urged him to shift his interest in breeding from chickens to men. The S.S. provided ample opportunity for one interested in selecting "pure Nordic" specimens. Although he had a large organization to run Himmler would still assess candidates personally; he only told them the verdict himself if they were accepted. By contrast with his male relationships, his marriage was stormy, a tenuous relationship punctuated by bitter quarrels. In the end they were estranged—in part, it was said, because Hitler's dislike of Frau Himmler threatened to upset Himmler's relationship with his Fuehrer. Himmler subsequently lived with another woman, by whom he had two children.

Himmler's third notable attribute was his penchant for semi-scientific hobbies, nearly all of which were pressed into public service. Taken together, these interests seemed to reflect a submissive superstition, mixed with concerns about vitality, purity, and identity. He was an earnest believer in nature foods, and when the S.S. began taking over firms that supplied it with equipment, the first company so acquired was a mineral-waters business. Himmler wanted his men to get soft drinks at a lower price, so that alcohol would not undermine their health.[13] He was also very much interested in astrology, and nagging uncertainties about the future drove him to various soothsayers and charlatans. On the whole the past offered more assurance: his fascination with Germanic origins seemed to go further than mere cultural attitude and received belief. At one point he insisted that the antecedents of S.S. recruits be known back to 1750, and he employed an investigator to work on his own father's lineage. His mother's ancestors were from Hungary, and some said that the features of mother and son showed strong traces of Mongolian. But it is perhaps a coincidence that he recognized the Mongolians as the only people not of "our own blood" to give quality to Russia, and that he was a great admirer of Genghis Khan.[14] This aside, his historical interests lay with the "Aryans." Himmler was intrigued with the notion that Vikings, Crusaders, and Teutonic knights were historical forebears of his S.S. elite, and his research into the medieval knightly orders was at pains to show that their origins were not alien and "monkish." As Kersten put it, he had to have "historical models" for his beliefs.

Although he could say that "intellect rots the character" (boasting that he had had to shoot some upper-class "cowards"), some of his historical interest involved scholarship. He spent much time developing the S.S. Institute for Research and the Study of Heredity, an organization whose subjects included archeology. But his interest also had a strong dose of the mystical. Himmler was fired with the idea of furthering the conquest of eastern Europe started by medieval princes. One of these, his namesake Heinrich I, became a virtual god to him, indeed more than a god. More than once he hinted quite seriously that he was the reincarnation of Heinrich I. He had a library on Heinrich, and built him a splendid new shrine.

On the level of behavior, it was racism that provided the chief link between his crank interests and his brutal aggressiveness. His statements about racial purity were often interspersed with allusions to physical health. A favorite slogan was "Back to Nature," which reflected his early interest in farms and chicken breeding! He sought for his racism all the authority of a biased "science"; hence his interest in the measurement of skulls, and his avid enthusiasm for Rosenberg's race-and-blood doctrines, with their contempt of Christian "weakness." Scientific authority helped him to justify brutal racist policies in the face of possible objections from others (and from himself?). Thus in 1941 he told his S.S. leaders that the task of running the concentration camps should be regarded as "fighting the subhumanity": "This will not be a boring guard duty, but, if the officers handle it right, it will be the best indoctrination on inferior beings and the sub-human races." Through the camps and extermination programs, Himmler also encouraged studies of death and human endurance. Some of these inflicted extreme pain on living and dying people. One experiment personally inspired by him entailed the freezing of prisoners to the point of death (or near-death), followed by an attempt to revive them through sexual intercourse, using the "animal heat" of prostitutes. When shown medically that this was impossible, Himmler retorted that country cures were often best and he could well imagine a fisherman's wife reviving her half-frozen husband by taking him to bed with her. This make-believe bears the stamp of a sadistic fantasy, in which a quest for health and strength conceals a fascination with death and deviance. It should also be added that, for all his use of doctors and his deep dependence on Kersten, he had long declared his dislike of the medical profession as a cabal of incompetents. Secondary rebellion thus encouraged him to persist with his scientific cruelties.

Even aside from these, there is considerable evidence of his desire to punish and dominate. Many little incidents show that Himmler the timid was also Himmler the bully, especially when he thought his inferiors were not showing him due respect or when they caused him inconvenience, however unwittingly. Although he punished subordinates for corruption and "unnecessary" brutality, he added his own personal touches to the cruel harassment of prisoners in the concentration camps and the Jews in Poland. At least once he executed an S.S. officer who let a prisoner escape, and after several warnings he had his own nephew shot for homosexuality, Indeed, one of the few times he became angry with Kersten was on the subject of homosexuals: he considered that they undermined the nation's morals and he wanted them either castrated or put in the camps. His political power drive was as enormous as it was nasty: he was constantly trying to get control over new departments and weapons, and as early as 1933 he was boasting that he had had Dachau's inmates excluded from a Christmas prison amnesty. It is significant that he personally wore the emblem of the long-service guard unit first established at Dachau—the "Death's Head," a skull and crossbones.

And yet to many, Himmler seemed one of the kindliest of men. He was considerate of the girls in his office, and attentive to the welfare of his S.S. subordinates and their families. Some of this had a touch of vanity (he wanted to be godfather to every German boy born on his birthday). But much of his kindness seemed to run deep, and it made the more difficult his complicity in mass killing. He blocked at least one attempt by Heydrich to instigate a pogrom, and there are indications that he was privately opposed to the "Final Solution" plan when he first learned it. His own preference was to restrict Jews to their own "culture" rather than wipe them out. When he first saw a mass shooting of Jews he was frenzied with shock and horror, though he concentrated his immediate effort on trying to save one victim, a fair-haired young man, on the grounds that he looked Aryan. He demanded that less cruel killing methods be used (the gassing vans may have resulted from this). But later, when the extermination programs came under his control, he threw himself into the work of supervising the facilities and justifying the work to his S.S. staffs. Fear of Hitler may have been an important factor in this, but to act in obedience to Hitler he had to deal with his own humane scruples. How he did so is crucial to an understanding of Himmler's authoritarianism.[15]

In considering this aspect of Himmler, we must digress to some basic observations about humane feeling, perception, and organized violence. It is normal in most cultures to feel sadness, pity, revulsion, or other emotional concern at the sight of living creatures suffering hurt or death, *if* in some wise they are felt to be like the beholder. To an extent that depends on cultural values, the humane feeling will be moral feeling, a matter of conscience—even the Nazis sometimes invoked an ethic of compassion toward their own elite race. (Thus, the concentration camp doctors carrying out their cruel experiments relied upon an official dogma that their findings would save German lives.) But moral feeling is developed out of impulse, a complex of basic emotional drives which include such related elements as the need to identify with others (to love and be loved) and a concern for one's own survival and vitality, leading to a projection of this concern onto others so that the victim beheld becomes a metaphor of oneself. It is, after all, partly through basic impulse relationships with parents and others—relations involving love, identification, and concerns for the self's vitality, whether or not sexual feelings are prime—that humane moral precepts are internalized and humane conscience developed. Himmler was not immune to these feelings: he was not the rare psychopath who has a stunted sense of identification with others, although like many people his revulsion at mass killing may have been reinforced by fear of his own destructive impulses, threatening an anarchy which might reverberate upon himself.

It would be wrong, on the other hand, to suppose that most people would feel serious humane pangs in every situation where they might see, or even abet, human destruction and suffering. The most obvious example is the killing of enemy soldiers where the context is viewed as being one of self-defense and a fair martial fight, so that the requirements of justice, survival, and identification with one's fellow soldiers can effectively exclude any pity for the fallen foe. Furthermore, in the heat of battle, when sadistic and aggressive feelings are aroused, in part as a defense against fear and fatigue, normally humane men may massacre quite unthreatening women and children without major qualms. To some extent this may be because destructive impulse simply swamps humane impulse, or disconnects its application. But, in both cases, there is an important *perceptual* factor which precludes humane identification with the victim. The victim is seen less as a living being like oneself than as a "foe," an associate of the foe and/or an utterly alien out-group. At the same time, emotions toward the victim will affect this cognitive element, will help to determine how the victim is perceived. Hate, blame, even respect ("he's a good fighter and he's taking his chances like you or me") may stereotype the enemy in a way that removes pity (although in the last case there may be a less compassionate form of identification).

So far we have focused on "hot-blooded" violence. But what of systematic "cold-blooded" brutality, away from the heat of battle? Again, it would be wrong to suppose that the witnessing of, or participation in, "cold-blooded" brutality always brings a pang to the normally humane. Thus, we should not assume that the great bulk of Roman spectators, reveling in the spectacle of Christians torn by wild beasts, were either incapable of humane feeling, or felt any great conflict of emotions. It is more plausible that cultural beliefs and attitudes so influenced them that the Christians in the amphitheater were not perceived as people closely akin to the spectators: they were near enough, perhaps, for the spectators to feel an enjoyable degree of sadism and vicarious horror, but not near enough for pity.[16] Even without reinforcement from blaming and stigmatizing, a person's culture can put a cast on his perceptions which prevents humane identification. In many societies, people may abuse animals more out of negligence than enjoyment; they simply do not consider the animal's pain to be significant, or do not really consider the animal at all. In our society the humane imagination about animals extends further but there are still limits: few of us who eat meat think much about the killing which precedes our eating. In part this may be a defense against revulsion; but the very language of the society, added of course to appearances, helps us to think of "meat" on the platter as a very different entity from live animals and living flesh. This example also shows how much easier it is not to think of the subject as a suffering victim when the infliction of hurt is well removed physically from us.

When these cultural, cognitive, and moral elements do not provide complete insulation, so that the accomplice in brutality is not protected from humane scruple, he may employ a number of psychological techniques to help suppress or confine these scruples, thus preserving a humane self-image and a sphere of human behavior while still supporting a brutal program. Indeed, the more humane feeling a person has, the more he may adopt these techniques to reduce awareness of inner conflict and unconscious fears that he will become generally brutalized, hence changed in identity. The range of employable techniques cannot be reviewed here; they include a spreading of blame and responsibility, denial of the victims' innocence, and a pre-emptive, qualified protest ("Isn't this terrible? I'm really helpless in the matter but I'm doing all I can to eliminate *torture*").[17] These techniques involve perception, but the very fact that they are suppressive means that they do not wholly dominate the individual's view of the victims; they simply make less conscious those perceptions of the victim which lead to human feeling. And they also suppress the humane feeling itself.

Authority, for its part, can suggest to the individual many of the suppressive techniques. In war, for example, governments and military leaders frequently offer rationalizations for brutal programs. At this point, however, it is not easy to distinguish authority's assistance to suppression from its success in preventing humane perceptions of the victim, and therefore scruple, from arising in the first place. The more sanctified an authority, the more complete its claim to represent social norms, and the greater its control over information reaching the individual, the more likely it will be to make suppression unnecessary. This is quite aside from the point that patriotic authority may offer sincere justifications of violence: even the appalling RAF fire-bomb raid on Hamburg could be seen at the time as (1) British self-defense, and (2) a prevention of greater suffering in the long run. Unhappily, times of military crisis promote a fear, a hatred, a callousness, and a submissiveness—among leaders as well as followers—which make it difficult for anyone to make a humane yet realistic assessment of costs and consequences.[18]

None of this necessarily involves authoritarianism. But where suppression is required, it can sometimes do so. This brings us back to the subject of Himmler and the Jewish extermination. Potent and pervading as Hitler's authority was, it could not so control Himmler's perceptions as to prevent him from feeling scruples when directly confronted with mass killing; certainly it could not when he had to confront it face to face. For one thing, the quality of mass extermination, its mixture of personal confrontation with helpless civilian victims and intensive organization of killing, was a stupendous departure from the pogroms and Blitzkriegs and other facets of previous German violence. (It is true that the Jewish extermination was preceded by a semi-secret killing of mental "defectives," but Himmler had reacted against this—see below.) For another thing, the Jews had lived for years among German Gentile neighbors; they had not been mainly isolated in ghettoes, stereotyping enclaves. In most observable aspects of human behavior the Jews were no different from their neighbors; they did not always even look different. Hence the particular reaction of Himmler when confronted with the most Nordic-looking Jewish victims. Despite the efforts of Nazi propagandists to dehumanize the Jews, to define them as "vermin" and an abstract, long-term threat to the nation, Himmler's sense of identification with them, reflecting his view of them as people, was by no means destroyed, although it may have been weakened. On the other hand, Nazi doctrine also suggested to Himmler ways of dealing with humane identification once it had shown itself.

In 1943 he addressed his S.S. leaders in this vein:

I also want to talk to you quite frankly on a very grave matter. Among ourselves it should be mentioned quite frankly and yet we will never speak of it publicly. . . . I mean the evacuation of the Jews, the extermination of the Jewish race. . . . To have stuck it out and at the same time—apart from exceptions caused by human weakness—to have remained decent men, that is what has made us hard. This is a page of glory in our history which has never been written and is never to be written.*

He also told his men:

The order to solve the Jewish question, this was the most frightening order an organization could receive. . . . [We expect you to be] superhumanly inhuman.

Although he said such things to allay qualms in others, the words

* Address at Posen, October 4, 1943. The point about remaining decent apart from exceptions of weakness can mean either (1) a concern for remaining humane toward one's own group, apart from lapses into general brutality; (2) a concern for remaining "hard" apart from "weak" lapses into humane revulsion (Himmler nearly fainted when he saw the mass execution); or perhaps (3), a vague mixture on different levels of (1) and (2).

read very much as if he were talking to himself as well, and his private talks with Kersten were marked by ambivalent concern about cruelty and strength. According to Hannah Arendt, the force to be "superhumanly" overcome was not so much a humane scruple derived from conscience as "animal pity" caused by the sight of physical suffering—in our terms, primitive identification with others, based on impulse.[19] One may accept the fact that Himmler tried to define compassion for the exterminated as animal weakness, thereby removing it from the sphere of conscience; but it would be rash to agree that the compassion had no element of conscience, that the qualms were not real scruple. It is very hard, of course, to distinguish the two since, as already pointed out, humane conscience is developed by social learning out of "affiliative" impulses. But we do know that Himmler, like many other Germans, was not insulated from the historic influence of humane, Judaeo-Christian morality. He remained a Catholic well into adulthood, and the charitable visiting he did as a student in Munich echoes the mercy errands to wounded French prisoners made by his parents. We have also noted the questions of conscience which a devout mother put to him. In objecting to the destruction of mental defectives, Himmler was quick to tell Hitler of the mounting public protest that this caused. The victims in this case were not principally Jews, but near the end of the war, when British troops liberated Belsen, Himmler told a subordinate, "I am filled with horror at the thought of what is coming," meaning that he feared the consequences of their outrage. To say that he projected recrimination onto the enemy would be purely speculative, but at least we can say that Himmler knew the force of humane opinion—and he was a deeply submissive man.

In short, Himmler seemed to be divided against himself, both in conscience and in impulse. Basic "animal" identification with others, reinforced by humane morality, was ranged against the impulse to dominate and punish, endorsed by the Nazi ethic of "hardness." Himmler's way of coping with the conflict was to pit the hardness against the compassion, and try to recognize the former only as legitimate. A few years after first seeing a mass execution, Himmler was described as showing no emotion in his face when he witnessed an extermination program at Auschwitz. He simply said, "It is a hard job, but we've got to do it."[20]

To support this inner alignment, Himmler used mechanisms of displacement. Hannah Arendt argues convincingly that Himmler redirected pity onto himself: "So that instead of saying: What horrible things I did to people!, the murderers would be able to say: What horrible things I had to watch in the pursuance of my duties, how heavily the task weighed upon my shoulders!" For his subordinates at least, and perhaps for himself, Himmler helped along this displacement by attempts to redefine the killing in heroic terms and to denigrate the victims. The extermination became "battles which future generations will not have to fight again"; the women, children, and old people who died in the camps were "useless mouths"; and on later visits to the camps Himmler would point out the "criminal" features and "inferior" bone structure of the Jews paraded before him.

An alleged wartime episode adds to the impression of anger and doubt displaced against scapegoats. A medical corpsman had written to Hitler, reporting in shock that he had seen Polish women and children forced to lie in graves and then massacred; he had been called upon to help fill the graves in. The letter was forwarded to Himmler, and according to a person who said he was in the office at the time, Himmler's first reaction was to exclaim, "Amateurish. There is no need to call in outsiders to help."[21] Politically this was a rational statement, implying that general German opinion could not be relied upon to accept such actions; but it was also an outburst in an emotional context. On the one hand, Himmler's initial first-hand reaction to mass killing had been very like that of the letter writer's; on the other hand, Himmler was terrified of Hitler and morally in awe of him—one contemporary account has it that Himmler at first tried to withhold cooperation in the Final Solution but changed course in a panic when Hitler failed to answer a telegram he sent querying the program.[22] Small wonder that Himmler should explode against "amateurish" henchmen who opened up the whole really very painful matter. It is perhaps relevant that Himmler blamed his rival, Goebbels, not Hitler, for the Final Solution concept, and that for all his attention to subordinates' welfare, he was apt in private to abuse his S.S. leaders —they were soft and disloyal and each should meet a "hero's death" at the front.

But Himmler was not entirely consistent in the way he managed his doubts. On one level, he tried to redefine "brutality" so that he could weigh in against it from a position that mixed toughness with humanity. "We must be hard . . . [but] no underhand cruelties." This refusal, or inability, to close out all humane considerations was played upon by his doctor. Kersten used his personal power over Himmler to obtain numerous concessions—expiations of Himmler's guilt: prisoners freed, Jews shipped to safety, death sentences commuted. Signing some releases for Kersten, Himmler once declared, "They don't deserve it, but I will do it for my own sake." Kersten's diary, in fact, has many statements by Himmler showing his acute moral division over the policy of mass killing. In the presence of Kersten, there were moments when he was prepared to recognize that conscience was not entirely ranged on the side of Hitler and the "requirements" of history. On a more unconscious plane, it seems fitting that physical ailments secured his exposure to the clever, humane influence of Kersten. When Hitler, in a rage at the Amsterdam riots of 1941, ordered the relocation of the Dutch in eastern Poland, Himmler's cramps took a sharp turn for the worse. Kersten persuaded Himmler that he was already overworking and that the job was too much for him. Hitler subsequently postponed the project till after the war; but, in romantic terms, we have here the picture of two strong male authorities competing for Himmler's soul. Is it too much to suggest that Himmler, through his pains, was really asking Kersten to deliver him from the other authority and its destructive demands?[23]

We can summarize Himmler's authoritarianism by concluding that he was an uneasy man, submissive and domineering, deeply ambivalent about violence and compassion, who felt unable to show aggression against strong male figures. To some extent he consumed his hostility in a general suspiciousness (useful to the "card-index mind" of a political police chief).[24] But he also concentrated hostility against various types of "inferiors"—in personal outbursts, sudden acts of punishment, and experiments whose pseudo-scientific status helped him to put aside his squeamishness and his fear of uncontrolled impulse. He longed to be a glorious military commander; he lacked the talents to be one; but the romantic culture of his youth coupled with the rigid demands of his personality denied him a real alternative. And so he became a policeman-executioner.[25]

RUDOLPH HOESS[26]

Unlike the other Nazi executives portrayed here, Hoess was only a middle-rung official, an S.S. colonel. Yet he is worth considering after Himmler for several reasons. First, Himmler personally recruited him for the S.S. and later picked him for work in the concentration camps, beginning with Dachau in 1934; later, as commandant of Auschwitz, he organized the systematic killing of about two and a half million people. In the second place, he was directly examined by a psychiatrist at Nuremberg (G. M. Gilbert), unlike Himmler, who killed himself before he could be imprisoned.[27] Third, his case shows how an organization, geared to "cold-blooded" mass brutality, could select an individual whose emotional makeup, coupled with a fairly efficient administrative mind, was fitted to its purposes.

In Hoess's brutality, punitive authoritarianism was not as central a factor as it was with the other authoritarian Nazis portrayed here. Of equal importance, perhaps, was a stunted capacity to feel affection or sympathy for others. In his youth, so he told Gilbert at Nuremberg, he had had no comrades and was happier with animals than people—and in early adulthood he became more and more frigid sexually. In other relationships, too, he was much withdrawn. This temperament helped him to face the task of mass killing; but he still had to deal with qualms, and the way he did so reflected his authoritarianism.

Three facets of his character stand out.[28] First, a repressed—or at least *suppressed*—rebelliousness. According to Hoess's own account, his father was a lower-middle-class merchant who, after contracting some disease abroad, had become a fanatic Catholic. His piety overshadowed his wife; that, at least, was how Hoess saw it later. Hoess said his father had a way of punishing him by guilt, trying to make him feel he had wronged his father personally for the slightest misdeed. Instead of being beaten, he was constantly made to do penance in prayer. Hoess had two younger sisters, and he learned much later that at the time of his youngest sister's birth his father had taken an oath, dedicating him to the priesthood and a celibate life.

Hoess's response to this oppression seems to have been a submissive withdrawal which affected his feelings about his parents thereafter. Deep ambivalence toward them was concealed by deadened emotion. Writing in prison at the end of the war, he said that when afflicted by nervous tension he would suddenly see his parents standing before him. In his childhood, he said, they had been very strict about details—"duty" was the highest value—yet he also declared that they "let me do more or less as I wished." He said he revered them but could not understand why he "was never able to give them the love" of other children.[29] With his sisters, too, he said he felt "no particular ties."[30] Occasionally, he would give vent to violent rage; on one such occasion, at the age of thirteen, he beat up a schoolmate and caused him to break his leg. There is also some slight evidence that he took out hostilities on his sisters.[31] His father died when he was about fourteen, on the eve of World War I, and during his teens he became increasingly critical of both his father's regime and the church. Yet paternal authority continued to hold him. When war broke out:

> my only thought and desire was to become a soldier one way or another. Here I must remark that almost all of my paternal ancestors had been officers and that the career of a soldier attracted me more than that of a Catholic priest. But since my parents' most ardent wish was to make me a priest, I was willing to become a missionary as a last resort.[32]

In the early 1920s he became a soldier of fortune and then a Nazi. He took avidly to the racial doctrines, reading Rosenberg, *Mein Kampf*, and other tracts; twenty years later, in prison, he said he was happiest when reading about race and heredity. He likened his faith in these doctrines to his former belief in Catholicism. At Nuremberg prison he showed a passive, docile quality; it may well be that Nazi dogma appealed to the submissive in him as well as the aggressive.

This brings us to the second important aspect of his character. Much of his morality was contingent on external authority, so that his main internalized ethic seemed to be loyalty to that power. We must be careful here not to overstate the matter: in varying degree, according to situation and stress, all people are liable to yield up conscience to an overriding authority; since our moral values were internalized from an authority in the first place, we recognize the claims of some moral authority or other in helping us decide what is good. But with Hoess external command was particularly potent because his internalized values were largely so weak. Although, at one point in prison, he absently mused as to whether Himmler really had believed the moral justifications he gave him for killing the Jews, this thought—the notion that Himmler might have got him to do something by pretense—moved him less than the fact that Himmler had committed suicide and deserted him. Perhaps in reaction against his childhood, when attempts to make him feel guilty had so oppressed him, he avoided problems of principle by leaving them to authority.[33] If authority said a violent act was necessary for its protection, or the protection of Germany, he was quick to accept this. He told Gilbert he had felt no guilt when, in 1923, he assassinated a traitor to the Nazi cause. It had to be done to defend the Fatherland. Mass extermination, however, was more difficult. In his prison memoirs, he told us the "doubts seething inside me"; the contrast between his own happily playing children and the world of the gas chambers was so unbearable that he would ride off on his horse alone "until I had chased the terrible picture away." (He also sought relief in drink.) But the job had to be done, the order for it had come in strictest secrecy through the Reichsfuehrer (Himmler) from the Fuehrer himself. Therefore it was right although it required "the stifling of all human emotion."[34] It was in this vein that he told Gilbert about the start of the program:

> For the S.S. men who participated in it, it was a terrible job. I often wondered about it and the men often talked to me about it. But the order of the Reichsführer [Himmler] and his explanation removed any doubts and gave me the strength to remain aloof from all the frightfulness that I had to witness. Of course none of the S.S. men who participated in this work cared for it, especially since most of them, like myself, were married and had children. But later one became desensitized.[35]

In these statements, Hoess may have felt that he should exaggerate the humane feelings of himself and his subordinates, and implicitly blame Himmler for his own protection. But the vividness of his story does suggest some qualms; the point is that the qualms drew practically no support from moral principle, since the humane elements of his conscience were so weak. After the war, his responses in psychological tests indicated a marked dependence on pat generalizations and a loathing of details which did not conform to these.[36] If this interpretation is true, one would indeed expect him to take uncritically Himmler's brief defense of the mass killing, and to suppress lingering doubts. All the more so as he reveled in the status of camp Commandant. Surrounded by aides, glittering with rings and decorations, he made the "strength to remain aloof" an ally of vanity.[37]

The third aspect of his authoritarianism was the focusing of aggression, in the name of moral authority, against rebels and underdogs. When asked about his brutal duties at Dachau—this was before the Final Solution—he said he had not found the work unpleasant because the inmates were mostly backsliders who had to be "educated." His memoir castigates the sadism of some S.S. guards, yet is full of jibes at their victims. He describes the sex offender, "a typical asocial" who "whined" before his execution; and he details with callous fascination what appears to be a nervous sexual frenzy on the part of a homosexual prisoner.[38] Professional criminals he had always despised, not just for their cynical ways but for "rough," dirty language. As Commandant of Auschwitz, he was suspected of having a Jewish mistress, a prisoner; when she became pregnant, he showed his distance by confining her to the "standing bunker," a punishment box.[39]

In his own account there is a note of displaced rebellion. He said that at Auschwitz, before he became Commandant, he felt sympathy for the prisoners, but could not bear to relinquish his black uniform. His memoir also said, in a very righteous tone, that unlike some S.S. men he hated to watch floggings—indeed he could not understand why floggings revolted him more than executions. From about this point in his memoirs, he builds up the attack on his S.S. colleagues and subordinates. Unnecessarily brutal, inefficient, "untrustworthy," they are "distasteful in every respect";[40] he withdrew from them socially; his aloofness seems justified. In fact the S.S. guards were highly selected for ability; efforts were even made to screen out sadists. *If his subordinates failed him, his very aloofness may have been responsible.* Among other things it does seem that he blamed his henchmen for the dirty work he was compelled to do. Nor was he above blaming the victims themselves. He told contemptuously of his surprise at the Jews' "indifference" to dying (although he recorded unemotionally the efforts of Jewish mothers to save their children) and he described as "utterly callous" the stoic impersonality of the Jewish inmates who had to search the corpses for gold teeth. All this from a man who, in the face of atrocities, cultivated an iron mask and declared it his duty to "exercise inner control."

It is an appalling fact that when a system degrades and dehumanizes people, it often makes them easier to loathe—and not just in the eyes of authoritarians. But it has also been suggested that concentration camp officials exploited this fact in dealing with themselves. By hating the inmates, they squelched dangerous empathies—a temptation to be lenient—which could subvert their role and bring retribution from above.[41]

JOSEPH GOEBBELS

The use of mass communications to manipulate popular feeling was a decisive instrument of Nazi power. After Hitler himself, the man most responsible for developing that instrument was Goebbels. In addition to being the political chief of Berlin, he was Minister of Propaganda from 1933, and by the middle of World War II he had become overlord of virtually all "cultural" activities. Just as the basic characters of Himmler and Hoess largely served their roles, so did Goebbels' emotional needs suit his—the steady buildup of an adored Fuehrer, the dramatizing of patriotic power, the pointing of mass hatred at the foe. Goebbels was a very different man from Himmler and Hoess. He showed much of the making of an intellectual, a considerable aesthetic sense, and in certain areas of private life a fair range of tender feeling. And yet with him too authoritarianism was a crucial element. His life demonstrated how potent a political force authoritarianism can be, and how ultimately destructive, when it is combined with cynical intelligence and superb oratorical gifts. Viewed over time, his behavior vividly reflected a clash between two cultural traditions—the humane individualism in Judaeo-Christian civilization and an ultra-Prussian ethos which increasingly defined tenderness as weakness. In the name of the second tradition he turned more and more against the first, but both were caught up in his basic feelings. Indeed, his authoritarianism did not clearly manifest itself—perhaps it did not fully exist—until his adult years, when German romanticism was acquiring its full Nazi harshness. Well before this, however, there were experiences which made him at least vulnerable to authoritarianism.

Joseph Goebbels was born in 1897, in the Ruhr. His parents were devout Catholic, lower middle class but from blue-collar families. Joseph's father, Friedrich, has been described as a stern, austere man with "a rather deliberate sense of humor."[42] He spent all his working life in a firm of gas-mantle makers, rising from office boy through various clerkships to a minor executive position, yet not receiving more money than the top workers on the factory floor. His wife, Maria Katherina, was a strong-minded woman, the daughter of a Dutch blacksmith. In later years Joseph professed great respect for her as representing "the voice of the people"; he of course concealed the fact that she was but a naturalized German citizen.[43]

At the age of four, Joseph was struck by polio. Despite an operation, followed by constant expeditions to church with his mother, one of his feet was permanently crippled and his physical growth retarded. Later, he filled out somewhat, but until then, his head looked abnormally large, and his physique remained short and slight. Pictures taken of him as a Nazi leader, in the midst of colleagues or a military escort, show a sallow-faced man dwarfed by the others—sometimes straining his head upward as if to escape obscurity. In childhood the afflictions of his polio must have been especially felt, for he was not able to run around like other boys and he had two older brothers who were quite healthy. (He also had two sisters, one of whom died when he was small.) But his handicap brought its own advantages. Shutting himself away in his little attic bedroom, he became a precocious reader. His parents ignored rather than encouraged him in this, but later, when he was about fourteen, his father suddenly presented him with a piano. The parents had noticed his enjoyment of music, and they had steadily saved for a piano over the years. Decades afterward, when Goebbels had reacted against his father's religiousness, he suggested obliquely that the piano accorded with Friedrich's ambitions: "It fitted very well among all the knick-knacks of the drawing-room, and I was allowed to go in every day to practise. . . . It was meant to be a stage in the plan of life mapped out for me."[44]

After his primary education, in a Catholic grade school, Joseph was sent to the Gymnasium in his town. He was a good scholar, but neither his teachers nor the boys liked him. He had a supercilious way of showing off his knowledge, and he was constantly and very obviously trying to impress his teachers. Like the young Himmler, he had the reputation of a tattletale. According to a contemporary, his lameness saved him from being beaten up by other boys. They nicknamed him "Ulex" after Ulysses, "the sly one." He liked the name; but in the long run, the role of clever deviousness was not enough for his self-respect. War broke out when Goebbels was seventeen, and in the excitement his contemporaries at school began challenging each other to enlist. Goebbels joined the queue of army volunteers. The result was humiliating. The recruiting station's doctor took one look at his physique and rejected him without even making the routine examination. Goebbels returned home, locked himself in his room, and sobbed like a child. For a day and night he refused to see anyone. After a while it was decided that he would remain at school, to qualify for the university and thence become a priest. Goebbels did not object; indeed, his scripture teacher said subsequently that he seemed very keen on religion at this age.

We might pause here to consider some parallels. Like Hung Siu-tshuen, the Taipings' authoritarian prophet, Goebbels had reacted bitterly to failure at an examination. The same happened with Hitler, who was rejected by his chosen art school. In all three cases, a great deal of identity and self-respect was invested in the test. We have already considered this in the case of Hung Siu-tshuen; in the case of Hitler, the self-image of artist seems to have been in part an effort to separate himself from the "herd" and to avoid ordinary, humdrum work. In the case of Goebbels, failure to pass the army test was directly bound up with a very real physical inferiority. There is some parallel here in the physical inferiority felt by the young Himmler; and we shall see in a later chapter how the values and demands of the society would intensify the resulting blows to self-esteem.

Goebbels' early manhood was a time of increasing rootlessness and searching, for him as for the nation. He moved from university to university—more than did most students. His interests were mainly literary and aesthetic, interlinked with a vain and pompous manner and a certain snobbery toward "the blind and raw masses." His letters of the period also show a reverence for "virile" character and an insistence that, when faced with disappointment, he is no cry-baby. At the University of Heidelberg, Goebbels studied under the celebrated Jewish professor Friedrich Gundolph, who was closely associated with the poet Stefan George. Although he later rejected the Nazis, George was a romantic anti-democrat, and some of his philosophy was in keeping with Goebbels' emerging attitudes. Goebbels now became estranged from Catholicism; in letters to his father he hinted that he was losing his faith and that perhaps his parents should reject him as the "prodigal son." Later, his parents became greatly displeased and upset at his growing apostasy, but his reaction seems to have been more a dramatic self-pity at the thought of losing their love than outright reproach against them.

At the time of his graduation, he was still attracted to elements of the Christian teaching, and through the influence of a college friend, Richard Flisges, he was greatly drawn to Dostoevsky and to a vague anti-bourgeois radicalism. Flisges had been badly wounded in the war and decorated for bravery. He failed to get into a university, became a laborer, and was killed some years afterward in a mine accident. To Goebbels he was a hero, later a martyr. Soon after he graduated, Goebbels began writing a novel, *Michael*, whose main character seemed to be a fusion of Flisges and himself; through Flisges he could realize the soldier's experience. *Michael* combines both the tender and the anti-tender. The protagonist is fascinated with Christ, but the Christ must be "hard and inexorable." He is creative, lonely, and philosophical, but he believes that "the Intellect has poisoned our people." He has a deep and passionate love affair, but it clashes with masculine friendship, and in the end it must give way to a mighty cause and a leader who can settle all doubts.

He on the rostrum glances at me for a moment. Those blue eyes sear me like a flame. That is an order! I feel as if I were newly born. I know now whither my path leads me. The path of maturity. I seem to be intoxicated All I remember is the man's hand clasping mine. A vow for life. And my eyes meet two great blue stars . . .

I have loved Hertha Holk, and I will probably love her for ever. But she isn't the comrade to understand one fully.

Some of *Michael's* "hard" side may have been inserted later, for although Goebbels started writing it in 1921, it was finally accepted by a Nazi publisher in 1928 or '29. But, even if they were politic insertions, they also reflected submissive-aggressive needs. *Michael's* allusion to a great unnamed speaker, with searing blue eyes, is very like the way Goebbels' diary describes one of his first meetings with Hitler.

These large blue eyes! Like stars. He is happy to see me. I am supremely happy. . . . This man has everything it takes to be king. The great tribune of the people. The coming dictator.[45]

Despite its emotionalism, Gobbels' "conversion" to Hitler did not happen all at once. Several years of depression and frustration, fear of failure, and a sense of moral aloneness elapsed between the time he first heard Hitler speak, in 1922, and what fairly can be called the final plighting of his troth. It was not until this period that a personal anti-Semitism emerged, fomented by Jewish publishers' rejection of his novel. It was also the period of a turbulent love affair which followed very much the lines described in *Michael*. Not least, these were the years in which Goebbels became a Nazi worker.

His first years in the party were spent serving the brothers Otto and Gregor Strasser, whose brand of National Socialism was generally to the left of Hitler's. Goebbels' attitude to his superiors alternated between cool skepticism, jealous feelings of rejection, and a hero worship which suggested some covert homosexuality.[46] The same applied to his attitude toward his immediate boss, Karl Kaufman. His first diary notes on Kaufman reveled in affection; later, he dismissed him as "unbridled," "soft," and too "good-natured." Kaufman's subsequent version of the matter was that Goebbels felt "as jealous as a woman" if his chief did not pay him his prime attention. Unlike the archetype authoritarian, Goebbels did not have the sort of mind which easily suppresses doubts about a superior. And yet he passionately craved a leader, a flawless but intimate god, to whom he could yield utterly. An early diary note about Hitler expressed some of this.

I would love to have Hitler as my friend. His picture stands on my table. I could not bear to have to doubt that man.

But doubt at first he did. After hearing another speech by Hitler, he wrote:

What a Hitler! A reactionary! Astonishingly clumsy and unsure of himself. . . . I feel like crying. . . . That was one of the greatest disappointments of my life. I can no longer believe in Hitler! This is the most terrific thing. My faith is shattered and I feel shattered.

This state was too unbearable to last. When the Strassers broke with Hitler in 1925-26, Goebbels began by taking their side, but ended on Hitler's, having adjusted his political views accordingly:

Well, he may have something in these arguments on foreign policy. After all he has thought it over a great deal. I am beginning to be quite happy. I recognise him as my leader quite unconditionally. I bow to the greater man. To the political genius.[47]

It has been suggested that Goebbels' move was largely opportunist, that he identified Hitler's wing of the party as the more powerful force. This may be part of the explanation, but it is also true that Hitler captured and then held Goebbels by deliberate personal flattery. He took him out to dinner and put cars at his disposal. He attended a speech of his; he constantly praised him. Goebbels was overwhelmed. Hitler's money resources impressed him, but so did the man. He told his diary:

I had flowers from him and he seemed ever so pleased. . . . He hugs me as soon as he sees me. He praises me to the skies. I think he really has quite a soft spot for me. . . . Farewell, Munich, I love thee!

The climax came in July, 1928, when Goebbels spent three rapturous days in the mountains with Hitler and friends.

He is the creative instrument of Fate and Deity. I stand by him, deeply shaken. . . . He spoils me like a child. The kindly friend and master . . . These wonderful days gave me direction and pointed my way. In deep anguish I can see a star shining. Now the very last of my doubts have vanished. Germany will live! . . .
We go down into the valley. He singles me out to walk alone with him and he speaks to me like a father to a son. . . . Thanks for everything! Thanks! Thanks!

A few months later, Goebbels took the post of political chief of Berlin, although he had wanted to stay with Hitler in Munich. He remained Hitler's man right up till his suicide in the Berlin bunker in 1945, shortly following the suicide of the Fuehrer.

The sexual element in Goebbels' loyalty is apparent from the excerpts quoted. So is the religious, and both are fused in the wish to be "like a child," caught up in the arms of a strong "friend and master." There is even a hint of masochism: "In deep anguish I can see a star shining." As with other Nazis, Goebbels' Catholic upbringing seems to have created a dependence on strong religious authority. When the specifics of Christian dogma failed to hold him, the intensely personal, charismatic quality of Hitler met the need. Hence such terms as "faith" and "star" came easily to Goebbels in connection with his Fuehrer. Writing of those three days in the mountains, Goebbels rhapsodized:

> He seems like a prophet of old. And in the sky a big, white cloud almost seems to shape itself into the form of a swastika. Glittering light all over the sky . . . Is that a sign from Fate?

It is also noteworthy that when Goebbels mentioned his own speeches for the Nazi cause, he often described them as "preaching" (*Predigte*).

Besides answering a need for direction and sense of identity, Goebbels' hero worship had specific authoritarian connections. After visiting Frederick the Great's palace in Potsdam, he wrote:

> My God! Frederick the Great! That is the big thing about him, that at all times he remained master of himself, that at all times he was the servant of his State. A soldier for seven years. Frederick the Unique.

The words "at all times . . . master of himself" may be interpreted in more ways than one, but their use by Goebbels, a man of violent impulses and turbulent desires, suggests a dependence on authority to channel and control his impulses—by emulating Frederick and by serving the state. Even more suggestive was his admiration for Rasputin, who had so wondrously combined sexual conquest with religious discipline. He was reading a book about Rasputin at the time of his alignment with Hitler; and he wrote, "How much elementary strength in [Rasputin], when compared with sickly intellectuals." Here was the turning against his own questioning and philosophical past, and against the "sickly intellectual" role which had been the refuge of a crippled schoolboy.

At about this time also, he visited Hamburg, where he professed shock at the prostitutes. He inveighed against commercialized sex, but this was not all that he found offensive. It was "lust. On the streets one can see blonde girls hugging Jewish pedlars. . . . Such is bourgeois society. All of it either lust or business". The notable thing is that Goebbels himself was one of the lustiest of men. On the very train ride back from Hamburg, he noticed "on the side opposite a lovely wench peacefully asleep. Quite a girl. Yearning? You bet!" His diary of the 1920s—less inhibited than the records he kept after he became a minister—is full of erotic yearnings and allusions to his adventures. Although several of these became serious affairs, he was quite happy to pursue several girls at the same time; and he kept up this pattern for most of his life. When one remembers his physical handicaps, his past concern with "virility," and his comparison between "sickly intellectuals" and the "elementary strength" of a Rasputin—and when one adds to this the general boasting and vanity—one may reasonably infer that he depended on sexual activities to shore up masculine self-esteem, while giving him other emotional comforts as well. Much of his amorous commentary has a self-centered indulgence, emphasizing how much he needs the girls and what they do for him. His love letters are likewise self-centered, and there are glimpses of a maternal dependence. By contrast with this, the concern about impulse control was expressed largely in the political and social sphere: e.g., the inveighing against "bourgeois lust" and the praise of Frederick's self-mastery.[48]

This is not to say that all Goebbels' affairs were shallow exploitation. His relationship with "Else" seems to have been deep and tender, although his diary suggests that he had casual love affairs with other girls at the same time.[49] Much later, as a married man, he fell deeply in love with the Czech actress Lida Baarova; he is said to have told Hitler that he was ready to resign his high offices and take a foreign service post if he could divorce his wife and marry her. Hitler refused to have any high official of his connected with divorce, so Goebbels ended the affair and tried as best he could to put her from his mind. In general, Goebbels showed an imaginative sensibility to the feelings of women; there is no evidence that he felt a need with them to be restrictive and domineering. (There is likewise no evidence that an "inverted Oedipal" pattern shaped his personality.) He was particularly fond of Maria, his younger sister, and he appears to have been a kind and playful father.[50]

These attributes do not disprove the notion of Goebbels as an authoritarian, since it has not been claimed that authoritarianism necessarily eliminates tenderness in all spheres of behavior. I would argue that in some spheres the adult Goebbels did show an authoritarian pattern. Four aspects of this may be noted.

First, general hostility. Throughout his career, Goebbels was a very suspicious man. He distrusted even those closest to him, and he justified this by aligning himself with his heroes. Frederick, Bismarck, and Hitler, he declared, all distrusted the men around them. He was disliked in many quarters for a malicious tongue, and after joining Hitler he became specially vituperative toward Gregor Strasser, although Strasser had done a great deal for his early career. More generally, too, he once recorded,

As soon as I am with a person for three days, I don't like him any longer; and if I am with him for a whole week, I hate him like the plague.

This was in 1925, and shortly thereafter he wrote, "The only real friend one has in the end is the dog. . . . The more I get to know the human species, the more I care for my Benno." His attachment to Benno reminds us of Hoess's fondness for animals—and Hitler, too, doted on a little dog. Among people whose human ties are attenuated, some may focus their basic needs for affection on creatures which neither "answer back" nor make complicated emotional demands. Since they do not talk, one can project all sorts of imagined motives onto them, and also enjoy vicariously their primitive aggression. Thus Goebbels:

Benno lying under the bed and snoring away. He is like me, alternating between complete inertia and wild bouts of chasing. In a way, this is what I really want. A bit of fighting for me is as important as water for a fish.[51]

A second, related aspect of Goebbels' authoritarianism was his concentration of hostility against "inferiors." His dislikes largely took the form of contempt and superciliousness. In 1925 he declared, "I have learned to despise the human being from the bottom of my soul." Both then and later, he was contemptuous of many Nazi officials for lacking his intellect and aesthetic sensitivity. He could be cruelly humiliating to subordinates, and his treatment of personal aides was temperamental and inconsiderate. There was at least one incident when he showed extreme callousness about the death of the ordinary soldier.

A third aspect was Goebbels' submissiveness and the diversion of doubts about authority. As the war tide turned against Germany, Goebbels became more and more superstitious. With increasing desperation, he turned to omens, horoscopes, and the lives of past heroes for prophecies that the present time of troubles was but temporary. His dependence on such magic is all the more remarkable when set against high intelligence. In part his superstition seemed to be a way of quelling doubts about Hitler's ultimate wisdom: he was constantly proclaiming that "Fate" really was on Hitler's side, despite the black reverses. Toward the end, as Hitler became more violently irrational, Goebbels did criticize his Fuehrer in private conversations with his aides, and even before this he was not above making little digs. An assistant to Goebbels commented, "I can see that criticism is the salt of life to him." But the criticism was only directed at specific decisions; Goebbels never lost his reverence for Hitler as a prophet. When he privately disagreed with Hitler, he often exonerated him by attributing his actions to bad health, or by displacing criticisms onto Hitler's subordinates. Goebbels frequently blamed the military men around Hitler for giving him bad advice, when in fact toward the end, it was more often Hitler who disregarded sound advice.

Goebbels did not, of course, criticize Hitler's most brutal policies, for these were in line with his own feelings. "The rubbish of small nations still existing in Europe," he noted in his diary,

> must be liquidated as fast as possible. . . . We Germans are too good-natured in every respect. We don't yet know how to behave like a victorious people.

Before the war Goebbels had helped whip up pogroms, but he did feel qualms when told of the Final Solution. The qualms were expressed in a stifled way, and he overrode them in familiar fashion: by blaming the victims and identifying sympathy with weakness. From his diary of 1942:

> The Fuehrer once more expressed his determination to clean up the Jews in Europe pitilessly. There must be no squeamish sentimentalism about it. The Jews have deserved the catastrophe that has now overtaken them.
> . . . The procedure is pretty barbaric and is not to be described here more definitely. . . . One must not be sentimental in these matters. If we did not fight the Jews, they would destroy us. It's a life-and-death struggle between the Aryan race and the Jewish bacillus. No other government and no other regime would have the strength for such a global solution as this.

The final aspect of Goebbels to be noted here was his moodiness and drivenness. In later life, as in the 1920s, he alternated between silent brooding and an outpour of talk. During his active moments, he virtually demanded to be kept busy. Ever concerned lest he be bypassed in Hitler's circle of power, he became anxious at any abatement in the flow of messages and telephone calls reaching his office. He liked to have absolute control over things as well as people: his desk meticulously tidy; his subordinates impeccably dressed (or else fired); and a host of detailed rules implementing his censorship of the arts, the press, and public speech. In this, his personal fussiness suited the political needs of totalitarianism, but the man within was not at peace with himself.

HANS FRANK

The character of Frank, master lawyer of Nazism, will be considered more briefly. With Frank even more than with Goebbels, there was manifest conflict between humane values and Nazi allegiance; but like

Goebbels he dealt with the conflict in a predominantly authoritarian fashion.

Frank was born in 1900, in southern Germany. His father was Lutheran, his mother Old Catholic;[52] but, according to Frank himself, he did not take his religious education very seriously. Not much is known about his childhood, but his father was a lawyer who had supposedly been disbarred or suspended for some malpractice. At Nuremberg, Frank described his father as an authoritative figure who inspired him with respect for the law at an early age. The relationship, if any, between the father's shady past and the son's subsequent compromises of the law, and his general ambivalence about authority, is a matter for speculation. We do know, however, that the father was partly Jewish. Both father and son concealed this during the Nazi era, but as we shall see, the son did a great deal more than just conceal it.[53]

As a student in Munich, first at secondary school and then at the university, Frank was even more eclectic than Goebbels. Lenin, Hitler, Oswald Spengler, the composer Oscar Straus—these and other influences fascinated him. He was apparently a bright but unstable student, with an excitable kind of intellectualism.[54] In the Munich *Putsch* attempt of 1923, Frank was among the student Storm Troopers who marched for Hitler; the *Putsch's* failure was keenly felt. After university, Frank became a lawyer, but opportunities were scarce in the postwar depression. For partly economic reasons, he offered his legal services to the Nazis, who had advertised for lawyers to defend them in various suits. He threw himself into the work, and within a few years he was head of the party's legal department. After the Nazis came to national power, he was appointed state minister of justice for Bavaria and he was largely responsible for remodeling the nation's legal system.

Before Frank became a Nazi lawyer, Oswald Spengler had warned him against the party. So had his old professor of criminal justice. Frank knew that Hitler had a basic contempt for law and for lawyers as a whole, and he retained some professional scruples. During Hitler's anti-Roehm purge, which involved people in the Bavarian prisons, Frank objected to the waiving of legal process; but he quickly gave in. Ernst Roehm and others were delivered to the S.S. firing squads. Shortly afterward, Hitler abolished the state ministries of justice and made Frank a minister without portfolio, in effect putting him "on good behavior." The "good behavior" was secured. Frank changed his tune about legal principle, and produced a stream of speeches and articles upholding Nazi concepts of criminal and constitutional law.[55]

During the late 1930s, Frank was an important envoy to Mussolini, and he then became Governor-General of Poland. Hitler's prescription for Poland was an extreme mixture of racism and exploitation. As an inferior people, the Poles were considered "especially born for hard labor." Their standard of life was to be kept at the minimum needed to produce that labor. Jews and "the intelligentsia" were to be exterminated. In supporting this policy, Frank identified fiercely with Hitler's master race concept. His private diary as well as his public utterances expressed enthusiasm for the Poland policy, and in his endorsement of Jewish extermination he hinted at a Final Solution for all Jews (not just Poles) well before this decision emerged from the secret councils of Hitler and Himmler.[56]

At one point his diary seemed to make a show of brutal indifference in order to suppress qualms. He wrote: "that we sentence 1,200,000 Jews to die of hunger should only be noted marginally." Why bother to say "should only be noted marginally" if such de-emphasis was the obvious course? On legal ethics even more, he was clearly divided against himself. Early in his governorship he told his staff:

Gentlemen, I must ask you to fortify yourselves against any sympathetic qualms. We must exterminate the Jews wherever possible, in order to uphold the general task of the Reich here. That will of course have to take place by other [than legal] methods. . . . One cannot transpose accustomed viewpoints to such gigantic events.

Legal process and its humanity was thus written off as a limited tradition. A while after this, however, Frank clashed with Himmler over control of the state police in Poland. Having failed to get Hitler's support in the matter, he made a number of speeches in various German cities, denouncing the police state and asserting that "ancient Germanic principles of law" cherished the citizen's "incontestible rights." In his stand for civil liberties, Frank spoke only of German citizens, but there was some difference between his praise of legal protection and his previous deprecation of "accustomed viewpoints." Hitler's response was to strip Frank of his party and political offices, and to make him civilian administrator of Poland, subordinate to Himmler's police powers. Cowed by this, Frank threw himself into cooperation with Himmler's S.S. forces, and his diary reveled in assertions such as "The Poles shall be the slaves of the Great German World Empire."

Frank was captured by the Allies two days after Hitler's death. He tried unsuccessfully to kill himself, and was later sent to Nuremberg to await trial. While in Nuremberg prison, he became a convert to Roman Catholicism. He turned vehemently against Hitler and Nazism, cursing them in the name of God for greed, sacrilege and other evil. Although he blamed himself for atrocities, he was much more vocal in blaming Hitler, other Nazi leaders and the German people as a whole, and in this there seemed to be some projection of guilt. He continued to be fascinated with Hitler—as the Devil. He reviled his co-defendants, "repulsive characters" for the most part; he praised his prosecutors: "Such fine men, those judges and the prosecuting attorneys—such noble figures the Englishmen—the Americans—especially that fine tall Englishman."[57]

Frank's change of allegiance was not just a conscious ploy to propitiate his accusers.[58] It reflected an unstable morality which enabled him to make passionate alignment with the prevailing power. When Nazism failed and was exposed, he replaced it with the most autocratic of Christian religions; yet he had doubts about that too, for he sometimes wondered if the notion of an after-life was not a myth. During his allegiance to Nazism, he occasionally challenged his superiors when his legal powers and professional identity were threatened; but his usual course was to squelch doubts by turning the more vehemently against "inferiors" and outsiders. Frank's "formative" years seem to have created a dependence on authority, and some susceptibility to guilt, without implanting a strong conception of the values that authority should represent. For the restless student, drawn to many doctrines, Nazism offered an adamant certainty, and perhaps that was something in itself. But there were also the functions of anti-Semitism. It is notable that one of Nazism's most ardent anti-Semites should himself, secretly, be partly Jewish. Granted, this might conceivably be mere coincidence; but we suggest that the role of Nazi lawyer and governor enabled Frank to dissociate himself from the racial "inferiority" (and professional failure?) of his father. And to dissociate himself in the harshest possible way, by attacking racial inferiors. This is not to say that economic incentive and political ambition played no part in his attraction to Nazism; on the contrary, these things were bound up with emotional need. The choice of Nazism as a way of furthering his ambitions had implications for his personality: it pressed him to deal with his feelings in an authoritarian way.

G. M. Gilbert's assessment of Frank at Nuremberg supports this diagnosis of authoritarianism. In psychological tests (the Rorschach), he showed much emotional turbulence. Hyperactive imaginings alternated with depression and withdrawal; aesthetic ecstasy would suddenly give way to morbid fantasies. There seemed to be a great deal of sexual conflict; it is worth noting here that Frank was unhappily married to a woman five years his senior. And from the way Frank talked about Hitler, it was clear that his submission to the Fuehrer had included a strong element of unconscious homosexual yielding.[59]

OTHER PATHOLOGIES

It should not be assumed that all the top Nazis were authoritarian. A borderline case was that of Rudolph Hess. His submissiveness and paranoia were very much an authoritarian's: a repression of hatred for a killjoy father; a dependence on "pure" male figures; anxieties about weakness and contamination, and obsessive fears of poison.[60] There is no evidence, however, that he directed his hostilities in a punitive way against external symbols of weakness, tenderness, or inferiority. It is true that the Nazis gave him outlets for aggressive self-assertion: he enjoyed his early days as a brawling Storm Troop leader; and fears of contamination may well have intensified his political anti-Semitism. But, again, he did not focus his aggressions on objects *despised as weak*, for to him the Jews were overwhelmingly a symbol of threatening power. He demurred against the Nazi trend to extreme atrocities; he was genuinely concerned about the killing of women and children in German air raids; and in his personal dealings with women and subordinates, he was considered to be gentle and chivalrous. It may be argued that his gentleness was a "reaction formation," a way of offsetting destructive urges, but even if so, there is no evidence that these urges included a special need to strike rebels or the weak.[61]

A very different character was Hermann Goering. Brutal and domineering he certainly was. He showed great enthrallment with military pomp and adventure—there was something narcissistic and undeveloped about his enjoyment of parades, fancy uniforms, and luxuried living. His fantasies revealed some sadism, and as a schoolboy he went in for Jew baiting so aggressively—turning his dogs on local residents—that he was punished by his teachers. Caught up in nationalism, he hated the Weimar Republic and resented Germany's humiliation at Versailles.[62]

Yet he lacked the kind of submissiveness shown by more authoritarian Nazis. With his penchant for bullying there went a capacity to criticize authority based on a cynical intelligence.[63] As a World War I air ace he showed bored irreverence for military traditions, despite his own romantic militarism. A pilot's role, of course, made this easier, but at school, even more, he had gained a reputation for being insubordinate. His father, a distinguished colonial civil servant, who came of a line of senior government officials, was stern in a traditional way, yet his rule does not seem to have been harshly inhibiting.[64] By the son's own account, on one occasion when his father did thrash him—for too much violence in his war games—Hermann protested openly, saying that courage should not be penalized.

This is not to say that his childhood relations were satisfactory. From the age of six months until he was three, Hermann was separated from both his parents. His mother left him in the care of her closest friend and rejoined her husband, who was then Consul General in Haiti. Goering's earliest childhood memory was of hammering his mother in the face with both fists when she came to embrace him after her absence. As a boy, he was jealous of his older sisters, who had visited the parents abroad. His general strutting and bullying must in part have been compensation and revenge for early rejection and deprivations. Once, when his parents disciplined him for persecuting his sisters, he sulked and then sought sympathy by pretending to be sick. In a much more humorous way he showed something of the same theatricality throughout his life. The combination, however, does not seem to have involved displacement of rebelliousness against underdogs. Like the others he felt Hitler's spell and G. M. Gilbert argues that for him too the Fuehrer was very much a father figure. But there was not the same earnest subservience to him, and in his personal life the latter-day Goering remained somewhat independent of his leader. He found his solace in palace orgies and drugs. He showed no great emotional attachment to Nazi ritual and pseudo-religion; nor did theories of race and national defilement preoccupy him. He was anti-Semitic as a matter of social attitude and economic policy, but he did not show much personal dislike of Jews, and he did not automatically reject people whom he knew to be cool about the regime.[65] While accepting brutality against the "foe," he was revolted by deliberate atrocities against women and children, and unlike a Goebbels or a Himmler he was not inclined to batten down his qualms by denigrating the victims. (He possibly turned to drugs instead.)[66] His callousness, in short, did not receive that extra, bitter twist given by a submissive and punitive alignment with authority.

Somewhat different from Goering, if only in degree, was the type of Nazi described by T. W. Adorno and others: the rootless, deeply asocial nihilist.[67] In this type the destructiveness and moral brittleness of the authoritarian, the cynical irreverence of a Goering, and the brutality and emotional deprivation of both were found at their most extreme. For such a person, Nazism provided opportunities for aggression, and perhaps a controlling channel for wild impulses; but it did not exact an authoritarian form of submission. Ernst Roehm, the Nazi "Storm Troop" chief who broke with Hitler and was murdered, may well have had this kind of nihilist character.[68]

15   ADOLF HITLER

To say that Hitler had many of the traits shown by extreme authoritarians is not exceptionable. The most obvious of these traits need only be summarized. First, he was a strained and touchy person, given to outbursts at the slightest rebuff, be it real or imagined. Though he capitalized on these moods as he developed his political skills, his violent and edgy temperament had been inflamed during early years of frustration, when he eked out a precarious, lonely existence in Vienna, an ambitious but unsuccessful artist living the life of a tramp. At the height of his power, his inner disquiet was still apparent; he suffered from insomnia and frequent stomach disorders, despite anxious dieting.

In the second place, Hitler had an immense fund of destructive hostility. His capacity for enjoying revenge was enormous, as when he watched on film the slow hanging of "July plot" conspirators. His sense of humor, too, was apt to be aggressively callous—his laughter for instance, when Goebbels told him of the latest humiliations meted out to Berlin's Jews. With this was fused a contempt for tender sympathies, and an equation of manly strength with ruthless brutality.

In the third place, he *had* to dominate. At private gatherings no less than public meetings, his friends were treated to lengthy tirades and brusque demands. As a young man he was said to have been shy and awkward with women;[1] later, he learned to flatter and charm them, but in the few close relationships he had, he was restrictive, demanding, and jealous. In political beliefs, the notion of social equality goaded him, for though he courted the masses he despised them for doltishness. A great deal of his destructiveness was concentrated against people expressly considered inferior: in line with this, the concentration camps took not only ethnic "under-people" and political heretics but gypsies, alleged homosexuals, and the mentally deficient.[2] Likewise, the "euthanasia" program stemmed directly from Hitler's mind. As far as sheer Nazi doctrine and "science" were concerned, the more publicized notion of sterilizing the mentally ill would have furthered national "purity" just as plausibly as extermination.[3]

Related to all these traits and needs was Hitler's anti-Semitism. It was more than a political tool, and more than just a culturally-learned attitude. It was an obsession. At the end of his life, when his world was literally falling to pieces around him, when his audience was not a nation but a few followers huddled in a bunker, he blamed the Jews above all else for his afflictions. Throughout his adulthood his conspiracy notions were centered on the Jews, though by no means confined to them. With no one else perhaps has anti-Semitic expression suggested more vividly the mechanisms of paranoia and projection. The "maggot in the putrescent body," the "bacillus" which dissolves society, the "repulsive, crooked-legged" seducer of "hundreds of thousands of girls"—so the imagery went, and throughout his career; "the Jew is the ferment of decomposition in peoples" was one of his favorite phrases. This imagery did not originate with Hitler; he learned much of it from Viennese anti-Semitism and, perhaps, from the sordid imaginings of Nazis like Julius Streicher. But the important point is the extent to which it captured him, and the readiness with which he made one people an "all-purpose" scapegoat, in private conversation as well as public propaganda. Behind nearly everything that Hitler attacked, from "pornography" and prostitution to Modernism in art, behold the Jew.

It has been suggested that Hitler's anti-Semitism was compounded by being born an outsider, an Austrian of uncertain antecedents (in part perhaps Czech, possibly even Jewish) who looked to Germany for greatness.[4] It is no less probable that there was some relationship between the sexual moralism in his anti-Semitism and an apparently meager sex life. The most obvious link would be the concern about vitality and purity: hence the racist specter of debilitating, defiling invasion. In like spirit Hitler became very anxious about his health: he had a horror of catching cold or any other infection; he avoided alcohol, coffee, tea, and tobacco, and he became an ardent vegetarian. It is impossible to say how primary and predominant the sexual was in these things. One might argue that his prime concern was social, a fear of being dragged down the gutter, of being lost in the common herd, without power, without identity. Such fears might be expressed in partly sexual images of dirt and defilement. But again one might suggest that several factors were primary; that the social and the sexual reinforced each other; that he felt especially vulnerable to loss of identity in the "herd" because at root he did not feel a man. In considering these possibilities, we move to one of the most difficult problems in assessing Hitler's character—the question of submission. To what extent did Hitler show submissiveness? What part did it seem to play in his makeup? Was it essentially authoritarian?

To make any answer to this, we must begin with Hitler's childhood. His father, Alois, was the illegitimate son of a farm girl and a miller who was constantly on the move. Alois was brought up by an uncle, but he left his household at the age of thirteen to become a cobbler's apprentice in Vienna. Five years later he joined the Imperial Customs Service, reaching in a relatively short time the top grade attainable by one with just an elementary education. He retired from the service when Adolf was about six, but continued to provide comfortably for the family; although he lost money from a smallholding.

Alois Hitler was a popular man with his drinking companions, and in the office he seems to have been a cheerful dictator.[5] To others he was somewhat different. As Alan Bullock mildly explains, "his domestic life—three wives, one fourteen years older than himself, one twenty-three years younger; a separation, and seven children, including one illegitimate child and two others born shortly after the wedding—suggests a difficult and passionate temperament."[6] He seems to have married his first wife, the one much older than he, very largely for her money; they were divorced after he had been having virtually simultaneous affairs with two other women. He continued to be promiscuous during his second marriage. His wife became tubercular and by this time Alois had acquired a reputation for callousness; it was said that he ordered her coffin before she died. His third wife, Klara, much younger than he, was the mother of Adolf. Five children were born to them; a girl and a boy died in infancy before Adolf arrived and a younger brother died when he was six. Only a younger sister survived with Adolf, but he had an older half-sister and half-brother (also called Alois).

In the home Alois was a constraining presence, moody, intolerant, short-tempered. He showed some affection for Klara, but he also tyrannized her. To an acquaintance of the family, she seemed a subdued, disappointed, and harassed person, but also loving—at least to her daughter. She kept an unusually spick-and-span house, considering that there were children; and she was quite possibly a more devout Catholic than Alois, whose religion was largely bound up with considerations of status.[7]

As one might expect in these circumstances, the young Adolf was cowed by authority but assertive in other directions. According to one eyewitness, Alois would bawl at his small son, who seemed very much in awe of him.[8] At his first school, Adolf was scared of authority but was deemed lively and intelligent by his teachers, as well as obedient. Among his schoolmates he was particularly keen on war games and he had his own small-boy gang which got into some minor scrapes. Personally, he was foxy rather than a fighter. At secondary school his teachers gave him good reports for obedience and moral conduct, but bad reports as a scholar; he was considered lazy. He was cantankerous with his schoolmates, hating contradiction and demanding that his friends be followers. Until the age of fifteen he was fascinated with Red Indians; and he was drawn to anti-Semitism while still a boy.[9] He showed no interest in women until well into adulthood.

Hitler's father died when he was not quite fourteen. Some years afterward Hitler began castigating his father as a tyrant, blaming him for his own failures at school and inventing stories of a conflict over his plans to become an artist. There is no evidence, however, that Hitler quarreled with his father when he was alive. As already noted, it appears that he was in general rather awed by authority. In the light of this, his subsequent outbursts against his father may be seen, in part, as a desperate attempt to resurrect an Oedipal role that he had failed to fulfill. When writing about his parents in *Mein Kampf,* he portrayed his mother as a strong and pure matron, but also a martyred figure—a widow left impoverished after her husband's death.[10] Since in fact she was left with a comfortable pension, the story's closest parallel in reality is that Hitler himself continued to draw money from her after he had left school, rather than find a job or any other regular pursuit. At another point, Hitler once told of beatings by his father, when he would amaze the family with his stoic endurance. In fact he greatly exaggerated the number of these incidents, and it has been argued that they did not happen at all.[11] It is clear that he was romancing when he described the little Adolf, cursing his drunken father and begging him to come home from the tavern.[12]

Throughout these fabrications Hitler seems to be denying that he was weak and that he did not stand up to his father. The denial was surely linked to his anti-Semitic complex about rape, defilement, and penetration. In *Mein Kampf,* Hitler draws the portrait of a laborer's child, raised in a poverty-stricken and overcrowded home, who must see shocking things happen, including the assault on his mother by his drunken father. Such an image—the pure Nordic woman defiled by a sot—may have served subtle propaganda needs, but there is a strong similarity between this picture and the hardship, oppression, and specters of drunkenness attributed to his own home in earlier pages of the same work.[13] Since his father did in fact abuse his mother, the fantasy seems to reflect an Oedipal fear of his father taking his mother, but does it not also suggest a fear that his father might emasculate or annihilate *him?* Consider again the context. A pattern in childhood and adolescence of submission to authority. A pattern in adolescence and early adulthood of sexual inhibition. The mental linking of alcohol with humiliation by one's father and the loosening of controls on a brutal husband. An emerging racist imagery expressing concerns about rape, invasion, and corruption. I suggest the following interpretation. First, Hitler felt emasculated by his failure to join with his mother against a tyrannizing father. Second, his submissiveness to threatening authority aggravated homosexual fears about being penetrated (it is worth mentioning here that an observer who saw Hitler speak before the war thought there was something indefinably "feminine" about him, for all his harshness).[14] In the third place, Hitler may have projected bottled-up hostility onto his father, thus compounding his own fear of annihilation by overwhelming authority. The number of deaths in his family may have reinforced a feeling of precarious vitality, for in addition to the young children who died, Hitler's mother died of cancer when he was eighteen, after years of ailing.

Does all this add up to a picture of authoritarian submission? Certainly it does not conform to the archetype model in which the adult continues to mute rebelliousness against a hard father. But we have already noted a German variation in which the adolescent turned to other hard authorities. And the early death of Hitler's father may have encouraged him to make more of a revolt against his father than he otherwise would have. As it was, the way Hitler behaved after his father's death was more often that of the paternal tyrant than one who had sympathy for the tyrannized. His deepest revolt seems to have been against his own past submissiveness and weakness. Viewed over time, this can be seen in part as a process of displacement. The resentments which Hitler did not express directly against his father were expressed largely in destructiveness against "inferior" out-groups, though also against the "bourgeois" world which had rejected him in his early career. His targets did include symbols of authority—mostly old and faded authority—but his contempt for the masses and his hatred of deviants reflected a wish to dissociate himself from the weak and outcast. Furthermore, in view of his childhood background, his adamance against softness and sentimentality and his restrictive behavior toward women indicated that his Oedipal role had not been resurrected very far—he still could not "afford" to get too close to feminine tenderness. This is not to say that Hitler never felt affection for anyone, but the conditions under which he did so were both limited and limiting.

So far we have only considered the factor of submission in Hitler's childhood. To go on from this and say that the adult Hitler too was "submissive" may at first seem a very far-fetched claim! There are indications, however, that Hitler felt extreme submissive needs through much of his life, although his power drive hid these needs from himself. It must be remembered, of course, that all people have urges to submit as well as assert. The fact that Hitler reverenced ideology, drawing from various nationalist and racist thinkers, does not itself suggest anything more than a "normal" need for authority, plus the political uses of that authority. What counts for our inquiry is the particular flavor and intensity of his submissiveness.

One revealing sign was the way Hitler spoke of providence and fate. At several points in his career, particularly when obstructed or threatened, Hitler told of the tasks imposed and the road laid down for him by "Providence." True, there was political advantage in citing a supernatural authority. But, as Bullock observes, "calculation and fanaticism" were closely woven in Hitler's character.[15] The myths he created for himself he came to believe in unreservedly; self-gratification concealed the submission.

"I go the way that Providence dictates with the assurance of a sleepwalker," Hitler once said, and this remark expresses two themes which recur in other situations.[16] First, an intoxicated escape from self, or rather, perhaps, a drugged immersion of self in a greater whole. The aspect of intoxication could be seen most plainly in the Wagnerian romance, the glitter of the Nuremberg rallies, and elaborate, racist blueprints for the world could spellbind him. Brought up a Catholic but lacking deep allegiances to the traditional church, Hitler felt a need to create his own religion, a harsher if vaguer religion. Hence the very personal references to "Heaven," "Fate," and "Providence." On a more secular plane, too, one could discern something of the same link between a sense of rootless drifting and the wish to lose oneself in authority. His reaction as a young man to World War I was the most striking sign of this. The war meant escape from loneliness and frustration into an exciting collective armed with purpose. Long afterward, Hitler spoke of "the stupendous impression produced upon me by the war—the subordination of 'one's own ego' to the heroic, common interest."[17] Taken by itself, this may not seem an unusual response to war, but as a political idea, the notion of immersing one's ego in the Volk was trenchantly repeated by Hitler. Here again, character traits and political doctrine are particularly hard to unravel, but it did seem that the doctrine found fertile ground in Hitler's own experience and character needs. With time, "subordination of the ego" became a prescription for his followers rather than for himself, but in many of his preachments he showed a knack for touching those springs in others which he too possessed.

A second theme in Hitler's supernaturalism is a "stop-go" motif—an alternating between assertive action and passive dependence. The sleepwalking statement, already quoted, showed both sides of this. So did his behavior in the years before World War I, when he swung back and forth between a depressed and moody indolence and an excitement about schemes that were never followed through. With his immersion in politics, the passive side was obscured but it did not cease to exist. One clue to its persistence was the strained quality noted by Bullock.

Hitler had nothing of the easy, assured toughness of *condottieri* like Goering and Roehm. His strength of personality, far from being natural to him, was the product of an exertion of will: from this sprang a harsh, jerky and overemphatic manner which was very noticeable in his early days as a politician. No word was more frequently on Hitler's lips than "will."[18]

Despite his emphasis on will, he did not, unlike many authoritarians, seek order and comfort in a detailed, disciplined routine. His self-image as artist permitted him to hate systematic, administrative work; his escape from inner uncertainties lay in messianic dreams rather than a meticulously filled schedule. As a result, the passive side of him could find some expression in tendencies to brood and delay. At the same time, his attention to military technicalia was so extreme that it sometimes interfered with his thinking about broader strategic questions.

Hitler's alignment with "Providence" and the Volk meant that his doubts about these external images of authority were inseparable from doubts about his own mission and himself. A process of displacement in dealing with these doubts can be seen in *Mein Kampf*. He tells of a crisis of faith, of the disillusion he felt on perceiving the working-class movement and its attractiveness to the masses.

All that I heard had the effect of arousing the strongest antagonism in me. Everything was disparaged—the nation because it was held to be an invention of the capitalist class (how often I had to listen to that phrase!); The Fatherland, because it was held to be an instrument in the hand of the *bourgeoisie* for the exploitation of the working masses; the authority of the law, because this was a means of holding down the proletariat; religion, as a means of doping the people, so as to exploit them afterwards; morality, as a badge of stupid and sheepish docility. There was nothing that they did not drag in the mud. . . . Then I asked myself: are these men worthy to belong to a great people? The question was profoundly disturbing; for if the answer were "Yes," then the struggle to defend one's nationality is no longer worth all the trouble and sacrifice we demand of our best elements if it be in the interests of such a rabble. On the other hand, if the answer had to be "No," then our nation is poor indeed in men. During these days of mental anguish and deep meditation I saw before my mind the ever-increasing and menacing army of people who could no longer be reckoned as belonging to their own nation.[19]

Rather than stand aside from his German in-group or face the specter of unclaimed masses, Hitler found a scapegoat—the Social Democratic leaders, dominated by Jews, who were corrupting the popular mind. "Knowledge of the Jews is the only key whereby one may understand the inner nature and the real aims of Social Democracy."[20]

It may be argued, of course, that Hitler's scapegoating of the Jews was a deliberate strategy. So it was, in that Hitler sensed the political uses of blaming them. But it has also been seen that the scapegoating had a strongly individual flavor; and in this particular context it enabled him to keep a persisting contempt of the masses from subverting his racist-nationalist doctrines. These doctrines, in turn, were not simply a conscious device for making Hitler's power aims popular. They affected the very definition of these aims. Thus, for all his urge to dominate, he was attracted again and again to the notion of an alliance with the British, fellow members of the clean, strong Aryan elite. Though at times he despised their leaders for what he thought was weakness, at other times his dislike had overtones of a rejected suitor.

In its definition of an in-group as well as an out-group, racism was for Hitler a very personal authority.[21]

In arguing that Hitler's character was basically authoritarian, we are still left with a major question—the matter of rationality, self-control, and self-insight. It is not simply that Hitler could be perceptive and flexible in military and political affairs, at least through 1942. It is also that he made shrewd uses of his own emotion. In meetings with subordinates or with foreign politicians, he would throw himself into frenzied rages, appearing to lose all control of himself—and then suddenly he would stop, straighten his clothes, and resume in normal voice. There seemed to be, likewise, a *knowing* trait behind his appeals to mass emotion. His playing to popular frustrations, fears and hatreds drew very much from his own feelings. He exploited his self-pity, and in *Mein Kampf* he declared outright that his early years had been years of loneliness and restlessness.

None of this, however, seems really incompatible with authoritarianism. Of course it was not of any archetype pattern, for Hitler was an extraordinary man and he allowed himself a range of psychological insight that many authoritarians "forbid" themselves. Nevertheless, there are no indications that Hitler was very conscious of his weakness feelings and his dependence on anti-Semitism to channel fears and resentments. As it was, the psychological insights which Hitler did have seem to have been intuitive and semi-conscious. He *sensed* the cravings of a crowd, but he did not consciously analyze the affinity between their needs and his. The same applied to his uses of rage and moral indignation. He had enough rational control to turn his rages off and on according to political expedience, but this did not mean that he perceived his underlying needs for such anger. In the political climate of his time and place, a self-control based on extreme alternating rather than steady moderation of impulses was no liability. And his moral brittleness helped all the more to make his righteous indignation a marriage of sincerity and opportunism. To some extent, he could make himself believe what was useful, politically, to believe; but this process required a certain lack of self-analysis.

It is not surprising, then, that Hitler consistently hated real discussion just as he hated contradiction. Debate swiftly became a monologue of abusive shouts. Intellectuals as a whole he distrusted, in part perhaps out of social envy, but also because they stood for a spirit of independent, rational criticism which he found distasteful and threatening.[22]

In the end these attitudes, allied with a more general distrust, helped to bring down disaster upon the Fuehrer, his aims and his country. As the military tide turned against him, he insulated himself more and more from intelligent advice, feeding himself instead on false hopes and delusions of power. Like Hung Siu-tsheun, he had the sort of mind which brings forth a vast new edifice and then destroys it.

16 CULTURE, CHARACTER, AND POLITICS

CULTURAL FACTORS IN GERMAN AUTHORITARIANISM

We have already considered some of the forces which seemed to produce much authoritarianism in prewar Germany. We can now pick out a more general theme.

The basic development follows the diagram of causes presented on pages 104-05, showing two broad types of influence, each acting upon the other and upon the individual. In the German case, these influences were as follows: On the one hand, there had been from the nineteenth century a series of economic stresses and social disruptions. On the other there was growing moral domination by an "ultra-Prussianism," a militarist ethos which bid up the "hard" traditions of aggressiveness, ascetic obedience, and physical toughness, while obscuring the equally traditional, knightly values of courtliness and chivalry—except on the most abstract plane.[1]

These influences jointly affected child rearing: for example, they sometimes made parents more repressive and socially anxious and they promoted the kind of "tenderness taboo" described by Henry Dicks. At the same time, we must not underestimate the relatively direct impact on character of social stresses and moral orthodoxies, operating in part after childhood. For instance, in the economic disruption which followed World War I, unemployment and financial straits could magnify a person's feelings of weakness and failure. Simultaneously, cultural beliefs offered an array of targets—Jews and so on—which encouraged a scapegoating response to frustration.[2] Likewise, long-established but intensifying political themes, such as anti-Semitism and the fear of national "encirclement," legitimized and developed personal paranoia. As we have already seen, the Jews came to represent various kinds of threat, from the political to the sexual. Hence the racism and embittered nationalism which formed part of Germany's political traditions did not simply influence behavior; in some cases, at least, it affected basic organizations of personality. Under a different cultural outlook from that which dominated Germany, insecure and emotionally deprived people—even those, say, with deep fears of impotence or defiling penetration—would have tended less to deal with their feelings by developing punitive wishes.*

This is not to say that cultural beliefs promoted authoritarianism without getting anything in return. By the interwar period at least, authoritarianism was surely prevalent enough in the population and among the new nationalist leaders to have its own harshening effect on widely accepted ideas. But there is no indication that authoritarians (as defined here) were *the* representative character type of the German people. Depending on individual circumstances and backgrounds, there were many kinds of response to hardening orthodoxy and social stress. Conversely, there were many kinds of people whose collective expression shaped the orthodoxy.[3]

To understand these factors, we must go back to before World War I. The top Nazi "Old Fighters" and their earliest disciples were born at or near the end of the nineteenth century; so their parents were conditioned by nineteenth-century influences. From the standpoint of social stress and disruption, a train of developments may briefly be noted. The industrial revolution came to Germany relatively late, but when it did so, she swiftly became the foremost manufacturing nation in Europe. With such change there went the tensions induced by changing social relationships and economic needs. In particular there was a difference of spirit between rationalist industrial expansion and the

---

* Cf. Gilbert's comments on the role of German history in personal paranoia and the complex relation between "clinical paranoia" and learned "cultural pseudo-paranoia." Gilbert, 1950, pp. 134, 270 ff. My own observations convince me that, even among people with somewhat paranoid fears of dirt and penetration, learned values can lead them to project feelings of threat onto power figures in a way which accommodates humane feeling and rebelliousness. Unconsciously or semi-consciously, they may even displace run-of-the-mill irritations with "little people" onto figures of strength who "can take it" or who "need putting down."

survival of great "feudal" estates. There was also considerable antagonism between middle and working classes, and by the end of the century there was a new *petite bourgeoisie* which felt squeezed by big business from the top and politically organized labor from below. Most of the top, authoritarian Nazis that we have portrayed came from this background, and though this is not a statistical sample, one would expect a disproportionate number of authoritarians to have had parents in the same stratum—people of precarious status striving to be "respectable." Hand in hand with class antagonisms went political intolerance: during the late nineteenth and early twentieth centuries, democratic institutions and customs were generally weak, and people of Social Democratic background—the largest political party, predominantly lower class—were arbitrarily excluded from the higher civil service.[4]

From the standpoint of ideology, there was in many quarters an intense German nationalism. This was fanned by a sense of precarious nationhood, for it was not until the latter part of the nineteenth century that a fairly unified political state emerged from loose confederation and the dominance of Austria. Even then it was a very defensive nationalism, as was shown in the 1870s' *Kulturkampf,* Bismarck's onslaught on Catholic practices and power which had seemed to threaten German unity and Prussian leadership. At the same time, a succession of romantic and philosophical writers helped develop German nationalism into a tremendous mystique, and toward the end of the century their influence was compounded by the rise of social Darwinism and scientific theories of Nordic superiority. Although Jews comprised less than one percent of the population, anti-Semitism had strong historic roots, as it did in other countries; and the exclusion of Jews from army and civil service showed how institutionalized it had become, despite a law of 1869 forbidding religious discrimination in public appointments.[5] After the financial crisis of 1873, numerous pamphlets appeared blaming the Jews and accusing them of fostering both large-scale capitalism and Marxism. Again, this expressed the squeezed, in-between position of various middle-class groups.

The German school curricula, with their emphasis on national history, provided a strong vehicle for militarist romanticism. This is not to say that all teachers had the same beliefs, but the school lessons did encourage and legitimize a patriotic channeling of aggression. It is notable that Hitler, Himmler, Goering, and other Nazis were enthusiasts about German history at an early age; they might have been so anyway, whatever their schooling, but their lessons at least reflected and transmitted some of the nationalist spirit of the time. Furthermore, at some prewar schools the students revived old militarist societies such as the *Fehme*, a group whose moral harshness and political intolerance gave it some resemblance to the Klan. By and large, the German *Gymnasia* lacked the extensive organization of games provided by British "public" schools; there was relatively little channeling of aggression into apolitical and unhostile behavior. Instead, there were long, hard hours of schooling, and a little playtime. It may be added that, according to some traditions, the German schoolmaster could be a neurotically harsh figure who took out on the pupils his resentment at a low social position and a restricted life. How much this stereotype really applied to the late nineteenth and early twentieth century is unclear; but it reminds us again that patterns of upbringing favorable to authoritarianism may have been entrenched well before World War I.[6]

And then, the interwar era. At the end of the war, Germany's economic disruption was accompanied by an increased hostility between different classes, and severe splits in opinion over foreign and domestic policies. Throughout the next decade and more, German attitudes were strongly marked by social envy. The colossal inflation of the early 1920s bore particularly hard on the working class and the small middle-class salaried man, whose earnings nowhere near matched the increase in living costs. The psychological damage was perhaps greatest for the *petit-bourgeois*—especially the clerical official and retired tradesman living on savings. Many of these people were abruptly reduced to the economic level of the proletariat. In the light of this we may consider Erik Erikson's impression that the German father was often not simply autocratic but harsh, owing to an "essential lack of true inner authority."[7] The martinet at home, making up for his insecurity in the world outside, might be just the sort of person to induce authoritarianism in his children. At the same time, however, the father's inability to provide much for his children's future may have played a part in the evasive, adolescent rebellion already mentioned. In the social chaos of the 1920s, the new generation tended to discount (overtly, at any rate) those "old generation" symbols of authority which were associated with failure. Partly as a result of this, but also because of a general breakdown in traditional relationships, the climate was not a good one for a deep and stable planting of values and loyalties.

These factors help to explain the mood of restlessness and anomie which affected the young Nazi leaders at Munich, but which also had an impact on the next generation. During the early twenties in particular, a welter of social creeds and authorities impinged upon the individual, and the decline of formal religion left a vacuum, to be filled in many cases by a newer, harsher authority. Religiousness remained; the Christian ethic of compassion declined. Hence, in part, the acute "religicizing" of the Fuehrer, his exaltation as an omnipotent god. We may note here that, among Henry Dicks's POWs, the chief religious influence reportedly came from their mothers. This jibes with other impressions of German upbringing, and one may speculate that it would encourage the authoritarian to reject church religion—as something associated with femininity. At the same time, consciously or unconsciously, he might feel a continuing claim by his mother's values, particularly when he felt a strong, if covert, maternal dependence.[8]

In this account of the postwar era, we have so far concentrated on factors of cultural and social disruption. The other side of the picture is the further hardening of a nationalist ideology, the declining influence of other doctrines, and the subsequent use of the prevailing nationalism as the rationale of totalitarian government. In part, this condensing and hardening process was the defense reaction of a threatened culture, a reaction led by organizers and communicators but based on many levels of need among the general populace—economic, social, emotional. It was a reaction to national defeat in World War I, to the losses imposed by the Treaty of Versailles, to the revolutionary yet alien force of Communism, to the specter of national encirclement, to social divisions, economic distress, and moral uncertainties. At the same time it drew on traditional ways of reacting. Although Nazism contained revolutionary elements, the romance of Fatherland and Volk was no more a break with the past than was the scapegoating of Jews.

World War I contributed to hardening nationalism in a number of ways. It came when the future leaders of Nazism were in their adolescence, old enough either to fight or to be disappointed at not fighting, and at an age when they were highly impressionable by romantic notions of manliness, patriotism, and martial adventure. All the more embittering, then, when the war ended not simply in defeat but in national discord and the breakdown of domestic morale. This did not necessarily apply just to future leaders. It has been variously suggested that soliders returning from the war resented the economic difficulties into which they were plunged, by contrast with the financial security and status they had enjoyed in military life; and that they felt they were owed better things for the hardship and danger they had gone through. Erich Fromm maintained that these feelings were especially marked among young ex-officers, for whom the professional market was saturated. Versailles, he contended, became a symbol of national frustration onto which feelings of personal frustration were projected. How extensive such a process was it is impossible to prove, but it does suggest a way in which individual feelings, not necessarily confined to authoritarians, helped shape a collective pattern of beliefs.[9] At the same time, the beliefs, involving a war-based nationalism, became bound up with institutions and hence a force capable of influencing personal behavior. In his study of a German town between 1930 and '35 William Sheridan Allen noted the "bewildering array of militaristic and nationalistic organizations" which existed on the eve of the Nazi accession to power.[10] Several of these, such as the League of War Wounded and the Society of Former Artillerists, were predominantly for World War veterans. Like other militarist groups, some of them adjuncts of the Nazi and German Nationalist parties, they staged parades, dances, and plays, a constant publicity for their outlook. Between them they recruited a sizable number of people, and sometimes they mounted a joint crusade—as in 1930 when they petitioned the state government to ban *All Quiet on the Western Front* from school libraries.[11]

At the universities during the first postwar years were students who had fought in the war; there were many others who wished they had. Despite the range of philosophies contending for the students' minds, academia did not by and large provide a strong bastion against nationalist intolerance. For one thing, Germanic nationalism had traditionally drawn strength from philosophers, racial scientists, and other writers; it had been elaborated in both intellectual and lyrical forms. Then again, at a place like the University of Munich, some student activities merged with youthful paramilitary groups. Many youths who otherwise seemed down-to-earth were captured by a heady patriotic romanticism well before any specific National Socialist doctrines became the prevailing dogma.[12] In other classes too, hardening nationalism fostered an acceptance of violence which later among some people became a *readiness* for violence, especially amid the fears of the 1930s' depression. At this point, Nazi actions became particularly important in the process of *legitimizing* violence. The party which claimed to uphold "Germanic morals," and which stridently identified the Jew and Communist as the national foe, was also the party which offered employment in its brawling Storm Troop echelons, and made exciting promises of economic recovery. Even if most Germans felt that they would not go as far as the diehard Nazis, the impact of National Socialism was to lead social ethics in a direction more encouraging to extreme authoritarian behavior.

This brings us to the subject of Nazism itself as a cultural influence on personality. We will concentrate on two questions—one, the extent to which Nazism was a traditionalist reaction; two, the conflict induced by Nazism with the personalities of its disciples. The importance of the first is that we have so far emphasized the link between authoritarianism and an ultra-traditionalist cultural orthodoxy. But is this relevant to the appeals of Nazism? Certainly there was much in the movement that was revolutionary and new. Its leaders were essentially antagonistic to the established chiefs of German society—industrialists, generals, professional civil servants. In the army, Nazi influences did much to reduce the social apartness of the officer corps.[13] Economically, the Nazi program offered benefits to farmers, workers, and other "little man" groups, and when the Nazis came to power, their rearmament program cut down unemployment. At the same time, they eliminated trade unions, and at a grass-roots level they often built their power by an atomizing process—the sabotage of various associations and clubs which bound men together. As a creed, Nazism was explicitly anti-"bourgeois," and it was opposed to traditional religion, although Hitler soft-pedaled his attacks on the Roman church for largely political reasons. Finally, the Nazi regime implemented new concepts of state power involving totalitarian surveillance and the use of mass communications.

In weighing these attributes, one must remember that the newness of any political movement is relative. Even Chinese Communism at mid-twentieth century has drawn from native political and educational traditions, for all its attack on the old order.[14] Compared with this, German Nazism was far less revolutionary. Despite increased public works and increased state control of business, large-scale capitalism continued to exist under the Nazis. As a whole the middle classes obtained more economic security, but the small businessman's sector of the economy declined and for the worker no radically new welfare state was introduced.[15] In its ideology, Nazism did not so much attack traditional authority per se as assail recent leaders who had "betrayed" their Germanic heritage. The substitute for bourgeois flabbiness was ancient Teutonic vigor; the antidote to alien Christianity was a nationalist mysticism which, for those who wanted it, included the *gottgläubig* religion.[16] While individuals like Himmler and Rosenberg helped formalize these trends, the sanctifying philosophy drew from a part-mythical, part-historical past. We have also seen that anti-Semitism and romantic nationalism had strong nineteenth-century roots; and even the harassment of the churches had some precedent in Bismarck's *Kulturkampf*. It is true that different people could privately emphasize different aspects of Nazi doctrine, and that some were drawn to the nihilist and rebellious aspects rather than to the "Wagnerian mystique."[17] Even so, ideology encouraged the rebel to attack bourgeois and democratic leaders as symbols of weakness and corruption, and to do so in the name of a historic Fatherland and its heroes—Frederick the Great, Bismarck. For the authoritarian, therefore, Nazism sanctioned "secondary rebellion" while providing traditional power images with which to identify.

The second aspect of Nazism is the moral and emotional conflict exacerbated by the ideology within some of its adherents. Despite the harshening of German nationalism, the Nazi glorification of power, ruthlessness, and "hardness" did not operate in a wholly favorable setting. As we have already seen, both in Germany and the civilization surrounding it there were enough humane legacies to give the ethic of brutality a defensive timbre. Thus Hitler, in declaring that "the Polish intelligentsia" must be exterminated, explained: "This, too, sounds cruel, but such is the law of life." As he was wont to in such statements, he leant on a social Darwinist tradition, but he also recognized that some might think his actions "cruel" in a pejorative sense. Now, virtually all modern cultures have contradictory traditions and values, but if some of the values are pushed to an extreme in a short space of time, it is harder for the individual to balance or fuse them. It is still harder if his upbringing did not provide him with a clear way of bridging the divergent values—for example, by assigning priorities to different values in different spheres of behavior. In the postwar disruption of German family life, when new influences on youth challenged old ones, these difficulties may have been particularly prevalent. Especially so if, as Dicks suggests, a "soft" maternal indulgence of the child was often furtively conducted and poorly jibed with paternal demands of toughness.

On the level of basic personality—the management of feeling—we have already seen that an alternative to jibing and balancing opposed values is a more simple reliance on repression and/or suppression. And this is what Nazism encouraged its adherents to do: to deny and deprecate the emotional claims of humanity in favor of "hardness" and vengeful intolerance. In support of these pressures, Nazi totalitarianism blurred the lines between public and private life, extending into the private the demands of "*Mein* Fuehrer"—as god, husband, father, and political Big Brother. This is not to say that the totalitarianism was anywhere near complete, or that its ethos rejected all expression of tender feeling. On the contrary, with some individuals, the aggressive claim on tender feeling levied by Nazi leadership could bring out a latent conflict between homosexual submissiveness and affection for women. We saw this in the early manhood of Goebbels, when his discovery of Hitler seemed to interfere with his feelings for "Else." Hans Frank, too, seemed to have felt a partly similar conflict.

Having said all this, I would leave the subject on a note of caution. For one thing, it should not be assumed that we have covered every major source of German authoritarianism. Second, there may well be other cultures, equally nourishing to authoritarianism, in which the important influence does not so primarily involve the sexual. In Germany, the "tenderness taboo" and the readiness to identify humane sympathy with weakness became culturally-learned values, although they were espoused more by some than others. As transmitted through the culture, these values easily lent themselves to mixtures of authoritarianism and homosexuality. Yet in other societies, too, there might be strong pressures to stifle rebellion and turn it against moral inferiors and social weaklings, without the same cultural labeling of "feminine" tenderness as sickly and despicable. These variations, however, are relative. Insofar as it affects child rearing, any pressure to repress rebellion and turn it onto "safe" symbols of weakness may implicate sexual relationships and feelings. For example, the child may make extreme identification with paternal authority against soft-seeming women, even though prevailing cultural values do not directly equate tenderness with weakness. Still more generally, it should be stressed that the sexuality of power is not peculiar to authoritarianism. In America's TV age, the sex-appeal factor in electing democratic politicians is widely acknowledged, but only as it applies to women constituents. One may ask, however, if the sexual element is not also widely present among male voters—for example, in the fascination with young, rugged-looking statesmen, and some of the concern with a strong defense "posture" against foreign threats. Until such questions are further explored, one should not assume that sexuality per se, or even homosexuality per se, was a distinctive attribute of Hitler's emotional appeal and demands. What did stand out was the extent and the particular quality of the sexual force he represented and the sexual needs his image met.*

A COMMON MATRIX

In discussing the relationship between authoritarianism and Nazism it would mislead to stress only the direct, mutually reinforcing ties between them. Obviously the two phenomena were also parallel products of a common environment. In other words, many of the cultural factors which fostered authoritarianism also created Nazism, and not solely through the influence of authoritarian character. Even *within* German society one might expect to find authoritarians concentrated in those social groups where Nazism was particularly popular—and would have been popular anyway without the influence of authoritarian pathologies. Hence many authoritarians would be well located for their emotional susceptibility to Nazism to become outright affiliation.

Several studies of voting in 1932 have shown that the Nazis drew disproportionate support from small towns. Indeed, "the larger the city, the smaller the Nazi vote."[18] Various studies have also shown that the Nazis drew disproportionate support from self-employed businessmen, lower-middle-class civil servants, white-collar workers, and small farm owners (but not farm laborers). The same went for actual membership in the party, except that small farmers were underrepresented.[19] In both cases—the small-town-rural appeal and the *petit bourgeois* appeal—Nazism tapped the fear of certain groups that they were losing out to big-city power blocs, especially organized labor and the cartels. Despite their statism, the Nazis captured nearly all the supporters of provincial parties which had opposed the centralized power of the modern industrial state. These parties, in turn, had been

---

* In view of the historical influences on character, one may ask whether authoritarianism has ceased to be widespread in Germany since World War II. Ivo Strecher has described to me the behavior of some contemporary German police, in which obsequiousness alternates very suddenly with snarling aggression. Is this just a liability of the police? The German slang "bicycle rider," denoting someone who pedals hard down on inferiors while presenting a high bottom to be kicked by his betters, suggests that authoritarians or persons very like them are common enough to leave their mark on language! On the other hand, the term *is* derogatory, and the type is not so common and accepted that there is no term for it at all.

largely based on middle-class support outside the metropolitan centers. They had expressly appealed to the artisan's and tradesman's fear of being made a "proletarian wage laborer" by the forces of capitalism from on top, socialism from below. Hitler likewise promised to defend *petit bourgeois* groups whose class identity was threatened by the depression and by previous economic stresses. His statements showed that he was well aware of the importance of status concerns. When talking to audiences of small businessmen, he could mask the Nazi antagonism to "bourgeois" values, while letting the epithet remain applicable to bankers and trusts. To some extent also, Hitler appealed to small-town and rural antagonisms of a more diffuse kind—resentment of urbanization, big-city liberalism, and any social change which seemed unfavorable. How important this factor was for the Nazis it is very difficult to prove; but it is striking that, in the small town analyzed by William Allen, the array of nationalist and militarist clubs, many of them not at first specifically Nazi, were most influential in middle-class life.[20]

In line with our thesis, one would expect both the small provincial community and the *petite bourgeoisie* to provide especially fertile ground for authoritarianism. Whether they in fact did so is a matter on which we have no direct evidence, but the strong possibility must be stated lest one oversimplify the relationship between Nazi appeal and personality. By and large, the small towns were a repository of traditionalism, yet amid economic disruption and social change their culture was on the defensive. At the same time, provincialism fostered an intolerance and a stereotyped outlook, which in turn could endorse an authoritarian response to stress. It is true that our "middle town" hypothesis as applied to America did not apply mainly to very small towns, but in Germany even rural traditionalism may well have had a harsher quality.

A somewhat similar case can be made for the notion of a *petit-bourgeois*-authoritarian link. According to tentative evidence put forward in earlier chapters, parental anxieties about status and clean-cuffed respectability can foster authoritarianism among the children, especially when the parents are anyway dictatorial. But economic stresses may also have fomented authoritarianism among the middle-class parents themselves, the immediate generations caught in the twenties inflation and the thirties slump. A desperate hanging-on to middle-class conventionalism and a fearful contempt of social inferiors—these might affect basic character in an authoritarian way, given a society where democratic and egalitarian values were weak, and where Jews and other outsiders were historic scapegoats.

In *petite bourgeoisie* and the provincial community, then, the following stresses and social attitudes may be supposed to have promoted both Nazism and authoritarianism: economic threat and the fear of losing status; envious resentment of the powerful, coupled with hostility to scapegoats and dissociation from the big-city masses; middle-class moralism and patriotic militarism; provincial narrowness; and a wish to revive the "good old days" when Germany was great and life supposedly more secure. In moving people toward Nazism, these factors may have weighed with different persons at different psychological levels. For some, supporting the party in response to these factors may have been primarily the result of political ideas and social and economic concerns. Among others, deep emotional needs do seem to have been important—for example, a feeling of degradation and self-contempt caused by economic reverses.[21] Not that all of these people were necessarily authoritarian. But, in the case of authoritarians, one would expect the class and community factors outlined above to have made strong contact with *a great deal* of the personality structure—for example, not simply by fomenting a sense of powerlessness and failure, but by shaping and endorsing a punitive conscience and the repressive diversion of hostile impulse (onto "socialist" workers, Jews, and so on). As a result, the emotional bases of their support for Nazism would have been particularly extensive in the personality, since their inner structures reflected so much of the social antagonisms and stresses to which Nazism was a politically organized response. This is not to say that, on the level of personality structure, authoritarian formations provided the only way of reflecting a great many of the social antagonisms and stresses. Nor must one forget that, even outside the smaller community and *petite bourgeoisie,* Hitler was very skillful at appealing to a variety of groups for a variety of reasons.

AUTHORITARIAN AND POLITICAL INFLUENCE

The ascent of authoritarians to the top of Germany's political power structure was obviously due to a complex of related factors. In the first place, it seems that Germany had a relatively large "pool" of authoritarians, when compared by rough impression with other Western societies of the same era. The larger the pool, the greater the chances of its throwing up individuals with the political skills required to take power. The same applied within the Nazi party, during the early stages when its top command was under dispute.

In the second place, the relative ineffectiveness of established government and the weakness of parliamentary institutions created a power vacuum into which essentially "unparliamentary" leaders could march. To cite just two elements—at the time of Hitler's accession to the Chancellorship, no party had an outright majority of Reichstag deputies; and the executive government had seemed unable to cope with frightening economic crises. Under these circumstances, and given the historic weakness of democratic traditions and political tolerance, the way was opened up for men whose programs suited their own authoritarian needs. (I include Hitler within the rubric of "authoritarianism".)

This brings us to the question of mass support. It would be a distortion to say that a mass following simply gave Germany's governance to Hitler and the Nazis. It was not until after Hitler became Chancellor that the National Socialists and their nationalist allies gained a majority of the Reichstag; even then it represented less than half the popular vote. The Nazis alone did not gain a decisive majority until the Communist deputies had been outlawed. Without shrewd political maneuvering, plus the mistakes of his opponents, Hitler would never have been made Chancellor and thence gathered the reins of supreme power. On the other hand, still less would he have attained supreme power without the popular following that he had. Apart from the use of mass demonstrations, the fact that by 1932 the National Socialists far outnumbered any other party gave him a crucial weapon for bargaining.

In cultivating popular support, and even more in recruiting demonstrators and party workers, Hitler benefited from the large numbers of people who shared many of his traits, frustrations, and needs—feelings expressed with eloquence by Goebbels and Hitler himself. In this psychological constituency, authoritarians were a central type. To one "side" of the type stood the immensely submissive person like "Fritz Muehlebach," prepared to execute or condone aggressive orders by authority, but not punitive toward underdogs per se.[22] On another side was the nihilist thrown up by social chaos, basically more amoral and less repressed than the authoritarian. This type, it has been suggested, was often found among the unemployed and also among professionals of danger—racing drivers, air aces, colonial adventurers.[23] In addition to these types there were other kinds of personality, involving various combinations of aggression, rigid obedience, and racial romanticism.[24] These types—mixtures of cultural belief and emotional need—were not entirely separate from each other or from authoritarianism; there must have been borderline cases. But one may consider the authoritarian a central type in Nazism's psychological constituency because it combined both the intensely submissive element and the vengefully destructive. And therefore authoritarians like Goebbels and Hitler, adept at sounding their own chords in others, were in a good psychological position to build a mass following.[25]

Hitler's own personality was also a factor in the rise of other authoritarians. In personal relationships no less than in mass communications, he had magnetism which was quite overwhelming. Various people who knew him have even suggested that his eyes had a hypnotic quality. Be that as it may, Admiral Doenitz' account of visiting Hitler echoed the impression made on other visitors:

I purposely went very seldom to his headquarters, for I had the feeling that I would thus best preserve my power of initiative, and also because, after several days at headquarters I always had the feeling that I had to disengage myself from his power of suggestion. . . . In this connection I was doubtless more fortunate than his Staff, who were constantly exposed to his power and his personality.[26]

Not with all, however, was the predominant reaction a wish to escape. We have already seen, in the case of Goebbels and Frank, how a deep wish to be mastered and enthralled by a strong male hero could attract people to the Fuehrer's service. In the case of Goebbels, we also saw how Hitler flatteringly played on this form of submissiveness. When one adds in other traits of Hitler's—his quick-tempered intolerance, his demand for ruthlessness, his pre-emption of much decision making—it is easy to see how authoritarians would be prominent among those who survived for a long time in high positions immediately subordinate to him. For some authoritarians, granted, the subservience might have been too obvious to suit their particular needs; one cannot imagine another Hitler serving for long under the Fuehrer! As it was, Goebbels fretted at times under Hitler's decisions. But the main point stands.

The actual influence on German life and events wielded by high-placed authoritarians gained from both institutional and psychological factors. Most obviously there was the political system itself, the concentration of power and charisma at the top. Although this primarily armed Hitler, some of his authority accrued to those associated with him. Inside the various sub-hierarchies headed by his top subordinates, faction fights, intrigues, and the opaqueness of vast bureaucracy caused some dispersal of power; on the other hand, the men at the top gained from the system's autocratic ethos and a general German tendency to respect rank and official command.[27] In the society as a whole, the totalitarian nature of Nazi power and ideology enhanced the top leaders' influence over personal lives. Himmler and his network of police surveillance, Goebbels with his captive mass media—men like these wielded enormous everyday power in the name of Fuehrer and Fatherland, without challenging Hitler's supreme authority.

Despite all of this, the influence of authoritarianism as such upon political and social developments is very hard to judge. For one thing, it is always difficult to tell how much of a leader's public action stems from his internal disposition as opposed to immediate external influences; in varying ways the two obviously interrelate. For another thing, as oft said already, authoritarianism does not monopolize the individual's disposition to all facets of his behavior. Therefore, to say that authoritarian individuals wielded great power in Germany is not logically the same as saying that the use of that power was greatly shaped by authoritarianism. In view of these difficulties, I shall mention just two specific developments which authoritarianism seems to have greatly affected.

The first is the evolution of Nazi doctrine as an influence on popular beliefs. The prominence of authoritarian leaders in the rise of Nazism, and the singular way in which Nazi imagery matched authoritarian needs and fervor, make it reasonable to infer that authoritarianism helped determine the *emphases* in National Socialist ideology. To be sure, neither reason—the prominence of authoritarian leaders or the matching of doctrine and personality—provides sufficient basis alone for our deduction. It is the combination of the two which is convincing. And it then follows that, through Nazi ideology, the authoritarianism of Hitler and others could influence the moral and cognitive climate in which young Germans were brought up. This is not to say that Nazism wholly controlled the climate, or—to mix the metaphor—that everyone received exactly the same kind of ideological dose. Nevertheless, the writings and oratory of Hitler and Goebbels supplied a central impulse to public propaganda. To this was added the Nazi focus on youth groups (Hitler Youth, the Nazi Schoolchildren's League, etc.) and the Nazi regime's influence in the schools.[28]

The second development which seemed to bear the mark of authoritarianism was a concrete event—the decision to exterminate the Jews. In this act, authoritarianism was surely decisive. In the anti-Semitism that *led up to* the Final Solution, authoritarianism can be cited as no more than a reinforcing element. Likewise, there is no evidence that the *carrying-out* of the Final Solution would have failed had there not been authoritarian personalities to play an important part in executing it. But the decision itself—that is another matter. It cannot be assumed that the preceding anti-Semitism had a momentum of its own which inevitably led to mass extermination. Not all persecutions of Jews, even those involving violence amid social stress, have led to massacres, and it is clear that the Final Solution stimulated rather than stemmed from the development of mass killing methods.[29] Nor can it be said that mass extermination was bound to result from the particular hatred, fear, and racism that held sway in World War II Germany, especially among Nazis. We have already noted the moral explanation that Hitler and Himmler felt obliged to give in issuing the extermination directives. This, and the secrecy with which they conducted the operation, testified to the presence of humane scruples at large, even though many Germans subsequently suppressed their inklings of the truth.

The decisive element was Hitler's paranoid obsession with Jews, his vengeful destructiveness, his need to punish inferiors and outsiders, and his self-immersion in a racial mysticism that could be used to support his aggressions. If Hitler really did believe that the Jews would in any sense destroy Germany unless destroyed first, this belief was the product of a delusion which exaggerated prevailing cultural fears of a Jewish threat. Until Hitler made it so, the mass killing of Jewish men, women, and children was not even a necessary adjunct to Nazi beliefs and values; the Nuremberg Laws and other policies had already served the needs of doctrine by isolating and subordinating the Jewish populace. Nor, from Hitler's standpoint, was extermination politically useful as a means of channeling German aggressions. Since the country was at war, there was no shortage of real enemies to hate, and the very secrecy of the mass killing meant that it was not a program for public consumption. It is true that the program stemmed, administratively at least, from "euthanasia": when the latter was abandoned for political reasons, it was safest for Hitler to divert the large euthanasia staff into the extermination of Russian and other Jews, thus keeping them implicated, brutalized, and all the less likely to tell tales. But, even if this political incentive was a major factor in Jewish extermination, it simply links the Final Solution to Hitler's euthanasia decision, which, it has already been argued, was a product of his personality.*

Of course social stresses and culturally-learned attitudes helped bring about these decisions indirectly, acting through Hitler's character. But these forces only led to the decisions because Hitler had reacted to them in an authoritarian way. In the long term, the pattern of cause was circular. A rare convergence of historical events, ideas, family circumstances, and (presumably) physiological makeup gave to a character its distinctive stamp. That character's way of dealing with its drives and emotions then affected history; it could only do so because social opportunities and demands combined with the individual's character traits to give him overwhelming political power.

* Economically, there was no clear advantage in total extermination of Jews, even from the standpoint of Nazi assumptions about Jewish productivity. For a somewhat contrary view of all this, tracing *lethal* anti-Semitism back to Medieval demonology, and also stressing anti-*father* hate in German anti-Semitism, see Cohn, 1967. (Was the anti-father hate a displacement onto weaker-seeming, easier-to-attack authority symbols?) Cohn is also interesting on the Jew seen as racial poisoner of the Russians, and he suggests that Hitler wanted Jewish extermination as early as 1919.

PART V

RECENT AMERICA

17 THE WHITE SOUTH*

More than twenty years ago, Helen McClean wrote an article on "psychodynamic factors in racial relations." She described white people of small Southern towns, subservient to a puritanical caste culture, living lives whose "emotional aridness" was only temporarily relieved by "hysterical religious and sadistic orgies." Sexually repressed, these people envied the blacks, whom they believed to be more virile and felt to be more able to express "genuine warmth." They sought contacts with blacks, but these contacts were fraught with a "terror of the forbidden." And so,

> their inflexible consciences, in seeking a victim to punish for all manner of forbidden impulses, must keep in subservience those who represent the temptations. . . . Occasionally a lynching [relieved] the corporate guilt of the white community.[1]

Although McClean drew on first-hand observations, we must of course beware the easy thought that one central character pattern underlies all Southern racism.[2] But, if we limit the sweep of her assertions, we can read them as suggesting that Southern culture, particularly that of the Deep South, has in some people promoted an authoritarian way of dealing with impulse. This will be all the more plausible when we come to note the moral ambivalence which has so often attended Southern submission to the segregationist code. The forbidden, imperfectly re-

---

* This chapter was prepared and written before the Nixon Administration came into power. I do not know if current social and political trends are reducing or increasing the pathologies described in this chapter.

pressed impulses mentioned by McClean represent potential revolt, which, if let out, would bring upon the individual a total obloquy ("nigger lover") mixed with physical danger. In the case of Tom Watson we have already noticed how harshly and internally these pressures could act upon a man's subversive humanity.

From intensive interviews in the late 1950s and 1960s Robert Coles's notes on white Southerners have indicated two types of authoritarianism.[3] One kind involved fairly educated people whose doubts about segregation were near the surface of consciousness, and who reacted with extra vehemence against white liberals and certain blacks who threatened to remind them of their doubts. Suppressive ire, directed at persons who might fan their own feelings into dangerous rebellion, enabled them to displace onto these people many of the subconscious irritations they felt at being put in a position of ambivalent conformity. Authoritarian processes thus served the white-caste way of life, not just in the obvious way of supercharging racism, but by quelling criticism. This is not how Coles put it, but the observations by liberal Southerners whom he quotes strongly suggested that pattern, for all the observers' subjectivity. One such observer was an Alabama college professor who had urged desegregation on his colleagues in the 1940s and early fifties when it was easier to get away with it. Since then he had kept his views very quiet, but silence did not placate the *"pure* Southern" family of his wife. He interpreted it this way:

They don't know it, but they're taking out a lot on me that they really feel toward Alabama's segregationists. I had my say a long time ago, and when I did they were surprised, but pleased. It's the climate here that has changed. I've even gone along with it by keeping silent whenever possible; but somebody has to be the enemy—and the representative of what is coming. My father-in-law feels I'm exposing the family to danger, risking our lives and welfare. Yet what he is really upset about, and can't dare acknowledge, even to himself, is not me but this town and the panicky people in it, including himself, and I guess at times me, too.[4]

Now, assuming these observations to have some truth, they might still describe more a "situational authoritarianism" rather than deep traits of character. But Coles reported another case where a deeper authoritarianism seemed to be involved. The observer in this case was a leading citizen of Birmingham, a liberal doctor. In the course of psychoanalysis, he had become aware again of the great love he had felt for, and received from, his family's black nurse. When he tried to tell his older brother about this, the brother "flew into a rage."

He told me I was coming out with nonsense, crazy nonsense it was. I could tell by his excitement I had hit upon a sensitive nerve.

Later, when the doctor took a quiet lead for desegregation, his brother angrily accused him of being a "god-damned nigger lover," always "soft on niggers," and having a stubborn anti-Southern streak. Perhaps he should go North where he belonged. As the doctor saw it, some of this vehemence originated in childhood. Their mother was impartial but distant; in a sense the nurse was their real mother, "until we were sent off to school after twelve."

Naturally, my brother went to school first, being older. He would come home on holidays full of jokes about niggers, how stupid they are, and animal-like. I never connected his attitude then with the fact that I was alone with Ruth, and he away from her. In his heart he must have felt the way I did when I finally did leave—homesick, and more for our nurse Ruth and handyman John than either of us dared admit to ourselves, let alone anyone else.

In continuing to attack blacks and "nigger lovers" so harshly, the brother may also have been attacking or denying more general feelings of maternal dependence and rejectedness. Be that as it may, the doctor said he finally stopped his brother's onslaughts on him by abandoning careful argument in favor of a simple, strong demand: "Why don't you leave me and the niggers alone? That's all I ask you, leave us *all* alone and find some other enemy."[5]

The second kind of authoritarianism portrayed in Coles's report involved less the diversion of doubts about segregation than the racial channeling of aggressions so as to shore up self-esteem and align the person with authority—and not just caste authority. One possible example was "Mrs. Patterson," a member of the mob which harassed Negro children in the New Orleans crisis over school integration. Poor, tired, and frustrated, suspicious and chronically obese, she struggled to manage a large family without much help from her husband. When he was not drinking, he would sit around the home, laconic and "tough." She made little criticism of her husband's habits; instead, she took out her frustrations on blacks: they were dirty, they ate pig food, they were lower than dogs: "I have enough to do just to keep going and keep us alive without niggers coming round." To Coles, who interviewed her directly at length, it seemed that her railing at the black schoolchildren, so isolated and oppressed, contained a cry against her own isolation and misery; and that being a devout Baptist, "she could only allow herself to express such despair and rage at a Negro."[6]

Another, very different example was offered to Coles by an upper-class Mississippi lady. In explaining how she had become an outspoken integrationist, she also discussed her older brothers.

> Perhaps it is because I am a woman that I feel the way I do, a woman who grew up with two brothers who constantly made light of what I could do or be. Instead of being their pet younger sister, I became someone they could bully, and call weak. My mother and I were close, though, and in her eyes she was weak, too. She believed that all women were weak because she believed my father, and he said so—often. He was a rich man, partly through money he inherited and partly through money he made in law and investments. My brothers worshipped him, and my mother obeyed him. . . .
>
> Actually my mother was silently strong; and my father was noisily weak, so weak that he had to scare everyone around him to compliance, submission, agreement, or at least a pretense of such behavior. Thus, neither of my brothers ever had a chance to be anything but lawyers, and anything but intolerant—about the poor, the North, Negroes, foreigners, and in a way, women.[7]

To a large extent, the brothers may simply have learned intolerance from the father with whom they identified. But the passage above suggests that the values learned from the father also endorsed an authoritarian management of aggression.

Among the Southerners most fully described by Coles was "John," a Louisiana militant who had taken part in mob violence. In conversation with Coles, he said that he would like most blacks exiled to Africa, leaving behind a few to be sterilized and employed in jobs suiting their God-ordained animal qualities. Some blacks he had wanted to kill, but these were working for the Communists. There was a war on between God and the Devil; "We may lose" as a punishment for disobedience, including "nigger-loving." John was also worried about other minority groups; he would ship the Jews "back" to Russia, and he hoped the Greeks and Lebanese who sailed into New Orleans would stay on their boats. In World War II he had been stationed in New Jersey, and he said he had gone frequently to New York to look at his enemies, the Jews and capitalists and blacks; he knew them well. He had never been against the Germans, he declared. Roosevelt was a crippled traitor.

Restless in his job—a state government clerkship—John had helped organize public protests against integration. Once he had even run for political office, losing but polling a sizable vote. He read constantly in the literature of racism and the radical right, but given his paranoid assumptions, he seemed by no means unintelligent. He was a moody man, now sullen, now cheerful, now irascible; he bitterly fought his son, trying to change his habits and hobbies and jerk him out from racial indifference. (In every little Southern group, and almost every family, some people are more racist than others; this simple fact alone surely says something for the personality factor in racism, even in the South.) Coles's own interpretation traced the racist needs of John to an accumulation of stresses; they included economic frustration following initial success, and domestic difficultes—a permanently ill wife, a bleak marriage. But they also included experiences originating in childhood and parents, and it is here that the authoritarian element, if such it is, can be perceived. He was an ailing infant, and later in childhood he had two bouts of pneumonia. A black maid nursed him through the first of these; by his own account, she gave him more sympathy than his mother did. The maid died when he was twelve, collapsing before his eyes; it seemed to Coles that he resented this sudden loss and repressed his affections for her. John was a middle child of three, and according to his own account, both parents discriminated against him in favor of the others. His first memory was of his father's strap, a punishment for pinching his baby brother. This was to happen many times: apparently John and his brother never got along.

His mother appears to have been nervous and fussily demanding; his father moody and mean, and a heavy drinker.

I never figured why Daddy picked on me. We got along fine when he was sober, but when he got liquored up, I got it first and hardest. I looked like him and helped him most in fixing things around the house, but he never remembered things like that when he was drunk. . . . I used to be afraid to say anything for fear it would get someone upset at home, I just kept quiet and ran my trains.
 . . . My sister and brother both favored Ma, and Daddy, he'd feel no good because he couldn't get a week's pay, so he had to hit someone.[8]

In many things, so it seemed to the interviewer, John's portrait of his father resembled himself as an adult. John resented his father's behavior, but he atoned whenever he expressed this. His mother and father were "the nicest parents anyone could ever want." He said his father was "soft on niggers," believing they should be protected like children; but "I don't blame Daddy, because, you see, in those days we had them firm under our grip." Much of this reluctance to criticize his father may have been principled love and loyalty in the presence of an outsider, but his whole behavior and account of his life suggested a compensation for weakness feelings by acting rough like his father, not by raging against the kinds of authority which had sown resentments in the first place. He, who had turned his aggressions on a cleaner, well-behaved younger brother, now defended God and cleanliness against niggers who "dirty the whole city up" (New York) and a sister's family afflicted by poverty and alcoholism—"they live like pigs." From an early point in his life the caste culture surely encouraged this focus of antagonisms, and once the channels were set, economic and other fears of adulthood could find expression along the same paths.[9]

In understanding what may produce Southern white authoritarianism, we must start with the most obvious cultural facts. First, the caste system involving proximity to human beings regarded as utterly inferior. And second, evangelical puritanism, a strain particularly fierce and prevalent in the South, which has worked upon the individual's early imagination; has been selectively used to defend "scientific" theories of racial inequality; has offered humane rationalizations where the hardening of hearts seems required.[10]

Against these central points of culture have been ranged historical threats and disrupting forces. Abolitionism, the Civil War and Reconstruction, the recent civil rights acts, and movements for black liberation represent a chain of political threats, first to slavery, then to the very practice of white caste superiority. More insidious has been the steady moral challenge of egalitarian values, espoused publicly by most Americans and largely embodied in the country's formal institutions. Southerners *do* feel themselves to be Americans—and as some episodes in the early 1960s showed, many of the most racist have not wanted to look too ugly on national TV.[11] Another source of cultural tension has been the mixture of religious puritanism with hedonism, a "southland" sensuality. In his classic *The Mind of the South* W. J. Cash declared that the contradiction between puritanism and hedonism became greater as the puritanism hardened, despite (one might add) the hedonist suffusion in revival meetings.[12] Today, the clash between puritanical standards and the encouragements of a consumer society are nationwide—consider the ambivalent treatments of sex and liquor—but in the South this opposition has had a special historic intensity.

Another disrupting element has been the nearness—historically as well as geographically—of a frontier violence in which sheriffs and other local leaders were sometimes virtual hoodlums. This is particularly true of Mississippi, which was part of the "wild west of the Old South"; but then all of the generalizations made here apply more to some areas and groups of the South than to others.[13] Comparing regional frontiers as a whole, Frederick Jackson Turner found that Southern colonists were less communal than their Northern counterparts: it was mainly in the South that efforts to create towns by legislation failed.[14] Such individualism, stressing personal morality outside the law, could support a humane concern for selected underdogs: the early Klansmen, after all, were often praised by Southerners as the chivalrous champions of the weak, especially the women and children of Confederate soldiers. But we have already noted the two-way potential of American individualism and the ethic of placing women on a gilded dais: these themes could culminate in the humane liberal, but also in the cruel, intolerant moralizer—and mixtures of the two. The main point is that "frontier" individualism (even today private gun ownership is especially prevalent in Texas and the Deep South) has offered a challenge to social solidarity. That challenge remains, despite the Southerner's famed friendliness to visitors of good will and to his own.

For the Deep South particularly, the list of social threats must include economic frustration. It is not simply that the Deep South is poor; it has been poor compared with the rest of the nation, and Southerners know it. Rural poverty rubs hard against agrarian myths which praise the small farmer as "the American." For many reasons it is not surprising that annual rates of lynching have in the past correlated inversely with cotton prices.[15] The poor white's fear about status and the black is well known; the Southern economy does not thoroughly support the caste system by assuring all whites an income far above that of most blacks. It has often been said that Southerners who have felt economically and socially insecure (not invariably the poorest) have had the greatest need to keep the black down and make him a scapegoat for their fears. But their insecurity is also a potential threat to the caste system; how much less dreadful the specter of social decline and economic failure might be if blacks were not deemed so inferior, if *at all costs* one did not have to keep above and apart from the black masses. As it is, a fraction of Southern blacks live at economic levels above that of most whites, though not enough to change the general comparison. We do not know that any whites have a repressed notion of ending the caste system as a way of alleviating status anxiety, but we do know that impoverished Southern white farmers once joined with their black counterparts against the white well-to-do.*

---

* In his biography of Tom Watson, Woodward (1963) tells of white Populist farmers riding in from miles around to protect a black ally whose life had been threatened.

Since the early days of slavery, many aspects of Southern cultural orthodoxy most relevant to authoritarianism have hardened or intensified. In large measure this has been a reaction to the social and cultural threats outlined above: it was not till the end of the nineteenth century that racial demagogues and a popular literature occupied with the black man as rapist and brute really flourished.[16] From colonial times, admittedly, the white-caste imagination had associated blacks with great potential of violence, and before the Civil War white Southerners showed a fear of slave revolt out of all proportion to its feasibility and frequency. But even these concerns were stimulated in part by abolitionist propaganda, private aids to escaping slaves, and, perhaps, the sheer fact of the South's union with so many states which did not countenance slavery.

Then again, since the Civil War the Confederacy has become the Confederate myth, a past elysium, a romanticizing of provincial convention. Defensiveness against the North accentuated the worship of martial heroes from Andrew Jackson to Robert E. Lee. W. J. Cash has claimed that with economic change and hardship the cult of the gentleman narrowed and ossified, and that the Great Depression, which hit the South especially, increased the number of those who sought escape in fanaticism. More recently in Mississippi, James Silver has described the great mass of educated citizens as looking to the future with foreboding, feeling that "time is fast running out" when the larger society will tolerate their ways, yet largely preoccupied with their notions of "athletic prowess, feminine pulchritude and evangelical religion."[17] This is Mississippi, the most adamant state: of course the white-caste behavior of many Southerners is softening, and with others there is an underlying, secret readiness for change. But many of these are in cultural limbo. They fell between the convinced integrationists —the crusaders and those few who can explicitly connect new treatments of the black with old patterns of Southern gentility—and the great number who hang tightly on to a hardened cultural orthodoxy.[18]

One sign of the cultural defensiveness has been the success of right-wing movements in the South—the votes for Goldwater and Wallace, and more extreme still, the flourishing of the Birch Society. In 1964 the

---

In Britain today, parents who scrape to send their sons to expensive "public" schools are not repelled by the idea that a lot of strain all around might be saved if the public school system could somehow vanish overnight—if the idea is not put in serious political terms as a socialist, "abolitionist" proposal, they sometimes are attracted in an amused, fantasy way.

sheriff of one Mississippi town told voter registration workers that the whole town was "private property," so they "better keep out." But the right-wing appeal extends far beyond the most obvious political offerings: the attack on civil-rights-minded Federal agencies, the preservation of private property against black demands, and the exalting of states rights. The view that all social critics are agitators or Communists—the terms are nearly synonymous— is traditional in an area where the cry once was "Scratch a reformer and you'll find an abolitionist." At the time, the 1840s and '50s, such simplification was not pure fantasy: there were many ties between abolitionists and other liberal and humanitarian movements which flowered during this period. The Southern response was intellectual suppression and social exclusion; new ideas were feared as subversive; and in later decades a breed of preacher-politicians arose to attack Yankees, atheists, Jews, and other faces of a common enemy.[19] The anti-Semitism which runs through so much of Southern radical-right expression today has some roots in the history of Jewish traders who exploited Southern farmers, and in the continuing reality of urban-intellectual, Jewish liberalism. But also, the racial right's concept of law-and-order and its specter of moral and social "slipping" will command great force where race fears inflame basic human concerns about anarchy, and where compromising can be labeled "mongrelizing." Many of these factors are not confined to the American South: in Rhodesia and South Africa, too, it is not surprising that white-caste defensiveness has produced radical-right censorship and demonology.

The interaction of orthodoxy and threat has produced, on the plane of individual character, some distinctive emotional tendencies. Taken each by itself, these are not confined to authoritarians, but they are surely conducive to authoritarianism in those cases where other factors —an economically, frustrated father, for instance—have enlarged the individual's sense of weakness.

A marked trait among some educated segregationists is a defensiveness which seems to mask doubt, moral anxiety, and perhaps even guilt. To the friendly visitor from the North or abroad, a Southerner may well start defending segregation before the visitor has mentioned the subject. The core of the defense is often a rationalization in conventional humane terms: "Relations between black and white are really very good." To this may be added a more bitter scapegoating: "All the trouble is caused by agitators and misfits." In New Orleans, I met a segregationist ex-marine who raised the topic by attacking South Africa: "It's terrible how they treat them there." In many of these cases the individual seems to be speaking to himself, anxiously seeking to disarm or deflect inner criticism.[20] The tendency of white Southerners to exaggerate the rebelliousness of Southern blacks, to read aggressive intent into the most minor accident, set off by the most docile individual, may in part reflect a guilt about the blacks' oppression.[21] It may also sometimes represent projection. From extensive sessions with Southern white children, Robert Coles claimed that they attributed to black children their own feelings of weakness or loneliness or angry defiance, and all sorts of things that the white child struggled to avoid: bad manners, disobedience, dirtiness, carelessness, and so on.[22]

Another tendency has been a fascination with black sexual power, coupled with rape horror and visceral reaction against the slightest sign of physical intimacy between races. Now to some extent these concerns reflect traditional beliefs rather than inner conflict. Where people are taught that "race mixing" is an assault on a cherished, even hallowed way of life, and a threat to one's personal identity, the smallest sign of miscegenation may produce horror without necessarily meaning that the person concerned has a "sexual hangup" or precarious self-esteem. And when people are told, as they have been, that black males have unusually large genitals and that black males and females are sexually free and extraordinarily potent, many of the same people may be expected to take vicarious pleasure in these "facts." The amount of conflict between desire and taboo or inhibition may be no more than the normal amount of conflict found in any society where curbs on sexual behavior help provide a market for celluloid and printed sex. As for the famous Southern "rape complex," this partly stems from beliefs about black male virility, and the concern itself has become a learned attitude.*

---

* In his nasty but useful novel *The Klansman* (1967), the Southern writer William Bradford Huie gives descriptions suggesting that far more sexual-racist beliefs may be traditional and relatively non-pathological, in a psychiatric sense, than many Northern psychologists realize. At the same time one can see in his caste of characters different mixtures of learned belief and desperate need.

As a reminder that sexual racism is found in the North too, we can turn to no less an exhibit than *The Making of the President, 1964*, by Theodore White (1965). "The biological anarchy" of Northern Negro families (a repeated and misleading phrase); the threatened New York "stall-in" by black drivers, described as reaching for the "groin" of the city; the praise of Martin Luther King and other new young black leaders for being so clean and handsome; the indiscriminate venom against Black Power leaders, contrasting with the thrilled description of most political leaders—and all this from a kindly liberal.

But the matter cannot be left here. Putting aside the question of how these sexual concerns first became a tradition—what sorts of personality advanced the process—there are signs even today that for some people the concerns can involve marked conflict and reflect emotional deprivation. And that for *some* of these people, the conflict is managed by sadism.

The Southern white author John Howard Griffin has told of hitchhiking in Mississippi, having darkened his skin so that he passed as a black.[23] It was much easier to get rides after dark, and of the dozen or so whites who picked him up, virtually all began pumping him for lurid sexual information. "They appeared to think that the Negro has done all those 'special' things they themselves have never dared to do." It was a "verbal pornography" and they had to have it; on the questions came, stripped of respect for the questioned. Griffin would try to change the conversation, plead he was tired and couldn't think—to no avail. Some of the questioners began obliquely, others were brutally demanding. One of the latter type clearly enjoyed the idea that the blacks must want white women, and vice versa: "There's plenty white women would like to have a good buck nigra." The potential conflict between this enjoyment and the fear of black sexual aggression is obvious, but there was also the immediate element of shame. In a car at night the driver could keep some anonymity; he did not have to face the questioner; and there were no witnesses.

This suggestion of furtiveness, coupled with the *"must* know" quality of the questions, did indicate some sexual maladjustment. One of the drivers who picked up Griffin showed a semi-overt homosexuality. An educated young man, he couched his sexual questions in the language of abstract scholarship, yet even here "the tone was subtly conniving": questioner and questioned would go about their sexual research together. Finally he asked his passenger to expose himself to him, saying that he had never seen a naked Negro. After a painful silence, the young man apologized in a numb, humiliated voice, anxious to explain he was no "queer." It is significant, perhaps, that this was one of the friendliest, most kindly-seeming, of that night's drivers. The others, on the whole much more callous toward Griffin, nonetheless did not press so far their vicarious enjoyment of his supposed sexuality. Did the more overt homosexual have less need to erect a defense of scorn against the object of interest? Patrick Gant, an English student who recently lived in Georgia and other parts of the United States, has suggested that overt homosexuality may be the tip of an important iceberg in the Deep South.[24] Around certain white college communities in Georgia he found more public signs of overt homosexuality than anywhere else he visited in the country (more attempted pickups and so on); but far more common was what seemed to him to be *covert* homosexual trends: indulgence in a sweaty, male fellowship, fascination with "perverts," virulence against "sex maniacs" and blacks who might assault their womenfolk. He also said he knew a number of white women who indicated that they or their friends were not really satisfied sexually by their husbands, who were apt to put them on pedestals of purity. Gant said he had noticed a surprising proportion of families where the man had married a person much younger than himself, quite late in life. Again, the wife was a symbol of delicate purity rather than direct sexuality.[25]

It is hard to know whether "covert homosexuality" is a fair interpretation; but more professional reports from previous decades give backing to much of what Gant said. Both Cash and Dollard stressed a Southern idealization of white women which dissociated them from sensuality.[26] Combined with puritan mores, it may have been self-confirming, so that some of the women actually became less expressive sexually.[27] Chivalry plus evangelicanism intensified a split image of woman which to some extent pervades much of Western culture: the woman who is a "good lay" is not the woman one loves or respects. But here the caste system intervenes in a way which increases the likelihood of conflict—value conflict, emotional conflict. In the white South it is the black woman who has traditionally been the "good lay" yet the sexual crossing of caste lines must be furtive lest it disrupt the social order. Dollard's study of a Southern town in the 1930s found that middle-class mores were inveighing more and more against such crossing, but it continued. Another source of conflict is the high value set on sexual prowess by Americans including Southerners. Blacks of both sexes really score high on this in the eyes of whites, yet caste codes demand they be considered inferior. The very existence of blacks thus dramatizes the old ambivalence about sex itself: it is good, it is vital, it is *performance;* it is dangerous, it is dirty, it must be hidden. In a broader sense—and this is more speculative—the worship of white woman as a mother figure may exacerbate conflict between passive dependence, nurtured by the "easy-going" emphasis of Southern culture and climate, and the drive to assert, magnified by American values on go-getting and muscular prowess. Economic frustration may enlarge still further a conflict over dependency.*

---

* Observers have described much heavy drinking and drunkenness in the South (cf. Coles, 1967; Banton, 1964), and other studies have connected high

Sadistic aggression against blacks, including both abuse and atrocities, has a number of possible connections with the sex and race conflict. It can reflect sexual jealousy. It can provide enjoyment of alleged black depredations in the very act of punishing them. And so it may couch sensual pleasure within puritan repressiveness. It is not surprising that some Southern prohibitionists used to revel in the specter of the drunken black rapist. A supreme example was the Reverend Wilbur Crafts, whose favorite sermon on liquor described a seventeenth-century Bavarian, supposed to have confessed on the rack that he had eaten thirteen children, having been turned into a wolf by a "devil's girdle." After detailing the wretch's tortures and execution—branded with iron and laced in twelve places for the twelve disciples—the Reverend would cry,

Ask yourselves what devil's girdle has changed so many negroes into sensual hyenas. Remember that during the four years of the Civil War the whole white womanhood of the South, in the absence of husband and brother, in the death grip of battle was at the mercy of the black population of the plantations.[28]

Today such propaganda may seem archaic, but the underlying appeal is not. Sadistic atrocities against blacks, including castration, have continued well into the 1960s and the use of torture in lynchings increased in the twentieth century. Cash argued that

the development of pleasure in violence, of sadism, and the notion that the practice of the thing was a grand way to be a hell of a fellow, probably never by itself produced a lynching . . . [but] it began to generate, among both common whites and planters, a type of deliberate nigger-hazers and nigger-killers, men who not only capitalized on every shadow of excuse to kick and cuff him, to murder him, but also with malice aforethought baited him into a show of resentment in order to so serve him.[29]

This suggests the development of specific personalities which responded to violent practice and took it further. In the past some lynching mobs have been quite large, with sadistic frenzy welling up in great numbers, pieces of the victim fetching a price as souvenirs, and so on. But lynch mobs have had leaders, and those most active in the cruelty may well have had particular traits. It also bears emphasis that lynchers have often shown little care for establishing the guilt of their victim, and

---

drunkenness and alcoholism rates with conflicts over achievement and dependency, including maternal dependency (Bacon, 1965; McCord, 1960), although other Southern factors must not be discounted (cf. Wilkinson, 1970). In a beautiful descriptive passage, Cash suggests a possible link between physical climate and Southern passivity and romanticism: Vintage ed., p. 48.

when the intended victim has escaped, they have sometimes marched to his home, raped his wife, murdered the family, and set fire to his house.[30] The burning need for revenge has easily been swiveled. So it was more recently, just before the murder in Mississippi of the three civil-rights workers. Missing the three in their first attempt, the killers took it out on some black people, who were badly beaten; then turned on each other in recriminations that nearly brought bloodshed; and shortly afterward burned a black church. Add this to the heavy consumption of whiskey accomplished before the murder and one may ask if this was not the behavior of men under tension, snarling and drinking to smother their guilt.

That murder, of course, was an extreme and publicized event. But how much terrorizing has gone unrecorded? "You can kill a nigger and toss him into that swamp and no one'll ever know what happened to him." The respectable-looking Alabaman who said this to Griffin when he gave him a ride had been taunting and half threatening him, insulting his rider's wife, and boasting about white man's freedom with black girls and the helplessness of blacks to do anything about it, yet in a curious way, seeking not just compliance but approval. Having satisfied himself that his companion was not "down here to stir up trouble" (because "you know what we do to troublemakers down here"), he supposed that his companion was just one more black who would take abuse and say nothing afterward.[31]

In connection with this, Griffin raised an important psychological issue. Could it not be that a man like the Alabama driver had shown but one side of his personality to the black person, that for the most part he was pleasant and easy, devoted to his children and grandchildren? With faith as much as knowledge, Griffin believed this could be so. But let us take the question to more technical aspects of personality. Might not many Southerners have an acute sexual complex about blacks, yet in much of their characters still be humane, and also at peace with themselves? Just because a conflict is sexual, must it therefore affect the personality's general integration and functioning? Many psychoanalysts would say yes, taking a stand opposite to the one implied by Griffin. For my part, I would take a position somewhere between the two but nearer to the psychoanalysts? Some characters more than others make fertile ground for a sexual complex about Negroes. A person who has this complex *may*, in nonracial relationships, be quite free of emotional stress, but these relationships are likely to be vulnerable: social and political forces may expand the way he feels about blacks into other areas of his life. For instance, radical-right doctrine on top of economic failure may encourage him to shun almost all new ideas as subversive, and to see in other targets besides blacks a symbol of revolt, defilement and repulsive/attractive sensuality. Unconsciously his feelings about blacks and the way he manages these feelings provide a model for other relationships, whether or not the model is ever used. But, even if he does use it, becoming neurotic and punitive in certain of these nonracial relationships, he may still be a kind father, grandfather, and so on, for the American ethos of manliness encourages a proud fondling of one's young.[32]

Admittedly, the extent of maladjustment can be exaggerated. And for some Southerners, right-wing ideology may help prevent inner moral conflict by presenting social problems in simple patriotic terms. In his novel *The Klansman,* William Bradford Huie describes a sheriff, a Korean veteran, whose patrol car is his tank. To him, "agitators" are the enemy—like the "gooks" in Korea—and the Southern "way of life" is a country to be defended. A childish, basically submissive man, he holds many of the sexual stereotypes of blacks, but he does not hate them and, unlike some other sheriffs, he is not extremely violent. This is a fictional portrait, but it draws on first-hand experience and it seems convincing.[33] Against this, a journalist has given us the nonfictional portrait of a Houston Bircher with a bee in his bonnet about "running checks" on people. Although Houston's left wing was extremely weak, he hired private detectives to protect him from subversion, and he once told the Salesmanship Club, "The John Birch Society does not see a Communist under every bed because American cowards have already taken all the room."[34] This man seemed to fear a more personal invasion than did Huie's sheriff, and right-wing doctrine helped him to point resentments at American softies, not just "the enemy."

It is easy now to imagine how Southern culture foments authoritarianism. For the frustrated it offers the imagery of paranoia. Its chief scapegoats are either racial underdogs, sexual threats and subversives —targets near at hand—or remote Federal authorities.* More hypothetically, we may see in traditional Southern stereotypes an Oedipal function rather like that portrayed by some interpreters of Nazism. The image of the beautiful mother figure defended against black lust may help a young white male to divert unresolved Oedipal feelings. The

---

* Griffin, 1964, describes his graphic experience of a "nigger-hazer" who backed off when challenged, and a bus driver who clearly took out his workaday irritations in a spontaneous piece of racial discrimination: pp. 36-39, 46-47.

racial drama becomes a disguised play in which he protects the woman from brute man (representing his father), but also enacts his own taking of the woman by projecting his desires onto an inferior brute (representing himself). This is just one more way in which learned belief and psychological need may entwine.

18   OTHER SETTINGS

The South apart, we have remarkably little American evidence of authoritarian character, as it is defined here. This is more a statement of ignorance than of fact. Authoritarian pathology may or may not be widespread in some quarters of American life; the point is, we don't know.

Much the same uncertainty applies to the past. In the lives of Tom Watson, Jonathan Edwards, and a few other figures, we have already noted what seems to have been an authoritarian dynamic. But we have no knowledge of authoritarianism among their followers. In my view, the most graphic portrayal of "common man" authoritarianism in a historical American setting is to be found in fiction—Sinclair Lewis's *Babbitt*. Babbitt is, I think, to be taken seriously, not as historical evidence, but as an illustration of possibilities. One-sided as it is, Lewis's creation of a Midwestern businessman shows how, in *some* cases, the social pressures and contradictions which came to a head in the 1920s—all of them very American pressures—foment authoritarianism.[1]

Before his home-town authorities, their business "ethics" and puritan morals, Babbitt groveled earnestly. Yet he resented them, how he resented them. He adored his town, the booming little city of Zenith, but Zenith also bored him utterly, so utterly he could only half admit it. He envied and partially disliked those socially above him, but he longed to receive their favors and be one of them. He spoke vigorously for what he considered a philosophy of individualism, but much of the time he felt happiest when he could cite the clear-cut authority of someone else for what he said. "Principles" meant a great deal to him, but he was extremely dependent on whatever group he happened to be with. He attacked those who did what he dared not do himself; in some spheres a tender man, he made himself narrow and intolerant. Usually repressed, sometimes impulsive, often guilty, he asserted himself in a blustering masculine way. Only with other men, close friends, did he seem to express deep affection—and then he was ashamed of it. His sex life followed a pattern of all-or-nothing control: he was nearly always a paragon of married virtue, but when he went on sexual adventure, he went headlong.

The story of Babbitt ended almost happily, and for an authoritarian, perhaps atypically. Finally recognizing his enslavement, he stood up for his son against his prudish relations. What is truer to the authoritarian is Babbitt's basic tenderness, though perhaps it was unusually overt. Had he been intolerant and assertive through and through—or as much as humanly possible—he might have been less in conflict and hence less authoritarian than an integrated autocrat. Again the irony strikes one, that he who combines humanity with harshness should, in terms of inner structure, be more maladjusted than a person of simpler brutality.

Sinclair Lewis says nothing of Babbitt's childhood, but he does portray a person who feels hollow and weak, unsure of his manhood and his identity. Whether or not it was responsible for these feelings in the first place, one can see how a Zenith culture—combining puritan repressiveness with business demands for assertion—might encourage a Babbitt to manage his weakness feelings in an authoritarian way. Furthermore, the very warfare in Babbitt's soul reflected conflicts in the surrounding culture—"integrity" versus business chicanery; democracy versus exploitation; puritan asceticism versus guilty enjoyment of the fruits of business wealth; acceptance of a prying public conscience, yet the liberal belief that one's own life and thoughts should be private. These themes run through the book; indeed, the portrait of Babbitt is largely of a man caught between competing demands. Some of this crossfire was traditional small-town stuff, the product of petty capitalism and parochial orthodoxies. But Zenith, like others of its kind in the early 1920s, was no longer just a small town. It had factories, the beginnings of labor troubles, and a small bohemian set. Thinking itself to be progressive (which in technical methods it was) it could not see that it had become a *defensive* small-town mind in a larger urban body. Many, indeed, of the stresses that afflicted Babbitt could be traced to a clash between old-fashioned small-town morality and the new freedoms brought by industrialism. Industrialism, in turn, was partly the native product of Zenith but also the vehicle of alien, big-city influences—a taste for high living, greater lenience over sex, radical ideas about labor.[2] Faced with this situation, Babbitt's very submissiveness made it worse. He tried to submit to all of the culture, and because the culture was so very contradictory, the culture's conflicts became his. This suggests a paradox. It is possible that Babbitt (if he existed) was socially abnormal (unusual in his community), not because he defied social norms, but because, on the contrary, he reflected too many of them too keenly.

As already suggested, a fictional portrait can say nothing about the actual prevalence or influence of authoritarians, in the 1920s or any other period. In the context of the 1920s one can give many reasons for supposing authoritarians to have been attracted to militant prohibitionism and, even more, to the resurrected Klan. There is no space here, however, to list these conjectures. Let us turn, instead, to more concrete, if scattered, indications of authoritarianism in more recent decades. We will focus on three very different phenomena: doctrines of political protest, police behavior under stress, and the situation of some Southern blacks.

POLITICAL PROTEST

A word, first, about biases. At the time of writing, it is fair to say that American psychologists have devoted more study to the radical right than to the radical left. With notable exceptions, at least until the recent campus revolt was well under way, they have been readier to ascribe radical-right behavior to "emotional needs" and the stock attitudes of specific temperaments—and left-wing activities to social and moral concerns that are not the special field of the psychologist. Although most academic psychologists are far from New Left, they are still further from Goldwater and the Birch Society, and it is always tempting to "pathologize" those persons most antithetical to oneself. It is also safer.

It must be admitted that the writer who most broadly applied *The Authoritarian Personality* to right-wing groups was not a professional psychologist but a historian, Richard Hofstadter. Unfortunately, he too showed some of these biases. In an influential essay on "pseudo-conservatives" in the late 1950s—extreme anti-Communists and nativists—he alleged that they sought scapegoats for their social insecurities and that, far from being *real* conservatives, they had strong though repressed anarchic feelings. Nowhere did he warn that his assertions were merely hypothetical, nor did he support them with biographical evidence, any more than he did his famous claim that the old Progressive leaders were motivated by status fears and social envy. This is not to say that Hofstadter's ideas, applied to *some* radical rightists of the fifties, were invalid; again, we just do not know.[3]

There have been no studies directly comparing American groups of different political persuasions in terms of authoritarian psychodynamics. Political groups have often been compared by investigators using psychological questionnaires, but these instruments have measured attitudes in a way that does not find out much about personality structure.[4] Perhaps the closest thing to a deep comparison involving authoritarian character is Ira Rohter's study of "radical rightists"—militant anti-communists—and "non-rightists" in a Northwestern city.

Although Rohter mainly relied on attitude questionnaires, he combined the results from a number of these with findings about social situation.[5] Large proportions of the "rightists" showed extremely punitive attitudes. Compared with non-rightists, they also tended to score high on scales designed to measure distrust of others, "intolerance of ambiguity," dislike of compromise, "sense of personal powerlessness" in society and the world, and "closed-mindedness" (including a submissive element). These findings held when rightists and non-rightists of the same class and education were compared.

Sociologically, Rohter found that the rightists tended to come from conservative backgrounds—small town and rural, religious fundamentalist. In their current lives, however, they had encountered stress and insecurity. Over a third—far more than among non-rightists—indicated that they had fallen well below the social class of their fathers; on the other hand, relatively large proportions of rightists in the middle classes indicated that they had risen a great deal. In short, the flux of both downward and rapid upward mobility. The rightists also tended to be either newcomers to their communities or oldtimers in declining neighborhoods.

In view of all these results, it is not surprising that Rohter's rightists were more apt than his non-rightists to say that they did not get the respect they deserved. A quarter of the rightists, far more than of the others, said they were not accepted in their community; and a study of their letters to the press showed that they were prone to praise great men of the past who, they said, had been unfairly treated. They were also apt to believe that influential persons in their community were cliquish and unfriendly. As Rohter saw it, the rightists' political beliefs stemmed from an interaction of traditional values, "authoritarian personality traits," and social anxieties. Ideology provided a way of coping with insecure social status: in response to frustrations they simplified their world and blamed scapegoats.[6]

Illuminating as it is, Rohter's research still does not clearly identify the specific mixtures of submissiveness and aggressiveness that we have called authoritarian. For a sharper identification we must limit our range of vision by using studies which focus on the personality and political beliefs of one or a few individuals. An early example is Nevitt Sanford's psychoanalytic study in World War II of an "American Quisling."[7] As a person who retained pro-Nazi sympathies throughout the war, he showed some independence of mind and spirit; yet, paradoxically, the political views that required this independence could be traced, at least in part, to deep-seated authoritarian anxieties.

The subject was a thirty-five-year-old mechanic—"downwardly mobile," for his father was a successful small-town dentist, his mother a schoolteacher. Very dogmatic, he had a strong tendency to blame others for his mistakes. In manner and speech he was fairly "tough guy," but was extremely deferent to male authorities and seemed to take out much of his general suspiciousness in contradictory accusations against his wife. As a small boy, he reported, he had been afflicted with shame at having to wear some of his mother's made-over underwear. In therapy with Sanford he showed much fear about homosexuality and a fantasy desire to take the woman's role in sex. His father, so it seems, had been prone to fits of violence, and would hurt his mother by boasting of sexual adventures in front of the children. But he worshiped his father; it was the alleged tyranny of his mother which he attacked. He may well have attributed to her some of his father's threat (in his dreams she appeared to have a penis).

American business power and its leaders thrilled him; he declared that, if the Japanese won the war, businessmen would still run the country under them. He often described the German and Japanese leaders as victims of Allied warmongers; but, more quietly, he would also suggest that Germany and Japan were irresistibly strong and that groups like the Jews had no business provoking Hitler. Sanford attributed much of this outlook to early fears of his father's strength and violence: his criticism of the Jews was very like a former irritation with his mother for provoking his father by "yapping about." It must be admitted that Sanford did not quote or cite his subject's political statements in any detail; he did not, therefore, support his inferences by showing the emotional overtones of the political statements made. On the other hand, Sanford's total interpretation does explain what is otherwise very difficult to explain. For the truth was that his subject was *not* a typical right-wing isolationist, an anti-Semitic America Firster of the kind that admired the new German might before the war. Rather, he combined elements of this type with elements of a very different liberal isolationism: that tradition, now again respectable, which would keep America out of foreign involvements in order to focus on humane domestic reform.[8] If he admired the right-wing Charles Lindbergh, he admired only secondmost Henry Wallace and his leftist-Progressive idealism. He once dreamed that his family were housing a Jew and that he was preparing to defend the home against the Gestapo. Quite late in his therapy he joined a picket line to get fair employment for a black. The therapy may have expanded these sympathies, but they were not created from scratch. According to Sanford's explanation, he had deep wishes to identify with underdogs, particularly the feminine oppressed. Feeling, however, that these alignments were dangerous, that they would bring punishment from strong male authority, he turned on the oppressed, the potential rebels —his mother, the Jews. This authoritarian betrayal he masked from himself by reversing the images of oppressor and underdog: his father became the "yapped" against, the Axis leaders the provoked.

This explanation should only be treated as tentative. It does show, however, how conceivably the same political attitudes may express opposite emotions uneasily bridged within one character. In the "American Quisling's" case, so it seemed, humanity was the very yeast of authoritarian reaction.

Moving forward in time to the 1950s, we come to the only published study (to my knowledge) which describes authoritarian character among left-wing political movements. This is Herbert Krugman's survey of psychoanalytic case reports on American Communists and ex-Communists.[9] Krugman gathered material on thirty-five persons in several cities. Nearly all of them were professional-class Jews (a fact not surprising since Jews comprised the great bulk of American Communist party members at the time). Krugman studied in greatest depth the case reports on eighteen people, ten men and eight women. It is not clear whether any of the women were authoritarian, but several of the men seemed to show a largely passive pattern of authoritarian behavior. Five of them evinced strong wishes to submit and "some slight history of overt, passive homosexuality" during adolescence. In more covert form, their homosexual feelings had apparently continued. According to Krugman, they feared "awareness of the feminine component in their submissiveness," while also being afraid to make direct aggressive challenges to authority. Their therapists described them as sado-masochist, turning much aggression onto themselves and, in two cases, onto their wives. Their self-images varied between extremes—from worthlessness to superiority and niceness, too nice to permit much personal assertion. With some of the five there was an attitude of martyrdom, a "bittersweet" anticipation of revenge (again, the sado-masochism). There was also a considerable amount of hypochondria, which was explained as a way of expressing fears of punishment by authority and of seeking fatherly care by doctors.

Although Krugman gave information on the families and social backgrounds of the Communists as a whole, he did not do so specifically for the five men just mentioned. In their cases, however, he did suggest certain ways in which Communist affiliation met the demands of personality. Drawing on the therapists' own inferences, he maintained that the party helped them to submit without guilt and to defer outbursts of hostility by anticipating a future revolution. For others who did not show so much overt submissiveness, the party's main psychological function seemed to be a guilt-free channeling of hostility. These connections, however, were little more than speculative, for the therapists seldom discussed politics with their patients. As a result, they could not pick up the emotional nuance of political belief in the way Henry Dicks did with Nazi POWs. It must also be noted that Krugman's sample was too small to show how prevalent authoritarianism was among all American Communists seeking psychiatric treatment.[10]

In addition to his own survey, Krugman assisted Gabriel Almond in some interview studies of Americans, French, and Italians whose attraction to Communism had seemed to rest partly on deep character needs.[11] In my view none of the published descriptions suggest authoritarianism, though in some cases too little information is given to make a judgment. What does emerge quite often is a variety of rigid *anti*-authoritarianism, some of it involving shame for a weak father rather than oppression by a paternal autocrat. Nevitt Sanford has said, likewise, that his psychoanalytic patients in the 1930s and '40s included Communists who tended to be rigid "Oedipal" rebels, not "inverted Oedipal" authoritarians.[12]

With the early 1960s we come to several studies portraying an authoritarianism of the radical right. An unusual type of study is to be found in Robert Lane's material on the political psychology of twenty-four college students. Two of them, both right wing, seemed authoritarian, and the unusual thing was that they themselves virtually pointed this out in written self-analysis. Both were concerned about how to channel safely their assertiveness, and in both lives an alignment with the powerful against the weak seemed to be connected with fears of ostracism and the harsh demands of their fathers.[13] My own study of a college student, "Roger Stanton" (reported at length in the appendix), tries to put some of these processes into cultural context.[14] The study describes one kind of relationship, or set of relationships, between Goldwaterite views and personality. Insecure in his ambitions and identity, Stanton was ill equipped to deal with the conflicts in values and loyalties that beset him in his long migration from a small-town home to a metropolitan campus. So he reacted against his new freedoms, selectively seizing the most ascetic and elitist of contradictory home traditions. Right-wing views thus facilitated an authoritarian defensiveness; but conversely, authoritarian feelings helped to push further right a political conservatism learned at home.

These individual case studies must be put in perspective. There is no evidence that anything more than a small fraction of the campus radical right has been authoritarian, in our sense of the term. This may be an illusion (authoritarians may tend less than others to volunteer for psychological study). But there is also the possibility that college right wingers, of the political stripe who supported Goldwater, have tended more to be "Jeffersonian idealists," genuinely concerned about aspects of individualism, than crusaders against communist conspiracies; and that the most authoritarian right wingers have been concentrated among the latter group. These two categories, of course, are by no means mutually exclusive, and to be cautious we should not apply them after the mid-sixties. But in my investigations at a West Coast private university I found that the first category prevailed among Goldwaterites interviewed. Few of them were very punitive politically, and only one or two seemed authoritarian.[15] This jibes with James Reston's impression of Goldwaterites who wrote letters to the *New York Times* during the presidential election of 1964. By and large, he reported, the letters fell into two groups—"temperate and troubled" arguments about the trend toward a planned economy and an increasingly powerful Federal government, and shrill polemics on policies toward communism and blacks. Obscene and abusive language, often expressed in the name of the Lord, was almost entirely confined to the second group.[16]

A study of campus "conservatives," done in 1963, supports somewhat the point made above. Lawrence Schiff interviewed and tested forty-seven students from nine varied colleges. They were all members of Young Americans for Freedom or "some equivalent conservative political action organization." Support for Goldwater constituted their central position, but they ranged "from moderate Republicans through John Birch enthusiasts to unreconstructed royalists."[17] Schiff found the most clear-cut instances of authoritarianism in the "relatively infrequent cases" where a militant anti-communism had been adopted in adolescence *and* had not declined in the college years. With these people, anti-communism seemed "most often a part of an underlying asceticism, an accentuated anti-intraceptive and anti-impulse orientation usually brought on by an atypically harsh and punitive upbringing."[18]

The other conservatives were not seen by Schiff as authoritarian in our sense, even though they seemed to share many of the traits found in right-wing authoritarianism. In various ways, their characters combined the following themes: One, "conversion" to conservatism at some point in adolescence or early adulthood, as an anchor amid uncertainties about role and identity—a reaction against the diffusion of self in a permissive and changing environment. Two, intense identification with the conventional values of success-minded fathers. (All but one of the group were either the eldest sons or the only sons in their families.) Three, tendencies to oblique and evasive forms of rebellion against the father, and sometimes an outdoing of the father by becoming more conservative or puritanical than he. Fourth, an ascetic outlook reflecting in part an anxiety about controlling sensual and rebellious impulses. And fifth, passive, security-minded attitude to careers and personal life, combined with a displacement of "risk-taking values" and a romanticized achievement drive in foreign-policy views that stressed brinkmanship and a hard line (the word "hard" was constantly used in this context). These reflected concerns about self-esteem and assertion.

This summary does not cover the many fine inferences made by

Schiff, nor does it indicate some important variations in the types studied—differences, for example, between adolescent and adult "converts." Schiff did claim, however, that none of the group, except the militant anti-communists already described, exhibited a strong desire to exclude outsiders or punish political deviance, and they did not seem to lack normal empathy. They were not cold and domineering people. Strongly prone to hero worship, deeply but ambivalently compliant, they found compensation in tough-minded but not punitive political beliefs.

It is on this last point that Schiff may have underestimated the amount of authoritarianism in his sample. In claiming that most of the group had no strong wish to "exclude," he appeared to base this argument on their lack of overt racism and nativism ("ethnocentrism"). He may have overlooked authoritarian types of aggression expressed somewhat obliquely against targets other than ethnic groups and communists and in ways which did not directly affront democratic convention. Schiff himself quoted a student from a Midwestern small town who traced his conservative conversion to shock at the "undesirable types" he saw in a poor section near his college. Schiff also argued that the "right-wing converts" in his group showed more "need to displace . . . internal aggressive impulses onto socially approved objects" than students in the same group whose political views had moved toward the center.[19] In conclusion we can say that Schiff pointed to a link between authoritarianism and a certain type of militant anti-communism; that the rest of his college right wingers exhibited some traits very like those found at the core of authoritarianism; and that he may have underestimated the number whose patterns of hostility put them into the fully authoritarian class.[20]

As we all know, American radical-right groups extol rugged individualism. Yet investigators of the John Birch Society have been struck by the amount of dumb obedience in and around that quarter, and in personal life I have known several middle-aged right wingers whose tough and angry politics seemed to compensate for curious passivities, an extreme avoidance of "plain talking" face to face, and—in some cases—a feeling that they should be more aggressive.[21] Today one can imagine that a really mean demagogue like George Wallace (behind the moral scourge, an "id" politician) would suit them very well. These elements do not necessarily make an authoritarian personality structure, but they may help to make right-wing milieus congenial to those who do have these structures. For a vivid presentation of submissive-aggressive imagery, complete with sexual overtones, I can do no better than quote two letters printed by the Birch Society magazine, *American Opinion*, in 1965. Neither was typical of *American Opinion* letters except in its admiration of the columnists and its political bitterness. Both were written by women, the first in response to an article on "sex perverts" and the mental-health movement.

A word of praise for a verbal trigger-man and intellectual giant, Jim Lucier ... a real knight with a thrusting sword. He did an excellent job in tackling that story, "For Morality" and calling the shots on the third-dimensional man (unmentionable creatures) described in his writings.

The bleeding hearts, stultifying the population and the air we breathe, make one physically ill. God give us more such men as Dr. Lucier to join the ranks of the courageous, to eliminate that foul element permeating our society, before everything worthwhile is destroyed.

Taylor Caldwell (Blaah!, December *American Opinion*) as always was radiantly profound! My irascibility is directed at females who kicked over the traces during the "bath-tub-gin-era" and assumed a role they are unfit to handle. These vacillating Eleanors browbeat their consort, and defy anyone to make a MAN of their sons. Society has reaped a clique of womanish-acting pragmatists who call themselves, of all things—men.

And I always thought that a young lady should marry a MAN—not a mother-in-law! Blaah![22]

Let me leave it to the reader to make his own analysis of these letters, and turn instead to some conclusions about authoritarian character and the recent radical right. I will confine myself to two points. First, the radical right seems to have been more important to authoritarians than authoritarians have been to the radical right. We have seen evidence that radical-right beliefs and activities have provided psychological services for authoritarians; we have not seen evidence that authoritarians have been a vital bastion of the radical right, be it as followers, leaders, or publicists. If such evidence exists, it has not so far come to light.[23]

The second point may at first seem to contradict the first. Authoritarians may well be overrepresented (compared with their prevalence in the whole country) in some of the key psychological and cultural constituencies of the radical right. Consider, for example, Protestant fundamentalists in the early 1960s. Several surveys show that these people tended more than others to be radical-right supporters and activists, and the findings hold when social class is allowed for and the South and small-town backgrounds excluded.[24] The fundamentalist origins of radical-right leaders in this period, and the revivalist tone of their meetings and addresses, have also been noted. Many fundamentalists may have held right-wing views very largely because of religious and moral doctrine: they wished to defend Protestant virtue—including the Protestant ethic of personal striving—against atheist communism and other "weakening" forces. But it has also been suggested that fundamentalism can develop, sanction, or reinforce a whole outlook conducive to radical-right belief. This is as much a matter of cognition as of morality. A division of the world into moral blacks and whites, the damned and the elect; the personification of evil; a conviction that sinners should be pursued; a belief that the very details of hallowed doctrine cannot and should not be adjusted to changing circumstance; a fear of heretics and those who would corrupt doctrine almost more than of the Devil (or communist power)—these and other attitudes may be magnified by fundamentalist belief. It is not surprising that right-wing American fears of communism and socialism have borne remarkable likeness to the puritan fears of Catholicism found in seventeeth-century England: the concern about feline Jesuit subversives, the specter of military as well as moral threat, the association of enemy doctrine with dirty, savage Irishmen. There is also a parallel between the monotonous, fascinated charting of communist successes and American sellouts by far-right speechmakers and the long cataloguing of sins in the old puritan diaries, not to speak of the apocalyptic detail marshaled in lengthy sermons.

It has already been argued that puritan creeds make a nourishing environment for authoritarianism, especially when social change puts them on the defensive and promotes personal insecurities. In America, then, as in Nazi Germany, a disproportionate number of authoritarians may have grown up in milieus where right-wing beliefs were ready to hand, respectably available for emotional service. This is not to say that fundamentalism has provided the only context in which authoritarian feelings and American right-wing beliefs are brought together; on the other hand, there is still no evidence that authoritarians have constituted so *large* a proportion of any rightist-prone constituencies as to have a crucial impact on radical right fortunes.[25]

POLICE BEHAVIOR UNDER STRESS

As an "urban problem" of the sixties, police behavior and its control has been much discussed. Only a few points on the background will here be made.[26]

In American democracy the police are a "minority group," called upon to do society's dirty jobs, and not all of them glamorous jobs. Their status and pay are *not* abysmal—many occupations are lower in both—but they are low in relation to the power they hold and the authority they must show.[27] Small wonder that they seem particularly prone to illegal violence when they believe the victim has shown disrespect.[28] Largely untrained to cope with race relations (at least until recently) or understand the complexities of modern-day poverty, they have, of course, a well-known record of prejudice and brutality, but they have felt aggrieved when blacks, liberals, and radicals seem to exaggerate that record and demand greater civilian checks on "the force." There is also the fact that many Northern police forces have large proportions of Irish Catholics, often of working-class background but aspiring to middle-class respectability. All the "backlash" anxieties —about black encroachments and black militance, about student "abuse of privileges," about inflation—would affect just these people.

Do police forces attract authoritarian personalities? Or do their unhappy status and the exigencies of police work simply produce intolerant attitudes, including a conformity to codes of tough behavior and attitude? We do not know the answers to these questions. The police may well tend to attract a variety of personalities, and I would not claim that authoritarians predominate among them. Hypothetically, however, it may be argued that (1) police jobs are particularly attractive to authoritarians in America; (2) some of the experiences encountered by the city policeman in America are liable to bring out any authoritarian tendencies that he may have. All this in spite of the fact that American policemen are *no* more brutal than their opposite numbers in many other countries.[29]

Certainly the chance to practice a pseudo-legitimate violence has attracted the sort of person who enjoys harassing "niggers," "shitty winos," "queers," and "punk kids"—"whores" too, as opposed to "nice women."[30] At the same time, policemen have been known to displace aggression from strong or authoritative offenders onto less-powerful persons—loafers, bystanders, photographers.[31] Then again, the clear-cut structure and requirements of a police force may offer refuge from the ill-defined and democratic relationships of civilian society. The same may apply to the military and to other strict command organizations, such as hospitals. The authoritarian secretary of a professor, described in an earlier chapter, was made very uneasy when she exchanged a previous career in the women's military for the slack and fluid relationships of an academic department.

All this suggests a paradox: that in the most democratic and permissive societies, important "command organizations" will house an unusually high proportion of people who are basically undemocratic and restrictive—among whom authoritarians are just one kind. How far a tight and hierarchical organization can *assuage* authoritarianism is not known, but one would not expect it to in the case of the police. On the contrary, the defensive moral position of police in many American communities, contrasting with the aggression demanded of individual policemen in their duties, may encourage an authoritarian response to doubts about their role. Unlike the military base, the police force is not a total institution insulating its members all round the clock from outside contacts and from the need to make constant shifts from professional to "civilian" roles. For the police, too, the public they serve can at any moment become enemies and quarries; no other occupation group has continually to face this sort of flux.*

Stresses like these are by no means peculiar to the United States, but American culture adds some special twists of its own. An extreme example, possibly involving authoritarianism, can be seen in the background of the Algiers Motel atrocity—the alleged police killing of three black youths, and the sexual harassment of their white prostitute companions, during the Detroit riot of 1967.† Of the three policemen most implicated, two served on a "cleanup squad" and were responsible for detecting and arresting prostitutes. Their duties, as such, were created by two somewhat contrary demands. On the one hand, they were aggressive enforcers of a puritan law against "accosting and soliciting." On the other hand, democratic safeguards for the citizen demanded clear evidence of accosting and soliciting (the customer, or "John," was not classed an offender). This meant that the policeman

---

* More than a century ago, Alexis de Tocqueville suggested that especially undemocratic Americans would find refuge in the military. The police, of course, may attract many authority-minded and romantically inclined characters who are still not particularly punitive. A successful London doctor who treated nervous disorders by auto-suggestion before the First World War claimed that policemen were particularly "suggestible," and indeed even too prone to become totally hypnotized (see Woolf, 1960, pp. 100-101). A psychologist, Max Levin, who spent some time with Los Angeles police; told me he found two salient groups: balanced and rational persons, keen on professional self-improvement, and a smaller group of criminal haters with strong dependency on the hierarchical organization. See also Stern, 1962, on West Pointers (pp. 692-694).

† The basic information for this analysis is taken from Hersey, 1968. Despite gaps in his account of the incident, Hersey's book is unusual in its attempt to follow through the lives of individual policemen, before and after joining the force. A police report of the episode cited witness of the killings by other law-enforcement officers. The policemen were brought to trial, but both a city court and a federal court acquitted them on insufficient evidence.

had to become a decoy, exposing himself to the prostitute's inducements in order to get evidence that would stand up in court. Yet the two policemen mentioned above were, in a sense, wholesome types; they valued order and cleanliness and "nice" women. There are some indications that their duties warped their sexual attitudes, increasing their distrust of women in general and inhibiting their relationships with the "nicer" sort. Most of the prostitutes they encountered were black, and blacks they generally despised and feared. Their very job associated sex and race with danger, for prostitutes occasionally lured customers into positions where their pimps could assault and rob them. In private, the policemen voiced various aggrievements at the system for which they worked, the impersonal demands, the meager rewards; yet they did not really blame the system. Add this to the panic conditions of the riot, its bewildering, warlike chaos, the killing of a patrol mate, and the upsetting orders which obliged them to be the passive witnesses of looting—every one of these an event which helped to disconnect morality from subsequent action—consider these things and the atrocity becomes explainable; the unleashing of sexual revenge served many needs. One is reminded that public office in America seldom enjoys that strong elite tradition which makes the office itself a reward, something above ordinary passions, in return for its protection from private exploitation by the holder. This, and the puritanism of some American laws, may make it easier for private moralisms to take over the policeman's role.

A connection between these "police pathologies" and right-wing animus can be seen in Bruce Jackson's study of "police on the junkie beat," a special New York unit assigned to drug offenses.[32] Jackson describes his time with "Sam," an undercover agent operating in Greenwich Village.

We walk to the Rienzi, where we are to meet someone named Wilson [Sam's] informer. Wilson isn't there, and Sam curses him, saying he can't stand an unpunctual man. [Just before this Sam had himself been an hour late.] He tells me the statistics reporting 60,000 addicts in the United States are all wrong, there are hundreds of thousands of them. I must have looked incredulous because he says, "Yeah, man, I'm serious. Look around you. Half these people smoke weed."

"You don't get addicted to marijuana. They're not addicts."

"Goddam right they are."

We walk down the street. Someone says hello to me, and I nod. Sam says, "I'll tell you who uses weed all the time: those folk singers. Bunch of addicts."

"Oh."

"You know any of those folk singers?"
"A few."
"They use weed."

We pass one place just as a four-man singing group is going in with their guitars. They pass in front of us. One of them sees me and waves: another says, "Hi, Bruce." I wave back. Sam looks at me queerly, then shrugs it off.

We go back to the Rienzi and talk about Court decisions [Supreme Court cases limiting police interrogations]. "Those bastards. What this country needs is a Hitler for a while. Get these people off the streets. Should have elected Goldwater: he'd have straightened that Court out. You know why I hate addicts?" I shake my head. "I'll tell you why: I got a nice wife over on Staten Island. She never heard a dirty word in her life. A nice girl." He says it with finality.

According to Jackson, several other members of the drug squad had very different characters. At least one of them showed empathy for real addicts. Sam's harsh and stereotyped views were not simply a product of police mores, for even within the one police unit the symbiosis of cop and deviant could take varied forms, depending in part on personality. On the other hand, police conditions and mores may well have developed Sam's punitive, defensive disposition by accommodating his morality and thrusting him at deviants.

As in the Detroit atrocity, serving on a vice squad may have imposed particular strains while attracting perversely the sort of individual most vulnerable to these strains. But the sanction for a punitive abhorrence of weakness and dirtiness is not confined to these humble reaches of American policedom. Over twenty years ago, from the directorship of the FBI, J. Edgar Hoover was inveighing against "crime-coddlers," "moo-cow sentimentalities," "convict indulging theorists," "hoity-toity professors," "mealy mouthings," whining pleas for sympathy," and (a favorite phrase) "mental halitosis"! Since that time, his aggressive concern about "weak" characters seemed to continue. and so had his exaggeration of Red conspiracies and his shrill glamorizing of selected criminals.[33]

THE BLACK OPPRESSED

In describing the scars wrought on character by the black person's suffering, psychologists—black and white—have emphasized a forced submission and its warping effect on the "handling of aggression."[34] Moral prejudice, the threat of social outrage, economic sanction, and physical terror have, in the past, not only diminished self-esteem and produced contempt for one's own, but have led to "oppression phobia":

a sense of foreboding, a fear of imminent punishment for being simply what one is.[35] Amid the present currents of black protest, it may seem insultingly out of date to speak to these problems; but I shall do so, even if the discussion applies to past and older generations rather than new ones.

In his famous treatise on slavery, Stanley Elkins related some of these themes to what may at first seem an authoritarian character type.[36] In comparing the treatment of black slaves with the breaking of prisoners in Nazi concentration camps, Elkins drew heavily on a source that we have already discussed as a document of authoritarianism—Bruno Bettelheim's concentration-camp report. Arguing along the same theoretical lines, Elkins claimed that the shock of uprooting from African cultures, the privations of the long sea journeys, and the special totality of the "peculiar institution" (by contrast with black slavery in Brazil), produced identification with the oppressor, a childlike dependence on the all-powerful master, and in other ways, too, an infantile regression. The result, Elkins contended, was the "Sambo" character type, or tendency. Other writers, by no means confined to Southern propagandists, have suggested that elements of Sambo, including a basic submissiveness—"white is right"—survived long past the days of slavery.

But in one respect the analogy between plantation and concentration-camp character types breaks down. Nowhere in his portrait of Sambo does Elkins depict the punitive aggression against fellow "inferiors" which so characterized prisoners of the S.S. Where the latter showed a harsh, moral pedantry, the former showed an easy-going sensuality—although this merged with the need for immediate gratifications exhibited by the German camp inmates. Some of this difference may be traced to the example and requirements set by the masters: the S.S. were more constantly brutal; the Southern overseers and owners were more prone to encourage a certain day-to-day self-indulgence among the slaves. A related element, long surviving slavery, may have been an Afro-American religious attitude which, though fundamentalist, stressed salvation rather than deep and utter sin. Religious teaching did not encourage a guilt-ridden assault on moral rejects; even the Devil was apt to appear a trickster more than wickedness incarnate.*

---

* Some of these points were made to me by Ben Sidran, a jazz musician who has studied black music in its social and psychological aspect. Cf. Sidran, 1970. In an F scale comparison of black and white freshmen in a Southern state, the only statement with which blacks tended to disagree more than whites was: "Every person should have complete faith in a supernatural power that he obeys without question." See Smith and Prothro, 1957.

From what Elkins says, it is conceivable that many plantation blacks turned their rebelliousness onto themselves in self-contempt. But hostility turned upon self can go with unauthoritarian tendencies—low need to blame others, *overt* view of self as weak and inferior, and some degree of self-probing and tender feeling.[37] (A contemporary comparison of college students found that blacks in the Deep South scored particularly high on "intraception," the opposite of the archetype authoritarian's self-censorship.[38]) In the late 1950s Abram Kardiner did produce from his studies of Northern blacks a picture of what he claimed to be a salient personality type, which resembled in many ways a passive authoritarian. As he saw it, racial discrimination often produced low self-esteem and tight curbs on aggression, which led among other things to general suspiciousness, a "fear of looking into anything too deeply," and an "ingratiating but removed" quality of behavior.[39] Kardiner also diagnosed a projection of self-hate onto other blacks, but he gave no evidence showing the extent of these alleged tendencies, and he assumed too readily that a black's contempt for other blacks meant dislike of self. In my opinion only one of the twenty-five Harlem case studies reported by Kardiner showed an authoritarian pattern of stifled and diverted anger (the case of "A.T.," a woman). Kardiner's studies, indeed, tapped many mixtures of dependence and assertion, and at least a few of his subjects showed a spirit of revolt that was far from authoritarian.[40]

More must be said, however, on the question of black hostility to blacks. First, it is a historical fact: among both middle- and lower-class blacks there has been a widespread tendency, conscious or unconscious, to be ashamed of Negritude as a symbol of moral inferiority.[41] The Black Power movements and the sign of the Black Panther do not contradict this; in part they are reactions against it. To a large extent, underlying contempt for Negro-ness has concentrated on traits popularly associated with lower-class blacks, but racial prejudice and class contempt are entwined. Blacks themselves have been apt to stigmatize skin color according to its darkness; in the recent past, at least, the higher the black's economic level, the lighter his skin tended to be; in part this may have been the result of white discrimination, but it also appeared to stem from the psychic and social handicaps inflicted upon the darker person by family, fellows, and self.[42]

The second point is that black contempt for blacks does not necessarily involve the full set of mechanisms underlying authoritarian hate. For one thing, racial contempt, like lower-class black hostility for other minority groups, has become a culturally-learned attitude. Hence the color slurs such as "black-assed" and "nigger" which young lower-class blacks have often learned to deploy in mockery or abuse among themselves. For another, when these learned attitudes are used to meet personal needs such as the wish to dissociate oneself from one's own disadvantaged group, this does not invariably entail displaced rebellion or projected self-hate. (As we have already noted, the social aspirant who turns from his own does not have to be authoritarian.) It should also be remembered that, despite underlying wishes to be "like white," a hostile stereotyping of whites was widespread among Northern blacks well before the 1960s riots.[43]

It is true that accounts of violence in black ghettoes, both North and South, have described patterns whereby general frustrations and/or aggressive feelings toward whites are taken out on safer targets, those nearest to hand—a wife, a child, a drinking companion.[44] To what extent this involves authoritarian character structure has not been shown; in some cases it may well do so. In the South there have also been reports, both in past decades and more recently, of a type of black who, by presenting a shining visage to white protectors, obtained power with which to bully his own race.[45] Not all of this, however, need signify authoritarian character. Some of the classic Southern submissiveness to whites was highly conscious and even exploitative: "yassir" could be a con game deliberately played to mock the white man or manipulate him in real or imagined ways. When this behavior was accompanied by domination of other blacks, the result could be a Dr. Bledsoe, the black college president so vividly portrayed by Ralph Ellison.[46] Another pattern, again not necessarily authoritarian, involved a temporary suppression of rebelliousness, so that the individual felt deferent when facing white authority yet angry soon afterwards.[47] But Elkins himself pointed out that deliberate compliance could merge with submissiveness based on inner need. The submissive person might not know all his motives for choosing the role of clever compliance; vice versa, the conscious or semi-conscious assumption of a role might alter the way feelings are unconsciously managed.[48] Thus the black who cleverly complied could play a greater psychic price than he realized: loss of self-esteem, for example, and the suppression of some doubts and resentments. So, even when he privately expressed rebelliousness against white power, some of the resentment and rebellion might still be controlled by displacement onto others. This pattern would amount to authoritarianism, if not the archetypical kind.

The most detailed evidence of authoritarian character in black individuals is to be found in the studies of New Orleans teenagers in the 1930s, by Davis and Dollard, and the follow-up studies of New Orleans adults in the 1950s, reported by Rohrer and Edmonsen.[49] Fourteen people in all were described in enough detail to let us make judgment about authoritarianism. Of these fourteen, I would suggest, two persons were strongly authoritarian, and three others showed some tentative signs of the character. The most common factor seemed to be a parent or guardian who amplified the more repressive demands of white conventionalism without being able, thereby, to protect the young person from the stress of being black and socially insecure. For reasons which we shall discuss later, it seems that females were specially liable to be involved in this pattern, both as oppressors and oppressed.[50]

We will look first at "Jeanne Manuel," one of the teenagers studied in the 1930s, and we will compare her with "Ellen Hill," a subject of the same original research. In some ways the two girls were alike, but in crucial respects they were not. Jeanne seemed very authoritarian, whereas Ellen was more directly and overtly rebellious. We will follow up this comparison with a commentary on "Ruth Lowell," a middle-aged and authoritarian hospital worker described in the second group of New Orleans studies, done in the 1950s. Finally, and more briefly, we will note three borderline cases drawn from both periods.[51]

Jeanne Manuel was Catholic and a "colored Creole"—Negro with a family history of French language and custom. Her parents were lower middle class, but high status compared with most New Orleans blacks.[52] Solemn and rather humorless, Jeanne was a snob, despising poor whites ("cheap ole pecks") as well as poor blacks. For whites as a whole she felt ambivalent envy. Being light-skinned, she knew she might be able to "pass"—some acquaintances had done so and found it "much better"—but she never tried it. Her mother had taught her to be proud being Creole, not to "play with them little black niggers," but not to try to look white either and especially to keep away from "pecks." Jeanne told her Creole interviewer that she thought "there should be three classes of people: white, Creole, and colored. It wouldn't matter if they had some dark ones in the Creole group, so long as they were nice, but I wouldn't go around with them."

Her family's economic lot was precarious, largely because of the bad health of her father. Her mother was something of a joiner, and it was clear from interviews with the family that she pinned social hopes on Jeanne. Unsuccessfully she had tried to hide economic worry from her four girls: she was determined that they should not get jobs or marry young. The family's straits were a matter of pain to Jeanne, a thing to be concealed. The home atmosphere did not seem harsh; the father was firm but generous and affectionate, and Jeanne said her mother talked more fiercely than she acted. Nevertheless, the mother administered a severe regime and this was reinforced by a grandmother. At an early age the children had their hands spanked for playing with themselves; they were put into tight panties at eighteen months with the express purpose of making this more difficult. At twelve Jeanne still did not know that babies came from mothers, and as a teenager her dating was controlled almost to the point of discouragement. From various sources she had learned that sex was dirty and nasty; she remembered her first menstruation as a painful time when "I kept on losing blood"; and the idea of sleeping with her husband was abhorrent to her. Inhibited at dances, she tended generally to withdraw from people, and even her own family called her "dry," a term they apparently used to mean lack of spontaneity.

In conjunction with her repressed nature Jeanne showed great uneasiness about challenging authority. From an early age she had been exceptionally unprotesting; more completely than many children, she adopted a pattern of doing whatever her parents wanted lest their love be withheld. She was now proud of her obedience, and extremely dependent on both mother and father. As a baby, she had been slow in learning to walk and this may have increased her dependence. At fifteen she was still afraid to go bathing unless her mother was there. But her coolness gave her some poise in emergencies: she was reliable; she did not lose her head. She prided herself on being more like her mother than anyone else could possibly be. By the time she was five years old she had become a "little mother," keen to learn about shopping so that she could go on errands by herself. Independence, when shown, was largely in the image of a parent.[53]

There were four girls in the family, and Jeanne was the second oldest. She was bossy to all her sisters, and not liked as a result. She had tried to stop the family calling her youngest sister "baby," and when the next youngest was born, she had been very jealous, demanding to be held in her stead, and so on. The sister became a spirited "little pepper" and Jeanne sometimes tussled with her. But the parents strongly forbade fighting (the family lacked safety valves), so when her sisters attacked her, Jeanne would usually complain to a parent rather than fight back. According to Jeanne, even her mother would say, "You are always telling your daddy when they hit you." Jeanne told the interviewer that she thought the second youngest was nice, but did not want her "getting feeling too big." And, in explaining why she did not like her little sisters to go anywhere with her, she exclaimed, "They're too disgusting, that's why." And she boasted, "I boss 'em around." She considered herself more mature than her older sister—"acts just like a child." Her identification with a mother's role made little room for the joys of petting an infant: she said she would have liked to have an older brother but not a little one. Jeanne constantly attacked her sisters from the position of model daughter–parent (she was sincerely the most religious of the girls). She once admitted that she wished she was the only child, and while many children may at some time wish the same, in her case, the feeling seemed to be particularly pronounced.

Much of Jeanne's bossiness, prudery, and snobbery she had learned from her parents. It reflected an in-between caste position—so nearly white and yet so far. This was entangled with economic fears; as the authors of the study pointed out, blacks were particularly vulnerable to class decline, owing to their weak bargaining position and lack of redress against employers. Despite these stresses, Jeanne was not *very* authoritarian along some dimensions: identification with her parents was relatively solid. On the other hand, maladjustment showed in sexual fears and in extreme jealousy of her sisters despite apparent favoritism by her father. Her concentration of hostility upon social inferiors and "babylike" sisters, coupled with great obedience to authority, suggests strongly an authoritarian displacement reinforcing the repressive attitudes she had anyway learned. As a result she exceeded her own family norm; hence, she was considered "dry" and her mother could remark on her telling tales to the father.[54]

"Ellen Hill" makes a fine contrast with Jeanne. She was a light-skinned fourteen-year-old, a year younger than Jeanne at the time of the interviews. (She and her family were interviewed by a black professional-class woman.)[55] Even more than Jeanne's her family was subject to social decline and economic stress. The father had been a waiter and baker, had lost jobs through drinking, and deserted his family just after Ellen entered junior high school. For some of her childhood the family lived with the maternal grandmother, a very matriarchal figure. The infant Ellen received from her mother a harsh toilet training; the authors of the study—Allison Davis and John Dollard—suggested that this produced her extreme concern with cleanliness and her "stubborn, retentive, acquisitive qualities." Her mother whipped her for handling herself and for playing "mamma and papa" and "having a baby" with her two older sisters. At the time of the interviews she had no social contact with boys. The male she did know, her alcoholic father, swung between generosity and aggression, but she learned to appease him. To both parents, indeed, she was winning and compliant, whereas she often attacked her sisters and was jealous of the two girls younger than she.

In much of this she resembled Jeanne. But there were differences. In childhood her main attacks were concentrated on an older sister, a "good" girl both at home and at school. She said she did not want to be like her parents, although this was partly on grounds of weakness; she became ashamed and contemptuous of her father and she declared that her mother cried too easily. But the main point was that her exploitative compliance with her parents never repressed an independent and rebellious spirit. Ambitious and insecure, appalled by her family straits, she sought to dissociate herself from lower-class acquaintances and to move among upper-class and light-skinned school friends; yet she was no "apple polisher"; she fought against class discrimination by teachers at school, and she attacked all "teachers' pets." Davis and Dollard argued that she abandoned compliance in favor of rebellion when the former did not work; her school was largely Creole and the teachers may well have discriminated against her personally on grounds of social class. But the authors also believed that she could not stand "*any* final subordination." Unlike many middle-class blacks of the kind she identified with, she defied some forms of segregation. While rationalizing her acceptance of a "colored" gallery at the movies, she was quite prepared to challenge to his face the shoe-store clerk who tried to segregate her from white customers. In shops and buses, her aggressive protest against discrimination was rare for any New Orleans black at the time, let alone a small fourteen-year-old girl. Her defiance went against the wishes of her mother and respected grandmother. She wanted to be a Negro champion, coupling that role with success as a doctor or lawyer.

Why did Ellen not respond to oppression in a more authoritarian way? One might cite a number of circumstances: the larger proportion of *older* sisters as potential targets of hostility; fainter family taboos on overt aggression; a weak paternal image and a mother who oppressed her but then seemed weak; a different school experience from Jeanne's; more outright economic hardship to be blamed on whites.

A particular *combination* of these and other experiences. Yet we would not have been surprised had Ellen's background led to authoritarianism. In this case as much as any, one may suspect that unknown, inborn traits were partly responsible for a different early outcome.[56]

We turn to the second set of studies, and to the case of "Ruth Lowell." At the time of her interviews she was forty years old and worked as a maid in a hospital. She lived with an aunt and was interviewed at various times by both black and white interviewers.[57] Outside of work her only social contact came through punctilious Catholic activities (apparently she was a convert) and a sewing club whose imminent dissolution she did not seem to regret. She had few real friends, other than her aunt, and evidently had never had a sexual relationship. Extremely submissive and always anxious to please her interviewers, she tried to avoid controversy. Rebellion was largely expressed in dreams, which had a strong current of violence. In an earlier interview, at the age of about twenty-three, she had said she hated whites, and in the 1950s she could tell a black interviewer of angry feelings toward a white interviewing psychiatrist. But her irritations were much more focused on blacks. She resented "uppity" blacks who, she felt, had often snubbed her; at the same time she was fascinated with elite black society. She talked constantly about upper-class blacks she had once met who were getting married or making a fortune. She also spent much time talking about the alleged immorality and violence of lower-class blacks; she despised the black patients in the waiting room and emergency wards. She had once been a nurse, but she had abandoned it for various jobs as waitress and maid because nursing seemed "untidy" and "unclean" and sick people "disgusting." She was very closed about herself, insisting that her life was highly satisfactory. In fact she was prone to crying spells, headaches, and diarrhea, and her mind teemed with resentments. She gave long narrations about work mates who imposed on her and teachers at school who had rejected her because she was poor. If these notions had a basis in truth, she at least was exaggerating. She feared that the principal of the school she left eighteen years before was trying to get at her, and psychological tests supported this impression of paranoia. Both interviews and tests portrayed a rigid person with low self-esteem.[58] She complained bitterly that New Orleans lacked places for recreation, when in fact she made little effort to use what facilities there were. At school she had dreamed of marrying a doctor; she was attracted by a larger social world than the small milieus she moved in, but she feared to enter it.

Ruth's mother had died when she was four, her father when she was seven, but from infancy she had lived with her paternal grandparents, who farmed a few acres in Mississippi. She had happy memories of them, but they too had died before she was twelve. In addition to this parade of death—three uncles had also died in that time—she herself, it seems, was not healthy. Going by her own description, she was a nervous and sickly child who suffered from "spells" of unknown cause until she was eight. She had one brother, a year younger than she, but they lived together only for a short time, and she retained virtually no contact with him. On the death of her grandparents she moved to New Orleans to live with her father's sister—the same aunt she currently lived with. Changing schools was described as a shock: having attended a one-room schoolhouse in Mississippi she felt backward in the New Orleans system, although in many respects she was not stupid. In addition to these stresses there was the character of her aunt, a prude whose sexual inquests, and fantasies about Ruth, helped convince the girl that sex was violent and dirty. To cap it all, there was the terrifying presence of her uncle, a vindictive adventurer, who would chase her out of the house, sometimes brandishing a knife. He died in 1938 but Ruth lived in the house with him for thirteen years.

Ruth did not talk warmly about her aunt, but she showed some emotional involvement with her. These feelings seemed ambivalent. She feared her prying, but rather than criticize her outright, was apt to blame their situation on other relatives. In many ways she was a more passive version of her aunt; as an insecure, rejected little girl she had taken over much of the older woman's character. Both women were long on moral indignation: Ruth, for example, disapproved of people who did not observe the Sabbath. Both devoted themselves to cleaning and tidying up the home; it was highly functional that the aunt, too, was a maid (for a white family). Both, indeed, were in slightly different ways the hangers-on of high-status groups while being isolated from their own. Again we have the situation of people in limbo.

In addition to Ruth Lowell and Jeanne Manuel, there were three cases that I have called "borderline" because of uncertain evidence about their psychodynamics and also because of behavior that seemed to qualify the main impression of authoritarianism. Information on one of these, a fourteen-year-old boy, was taken from the first set of studies, done in the 1930s. A "bad kid" from an ill-kept, impoverished home, "Judy Tolliver" was terrorized by his father and in awe of both his parents. Constantly spoiling for a fight, he harassed his teachers and attacked middle-class blacks whom he suspected of selling out to whites. At the same time, there were some indications that he displaced aggressiveness onto relatively weak authority figures—teachers, older girls, his grandmother—who could not punish him as his father could. In view of all his hardships, and in the way he reported his fears and dreams, he was (to me at any rate) an appealing person. Perhaps he was at the border between authoritarian and nihilist rebel.[59]

A very different individual, at least in social station, was "George Morgan," a young professional man in the 1950s. His life had a fluid, almost rootless quality, shuttling between a respectable profession and lower-class, gangland cronies. Vain, showy, and promiscuous, he was extremely dependent on a possessive mother, a socialite active in good works. Like Judy Tolliver, he was persecuted by fantasy fears of pursuit and injury. There were some signs that he had displaced hostility from his mother onto younger, weaker women, including his wife. Quite lacking in tenderness, he was ready to join hands with caste authority against social criticism, when it was safe and rewarding to do so. A materialist to the point of amorality, he may have been more a psychopath—in the deepest sense of that term—than an authoritarian.[60]

The third of our borderline cases was "Florence Lewis," a domestic servant at the time of her interviews in the 1950s. Raised in an unstable lower-class family (absent father, replaced by a series of other men) she had stayed very much under the thumb of a strong mother, who seemed to prefer two younger, lighter-skinned half sisters. Florence Lewis despised her siblings for living (allegedly) in chaos and squalor. Jealousy and displaced resentment of her mother may have been mixed up in these feelings. On the other hand, her treatment of children was lenient and she did not despise her own ethnic group. Often submissive, she was still capable of standing up to white employers and others who she thought had abused her. The authors of the study—Rohrer *et al.*—saw this as a reaction against her own felt submissiveness, but though the interpretation fits, no evidence was given for it.[61]

In the case studies reviewed here, the main immediate power pressing the individual toward authoritarianism was more often a female relative (mother or guardian) than a male either inside or outside the family. Both the New Orleans research and the Harlem studies reported by Kardiner and Ovesey included adolescents in male gangs, but these seemed too rebellious to be authoritarian; and the gang and its leaders lacked the repressive qualities of the snobbish mother or the prudish aunt. The numbers covered by the case studies are probably too small to support a statistical test of the matter, but when these impressions are added to findings from other quarters, we may expect even today to find a special relationship between female sex and authoritarian character among blacks, both North and South.

In the first place, black families are more likely than white families to be female headed (the father absent, often unemployed). The historical and economic reasons for this have been discussed so much elsewhere that they need not be stated here. Some have argued that it is more a feature of poverty than of black life per se, but for our purposes this comes to the same thing, since a disproportionate number of black families are very poor; and some observers argue that matriarchal patterns have carried over into the black middle classes.[62]

The second point is that strong feminine authority in the family would seem more likely to obtain extreme surrender from a girl than a boy. Very close identification is usually more possible with an authority figure of the same sex. A strong mother can say, in effect, to her daughter, "Be a proper woman by following me," more commandingly than she can say to her son. "Be a proper *man* by following me." This is only a likelihood (we have already noted cases where a possessive mother can help engender male authoritarianism).

The third point is that black lower-class women have been more likely than black lower-class men (in both sexes the great mass of blacks) to identify with mainstream values of the larger society against the goading privations of their own lives. This affects the woman both as family authority, potential promoter of authoritarianism, and as potential authoritarian herself. Owing partly to employment patterns—openings in domestic service and certain clerical and sales jobs—black women of the urban lower classes have been more involved in traditional American work values stressing "achievement" and "self-control."[63] To this is added the main brunt of child rearing and the attempt to keep a home together, creating the conservative anxieties of the nest protector. Mainstream standards of sexual attractiveness intensify even further the special pressures on the woman. It is black girls more than black boys who have been made to undergo, at the hands of their mothers, the physically painful process of hair straightening, and the equally painful symbolism involved: "To get more like white I must be hurt; how ugly I must really be." The potential for various kinds of sado-masochism can be imagined. For boys, on the other hand, mainstream canons of attractiveness permit a much greater carelessness about appearance.[64]

As a result of these factors, it has been the ghetto woman who could most easily invoke anti-black stereotypes: the unemployed male seen as a lazy "no-good nigger."[65] Observations of this come mainly from the North, but it is relevant that in a survey of Southern black freshmen from lower- and lower-middle-class families, women as a whole scored considerably higher on the F scale than men.[66] This is a striking fact, for women do not usually score higher on the F scale than men of the same social group, even though women have tended to be more conservative politically, going by several indicators in various Western countries. The difference in overall F scores between men and women does not necessarily mean that the women showed more authoritarian character, but it does suggest that they were readier to agree with statements reflecting a harsh, authority-minded form of mainstream conventionalism. This would help to make a good background for the shaping of authoritarian character in offspring.

COMMON FACTORS

Authoritarian pathology is curiously democratic. It touches here a Northern white policeman, there a black Southern girl; it works through the frustrated and oppressed; they become the frustrators and oppressors. Different though they were, nearly all the milieus covered in this chapter shared, in gross terms, common elements. On the one hand, their members were especially subject to the strains and conflicts of a mobile and diverse society—insecurities of status, clashes of morality, or both. On the other hand, they were dominated by conventional, even old-fashioned codes. In a way, they got the worst of both worlds, the world of failure and deprivation and the world of mainstream respectability. Fearful of losing or being left behind, they could not simply "cop out," for their dominant morality and rigidity of outlook drove them to prune themselves that they might compete in middle-class ways. If they could not prosper, at least they could be proper, attacking "delinquents," who in some ways enjoyed more freedom than they. Their unhappy conformism may, in part, have been impelled by the old-fashioned American myth that everyone can "succeed" who wants to; but it was also due to specific upbringings, combinations of parents and other childhood authorities, which transmitted American values in a particularly demanding and restrictive way.[67]

This interpretation does not apply to all the individuals covered here—it does not, apparently, to the communist authoritarians although little is known about their backgrounds. Also, our emphasis on social and cultural insecurity may reflect, in part, the bias of past studies. Psychologists and social scientists tend to study "problem people" (the poor, the protesting, the violent, the deviant) and our stress on intensive studies of individuals—always a slow business—means that we have had to rely to a great extent on work by other scholars, in order to accumulate enough material to support generalizations. Our findings are thus especially influenced by the orientations of others.

Even so, the factors in American authoritarianism which we have so far emphasized—the interplay of social stresses with demanding traditions—are not confined to those groups which are obviously deprived or affronted. Fictional though it is, the story of Babbitt comes back to remind us that successful *homo economicus* may win his very triumphs at the price of inner turmoil and self-repression; that conversely, his very lack of social deviance may reflect a desperate need to conform, as he seeks to lose his doubts and secure his identity in the tangible products of work; and that such a person's respectable addictions—to work and sociability—may be a veneer over conflicts of value which he has "caught" from the surrounding culture. Today such pathologies may be found among successful professional men no less than among business executives.*

---

* In Arthur Miller's recent play *The Price*, it is significant that the successful man trapped in this kind of net is not a Babbitt businessman (as in *Death of a Salesman*) but a professional man, a research-addicted doctor.

EPILOGUE

AUTHORITARIANISM

AND THE FUTURE

It is impossible to predict whether Western industrial society will become, in the next fifty years or so, more or less hospitable to authoritarian character—encouraging to the behavior, conducive to the disposition.[1] Even with more knowledge of the causes of authoritarianism, we would still face the basic pitfalls of prediction. We simply cannot tell which of the current social trends that are strongest today —evolutions of belief and organization —will be strongest in several decades' time, and in what spheres the strongest counter trends will emerge. We can, however, list some trends according to their possible effect on behavior and personality. In doing this we must consider the possibility of strong cultural reactions against some of today's trends, while remembering that such reactions may have seeds in the very traditions which they challenge—in short, a dialectic.

The following speculations apply primarily to the United States, but in varying degree to most Western industrial societies. In the main they apply to other sado-masochist and submissive-aggressive pathologies besides the pattern we have labeled authoritarian. We will not be able to distinguish much between formative effects on dispositions and "climatic" influences encouraging or discouraging certain types of overt behavior; as already stated, the two effects are apt to merge. Let us first consider, then, some aspects of current trends which may be expected to help prevent or limit authoritarianism.

Accelerating social change, the "generation gap" and other related factors are reducing the authority of elders and loosening still further the nuclear family. This should broaden the focus of a young person's dependency feelings, de-emphasizing the old, intense concentration on parents. At a progressively younger age, allegiance may be spread over more, immediate authorities, so that no one authority seems quite so crucial and unassailable. Styles of leadership, carried into the home from industry, may promote this trend—the overt stress will be on persuasion and diffused authority (à la committees), on motivational "understanding," on psychological techniques which include outlets for protest—in a word, manipulation rather than coercion and threat. We see here the values of "other direction," of the media professions, and of a mass culture so afraid it is falling apart that already a Governor Rockefeller could tell it what it needs: a "sense of purpose *communicated*" to the people—*what* purpose he did not say.[2] Coldly analyzed, such blandness may look silly, but the very discounting of moral specifics in favor of communication per se promotes ideological tolerance. There is a fluidity to modern leadership which runs against the authoritarian's sharp dichotomies, and the spread of education and the more empirical sciences may make it harder for authorities to weave a mysticism which hides the boundaries of their power and taboos rebelliousness. Over the long term, too, science and scholarship may promote an understanding of ethnic variations. Even faster, cheaper travel may affect basic habits of thought and feeling, and reward a person's less-authoritarian tendencies.

Then again, there are the facts of industrial affluence. Expanding leisure, and growing cultural emphasis on the experience of consumption rather than the problems of production, must surely weaken puritan authority and inhibitions. Even the remaining problems of distribution, the concern about inequality, support an ethos of "spreading the fruits" rather than "conserving oneself for grinding effort." It is true that many middle-class Americans, and perhaps other "Protestant ethic" groups, seem ambivalent about consumption, and that they draw into the consumption interest their old values of status and achievement. One must drink or drive modishly; one must *achieve* a sexual climax; and so on. But these mixtures may be transient. The future, too, may see an expansion of some current trends which work against the pressure to succeed and the fear of failure. The part insulation of "deviant subcultures," the upgrading of office ranks, and the proliferation of middle-level experts and advisers vis-à-vis straight bosses and subordinates (so that "everyone" becomes either a vice-president or a specialist); even the niche-finding cult of home and hobby—all of these may help more and more people to do "their own thing" and thereby maintain self-respect.

Somewhat allied with increased permissiveness is the spreading influence of sociology and psychology, with their stress on understanding the pressures behind a person's actions rather than blaming him individually for his misdeeds. In the world of social science, moralism against individuals is officially at a discount, unless—inconsistently—the individual holds power. Again it must be admitted that these tendencies cause ambivalence, even confusion. This confusion is rooted partly in a clash of principles. Under what circumstances and in what sense should one blame or punish? In the late 1960s, editorials and commission reports on the black riots were full of ambivalence about these matters, and the most humane jurists cannot agree on them. Even so, the gradual trend in criminal law and penal practice is away from the notion that to "make the criminal pay" is *inherently* just quite aside from values on social protection and the transgressor's reform. Although most people cannot live without simple concepts of moral fault, the long-term trend does not seem entirely confined to intellectuals. Many deviants thought worthy of punishment in a past age are today generally deemed worthy of "care" or suitable for "treatment" today; their stigmata remain, but the most punitive edges of convention are blunted.[3] This tendency reflects not just the advance of human science, but the growth of large-scale and dense organization, in which the individual seems less important and therefore less accountable morally. From the Nazi experience we know that this can lead to a callous submission—the yielding-up of conscience to an organization—but on the humane side, and in the long run, it may make it harder to find "blameworthy" persons to scapegoat. Whatever the reasons, it is clear that Western societies have in many ways become more humane than they used to be several hundred years ago. In the United States today, even the South does not compare to Stuart England with its legitimized and publicly enjoyed cruelties —animal baiting, public floggings, and the slow hanging of prisoners witnessed by carnival-type crowds. If today's violent films are their substitutes, they are not the real thing and they seldom display such continuous torture and punishment.[4] As mortality rates fall, and our general living becomes less rigorous physically, human life and general vitality seem more precarious. Even in America, where many states have resisted the modern Western tendency to abolish capital punishment, frequencies of lynching and official executions have both steadily declined.

We turn now to some possible trends which may accommodate and encourage authoritarianism. At the risk of seeming to wallow in science-fiction gloom, I will dwell at more length on these possibilities, for they are less obvious. It must be repeated: I do not predict that these possibilities *will* come about; but I do contend that their coming-about is conceivable in the light of what we know about our present society.

First, some of the trends already mentioned may produce reactive anxieties; one way of expressing these may be authoritarian behavior, encouraged simultaneously by other types of reacting personality. Accelerating social change, "permissiveness," the diffusion of authority, the assertions of youth, the impersonality of large-scale organization, all may cause fears about identity, anarchy, and the control of impulse, and a craving for tight-fisted authorities. The decline of organized religion and clear-cut religious belief (well documented in the United States) may spur a turning to new heroes, and on some fronts we may expect the authoritarian to merge with the sort of rebel who castigates "the system" but longs for strict guidance from men he can admire.*
Lacking the traditional restraints on leadership that build up in more slowly evolving organizations, new movements of reaction or protest may provide heroes especially appealing to the authoritarian.

What may happen, then, is that trends which for most people will work against authoritarianism will for some people promote authoritarianism by reaction. There is a parallel here in Robert Lifton's concept of "protean man." Among other things, he suggests, a "flooding of imagery"—an eclectic, superficial intake of messages, accelerated by mass media—is producing a sort of person whose very self-concept rests on the notion of change and experiment. But Lifton also argues that some react against these disparate influences by closing their minds and narrowing their self-concepts. One may expect those people whom personal circumstance and inborn traits have made rigid to be in the second group—among them, authoritarians.[5] More specifically to our subject, the very extension of humane thought and knowledge throughout the culture may, among resisters to these trends, put a premium on

---

* I am reminded of a college student who wrote dogmatic semi-Marxist attacks on American business, and when his work was criticized, blamed the academic "system" for giving him too much freedom to make mistakes in.

authoritarian processes. As the mass media, spurred by affluence and social-welfare values, expose more and more hidden pockets of suffering and cruelty (from famines and military atrocities abroad to abuses of the poor and sick at home), so it becomes harder to ignore or even simply close one's mind to these upsetting claims on one's humanity. Faced with this knowledge, a rigid person who does not like to be upset may sometimes find it easiest to react against his own compassion. Refuge may be sought in a submissive cynicism ("wars are like that—they probably had good reason to kill them") and/or an anger displaced against reporters of the bad tidings and those who protest against them. Such reactions can even be hidden in professional and other euphemisms which pay lip service to community welfare. The ethnocentric are growing more and more adept at talking in this code. Ghetto youth are no longer "immoral" but they lack "positive attitudes"; civil-rights laws (both in Britain and America) are seen to discriminate and "inflame"; and so forth.

But we must not assume that social trends will only foster authoritarianism by way of reaction. Depending again on predisposing, personal factors, some people may find direct inducements to authoritarianism in the mainstream trends of the culture. For example, in some milieus, the development of leadership by subtle manipulation may make subordinates feel so guilty about rebelling that they will displace onto other targets—the wife, say, or the children—their real irritations with "the boss" and the system for which they work. More dangerous, perhaps, are the potentials of scientific programs, theories and experiments.[6] Scientists, for some time, have been replacing priests as the exorcists of cosmic fears, and in an age of much questioning, any authority which seems to base its messages on rational but esoteric proof offers the relief of *unquestioning* acceptance; at the same time, the acceptor can vaguely believe that he is being more critical than he really is, on the grounds that science itself is supposed to be questioning. And when the authorities are only pseudo-scientific, how much more can they abet this self-deception. Thus, in the 1960s, American politicians and advertisers, exploiting the idiom of intellectual and scientific honesty, greatly expanded the practice of "poor-mouthing" and the "reverse sell": they "knocked the product," they knocked themselves. Or rather, they seemed to. For what they were really doing was a *pre-emptive* self-criticism, a sort of verbal judo—disarming criticism by making their own superficial and humorous self-critique. Ploys of this kind differ, at least in degree, from what we might call *pre-emptive introspection,* in which an individual makes a deeper, though still limited, analysis and confession of his own defects to ward off more painfully searching examinations, by himself or others. On both scores, however, we may expect the growth of a new type of authoritarian character for whom the lines of defensiveness are drawn closer in.

Something more here must be said about behavior and the authority of science. Even at its most probing and genuine, science can assume a legitimacy that rests on emotional acceptance—a moral mystique based on such ultra-rational, implicit values as the innate goodness of learning and exploration. Backed by this authority, scientific investigation can involve individuals in brutality, both by depersonalizing the victims under study, and by providing authoritative rationales. Thus there have been instances in recent years when a social scientist has witnessed atrocities in the group he was studying without intervening—even when he could do so safely and effectively—on the grounds that to intervene would be to "interfere with the subculture," spoiling his scientific material. (In one or two cases even the subsequent report of research made no effort to draw attention to the atrocities.) Perhaps few social scientists would go as far as this, but it shows how "Truth" can become the cruel master of certain temperaments.[7] Another example is better known yet perhaps still more disturbing. Adults from widely differing milieus, asked to take part in experiments involving punishment and memory, have been willing to give what they thought were increasingly painful electric shocks to students who made mistakes in a learning program. Many continued reluctantly to give these shocks, on command from the experiment supervisor, even when the victims cried out in pain and implored them to stop. (In fact the electrical leads were not connected and the "victims" were accomplices of the experimenter.)* I do not claim that these cases must involve authoritarianism; on the contrary, they show how a controlled, scientific setting can so affect perceptions of the victims and self in

---

* See Milgram, 1965. Many relevant aspects of his experiments cannot be summarized here, but the amount of compliance seems to have depended on "other-directedness" rather than the exact amount of institutional prestige possessed by the experimenting authorities. It also depended on the volunteer's distance from the victim, and his proximity to the supervisor. Sometimes the volunteer would only go on when the supervisor agreed to "take responsibility." Much of this is relevant to our earlier consideration of Himmler.

Milgram took careful steps after each experiment to ensure that his volunteers were not hurt psychologically, but ethical questions remain about the initial deception involved.

relation to an authority that many sorts of character can overcome humane qualms, albeit with guilt and extreme tension. On the other hand, the experiments showed that some volunteers could be induced to go further than others in the amount of pain they thought they were giving, and a development of the tests indicated that the experimental situation could provide an outlet for the volunteer's own destructive urges.[8] One would therefore expect the situation to elicit submissive-aggressive behavior from those especially predisposed to it.

Another potential of scientific authority is to conceal aggressive moralism. In the long run the very concealment, based on a sincere notion that scientists do at least *try* to be "value free," may make it harder to control and moderate aggressive moralistic urges, in oneself and in others. Even where scientific practitioners openly avow humane motives, this espousal of specific values can hide other values. In mental hospitals, for instance, punishment and blame are used against some inmates, not simply as part of a learning process designed to relieve their unhappiness, but to keep them quiet (make the hospital easier to run) and induce social conformity for its own moral sake.[9] Those practitioners who recognize and accept the moral biases of their regimes are still somewhat screened from most laymen, who assume that what goes on in the special treatment centers is indeed "treatment"—medical treatment—and not punishment and indoctrination. At the same time, the spread of scientific treatment approaches and facilities into the field of penal administration may increase the opportunities for professionals, consciously or unconsciously, to administer punishment under the aegis of medical and psychological caretaking.

One must admit here that the psychiatric and mental-health professions have themselves produced strong prophets against these tendencies. Some of these critics have indeed overreacted by arguing that mental illness does not really exist and that the real purpose of mental institutions is to take away people whom society wants to be rid of, for defensive rather than compassionate reasons.[10] Despite these simplifications, the critics do have a point in warning against the use of medical (or quasi-medical) institutions as substitutes for courts and prison without the latter system's supposed safeguards for individual rights and due process. There is danger likewise in the attitude of some determinist social scientists who, at the same time that they deprecate the notions of culpability and criminal intent as a standard for convicting lawbreakers, are prepared to lump most legal offenders with the mentally ill as people who need psychological treatment.

Without amendment by new safeguards, this kind of thinking and policy might lead us back to the primitive non-individualism of the Oedipus legend, in which a man is stigmatized for what he does, however unwittingly and whether he could apparently help it or not—stigmatized in a subtle and less atonable way that permits some to show him loathing, some sympathy, and all revulsion.[11]

Far short of these things, we can already see how scientific labels, used overtly to diagnose rather than condemn, carry increasingly moral connotations. The word "sick" has gone so far in this process that it is nearly as derogatory as those terms of a less-enlightened age —"lunatic" and "idiot." The same fate has befallen "neurotic," and it is now happening to "neurosis." (Nouns describing a condition are usually less stigmatizing than adjectives directly describing a person— the adjectives seems to embrace the person's whole identity—but a few years ago, even the chairman of a giant British fiber company quarreled publicly with the management of a rival concern, charging them with a "neurosis" about his own firm.) What seems to be occurring is a *chase through language*: terms introduced to help us understand or even de-stigmatize a person or condition (thus, the "disease concept" of alcoholism) are pursued by more stigmatizing senses.[12] It is as if our better natures introduce words to promote tolerance and compassion, but residual needs to blame and stigmatize will not be stopped. This, of course, is a simplification: different people use the same words differently, and there are many social scientists and professional caregivers who resist the worst stigmatizing corruption of their words as long as possible, and then move on to new words. Thus in recent years some psychotherapists dealing with neurotic patients have talked of "your difficulties" rather than "your problems," for "problem child" and so on have become derogatory terms. But, for laymen and some professionals, shifting usages may simply involve uncertainty about the relative claims of compassion and moral sanction, tolerance and blaming, and it is of such uncertainty that authoritarianism can be made.

Liberal and left-wing social scientists who have written about these usages have nearly always assumed that the moral bias behind the "sick" tag, as behind the mental institution, is essentially right-wing— a weapon wielded by mental-health authorities against deviants from conventional morality.[13] This, of course, is not how radical-right groups of the American sixties saw it, with their attacks on the "mental-health profession" as a source of amorality. In fact the social-science critics have underestimated the popular and politically varied market for moral "pathologizing." It is true that social workers and psychotherapists tend to use a middle-class morality in their judgment of proper psychological functioning. It is also evident that psychoanalysis has provided an intellectual opium for some social workers who might otherwise be more critical of the institutions surrounding the deprived "problem" person or family. In these cases it provides an intellectually satisfying system of terms and concepts which subtly deprecates the individual for not adjusting to society as he should; at the same time, by focusing on the individual and his "lack of insight," it can divert the social worker (including some of the most educated ones) away from an intellectual (but politically frustrating) critique of the social and political institutions that help cause the individual "problems" in the first place.[14] In recent years, both in Britain and America, more sociologically minded social workers have attacked this pattern, but the temptations remain. On the other hand, we have already seen how *academic* psychologists—teaching and research people as opposed to active caregivers—have tended to take a more left-wing stance, using their tools of analysis to attack bigots and inveigh against the psychic costs of capitalist conformity. On a more popular plane too, the use of "sick" terms against opponents is becoming established on both left and right, not to speak of the center. "Paranoid," "pervert," "psychotic," "screwball," "misfit," "hysteric," "hung up," "martyr complex," and, of course, "authoritarian" are now equal candidates for any good lexicon of political abuse.

At the gloomiest, we may have more and more situations in which competing social and political doctrines "pathologize" each other's disciples—reflecting not so much the hold of a mental-health "power elite" as a polity of "veto groups," each using the psychiatric smear to discredit its opponents' motives.[15] (The very term "authoritarian" has already been used in this way. In a debate on America's agrarian populists a left-wing and pro-populist historian accused Richard Hofstadter of projecting his own "authoritarian" traits onto the populists, thereby exaggerating their bigotry. The characterization was implausible, to say the least; the accuser was perhaps goaded by Hofstadter's varying uses of the "authoritarian" and related concepts.) A further outcome may be the flowering of pseudo-scientific cults, mixtures of scientific imitation and anti-science reaction, whose leaders wrap exploitative designs in prescriptions for health. (We have already seen this in Scientology and one or two California cults.)

The possibilities in all of this for authoritarian behavior are threefold. First, the cheapjack use of psychiatric language encourages not only a covert moralizing but a dogmatic sort of cynicism. By clever reference to a self-consistent and aggressive system of "insights," one can discount what a person says or believes, attribute his actions to unconsciously *interior* motives, and defensively thereby avoid the discussion of specific issues between that person and oneself. Like any cynicism, this kind feeds on itself, for the person who distrusts others will soon have good cause to.[16] At the worst the process may lead to a psychological imperialism. From saying "you don't *mean* that, what you *really* want is" it is a short step to a tacit "*I* will say what you want—*I* will determine your real identity."

In the second place, the language of psychiatry and mental health provides a way of attacking others through an authority which may seem absolute. If, in the modern era, one calls an enemy "evil" or "dishonest" or "cruel" or even "cowardly," the charge may seem so subjective and fallible as to lose its force. But, if one can tag the enemy as objectively *weak*, by using a scientific or quasi-scientific label of sickness that seems to be above moral and personal bias, one has more chance of hurting that enemy by penetrating his own needs and wishes. It is a sign of civilization, after all, that we often try to hurt our enemies psychologically rather than physically. This is becoming harder and harder to achieve through religious or other overtly moral language, for the decline of the churches and the pressing-together of different cultures are making almost all morals seem relative rather than absolute and enduring, good for all men and all situations. For a morality to seem absolute, it must be linked with forces that order the universe; this used to be the privilege of religion; it is now as much the province of science.*

And yet even scientific elders do not agree. The gods and their priests war as much as they ever did. This brings us to the third possibility for authoritarianism. It will apply to a rather different set of people from the first two possibilities mentioned above. As the practice

---

* A study of films and fiction could tell us much about the dynamics of revenge in modern society. Some of it is vividly illustrated in Ian Fleming's *Moonraker*, where James Bond can only "draw blood" from his adversary by mocking him for his psychological, and related physical, defects. The book, appropriately, makes a worship of the frightening beauties of scientific technology and revels in the professionalism of its classless hero, who can master, by sheer learning, the norms of any subculture. The patriotic and cold-war morality of the hero is more rarely mentioned than the tension between his libido (including tenderness) and his job.

of pathologizing and counter-pathologizing develops, the result in some quarters may be a disillusionment, not only with the concept of mental disorder, but with the whole idea of applying to human conduct a language and analysis that at least try to be scientific. We may have, in other words, a reactive return to overt moralizing, in which a backlash against the hypocrisies of psychology drives out its compassions.[17]

It must be granted that even if these trends (and counter-trends) flourish, they may be of only secondary importance to authoritarianism. In other words, they may accommodate authoritarian behavior and provide authoritarians with political opportunities rather than shape basic dispositions. But this in itself would be no small thing. My main point is that a culture which pays homage to science and intellect will not necessarily be less congenial to authoritarian expression. There is many an American academic who prides himself on his tolerance and lack of "ethnocentrism," when in fact he despises the failed and fears the outsider no less than the ordinary, old-fashioned small towner. The only difference is that he attaches in-group and out-group feelings to different people. Policemen, "pollyannas," and the person who is "not very bright" and deprecated or scorned in the place of Jews, blacks, and intellectuals. By attracting people who have recoiled aesthetically from bourgeois America, the universities tend all the more to become oases of snobbery.

These tendencies are confined neither to the United States nor to faculty. In a fairly new British university, I have noticed a syndrome of student attitudes which cuts across middle-class snobbery and intellectual liberalism. It combines vague rebelliousness against capitalism and "the system," extreme deference to individual faculty, loud inveighings against racists and "Victorians," and yet (in some cases) a virtual contempt of the college porters—dull underlings of authority who will persist in cleaning away all those lovely political-pornographic graffiti. When advanced industrial culture sets more and more store by intellectual achievement, narrowly defined and tested, it may become more permissible to deprecate those of humble station—not *overtly* because they are "lower class," but because they are "stupid" or "naïve," and stupid or naïve by their own lack of merit. In just this tenor I have heard artisans—conscripts in the Royal Air Force—denounce a lower-lower-class Cockney as "ignorant." The term had a special meaning, for education was greatly respected

EPILOGUE 281

among these men. It was not a term of caste patronage ("it's not his fault, he doesn't know any better")—instead it meant "crude, uncivilized and vulgar"; it implied that the person was too lazy or obstinate to educate himself into a better state. The meaning rested on the myth that education reflects achievement rather than fortune; if a man "didn't know any better," it *was* his fault. Extending this motif, one can imagine a technocratic culture so scornful of stupidity that individuals anxiously pursue credentials, displacing all doubts onto the slow, the sick, and the "cop-out."

Finally, we must consider the demographic and economic. If current trends continue, a few, increasingly rich Western nations—plus Japan—will face a world exploding with people, rent by famines, and charged with nationalist militancies. To some in the Western nations, depending in part on the beliefs they learn, the idea of sharing wealth and culture will seem like the myth suggested to King Canute. Siege mentalities, a horror of "the horde," will be encouraged; and the leader emotionally drawn to the idea of ethnic exclusion will have his chance. It would be a somber day were this to unite with a new eugenics, compulsory birth control in quality as well as quantity, appealing to those with special horrors of the weak and "inferior."

All these attitudes may go hand in hand with "law-and-order" concerns, as rapid urbanization continues to foster crime and press different cultural groups upon each other. Fears of anarchy are no less universal to human character than fears of weakness, the alien, and the "different"; they all involve basic feelings about vitality, security, and identity, and a wish to predict comfortably and cope with the responses of others. Nevertheless, it has already been argued that some people are especially anxious about these things; their imaginations seize and magnify what real social dangers there are. And, on a more formative level, publicized specters ("crime in the streets," "the yellow horde," and so on) may actually influence dispositions, for example by offering a threat complex as a way of displacing or projecting myriad anxieties.[18]

PREVENTION

With authoritarianism as with most other psychosocial problems, it is easier to analyze the phenomenon than to propose ways of attacking it. After so much diagnosis a few pages of remedy will not be very impressive. But we can make a start. The following suggestions outline very generally some efforts which could be made to prevent and limit authoritarian behavior at diverse points in the life cycle and cultural system. Preliminary and scattered though these proposals are, they speak to a much wider arc of human stress and suffering than is manifested purely in authoritarian character.

We must begin with a statement on child rearing and social ethics. In the case of most parents, "doing what comes naturally" seems to cause little harm to their children. It is nonetheless appalling how much power and freedom parents have to be unspeakably destructive toward their children, whether through design, negligence, or ignorance. And, for every childhood of physical ill-treatment, there must be scores of homes where other sorts of parental behavior have in effect destroyed part of the child by stunting and disrupting. This state of affairs is protected by laws and customs which affirm the privacy of the home from outside interference—a value only qualified by dire economic need or extreme abuse very visibly brought to the notice of public authorities. Within these limits, parents enjoy virtual rights of private property over children in their early years. They do so partly because our form of society has in the past favored the "nuclear" family (mobility, for example, works against the "extended" family group), but also because parents are more publicly articulate than young children.[19]

Today, I suggest, we should no longer tolerate such a system without qualifying it further. In this the values of compassion and social stability come together. A world where people increasingly press upon one another (the provocations of overcrowding) and where more and more destructive weapons are distributed (nuclear for the mighty, cheap revolvers for the lowly) simply cannot afford to give the private home free rein to become a nursery of hate, destructiveness, and extreme sado-masochism. But what can be done? The most radical solution would be to collectivize child rearing in community nurseries so as to remove all special relationships between parents and their offspring; parents could still take part in the nursery child rearing, but not exclusively with their own children. Before we turn in horror from such a proposition, two things might be said in its defense. First, a professionally-run community arrangement would not necessarily fail to give a child the sort of love and attention he needs for his happiness and creative development; on the contrary, it might be happier for most children to spread their affection among three or four "parents" rather than depend intensively on just two. Secondly, the egalitarian must in all logic support the idea. The greatest bastion of unequal opportunity is the ability of social leaders to pass on to their offspring, not money and contacts (important as these are), but those special ways of thinking, communicating, and acting which win success—and to inculcate these from an early age.

But for most of us, surely, the price of this system would be too much. It would bring us that much closer to the uniformities of a Brave New World, and it would deprive many parents of what has become almost their only creative function, the sense of which may indeed be enhanced by the biological tie. *Hypothetically*, it might also be argued that completely equal social opportunity might, on a deep level of character, actually increase the suffering of persons with low-status jobs, since they could only blame their own qualities for their lack of success. These qualities would still be unequally distributed, genetically rather than socially, and we know that people can feel ashamed of the most physical shortcoming. Allowing for all these points, the best solution might lie in some form of compromise between private and collective child rearing—for example, some move toward the version of the *kibbutz* arrangement wherein parents live with their children for part of each day, but public nurseries take on much of the brunt of child and baby care, freeing the mothers for other activities. If governed by humane values and inquiry, the system would speak to all the requirements mentioned above—safeguards for the child, satisfactions for the parent, social opportunity and variety—without perfectly fulfilling them all.*

Even well short of a full *kibbutz* system, there are many degrees and variations of the nursery and pre-primary-school arrangement that are worth consideration: see, for example, the Danish network. Research and innovation in this area should be a top-priority matter for any government in Western society that wishes to develop human resources and forestall social problems as economically as possible. Inherent obstacles—for instance, clashes between home and school child-rearing values—are not of the kind that cannot be overcome by

---

* No institution, *qua* institution, can guarantee more-enlightened practice (however "enlightened" is defined), for the institution will to some extent reflect cultural values. If convention accepts or prefers child-rearing practices that produce anxious, destructive individuals, a public nursery system may simply carry on these practices. On the other hand, it can guard against more random and concealed formation of pathology. In Germany it could not have prevented Nazi-type behavior, but it could have modified the special family circumstances needed to produce the extreme cruelty and destructiveness of a Hitler—and it could have done this within German tradition.

sensitive study, siting, and staff recruitment. In any event there is going to be increased demand for some such institutions and on more than one social plane. By present indications of restlessness, large numbers of college-educated mothers will not accept adult lives in which their energies are overwhelmingly concentrated on the routines of child care. For better or worse, they are being educated out of it. Unless complementary systems of infant care are enormously developed, we shall have more and more frustrated and guilty mothers, with consequent damage to the children. (This need, of course, is the other side of the coin to the widening of occupational opportunities for working mothers; advances on the two fronts must go together, and to some extent they already are.) We must recognize, however, that middle-class women can shout louder, more influentially, for what they need than can ghetto and working-class women, whose cramped conditions and limited cultural resources make assistance in child care a pressing need. Educational "consumerism" must come to the lower-class neighborhood, by private organization if not by public; but it is also important that public and educational agencies make sure that working-class mothers know about the child-care facilities that do exist and not find them strange and inhuman. Even in Britain, with its relatively well-developed welfare state, the free pre-primary schools tend to draw least (per child population) from those economic groups that, in a sense, need them most.

Apart from this, in both America and Britain, as elsewhere, it is shocking how few resources, both intellectual and financial, are devoted to early education compared with higher education. This is one manifestation of a general theme we will come to later: the way in which higher education has oversold itself. Since articulate thinkers about education are apt to live in universities—and to be adults—it is not surprising that they should tend to focus on their own institutions and more recent experiences and by their very articulateness draw the public attention away from the crowded classrooms and low-paid teaching of tiny tots—particularly when it is so much easier (though not more valid) to see a relationship between the nation's manpower requirements and college (and even high school) curricula. Perhaps government agencies and the great philanthropic foundations should try harder to offset some of this focus. I am not saying that national governments should abandon their support for research and development in higher education—but I do know that, for all the recent cutbacks, the U.S. Federal Government has supported some incredibly trivial research in higher education compared with the added work it could be supporting in the field of early childhood.[20]

In the meantime there are several things that can be done within present family and child-care arrangements. In some middle-class homes, as their affluence rises, one solution may be to have a younger unmarried sister of the wife, or a female student on the British *au pair* lines, live in the house (sharing in the household while perhaps having her own bed-sitting room) to take care of the children for specified hours in return for board and lodging. If the child in effect has three parents, intense dependency on any one of them may be avoided without necessarily reducing his *love* for any one of them. For the same reasons, families should be encouraged to have their grandparents live near them. But, in any event, I think we must insist that all people undergo some kind of practical preparation for the obligations of marriage and parenthood. Exactly what form the requirement should take I do not know; certainly I have no wish to make one more sphere of life subject to the potential straitjacket and banality of exams and credentials. Nor do I claim that parental education can eliminate the "pathogenic" effects of depressed social circumstances. Nevertheless, influence, comfort, and status do not seem to prevent some parents from doing all sorts of stupid things to their children—often with the best, or nearly best, intentions; and even in the slums and ghettoes, it would help to give parents or future parents much more information than they presently receive, from knowledge about welfare rights and agencies to some basic points about health and psychology.

As regards the content of parental education, I will confine myself to just a few of the needs of middle-class families, and those needs most relevant to authoritarianism. The suggestions that follow are in some wise merely an extension of the "Spock ethos"—that is, the *real* Spock ethos, which respects the natural intuition of mothers, deprecates excessive psychological worrying, and recognizes the child's needs for both authority and independence. The huge sales of the Spock books might seem to preclude the need for any further proposals on parental education, but not *every* parent reads them—even in the middle classes!—and anyway certain points should be stressed and put in broader context. First, parental authority should as much as possible be firm and consistent, so that the child "knows where he is" in relation to that authority. At the same time, parents should not eschew all conflicts and rebellion. Households should have safety valves; within limits, quick flareups are better than covert grudges. But parents should also encourage children to show aggression in ways which separate it from hostility; times of general rowdiness should have their place. It would help, too, if parents accepted the knowledge that they, as adults, can easily fear children for their turbulence and probing candor. To allay these fears, parents can retreat behind sophistication, mystery, and excessively oblique threat, all of which can stifle the child and cause anxiety. (I know how much easier it is to say these things in principle than to act on them amid the buffets of daily living; but they ask to be stated nonetheless.)

A special word should be said about achievement pressures. We have already noted how parental ambition, projected onto the offspring, may diversely contribute to authoritarianism. But the answer is not to attack the achievement ethic, nor to ask that somehow parents forgo the wish to have their children "do well." To demand these things would be to order an impracticable frontal assault on the culture's central values; and I, for one, would not care to argue that society would be better off, on balance, if pressures to achieve were reduced. What we can ask is that the criteria of achievement be diversified, and that parents and schools give young people more leeway in which to pick their criteria, their pathway of effort, and indeed their identity. If this is to be done, those fathers who are inclined to be tough-minded about achievement must broaden their ideas of what is manly.

This discussion leads us to two subjects—stresses on the individual generated at school and college, and (especially applicable to America) the broad cultural pressures on men to be and look "tough."

I have little to say about teaching and education in the schools, but this is not to imply that they are unimportant factors in the prevention of authoritarianism and other destructive pathologies. With regard to the urban poor, George Dennison has vividly shown how an experimental school with small classes and flexible yet firm teachers can break the emotional vicious circles that inhibit learning and, in some individuals, accompany a submissive-aggressive behavior.[21] Let us focus, however, on the very different world of higher education, on the assumption that the college years are not too late in life to affect an individual's basic behavior patterns, and that the colleges will increasingly influence the high schools as they take more and more of their nation's youth. Most of the argument that follows applies equally to America and Britain; in varying degree it may apply to other Western nations too.

We have already noted how, in several famous lives, failure at examinations or other tests catalyzed authoritarian behavior and perhaps expanded an underlying, authoritarian disposition.[22] Such tests were merely the tip of an iceberg of pressure on the individual. As such they are by no means absent from colleges and universities today: it is well known that more and more academic credentials are being required for more and more jobs, and the pressure does seem to be reflected in student statistics of psychiatric illness.* Apart from the testing, it is surely ridiculous to expect most youth, even intelligent youth, to really *want* to spend most of their waking hours for four academic years reading heavy books, on top of thirteen years or so prior schooling. Yet the college student can easily feel he is "stupid" if he does *not* enjoy this. All the more so when he finds that his teachers weave a vague and remote yet insidiously personal power. Persuasive and articulate, eager for apprentices, solemn in the sanctities of scholarship, they represent an authority—success through specified learning—which is much harder to attack persistently than the actual administration and social policies of the college. For some students, the result is a type of compliance in which a feeling of irksomeness at the system is suppressed, in part by focusing on the series of specific tasks and blotting out wider possibilities.[23] Such people are not necessarily punitive, but in the long run one might expect some of their kind to be reactors against radicals, hippies, and others who dared to take the short cuts they did not. (If this seems but a vague possibility, one might consider that in a fast-changing society the prevention of psychological disorder will be most effective if it tries to head off future contingencies.) In any event, we know that the academic system does generate an immense amount of psychic stress.

Despite the past decade's political onslaughts on the universities, policies to cope with students' psychiatric problems have focused more on adjusting the individual (through improved counseling services) than adjusting the college institutions around him. Yet it

* The big increase in psychiatric disorder among adolescents does not seem to be due solely to trends in self-labeling and the growth of school and college counseling and psychiatric services. In America at least, suicides and peptic ulcers are among the adolescent disorders that have increased. A study of persons seeking private psychiatric help has shown a big jump among adolescents in those citing educational stress as their chief problem. See Lipset and Altbach, 1966, for these and other points. It is possible that some students reporting sick may be unconsciously choosing a role which makes them seem more interesting and less anonymous and gives them an alibi from academic failure and the stigma of stupidity. But such a role might well produce conflict with other expectations that play upon the individual, thereby producing more emotional disorder within the individual.

would make more sense to concentrate on the latter, and it would continue to make sense even from the standpoint of the quasi-capitalist values which dominate our culture. The fact is that, as providers of leadership, the colleges and graduate schools have been overvalued by their own salesmanship, popular faith in education, and the laziness of employers. There is no evidence that four years at the colleges we know today—still less, high grades at college or exposure to graduate school—are necessary to many kinds of business and administrative leadership, even leadership of an "enlightened" variety. It is therefore consonant with both conservative and radical values that universities and the major employers should develop variations upon the academic treadmill. I suggest, in the first place, that big corporations spend more time and ingenuity finding and assessing nongraduates for management. This in turn requires changes in work units so that management has more contact with "men on the floor." Except where the need for a specific, technical skill absolutely requires it, management recruiters should never interview on a "graduates only" basis; if graduates *tend* more to have the abilities required, then let this fact be shown in the interviews, company tests, and subsequent performance, rather than taken for granted in a way that screens out the atypical individual. In the spirit of this approach, employers should never grant pay increases—as they do in some American and British schools—automatically with the attainment of certain higher degrees. If the work for such a degree improves the individual's performance, let him be rewarded for that.[24] In the second place, despite recent university innovations, there is much more that the colleges and universities could do to make contact with varieties of individual needs, especially with differing rhythms of individual development. They could make it easier for dropouts of some promise to return to the university (this is particularly needed in Britain, which lags behind America's leading colleges in this regard). And they should be receptive to candidates who have taken some time out between school and college. Certainly they should develop the kind of work-study combinations pioneered by Antioch, in which students relate the experience of their working terms out of college to their academic works when they return. This has the added advantage of giving students more information about careers on which to base their choices and thus avoid the trap of preparing long and working for an occupational authority that one really does not like, with all the attendant stresses that can flow from such a situation. Finally, the leading colleges and universities might consider ways to develop the night school and adult education. (For example, if nights make for thin education, why not weekends, or at least Saturdays, allowing a more collegiate use of campuses?)[25]

Put so briefly, these suggestions can only serve as pointers. Their brevity, however, should not be taken as a downgrading of university scholarship. On the contrary, it might well be argued that, if the colleges were less tied to a rigid and oversimplified system of credentialing, and thus less directly the servants of other employers, they might be less exposed to anti-intellectual attacks.

From credentials and the pressures to achieve, we move to a less tangible area—the problem of strength and tenderness in the culture as a whole, particularly as it applies to males. The American male's concern with toughness is itself an enormous subject for cultural study. In many cases the toughness value does not work against tenderness: the two are often jibed in the image of the strong man who stands up for the oppressed. It is still true to say, however, that a very great emphasis on toughness—and *looking* tough—requires clear guidelines for behavior if it is to be happily fused with traits of tenderness, gentleness, and sensitivity. This is not easy to ensure in a fluid, affluent, and unmartial society, where few guidelines of any sort are very clear and there is relatively little call for the most obvious, physical types of toughness in clearly demarcated areas. By example and implication, therefore, parents and other authorities must define "strength" so that it *includes*—not just *accompanies*—the notion that the strong men can afford to be gentle much of the time. Without this morality, however tacit, a young person is more likely to repress the "soft" side of himself and, in some cases, to mount punitive defenses against it. On the other hand, those parents who try to teach their offspring that loving and giving are all, without preparing them for the realities of aggressiveness (both in self and in others), may produce the sort of person who has not learned how to show aggression in moderate form, and whose ambivalent hostilities are papered over with a superficial friendliness. The trick, then, is to establish a fusion between the tough and the tender so that neither is furtive. This, surely, was the great achievement of Jesus of Nazareth, who helped redefine certain tender qualities —compassion, sensitivity, humility, forgivingness, patience—so that they were not just the necessary opposites of strength, but an integral part of restraint, vision, and endurance. His wrathful attack on the temple moneychangers was still needed, for even the gentle must sometimes push.

These considerations apply not only to the formation of character but to the limitation of authoritarian *behavior* in the larger society and its containment as a political element. Specific public policies aside, what American male would not rather be thought a "hawk" than a "dove"? Or would have preferred this before the terms themselves became hopelessly political? To say that he *should* have preferred to be a "dove" would be as naïve as suggesting that the American eagle emblem and the British lion would be no less satisfying emotionally if they were redrawn as lambs.[26] But the real misery—miserable because more avoidable—is that in American foreign-policy debates the crudest, most fearful overreactions to communism have been allowed to monopolize the symbols of strength, while those who would define and defend the national interest with more sophisticated policies have been called "appeasers" and "nervous Nellies." In part this is their own fault: at the height of the war, some of the most distinguished opponents of American Vietnam policy made a defeatist-sounding argument unnecessarily central to their cause: "We can't win in Vietnam." In terms of psychological appeal, it surely would have been better to extend rather than to spurn the attractions of "strength": to stress that a cooler attitude to Vietnam might go just as well as any other with a value upon fortitude and national honor and security; and to suggest that to blitz outnumbered enemy guerrillas (not to speak of civilian neutrals) with an enormous preponderance of metal, fire, and chemicals, to "protect our boys," was not an action of strength. This is not to say that all defenses of the war policy are irrational and inhumane, but simply that critics of the war have been unnecessarily vulnerable to authoritarian-type charges as well as to the kind of *anti*-authoritarian war defense which sees America as the strong champion against aggressors.*

Likewise in some domestic issues. It was all very well to excoriate the "police riot" which occurred at the 1968 Chicago Democratic convention—and which drew no little public support. Both the provocation and the brutality had of course to be pointed out. But it should also have been said that in the eyes of the world the Chicago police looked,

---

* Much of this applies not just to Vietnam. When the quiet Premier Shastri of India died, my wife—who had been writing at Stanford an undergraduate thesis on his leadership—wrote his obituary for the local California paper. In passing she mentioned his strength in resisting India's warhawks and choosing conciliation with Pakistan over Kashmir. Other papers called this weakness.

not like tough guys, but like panicky green troops whose fractured discipline allowed private vengeance and unofficial moralism to take over. I am not saying that these sorts of argument would have any immediate effect on policy and opinion, but for future issues they might gradually make it harder for the simple "get tough" proponents to operate effective levers on public feeling.

My last suggestion applies to the dogmatic and self-censoring aspects of authoritarianism. It speaks again, however, to a general need in education, and it might provide a way to discourage the glib and defensive use of fancy psychological language.

Even among those institutions which dedicate themselves to "questioning," there is a tendency to confuse questioning with the replacement of conventional wisdoms by new dogmas of the social sciences. While accepting the fact that basic ethical concerns are not amenable to scientific validation, one may still ask that individuals be encouraged to become more aware of their basic premises and to think about the personal influences which have shaped their prejudices and behavior. At college, especially, it is remarkable that the psychology student is never—in the usual course of events—called upon to write a paper on his own motives and conditioning; that the sociology student never has to ask what "subcultures" and "reference groups" helped make him what he is; and that the political science student very seldom has to think about the economic, cultural, and psychological sources of his own political attitudes and behavior. Yet existing curricula could easily absorb these requirements, and they would suit general and introductory courses in the social sciences, thus reaching far more students than those majoring in psychology, sociology, and political science. In terms of learning and intellectual development alone, would we not be justified in asking the student to spend just a small part of his time considering things nearest to home, from which he could then build, with humility, to an understanding of other men and alien groups?[27] In terms of preventing authoritarianism *and* a more general dogmatism, this proposal is not suggested as a simple cure, but as a longer-term influence whose effects would grow as more and more of the population went to college. The effect would not just be upon individuals as personalities, but as future parents and leaders whose basic outlook, their degree of openness, will influence successive generations.

We must anticipate, however, some resistances. Self-exposés cause embarrassment, as the more frenzied critics of Norman Podhoretz have shown.[28] Perhaps this explains why behavioral scientists so seldom write about themselves. Although we have had studies in the psychopathology of politics, and even in the psychopathology of art, we have not yet had real studies in the psychopathology of research. (Is it not possible, for instance, that some people study power because they want to enjoy it vicariously, feeling unable to handle the real thing?) I do not suggest, however, that self-study as an exercise for students need focus on pathology—in any event, deep motives are not necessarily sick motives. The point is to get people writing thoughtfully about themselves in their background to the extent that they feel able and willing to do so. As more of this is done, the academic community should be able to develop norms distinguishing such exercises from glib and sentimental attempts at confession, on the one hand, and educational invasions of privacy, on the other.

Another obstacle may consist of that tendency in American education to treat learning as a production and distribution problem, a matter of knowledge units to be piped into the individual under maximum pressure.[29] But here in fact America has enjoyed two very opposite traditions. One theme, certainly, has been the praise of external achievement, of getting and having, of making one's mark (and grade) without worry about fine feelings, the more reflective values, or what Peter Ustinov has called the "shy thought." This side of America has indeed been hospitable to the closed-minded, compulsive aspects of authoritarianism. But there is also another tradition whose constituency somewhat overlaps that of the first. This second motif is the ethic of self-improvement and self-scrutiny. It is reflected in the special popularity enjoyed by psychoanalysis in America: both the real thing and the popularized snippets of neo-Freud. It is likewise seen in the books of self-improvement (from sex manuals to Norman Vincent Peale), and it is extended to the collective self-criticism in which Americans so fiercely lampoon their own culture. To some extent, perhaps, it attracts people as a refuge from the materialism of the first tradition; but both traditions share common sources, not least in puritanism and in scientific application (in *Poor Richard's Almanack* we have an early fusion of the two traditions).

It is in this light that innovations for self-study might be viewed—not as a general movement toward passive introversion, but to give wisdom to the busy. And to the committed. For, if by themselves these innovations might encourage a tendency to moral relativism, in fact they would be instituted in a college environment marked by a growing student and faculty involvement in national affairs and urban/social problems. This promises to be a powerful and long-term trend, and against it the proponents of self-reflection could offer a balancing force, preserving the idea of free inquiry for its own natural sake.*

---

* One danger in cultivating self-study is that of superficiality: it might become simply an application to oneself of psychological clichés, which reinforce feelings of disability and justify one's "problems." But this danger is abroad anyway; systematic self-study could get past the superficial stage and produce wiser understandings about the self in social context. I would also argue that the world will be safer and happier in the long run if it has fewer people who are closed about their prejudices and bottle up many feelings, even if the price is an increasing number of people who "overpsychologize" their unhappiness.

APPENDIX A

Character and Cultural Conflict:
Two College Students

"Roger Stanton" and "Jerry White" were members of the same university class. They were interviewed in the period 1961-65 twice annually during their four undergraduate years, and were also studied through questionnaires and friends' and teachers' comments. While at college, both supported Goldwater for President even before his nomination, and in their freshman year they scored very high on the F scale.[1] In many ways they were people caught between provincial proprieties and a more metropolitan liberalism; each, in his own way, reacted against that liberalism while absorbing some of its values. Of the two it was Stanton, perhaps, whose reaction was most fully authoritarian, but in other ways he was less authoritarian than White. He was by no means a wholly closed and submissive person; nor is this surprising, for the interviews were both lengthy and voluntary, and a person who shunned great inner probings would be unlikely to seek the experience.[2]

In considering both characters one must bear in mind the political climate. The study took place during the Kennedy and early Johnson administrations. Vietnam only became a major national issue toward the end of this period. The first of the big-city riots—Harlem, 1964—occurred also toward the end of the period, but the main run of riots, including the early outbreak at Watts, happened afterward. The first wave of campus sit-in protests occurred in the study's final year; the penultimate interviews reported below, conducted in the fall of 1964, were done just after the Berkeley "Free Speech Movement" crisis. It is fair to say that the study was concluded well before campus violence and "law-and-order" reaction had become widespread. As a result it was easier then than now to judge the factor of individual temperament in expressions of concern about rebels and protestors.

The report that follows gives most of its space to Roger Stanton; only his account offers some sense of change and continuity over the college years. For reasons of length, Jerry White's case is reported in more summary form, as a comparison with that of Stanton. Taken together the two cases shed light on the complex relationships between puritan morality, cultural change, and individual management of impulse.

ROGER STANTON

Stanton came from a medium-sized city in the West. His father used to be a traveling salesman for a big chemical corporation; at the time of this study he owned and ran a couple of hardware stores. In his senior year at high school, Roger Stanton won a scholarship enabling him to attend a university out of state.

His manner during the interviews was generally unemotional and passive. Yet his declared aim in life was to be a go-getter, rising rapidly to the top of a big airline and then launching into politics. In the interviews, too, his manner sometimes became more aggressive. When talking of his father, for example, he once said very emphatically, "He *gets—things—done*," thumping the interviewer's desk at each word. More usually he had the habit of starting a remark in a very firm voice and then trailing off into hesitance.

Freshman-year interview. Questioned about his senior year at high school, Stanton talked very much of a group that he "hung around with." They numbered eight to ten but he said he also felt "really close with a larger group on the periphery." Within these circles, however, there were no particular intimate friends.

Stanton said that he applied to colleges independently of his parents: "I preferred it that way." On the other hand, he had "plotted to come here with a group of friends" and some had got in with him. As Stanton described it, the high school group was in many ways not at all conformist: it embraced a great variety of political opinions and religious attitudes. Like Stanton, though, most were classical "music lovers"; and he added proudly, "None of us were really normal or average. We all had some outstanding characteristic."

Talking about friends at college, Stanton again described a group of "really intimate friends," ten to twenty in number. Among these, he said, "there are none I draw closer to than any other." This suggested that so far Stanton did not have any really close friends at college; and indeed he was inclined to talk of acquaintances as members of a group rather than as individuals. He was also apt to talk of a group rather impersonally, as a sort of consumer service. Though he had only been at college a few months, he said that his new friends compared "real favorably . . . excellent replacements for the group I knew before."

The conversation turned to girls. He was very deliberate.

"Several very nice girls within my classes and so on, and they're interesting. I'm sort of scared, however, to engage in a lot of dating up here. Usually I do date occasionally; here I haven't yet, though there are going to be some social events next quarter at which I will—but I'm rather reluctant to get involved in the circle, for fear it'll really cut into my studies. I mean, I've seen it, this is a problem with some people around the house . . . but next quarter I will—I've sort of held off on everything last quarter to see what's going to happen around here, and now that I know, I think I can date once every two or three weeks without hurting my studies, without affecting anything for me."

The university Stanton attended was very high pressure academically. Bombarded by tests and weighed down with lengthy required-reading lists, the students as a whole showed some anxiety about grades. Nevertheless, in the same interview, Stanton admitted that his aim of keeping a B average was "taking a lot less work than I suspected it would." Even without dating, he apparently spent a large part of each weekend away from the books. To some extent, therefore, his carefully-put reasons for not dating seemed to be a rationalization—and indeed later interviews revealed considerable inhibitions about the opposite sex. But the way he talked about his studies reflected other traits, too. Stanton was a person who wanted to get a great deal of his life planned out just so; he had a considerable fear of slipping, of losing control. In part, he feared losing control of himself. He said he could be "pretty cold . . . pretty mean" to people outside his own group of friends. His own "sarcasm" scared him, so much that sometimes he went back and apologized to people he thought he had offended. "I find myself slipping and allowing myself to say things that I really shouldn't . . . lack of self-control on my part." Just before saying this he emphasized that since he meant to become a politician he just couldn't afford to "go round snipping [other people] off." In all this he was remarkably like one or two of the right-wing students studied by Robert Lane.[3]

The same concern about self-control colored a particularly vivid incident which he described to the interviewer. When he was at high school he read or heard about some temperance propaganda claiming that a good 15 percent of the population were alcoholics. This made a great impression on him. He heard that if he once touched alcohol he might be unable to stop. At a family-reunion party in Iowa, he quietly emptied all the liquor bottles he could see, or so he said. His father, not surprisingly, was furious.

In politics and religion he again showed concern about slipping from a firm and fixed position. "At present I'm an arch-conservative, bordering on reactionary, and [this campus] is not known for graduating reactionaries or conservatives. . . . I suspect some of my political and some of my religious feelings will undergo change." He described himself as a "very strict Presbyterian" and said he went to church every Sunday; but he added: "This position is going to be under attack for the next four years from my friends, from the courses, from the faculty and so on. And so I suspect that I'll probably weaken. I'll try not to, I know that. I may or may not weaken. I'm quite orthodox, in other words; my church-going is quite sincere. I'll try to hang on but I don't know how well I can do this." As in the matter of politics, he said, "you can expect to change when you have certain cherished beliefs which may not stand up in the light of reason."

There are several things to note here. First, when Stanton called himself an arch-conservative, he meant the Goldwater type of conservative. He was a champion of individualism against powerful government authority, though in later conversations his statements about government showed a striking inconsistency. The second notable point is the sheer amount of concern and conflict he expressed about change in beliefs per se. Although he exaggerated the anti-conservative nature of the student body, his anxiety was the reaction of a person plucked from a fairly narrow culture and plunged into the urbane rationalism of a major campus. He was expressing, in short, the pain of cultural and social change, and he was expressing it with rather more intellectual self-awareness than authoritarian people may be expected to show. At another point in the interview Stanton said that he often had breakfast discussions about political and philosophical matters. Recently he and his friends had argued about whether it was wrong to change if one thought at the time that the direction of change was wrong, even if one didn't think it was wrong afterward. "This sort of bothered me," said Stanton. "Right now I'm horrified by the thought of political liberalism, but if I come out of here a liberal was the change for the good or the bad?" This is Stanton at his most self-questioning perhaps. Later on he did not allow himself such probings.

His speculations revolved about several conflicts of mind. For one thing there was a clash between moral absolutism and moral relativism. With his fear of "weakening," Stanton felt a marked need to keep to old and familiar values, yet he wasn't sure if those values were good in themselves (absolutes) or only good if he thought them good at the time. Another, related conflict was the clash between what he wanted emotionally and what he feared would be the dictates of reason. Intellectually he did not appear to have much confidence in his "conservative" beliefs: hence his suggestion that they might not "stand up in the light of reason." Yet he continued to view any move away from his customary beliefs as a sign of weakening and something to be resisted. In Stanton's personality, reason and emotional need were not well integrated.

There may also have been a conflict between old and new authorities. In spite of wanting to adhere to the old orthodoxies, Stanton showed a certain fatalism about the effect of new, campus authorities—courses, instructors, his peer group. It was perhaps because he recognized his interviewer as a "liberal" academic that he called himself "reactionary," with light deprecation.

And yet: part of Stanton seemed quite deeply to respect individualism. This came out at several times during the talks. On one occasion, for example, he said he liked the fairly large size of the university, in part because it accommodated a more-varied program, but also because he liked to lose himself in a crowd and be by himself every so often: to "retreat into your own shell, and reconsider yourself all alone." Despite his much-emphasized group of companions, the way he described his weekends—hobbies, reading, bicycle rides to the other side of town—gave the impression of a loner, and his whole manner and the way he talked of people suggested a person who did not make friends easily.

Sophomore year, fall. By his second year at college, Stanton was taking a much-harder position on the subject of political beliefs and change. He said that he read *The New Republic* and the *Progressive* as well as subscribing to *National Review,* but he denied that he read the more leftist magazines to help decide his political views. "My own mind is more or less made up," he explained. He read some magazines just "to find out what the other side is thinking." His interest seemed to include both a genuine intellectual enjoyment of debate and the puritan's slightly horrified fascination with enemy beliefs. At the same time he appeared to be staging a reaction against former doubts. When the interviewer gently recalled, "Last year you were a little worried about becoming too liberal . . .," Stanton interrupted him: "No problems." He said this very sharply, as if to shut off the line of conversation. "Do you still feel the same way about Goldwater?" the interviewer asked. "Uh-huh," Stanton replied quickly, jauntily, again with a tone that seemed to say "No more questions needed."

The interviewer then asked him, "How has this last week been for you?" (The Cuban missile crisis had just ended.) Stanton said he had listened to the radio reports mainly with "amusement" though also some "concern" at times. He generally approved of Kennedy's moves but thought they amounted to too little too late. He would have preferred a general blockade of Cuba to Kennedy's selective "quarantine" of offensive weapons; and he added: "I wouldn't have objected to invading if we'd had to." Asked if the chance of a general war concerned him at all, he said, very fast, "Not at all, no. I think general war's only a remote possibility."

"Does the idea of nuclear warfare bother you?" the interviewer queried in a neutral tone. Stanton again said, very quickly, "Not at all." In answer to a question about casualties, he replied, "If you could see it building up . . . I suspect it would be something around forty or fifty million [in the U.S.]." He said he was against a first strike because there were ways to "start winning without blasting Russia off the face of the earth." If we did blast them, "they would blast back, and while we would win, there would be a question of what would be left." On the rightness or wrongness of nuclear war, however, "If it's necessary, it's necessary. . . . And if we can win—win, win—all right." He added that he had "no special horror" about nuclear weapons; they were "just one more weapon in the arsenal of nations." When Greek fire was invented, people called it something special, but it wasn't; it was "just another weapon." Stanton went on to argue that giant nuclear weapons were, in any case, being partly superseded by more selective devices such as atomic hand grenades.

In talking of war, Stanton expressed views no more and no less aggressive than the doctrine held by many U.S. military officers; and it is not my contention that authoritarian personalities dominate the "hawk" line in American defense debates. What is more important is the *way* Stanton expressed his views. Although given every chance to do so, he refused even to admit that nuclear warfare was a terrible thing, however "necessary" it might conceivably be. He declared, in effect, that the human price of war did not much concern him. His whole approach to the matter was one of nonchalant, impersonal brutality; he quickly shrugged off any suggestion that there might be dilemmas; his main interest was in winning and in military hardware. Yet, as far as his personal plans were concerned, he was no militarist: he said with cold distaste that he had no interest in joining the ROTC, still less in being drafted. He showed a traditional American dislike of being consciously regimented.

It must be remembered that Stanton did not think nuclear warfare was likely to occur. Foreign-policy matters could serve him as a safe fantasy region where he could indulge desires to be a tough guy. An acquaintance with other Goldwater supporters has persuaded me that there is a passive type of person, often more apolitical than Stanton, who unconsciously sees politics as a world removed from real life—a realm where he can express aggressive urges that he is too inhibited to show in personal relations. At several points later on in the talks, Stanton indicated that he did not inwardly feel as dynamic and independent in ordinary life as he would have liked.[4]

On the subject of his parents, Stanton expressed a mixture of subdued irritation and loyal dependence. The previous summer he had worked in his father's main store. Asked how he had enjoyed it, he confessed that he really did not enjoy working with his father. Both of them were very much alike, and since they had strong ideas about what to do, they were inclined to "run head on into each other." Stanton said his father tended to "sit on the business and keep an eye on details," while he himself had "independent ideas about efficiency and so on." Over other things too, like the best way to mow the lawn, they had little disagreements. But Stanton emphasized several times in the conversation that they only disagreed on "petty things" and it was because they were both stubborn. He said wistfully, "He's an awful lot like I am. Only child and all that." He added at another point that he really didn't mind the friction at work, and anyway the money was a compensation. Some of this might be put down to ordinary loyalty, but Stanton, in effect, minimized the friction by identifying with his father. Talking about other employees in the store, he very much took his father's position. He mentioned one person, a high-school dropout, for whom he had to draw maps to prevent him getting lost on errands. "He's really not very bright," Stanton observed contemptuously and rather pompously. "My father is thinking of discharging him."

In fact, Stanton seemed to be more dependent on his parents' authority than he realized. The previous summer, he said, he wanted to take a short automobile trip with some friends. He added happily, "I thought [my parents] wouldn't approve, but they did." Likewise at college, "When I suggested that he let me drive to —— with the band next week, why there was no problem at all." It is interesting that Stanton, attending college more than two hundred miles away from home, still felt he had to ask permission for such a thing. But Stanton mentioned it to show that his father "doesn't give me detailed instructions—he has confidence in me."

Just before this in the conversation, he said his father "was very excited about the fact that I was going to college, and I should make the most of it—you've the chance once, be thankful." Stanton paused, and then went on, quoting his father: "And just mind that what you do doesn't come back to haunt you someday—and guide yourself accordingly." Asked what exactly this meant, Stanton replied, "Oh, the Young Communist League and other rash activities."

In the previous interview, Stanton had said that his parents were inclined to "snip at each other a bit" over the value of college. His mother, a junior-college graduate who had formerly taught school, appreciated college from the standpoint of "a good education and personal habits." His father, who had never gone to college and who had grown up during the Depression, took a more hard-boiled approach. For him, apparently, a college background meant "position" and a chance to make more money. Stanton said he tried to "strike a happy balance" between his two parents' views. When asked at another point what he did value in college, he replied, "A degree, friends, contacts, a broad base of knowledge so that when someone speaks about a topic I will know at least something about it." Among American college students these motives are not unusual; the only distinctive point, perhaps, was the stress laid on power and status in conversation. He repeated very definitely that a broad education was primarily useful because it meant he knew about a subject when someone else mentioned it. Status in the small group was very important to Stanton. When *writing* about college, however, Stanton hewed much more narrowly to his father's standard. On a sophomore-year questionnaire, he wrote: "Personally, I trust —— University will cause money and a job. That is all I ask of it." One suspects that, when he did not have to face an academic interviewer, he was readier to take a hard-boiled line, reflecting in part a strong pressure from his father to make good. At subsequent interviews, by contrast, he continued to mention the intellectual advantages of a broad education.

Returning to the first sophomore-year interview—it was noticeable that Stanton talked very little about his mother. To some degree there were external reasons for this: owing to work, he had spent more time in the summer with his father. On the other hand, he said he found more to talk about with his mother. He described her briefly as cheerful and accepting. He said he discussed news and business with his father; but he added, with an apologetic laugh: "We really don't say that much to each other. . . . We sit and watch television—sit and stare." Trying to make it objective, in a slightly hurt, eager voice, he explained: "Usually my father's rather interested in a TV show, and so am I."

From all that Stanton said about his parents, it appears that he did not submit to them utterly in an extreme authoritarian way. He was prepared, evidently, to voice disagreement with his father, and to say that he did not enjoy working for him. But what counts for authoritarianism, even more than the amount of rebellion overtly expressed, is the way the personality deals with the rebellion *not* expressed, and how the individual really feels about it. As already suggested, Stanton minimized what rebelliousness he did show by identifying with his father—especially with his father's hard-boiled intolerance. Remember, also, that at the times of the interviews Stanton was acquiring new authorities, not all of whom fitted easily with the old. We have little knowledge of how he responded to his parents in childhood and youth; he might generally have been much more submissive then than later. True, in the episode of the liquor bottles he must have known he would infuriate his father. But his action was in obedience to the even more severe authority of Temperance.

Sophomore questionnaire. This asked questions about a person's beliefs, aims, and values, and it gave the respondent space to answer in his own words. Stanton took it early in the new year.

In sexual matters, he said he had become "more permissive," but his views appeared to be almost entirely dependent on imitating respected figures rather than on principles.

> I always thought that gentlemen did not engage in premarital intercourse, but some of the finest people I have met have told me quite candidly that they are very free sexually. I always thought being "nice" and being sexually free were mutually exclusive. I suspect that I got this idea from high school where those who practiced the habits above were always the "trouble-making" element. My parents are rather puritanical about sex and I suspect that they are responsible for some of these old values also.

Another theme that emerged from Stanton's sophomore questionnaire was an affirmation of the "Protestant ethic," coupled with lack of confidence about succeeding in terms of that ethic. Here again, Stanton showed some intellectual honesty about himself. Asked what he would consider a "good life" in ten years' time, he wrote:

> The good life consists of having enough money to be independent and socially useful. . . . [But] money should not be so plentiful that one can buy everything one wants to. Part of the good life consists of struggle to achieve desires: they shouldn't be readily available. Victory gives happiness.

Further on he wrote, "I am not sure of my leadership ability. This is a must in the business world, and failure there could mean failure to achieve success in money or job, which would jeopardize the rest of the relationships." At the same time he admitted, "I tend to have a rather domineering personality; this could cause problems with marriage and friends." In terms of *The Lonely Crowd*'s categories, there seemed to be conflict between the inner-directed, desk-thumping "moralizer" and a modern other-directed type, highly tuned to the modes of his peer group—or, to borrow from William H. Whyte, a clash between "Protestant ethic" and "Organization Man."[5]

On the subject of politics, Stanton answered the questionnaire as follows:

> I have become even more conservative than when I first arrived here. I feel that this is due to my reaction against professors and their political beliefs. I have had several professors who do not make any attempt to divorce their political opinions from their course material. Generally, their arguments, when presented in this manner, are so sketchy that I can see through them right away. This leads to a certain self-assurance on my part.

Stanton said he was now more conservative than his parents (his father favored public-welfare programs while being fairly right wing over Communism). In religion, he said he agreed with his parents: he went to church and was a "firm believer." Biology and other courses had only confirmed his belief.

It is worth noting here that, although Stanton scored very high on the F scale when he took the test his first year, his score was even higher when he took the test again his senior year. In this he differed from Jerry White, the other student considered here, but was similar to many high F scorers studied at the same college. By contrast, the scores of most college students appear to fall during their four years. This does not mean necessarily that Stanton's basic psychodynamics became much more authoritarian; indeed, the scores of Stanton and other high F scorers on a second authoritarianism scale suggested very tentatively that no great intensifying of the disposition had taken place.[6] But it does imply that Stanton's heightened conservatism was not only a reaction to the bias of his professors. Stanton's move rightward was surely part of a more general reaction to all that the professors and their community stood for—rational questioning, secular uncertainty, and a modern challenge to the free-enterprise faith. It was a general ideological hardening, very much in character with authoritarianism though by no means peculiar to it.

Sophomore year, spring. Stanton said that in religious beliefs he had become more fundamentalist and closer to the teachings of Calvin. His best friend, indeed his only close friend at college, was a conservative Baptist, and this, he felt, had influenced him. Darwin's theory of evolution, he declared, was "riddled with holes," although there might be something to the "idea of mutations."

He showed no anti-Catholic feelings; on the contrary, certain parts of Pope John's encyclical impressed him. Politically, he was more intolerant. Asked his opinion about some current mild peace demonstrations on the campus, he said snidely, "It's a rudimentary test of intelligence to know when to come in out of the rain." (This was several years before student protest groups at the university resorted to physical obstruction.)

In talking about authority and freedom, Stanton was inconsistent. He praised Goldwater for representing Jeffersonian principles: Goldwater would maximize individual freedom—and individual wealth. Yet on the subject of college authority he took a very different line. The university administration, he said, should be more "awe-inspiring"; it should make students realize that "it is indeed the administration." The authorities should not try to be friends of the students; the proper relationship was "teacher and learner." What the students needed was more guidance and direction, not more independence. (Yet, not long after this interview, he was involved in a piece of vandalism which cost the university some equipment.)

Even within the sphere of politics, he showed inconsistencies. At one point in the conversation he said that the Federal Government ran seven hundred businesses which ought to be liquidated. At another, he argued that the government should take over the railroads, even though he mentioned alternative ways in which the railroads might get out of their financial difficulties. He also supported the Johnson proposal to subsidize a new rapid-transit system between Eastern cities. He realized his position was "terribly inconsistent" with his political views, but he explained that his love of transport matters came first. He even envisaged a possible management career in a nationalized transport corporation. Asked whether this didn't raise "an interesting dilemma," he said he didn't think about it.

On the subject of foreign policy, he again took a tough line, and his tone of voice became more cryptic, tough-guy, when he was discussing it. His most-admired historical figure was Theodore Roosevelt.

Junior year, fall. Stanton said he was taking a course in French politics, partly because he was very much interested in De Gaulle, partly because he liked the professor. He said of another professor whose course he was taking (a young political scientist with a rather bullying manner to students): "He has a class of cynicism which I like." But he was quite prepared to criticize the political-science faculty for not taking enough interest in undergraduates, and he apparently enjoyed and took part in lively class discussions. When the subject turned to exams, however, he said he hated essay questions which were too broad. Although he felt little aptitude for science and mathematics, the fruits of large-scale technology held a fascination for him that was partly romantic. He was particularly interested in transport and telephone systems, and he said he had a "passion for industrial towns."

Junior year, spring. This discussion focused mainly on Stanton's friends and acquaintances. His best friend, "William MacIntyre," was a person he had known in high school but only got to know well at college. As a staunch Baptist, MacIntyre disapproved of dancing and smoking, but on many matters Stanton admired him for having an independent mind. He was much more rebellious than Stanton: "He treats his parents like dirt," Stanton said without disapproval. To some extent Stanton took the side of the parents, reporting proudly that they often held him up as an example to their son. "Bill has confessed to me that in most cases the advice is warranted, well deserved." MacIntyre was very disorganized and Stanton said he was apt to "run [MacIntyre's] life for him." "I lead him by the hand . . . c'mon, Bill, let's get going, it's late, wear *that* tie." Sometimes he pushed too far, MacIntyre got mad, and Stanton would apologize. MacIntyre also got mad once when Stanton was talking to a "hot-rod type" in the latter's own language—again a shift into tough-guy talk. "Be yourself," MacIntyre told him. "Don't try to play the other fellow." Stanton reported this very honestly. Asked what in general he got out of the friendship, he said, "A good deal of knowledge and a good deal of enjoyment; I really enjoy talking with him." This valuing of friendship for the knowledge it gave emerged when Stanton talked of other friends, too. But the friendship with MacIntyre also enabled Stanton to dominate, taking the role of a stern parent, while at the same time enjoying MacIntyre's rebelliousness.

On the matter of dating, Stanton said he saw one particular girl quite often. Asked to describe her, he gave a short physical description ("very good looking") and then went on to say that she came from his home town and he knew her parents. Like his best friend, she too was a devout Baptist. When the interviewer asked him to describe her as a person, he said she was gregarious, vivacious, and talkative—"at times, too talkative." He also found her "a little immature," inclined to do things which would embarrass him "in a group." She lacked social graces, he said. In general he did not talk of her with much affection; her vivaciousness seemed to be too much for him. They necked a little on dates, and she had confided personal feelings to him; but "I have never reciprocated."

Later on in the talk, Stanton described the kind of wife he would like to have.

> Good cook, good looking, good housewife-manager type, one who enjoys the same tastes as I do, like music and so forth. Essentially the kind of woman whom you wouldn't be afraid to present in any sort of company of friends; someone who could hold her own in a strong intellectual discussion; who can hold her own in a circle of business friends, or bridge playing or gossipy-type women: this sort of thing. . . . I don't like career women.

Stanton talked about sex itself in a surgical way. As yet he had not gone to bed with anyone, but he had learned how it was done, had read about it, and felt he could "go through with it without any difficulty." He added: "I would like to engage in it—simply clinical curiosity about it." Despite the limited affection he showed his girl friend, he said at another point that he was ready to go as far as she was, sexually. "On the other hand," he said, "I have long felt that the prohibitions against adultery are also meant for premarital intercourse. . . . If there were some 100 percent effective contraceptive device, I would *probably*" (here he slowed down for thought) "feel a little less compunction about engaging in it." In the meantime, "it's probably better to wait from the standpoint of psychology and economics, and there are probably good moral grounds for waiting as well. But I would probably ignore them if the opportunity arose." Beneath the cool manner, the ambivalence and uncertainty in all of this is plain. His attitude to girls and sex was a mixture of inhibition, anxiety, exploitativeness, contempt of spontaneity, concern for social position; and all these components seemed to reinforce each other.

The conversation turned to politics, and the interviewer asked Stanton about his "feelings around the Kennedy assassination." Stanton showed some of the same impersonality that he had over sex. First, he said, "it was a sense of overwhelming relief that the assassin was a leftist and not a rightist." He then went straight into a discussion of the assassination's impact on party power, without making any mention of the shock and tragedy of the event. He argued that it hurt the Republican party since Goldwater could have carried the South against Kennedy.

Stanton said he would support the John Birch Society if it were not for doubts about the Society's leader, Robert Welch. He also said he was opposed to the current civil-rights legislation; and he opposed measures to end discrimination by private landlords. He admitted that "in many cases the Negroes have been denied their rights"; but he added: "Now they are . . . asking for privileges." Groups like CORE, he said, had demanded "not equal employment but preferential employment."[7] He didn't object to "quiet

Negro sit-ins," but some of the bigger demonstrations [albeit non-violent] were doing more harm than good to the Negro cause. "I dislike them intensely." In all of this, Stanton showed no sign of racism. He expressed concern for a fundamentalist reading of the Constitution rather than great feeling for the Negro lot; but that is not the same thing as racist aggression. We have no evidence that he would have been more hostile to blacks had the college climate permitted it. The fact remains that the values of Stanton's friends and acquaintances did not condone racism anyway; and, as the next interview report shows, Stanton found other targets for his hostility.

Senior year, fall. Stanton was asked to describe the general run of students at the university. Could he categorize them? Unlike many other interviewees asked this question, Stanton said without reservation that he could. He went on to portray several types, all of them with some contempt.

> There's an activist type—which I tend to associate with the beards and sandals variety. Then a middle class, apathetic, just-come-from-nice-suburban-home type, just come here to get an education and not a lot else. Another type would be the impresser. . . . And then I suppose I can *lump* all graduate students into some sort of category, not too favorable with exceptions. I tend to associate them generally with the beards and beatnik type . . . and all sorts of *activist* things. . . .
>
> As far as the beards and sandals type are concerned, ship them off to Berkeley; they deserve each other. . . . It would be quite fine if everyone fell into the other two categories.

Thus, for all his professions of individualism and his deprecation of the prevailing student categories, he was prepared to accept a conformist student body, dominated by the less-offensive types. It should be added that Stanton's university at the time was no great center for beatniks or strident left-wing activity.

Asked about his own friends, Stanton said he would put himself in "a *very small* group, I suppose an offshoot of the middle class here-for-an-education type." "Realistic-nice-guy-activists," he said humorously; and then in a more serious vein: "They're effective in a quiet way—no big riots or such like. I feel they operate at a much higher level of activity." In an earlier talk, Stanton had said that most of his friends disapproved of beatniks. In general, his opinion of other students on the campus drew a sharp line between a small in-group and a herd of crudely stereotyped outsiders. Yet his acceptance of the in-group was ambivalent: at one point he said that he found it hard to go against the group and that this often bothered him.

Senior year, spring. The interviewer asked Stanton what rights he thought students had in the college community. "Very little," Stanton replied. The college administration should set up what was required; it was then up to the students to take it or go elsewhere. "Student government's a farce; the board of trustees have all the power." The idea that student government might wield some influence through publicizing issues did not impress him.

At home, however, Stanton thought he was more independent of his parents than earlier. In the interview, certainly, he criticized his father more directly than before. "He has an obnoxious habit of getting people to do little things for him, like changing the TV channel when he wants a new program." On such occasions Stanton would take evasive action, burying his face in the paper and pretending he hadn't heard. In politics, likewise, Stanton said he avoided arguments with his father. "I quietly agree with him, and that is that." As in earlier conversations, he stressed that the friction with his father was on "trivial things mostly" and that they had the same stubborn streak. "We tend to run head on." Yet another point, he said he admired his father but didn't think they were much alike. "My father doesn't think I work hard enough," he added. He said his father was an "awful hard worker"; indeed, he was practically a "nervous wreck" when not working. His mother was "outstanding" for the way she got along with him: "She follows along and supports him." She let him make the major decisions, and rarely argued. Sometimes she told him he was working too hard, and on occasion she gently told him off when, indulging his habit, he asked her to do unnecessary little things for him. But she insisted on keeping the house "spick and span," and according to Stanton she worked all day at it.[8]

In a more general context, the interviewer asked Stanton who or what he found most irritating. He immediately replied, "Stubborn or obnoxious people." Stubbornness, it will be remembered, was a trait he attributed both to his father and himself, and an excuse for the friction between them. In this sense he talked of it neutrally; he was only prepared to attack it outright when he could identify it in others.

Stanton's scores on a self-rating questionnaire are worth noting here. Around this time he was given the questionnaire which asked him to give himself a rating on various traits—from "very low" through "middling" to "very high" on each.[9] With his permission a friend of his was asked to rate him also. Stanton described himself as very low in "rebelliousness," i.e., unrebellious. (His friend did not check this item.) On the quality of "drivenness, lack of peace with oneself, restlessness," he put himself high, but he put himself low in "emotional conflicts with self and others." His friend put him high on this, though, and Stanton himself thought that in his freshman year he was high on it. In both "self-esteem" and "intellectual sophistication," Stanton rated himself high; his friend put him low.

At the end of the last session, the interviewer asked Stanton about the talks they had had together over the four college years. What effect had they had on him? Stanton's first answer was that they had given him a certain status in his group of friends. He then added that they had given him some insights.

STANTON'S AUTHORITARIANISM: AN APPRAISAL

Stanton was not, in general, very self-confident, and his feelings were poorly integrated. Among other things, there was considerable clash between drives for "manly" independence and a submissiveness to authorities. The authorities included a traditionalism which, in the "Protestant ethic," demanded an independent showing and thus exacerbated the conflict.

Hence he could show some overt rebelliousness to his parents and still feel basically degraded by the extent to which he had *not* been rebellious.

There was also tension between the messages received from different authorities. Campus liberalism threatened to undermine the puritanism learned from parents and home-town life. At first he admitted the uncertainties this created; then his mind seemed to close. In the interviews generally, and by comparison with many other interviewees, he gave little direct description of moods and feelings.

In his heightened conservatism, and his tough-guy talk about politics, there appeared to be a squelching of doubts. He held on to his ideology as if he were gripping an anchor that threatened to slip away or fall apart in his hands. If it did these things he would be lost, without a sure sense of identity. In sexual values, it is true, he felt himself to be more permissive; but his new stance of the surgical explorer jibed with the need to dominate and to minimize tender feeling. Emotionally, his sexual values were *not* very permissive: they did not promote a wide play of feeling. (About his actual sex experience we know little.)

The same minimizing of tenderness appeared in his remarks about the Kennedy assassination. Although asked to portray his feelings at the time, he mentioned no sense of sadness or shock. This is not to say that Stanton had no tenderness; there was, for example, the fleeting glimpse of a love for his father, ambivalent and wistful though that love was. But, if Stanton's account of his father is accurate, it appears that the older man was not the sort of person to accept tender feeling from his son. And so, to feel close to his father, Stanton had to emphasize the tough qualities they had in common—the "stubbornness." And, just as he aligned himself with his father in contempt for a feckless employee, so he identified himself in general with a tough-minded conventionalism. This showed itself against student protest and the spontaneity of a girl friend. Yet specific targets were not enough to drain off his hostility. His identification with a small in-group of students enabled him to widen the target area; he viewed the student body at large as a rather scorned out-group.

Stanton's childhood reactions to his father, who was apparently an intolerant, demanding, and "driven" man, may well have formed much of his authoritarian disposition. It is not clear what relationship he had with his mother, and what specific effects it had on his personality. By adolescence, however, Stanton desired a more ascetic and tough authority than his parents alone could provide. This was true, at least, over drinking and in political ideology. In part this may be traced to a fear of weakness and of losing identity, which in turn was linked to concerns about impulse control. The teenage fear of drunkenness, and the alarm at his own "sarcasm," seemed to reflect an anxiety about becoming vulnerable. Vulnerable, that is, to his own emotions as well as to external forces— the two threats being much entwined. If he "went around snipping [people] off," it might hurt him socially; and if he lost control over his aggressiveness, his image of himself and his precarious relationships with others might be swamped by forces from the unconscious.

Having made all these points, we must reiterate that authoritarianism does not embrace the whole character, certainly not in the case of Stanton. In some areas of behavior, he acted humanely and thoughtfully; and what some would call rigidity others might call tenacity. Had his character been studied from another standpoint from that of authoritarianism, a more friendly portrait might have emerged. As it was, given the conflict and strain he was in, it was remarkable that he should offer himself for extensive interviews and so provide the illumination he did.

JERRY WHITE

The son of a Baptist clergyman, Jerry White came from a small agricultural town in the West. His disposition might be considered "borderline authoritarian," for on the one hand, he seemed to displace rebelliousness *away* from authority onto rebel images, but on the other, he had fairly deep humane values and he showed no contempt for the weak and inferior per se.

He was very submissive. He disliked criticizing any constituted authority, and when he felt disagreements he tried to suppress them; this came out vividly when he discussed his teachers, past and present. Asked about "conflicts or disagreements" with his father, he was anxious to minimize them. Thus, in the previous vacation, "I remember we had some kind of conflicts over something—I can't remember what it was. Oh they weren't serious or anything—just little frictions, nothing bad. We're not a fighting family or anything. Just the usual."[10] All this was said somewhat defensively. As White described him, his father was talkative, articulate, a very good host. From various things he said, White showed that he felt inarticulate and generally inept, compared with his father. He was also very dependent on his mother, whom he described as a happy, buoyant person who sang a great deal around the house.

Repressed and rather *de*pressed, White retreated from sociability rather than trying to emulate his father's graces. At college he "enwombed" himself in the Baptist youth club, studied voraciously, and avoided parties whenever he could. He had a marked fear of emotional expression. In several letters he wrote the college before he was admitted, he seemed to be keeping himself at a distance by using the third person—"the applicant," "the writer," "he," and so on. Again, when he described a Billy Graham meeting to his interviewer, he repeatedly praised the lack of "emotionalism" with which people made the decision for Christ; and his chief indignation was saved for wild and unruly behavior.

Unhappily for White, his cocoon of religious asceticism did not protect him from contrary tugs. In a very traditional, fundamentalist environment it might have; but the college was not such a place. Even the Baptist youth club had its bowling parties, and when one was coming up, White told the interviewer: "I'll *have* to go." But, since he was going, he seemed even sadder that he would be dateless. "Sort of a *lone* wolf," he said mournfully. He seemed ashamed of how little dating he had done, attributing it to poverty; but when asked to list the fifteen things he valued most in life, he put sex near the very bottom. At another time, he regretted not being "as socially integrated into the [college] community as I would have liked." He blamed the failure on the academic workload, but his dormitory resident (a teacher) said there was "something within him" which prevented his "making any effort to get to know others."

His position as a clergyman's son did not lessen the ambivalence—at least not the way he interpreted the position. He said that being a "P.K." ("preacher's kid") was difficult: he could not do anything which might reflect on his father, and anyway people treated him differently. According to acquaintances, on the other hand, he magnified these liabilities unnecessarily by being humorless and pompous about the whole "P.K." business.

As already mentioned, White was vehement against rowdy behavior and gadding-about. He said he disliked "backslappers" and he did not want a wife who would "chase off all the time to parties." In describing the ideal house, his prime concern was with having a quiet place for himself—away from "noisy kids." Asked his opinion of smoking and drinking, he paused, sucked in his breath, and then blurted fiercely, "I-don't-know, it's kind of *inane.*" The opinion itself was not remarkable, given his family traditions, but the way he said it suggested a fear of expressing too much aggression, a bottling-up and then a release of hostility when he confirmed that it was on the side of moral order. Perhaps also his hyper-concern about rowdy party-goers reflected an envy of people who had the sort of good time he could not manage.

Having said all this, it must be stressed that White did not seem a generally punitive person. Although a teacher said he could be "bitter with the world at times," he refused to stereotype his fellow students as Stanton did. Likewise, he talked about the afflicted and weak with a matter-of-fact sympathy that did not suggest a superficial kind of "reaction formation." He told, in this vein, of how he had accidentally frightened a woman, a co-worker in a fruit-packing job the previous summer. Without contempt or condescension, he explained that she was highly nervous and screamed at the slightest surprise. More significantly, he accepted with some imagination his parents' adoption of an adolescent, who was about the same age as he. This "foster brother," as he called him, had a mentally disturbed mother; she had been in and out of hospitals and the boy had had a very uncouth and mixed-up childhood. Of course, as a dutiful son, White could not be expected to oppose the adoption, but his sympathetic yet ungilded description of the stresses involved seemed to go further than superficial loyalty. His whole attitude to the matter reflected the humane values of his parents, the values responsible for the boy's adoption in the first place. It is not surprising that White supported the current civil-rights movements, though he joined his parents in liking Goldwater. Nor does it seem inconsistent with any of his personality that, when at last he found a steady girl friend, she should be a disabled person, a vivacious, pretty girl whom he admired in a very platonic way but with no trace of patronizing. He even approved of the idea that girl students, like the men, should be allowed to live off campus—though he said this hesitantly, with amiable surprise at himself, perhaps because college rules forbade it.

In drawing some conclusions about White, let us focus on two aspects of his behavior: the retreat from sociability and great emotional expression, and the occasional outbursts against party-goers and "rowdies." From the context of these outbursts and the defensiveness of their style it must now be obvious that the two aspects of behavior were linked. The question remains: what precise mechanisms were involved in the linkage? There may be several answers, none of them mutually exclusive. In the first place, White lacked social self-confidence. He seemed to wish that he had more social facility, like his father; but having retreated from the arena, he hotly resisted campus demands that he be more active and thus expose himself to possible failure. A puritan stance against frivolity came easily to him, since he had been raised in a fundamentalist tradition. The stance now served to justify his retreat. In the second place, however, there was a part of him which wanted to break out, to enjoy a wider range of social and sensual freedom. His very emphasis on rowdiness suggests that he had to fight hard to keep down his own "rowdy" urges. His self-control relied so heavily on repression and suppression that it was all or nothing; he feared that if he let out too much feeling it would get away from him.

These explanations do not necessarily involve the authoritarian elements of displaced rebelliousness. But we come now to the third explanation (or partial explanation). As already observed, White was very submissive, and even anxious to minimize conflict within his family. Given this fact, and given the other incentives for his attack on "gadabouts" and the like, he may well have used these targets to drain off unexpected rebellion as well—the "normal" rebellion offered by most American sons at some points. In this limited sense, White may have had an authoritarian tendency. But I say "limited" because he did not show any urge to identify with a punitive authority against humane feeling and tenderness; he did not, so far as one can tell, have a great need to dislike underdog symbols of weakness. His learned belief and values reflected a tender side of puritan Christianity, and these in turn appeared to have a deep effect on the way he dealt with his aggressiveness. One is reminded that psychodynamic processes cannot be fully discussed without reference to learned systems of belief.*

CULTURE AND IMPULSE CONTROL

Both Stanton and White showed concern about aggressive or "wild" impulse and its control. In the case of Stanton, anxiety about controlling his own aggression was explicit. In White's case, aggressiveness was bottled up and wild behavior in others was intensely feared and disliked.

* In White's case, as with Stanton, various Oedipal explanations offer themselves but the interview material on this is not substantial enough to warrant promotion to the text. One may conjecture, for example, that White retreated from Oedipal competition with his father, not so much by harshly aligning himself with his father *against* women (his father's values were too truly Christian for that), but by a more complete abandonment of the sexual and sensual arena.

It appears that both individuals came to college with a "Victorianism" that did not sit easily upon them. They depended upon strong moral and social authority for many things, not least for a reinforcement of self-control. Yet at college most of the new authorities which laid claim to their dependency feelings endorsed a more "permissive" way of life, a freeing of impulse, moral relativism, tolerance of ambiguity.

We have seen that the two young men reacted to these stresses in different ways, in part because they brought different dispositions to the college situation. To a large extent, college life only seemed to exacerbate tensions which were already there. Brought up to obey and "be good," they had not really learned, consciously or unconsciously, how to integrate obedience and dependency with other inducements and feelings. In part, perhaps, this was the fault of parents who did not involve themselves with their children in a consistent and supporting way; but it suggests that the very subcultures from which these individuals came did not provide well-integrated norms.[11]

APPENDIX B

Luther and Cromwell

The lives of Martin Luther and Oliver Cromwell remind us that there is no one set of relationships between puritan Protestantism and personality. Despite Cromwell's autocratic traits, there was much more of the authoritarian in Luther. The difference in this respect between the two was at least partly the result of family background and social circumstance.[1]

On first thoughts, Luther seems far from authoritarian. He revolted, after all, against a mighty authority, the leadership of an organization commanding vast social influence and supreme priestly power. To Luther, religious faith was an intensely personal experience which the forms and conventions of a traditional church could easily hinder. In consequence there was a side of him which genuinely wanted religious and intellectual freedom:

> Heresy can never be kept off by force. . . . God's word must contend here. If that avail nothing, temporal power will never settle the matter, though it fill the world with blood.

Until his cause prevailed, Luther was a clear champion of the individual against authority, even to the point of inciting political revolution.

> The common man has been brooding over the injury he has suffered in property, in body and in soul. . . .
> What do they [priests and bishops] better deserve than a strong uprising which will sweep them from the earth? And we would smile did it happen.

But there was another side to Luther, although it only stood out when he was aligned with established power. During the peasants' revolt of 1525, he put himself whole-heartedly behind their bloody suppression. Thirteen thousand peasants were massacred at about the same time that

Luther published his pamphlet *Against the Robbing and Murdering Hordes of Peasants*. One sentence reads:

> A rebel is not worth answering with arguments, for he does not accept them. The answer for such mouths is a fist that brings blood from the nose.

Of course the mere fact that Luther respected civil power does not by itself point to authoritarianism. On a purely rational basis, Luther had come to accept the position that religious faith could not survive without the support of firm civil government and a measure of church discipline. But his statements about civil disobedience showed an extremism and intolerance which cannot be explained by rational philosophy alone; he was appalled to think that his words might cause a defiling, engulfing eruption of the serfs; and his fear turned to frenzy:

> Let all who are able, hew them down, slaughter and stab them, openly or in secret, and remember that there is nothing more poisonous, noxious and utterly devilish than a rebel. You must kill him as you would a mad dog; if you do not fall upon him, he will fall upon you and the whole land.

Long after the rebellion had been suppressed, Luther castigated the class from which his own family had risen. "A peasant is a hog," he declared in 1532,

> for when a hog is slaughtered it is dead, and in the same way the peasant does not think about the next life, for otherwise he would behave very differently. . . .
> The peasant remains a boor, do what you will; (he has his nose, eyes and everything else in the wrong place).[2]

Luther's reverence for civil power had now hardened beyond reason.

> Because God has given a law and knows that no one keeps it . . . the authorities must drive, beat and slay the people, Messrs. Omnes, hang, burn, behead and break them on the wheel, that they may be kept in awe.
> There are no better works than to obey and serve all those who are set over us as superiors. For this reason also disobedience is a greater sin than murder, unchastity, theft and dishonesty, and all that these may include.
> The princes of this world are gods, the common people are Satan, through whom God sometimes does what at other times he does directly through Satan, that is, makes rebellion as a punishment for the people's sins. I would rather suffer a prince doing wrong than a people doing right.

Thus did the champion of religious freedom urge a harsh turning back from the new spirit of secular freedom which his words had helped bring about. Even in religion he came to the conclusion, however reluctantly, that "heretical" beliefs must be suppressed by force. Yet his respect for high power was combined with some hostility to the men who possessed it; he once remarked that rulers were "generally the biggest fools and worst knaves on earth." Something of the same ambivalence, the other way about, marked his dealings with churchmen. For all his strong speech and defiant ways, Luther could be exceedingly deferent to high Catholic dignitaries.

His very revolt, indeed, combined heroic courage with extreme submission. When he rebelled against Rome, he did so in part because he found it too harsh. Luther's age was a time of great rootlessness; the crumbling of feudal ties had thrust man upon his own individual being.[3] Appalled by the weakness and worthlessness he saw in himself, Luther sought personal meaning through submission to the church (his decision to enter the monastery had actually been made during a religious panic in a thunderstorm). For all its external discipline, however, the monastery did not give Luther the solace he craved. His obsession with past sins, a guilt colored by outright terror at the thought of God's judgment, went far beyond the requirements of his confessors. Their advice that he be more tolerant of himself only increased his anxiety. In effect they told him, "Confess and repent as much as you can, but then be at peace. Christ is forgiving and He bids you have hope." What he wished them to say, it seemed, was "Yes, you are worthless; you are right to condemn yourself; you can only find meaning and strength by forgetting yourself in God's holy power." The very tolerance shown by his superiors thwarted his deepest urge to submit, by bidding him live with his imperfections as a self-accepting individual—a course which threatened to bring down the wrath of a jealous God.[4]

This image of authority, as a punitive power which may attack on the slightest sign of disaffection, lies at the heart of much authoritarianism. The harshness of Luther's God was in some respects like the harshness of his father, a figure whom the adult Luther half repudiated, half revered. Born a peasant, Hans Luther had become a coalminer and thence pushed his way into the class of small industrialists. His relationship with Martin showed how early capitalism could foster both Protestantism and authoritarianism. (Even if Protestantism then served to encourage capitalism as it did authoritarianism, this notion reverses the main sequence of cause postulated by Tawney and Weber in their writings on capitalism and the "Protestant ethic.") A tough, competitive man, Hans Luther was immensely ambitious for his son, and for himself. Little Martin was frequently beaten and, more important, he did not always know the reason why.[5] The whippings made him resentful, but his father had a cunning which, on a conscious plane, could always win him back.[6]

The complexity was repeated in adulthood. By Luther's own account he entered the church to get away from his parents' severity; yet the escape route seemed to reproduce his earlier submission. We find him yielding first to monastic discipline, and then to a God whose moral fierceness matched that of his father. Beneath the submission lay a fear of authority which had become so much a part of conscience that it actually sought new authorities to be afraid of. Fear—religious fear—seemed to provide among other things a rationalization for the feeling of weakness which severe parents and brutal schoolteachers had planted within him.

For Luther, weakness of soul was inseparable from weakness of body. There were times when his heart seemed to palpitate and when he broke into sweats, both conditions often occurring with fits of nervous and religious anxiety. He also suffered from indigestion, kidney stones, and hemorrhoids, and his famous constipation begot if it did not also reflect an immense anal concern. He was obsessed by images of anal dirt: his portraiture of enemies, from papal executives to the devil himself, abounded with vivid fecal prose. Given the other aspects of his character, this adds to an impression of authoritarianism, although by themselves "anal tendencies" are not necessarily authoritarian. More speculatively one can see their genesis in the childhood of a harshly treated small boy desperately trying to keep out of trouble, the son of middle-class *nouveaux* who had made cleanliness a creed.[7]

It must be said that in several important spheres Luther did not behave in a manifestly authoritarian way. As far as can be observed, this was true of his relationship with his wife, and it certainly applied to his intellectuality. He was confident enough of his intellectual powers to welcome full debate with the Pope's representatives, and he thought much about his own character. Although he did not fully recognize his wish for power and aggression, and although his bodily ailments would seem to reflect repressed anxieties, yet he did to some extent recognize his feeling of weakness and his deep dependence on God's authority. On the other hand, when he called himself weak, he primarily meant weakness before God and as a mortal, not as a man compared with other men.

We cannot really know to what extent, if at all, Luther's castigation of peasants and rebels provided a means of diverting rebellious impulse. Some of his vehemence does sound like an attack on his own rebelliousness, coupled with oblique warfare against his father, striking that part of Hans which could be labeled "inferior peasant." All one can say for sure is that he was a very aggressive man who, having made submission, turned his hostility—a sadistic adamance—against a temporal rebelliousness of the sort he had once himself expressed. It is nonetheless interesting how even this minimal pattern suited Protestantism. As it is, perhaps we should think of Luther's personality as a borderline, and very complex, authoritarian example. Had he been less sensitive and understanding than he was, he could not have been so creative and wise an architect. Yet, had he been more rational, more balanced, more at peace with himself, how could he have stoked the fires of anger and fear which helped destroy Catholic supremacy? In our secular age it is almost impossible to understand the magic hold which the late medieval church, for all its decadence, exerted on every walk of life. To defy the magic a driving, raging passion was needed, and an obsessive fealty to an even higher power.

Oliver Cromwell was in some ways very like Luther, but the concept of authoritarianism does not really illuminate his personality. It is true that "the man who killed the king" made himself a dictator, and that the rebellion he led was in part a battle to restore the traditional power and privilege of a gentry elite. It is also true that Cromwell was a man of pentup violence and hatred, as an M.P. one of the most insulting speakers that the English Parliament ever knew, and a commander who did to the Irish what Luther wanted done to his peasants. Yet long before any fighting broke out Cromwell proved himself a genuine defender of the underdog. He successfully championed the marsh dwellers of the Fens when a land corporation threatened to drain away their livelihood. By itself this might be put down to local patriotism, but in a spontaneous and quite unpatronizing way he performed small acts of kindness to poor villagers, and his concern for the weak and oppressed was so emotional that it seemed almost feminine. As Lord Protector of England he put an end to the cruelties of bear baiting and cock fighting; as a father, he combined Biblical earnestness with affection and laughter.[8]

The same man massacred the Irish defenders of Drogheda. Cromwell himself gave two reasons for his conduct: "the heat of action" and a strategic judgment that "it [would] tend to prevent the effusion of blood for the future"—the same argument used for modern war policies by many types of men. Cromwell's prejudices against the Irish probably made it easier for him to massacre them in the heat of battle; it certainly enabled him to condone a second slaughter in which he did not play a direct part, the killing of soldiers and civilians at Wexford. On the subject of Ireland Cromwell accepted the stock attitudes of English puritanism, the hatred which stereotyped Irishmen as barbaric outsiders, defiled by a subversive papist heresy. These attitudes had become part of English puritan culture: even to men like Milton and Spenser the Irish were a subhuman race which must be controlled by harsh measures.[9] Cromwell showed his own bias by castigating the Irish for atrocities perpetrated in their rebellion of 1641, yet ignoring the cruel English record in Ireland and forgetting the puritan soldiers' massacre of Irish women camp followers after the battle of Naseby in England. Naseby, indeed, showed how nearly the mixture of puritanism and war savagery could produce authoritarian behavior. As G. M. Trevelyan put it,

> the brute instincts of the natural man, which the Puritan warrior thought he had tamed within his breast, were often aroused in special forms by the very religious principles which restrained him from indulging the greed, cruelty and lust of the ordinary soldier.[10]

Hence the same troops who treated most civilians with unusual respect were capable of lynching defenseless Catholics and women suspected of witchcraft. To what extent this involved the displacement of tightly curbed impulse we simply do not know; it seems likely. Even if such displacement did occur, it would not necessarily, and in every case, signify the special relationship with authority that marks authoritarian character. However, where this relationship existed, one would indeed expect puritan anti-Papism to *catalyze* authoritarian aggression.

It is with these points in mind that we should consider Oliver Cromwell and the question of authoritarianism. Drogheda and Wexford were far less central to Cromwell's psychological development than the Peasant War was to Luther's. Luther, after all, continued his castigation of "Messrs Omnes" long after the heat and fear of the peasant uprising had passed. Cromwell, for his part, grew more and more tolerant of Catholics; his dictatorship gave them greater freedom than they had enjoyed under Parliament in the last days of Charles I, and his rule showed much more respect for individual liberties than the postwar Parliaments it succeeded. In religious tolerance Cromwell was ahead of his age and in stark opposition to the narrow puritan sects which fought with him against the king. His famous saying "No man can look into another's heart" expressed a belief that he battled for practically all his adult life.[11] Martin Luther paved the way for such a battle, but Cromwell was the more adamant rebel against a hierarchical and formally organized church. Both men had explosive tempers, and in both, perhaps, their angry outbreaks could be traced to repressed impulse, nagging doubts about being saved,[12] and the frustration of dynamic minds thwarted by petty men. It also appears that Cromwell displaced guilt and aggression in rowdy horseplay—as in the way he buffooned when signing the King's death sentence, a blustering from his own divided feelings. But in face-to-face confrontations Cromwell was more apt than Luther to express his hostility against people of power and position. He could be incredibly rude to superiors, and in Parliamentary debates about bishops (whom he hated) he was so vituperative to other M.P.s that the House nearly had him censured. All in all he acted too directly and consistently against authority to be counted an authoritarian as we use the term.

In social rank, Cromwell was a wealthy squire of inherited means. His father, Robert, was no Hans Luther, no self-made capitalist competing with his son and yet pushing him to social conquest. Robert Cromwell came of a distinguished Huntingdon family, landowners, magistrates, and Members of Parliament. He is said to have been a quiet, reflective man, and he died when Oliver was eighteen leaving him the only male in a large family. Throughout his life Cromwell's strong-minded mother remained his close confidante; there was none of the authoritarian's tendency to dissociate himself from womanhood.[13]

Cromwell's upbringing seems to have built inner strengths which survived the sermons of his grimly puritan teachers. As a young man he was fearless enough of the Calvinist God to become a reckless prodigal; later he underwent what appears to have been a religious identity crisis in which fever, nightmares, and intense remorse merged together; yet unlike others of his theology he never sought to lose himself in extreme self-denial. The most joyless English puritans, the close-cropped "Roundheads," who dressed as somberly as they lived, were to be found mainly among the urban middle classes.[14] It is symbolic that Cromwell, a landed gentleman rather than a bourgeois, wore his hair to the shoulder; that as a new M.P., he dressed so untidily that a Royalist legislator called him a "sloven"— and that his favorite daughter, Elizabeth was incomparably his naughtiest.

Of course Cromwell was a *puritan,* supporting moral codes which even by many contemporary standards seemed oppressive. Under his Protectorate, adultery was severely punished, and evidences of "merrie England" such as dancing on Sunday were put down. But he also abandoned capital punishment for all except convicted murderers, and other laws too he moderated. He was a dictator, not a sadist.[15]

NOTES

FOREWORD

1. Written in collaboration with Betty Aron, Maria Levinson, and William Morrow, and published by Harper, New York, 1950.
2. Fielding's account is in *Tom Jones,* vol. I, chaps. 5-8. Butler's is in *The Way of All Flesh,* which was written in the 1860s though not published till much later. *The Authoritarian Personality* drew ideas not only from Freud directly, but also via Erich Fromm from Wilhelm Reich and from Harold Lasswell, A. H. Maslow, and many others.

1. INTRODUCTION

1. "Authoritarian" is not a good term for our subject in view of its general meanings, applied to institutions as well as people. Still, in absence of a good alternative, I have kept it to make a clear connection with *The Authoritarian Personality*. Perhaps the best alternative is "ecomanic" but this, as yet, is too obscure for a general readership. "Submissive-aggressive" is unwieldy and too broad a category, "sado-masochist" too exclusively sexual and again too broad; sado-masochists are not necessarily authoritarian.
2. See, however, the studies of Luther and Hitler by Fromm, 1941. Since my writing this book, work on other types of psychopathological behavior has led me to formulate more systematically the different ways in which culture and society produce behavioral disorders. Some of this is relevant to authoritarianism but must await publication in a separate work.
3. These and other confusions of terms are pointed out at greater length by Greenstein, 1965b and 1969. To clarify matters Greenstein distinguishes between "cognitive" and a more emotionally-fraught "ego defensive" authoritarianism, but the two are not mutually exclusive, as we shall see.

4. Perhaps the nearest to this is a study by Stern (1962), using a questionnaire quite like the F scale. The Student Development Study at Stanford and Berkeley used extensive interviews as well as questionnaires, including the F scale, but its published work did not relate the two in studies of authoritarianism. Cf. Katz, 1968.

5. See the study of "Mack" in Adorno *et al.*, 1950, pp. 32 ff., 529 ff., 788 ff., and elsewhere. Since then, to my knowledge, the only published case studies done explicitly in terms of authoritarian psychodynamics are Frenkel-Brunswik's study of "Karl" (1951), Sanford's study of "Pat" in White (1954), and a few "Faces in the Crowd" portrayed by Riesman (1952). Riesman's studies do not clearly show authoritarianism, as defined here; the other studies are discussed later. The main surveys of research on "authoritarianism" (Christie and Cook, 1958; Kirscht and Dillehay, 1967) simply omit clinical case studies!

6. But cf. Pettigrew, 1958. Fromm (1941) and Dicks (1950) related social and cultural factors to concepts of deep-seated authoritarian character, but this has not been followed up since *The Authoritarian Personality* was published.

7. Several of the F scale "items" (questionnaire statements with which authoritarians are expected to agree, thus producing "high F scores") are exactly the same as statements used by the Lynds in their 1930s study of Muncie, Indiana, to illustrate Middletowners' cultural beliefs. It is quite clear that right-wing ideology will often push up a person's F scale score, whether or not his ideology reflects authoritarian psychodynamics. A newer, longer questionnaire has been developed which, aside from its religious items, seems on the face of it less vulnerable to learned ideological biases and more squarely focused on authoritarian psychodynamics. On this scale authoritarians are supposed to score low (it is sometimes misnomered the Social Maturity Scale, which says more about the users than the subjects of study) but it has not really been shown to work by testing it against depth studies of individuals.

For more technical criticisms of the F scale, see Christie and Jahoda, 1954, and Kirscht and Dillehay, 1967. On the cross-cultural limitations of the scale, see an interesting Arab-American study by Melikian, 1959.

8. Little reference will be made to advance research in perception, learning, and conditioning—in some respects it complements the ideas presented here. I do not doubt, for example, that mixtures of situations, social pressures, and individual psychodynamics can affect perception to the point of altering what we "physically" see with our eyes.

9. Fromm, 1941, and Dicks, 1950. My treatment of leading Nazi characters has not benefited from Albert Speer's memoirs or from Joachim Fest, *The Face of the Third Reich, Portraits of the Nazi leadership*. These works appeared too late to be properly used here.

10. Not to be confused with Rudolph Hess.

11. I am grateful to Craig Comstock for the nucleus of this point.

12. In my search for evidence of authoritarianism, I have not explored the studies of individual behavior in small groups; I realize too late that

this may be a grave oversight. It is also possible that a development of George Kelly's "personality construct" tests might produce a valuable indication of authoritarianism in some people. Some studies of behavior in experimentally contrived situations are reviewed later.

13. For research purposes, psychoanalysis of a living patient does enjoy a great advantage over historical study in that feedback from the patient can be used for more probing questions. This, however, may become a "leading" of the subject. See Greenstein, 1968, especially pp. 272 ff., for a brief but balanced discussion of these and related problems. In his subsequent book Greenstein (1969, especially chap. 3) has set out some ways of judging and fairly presenting the psychodynamic factor in the action of a historic figure—he proposes a more systematic and, in a way, more advanced procedure than I have usually followed. On these problems, cf. Erikson, 1969.

2. PORTRAIT AND CONCEPT

1. Butler's portrait of Pontifex was based on his own father, but it is not clear how much he was simply drawing from his father in describing a general type. In her splendidly written book, Garnett (1926) argues that the father, though a strict and proper Victorian, was more amiable than his son made him out to be. The portrait was very much Butler's *image* of his father. Garnett does, however, admit that the father did not like children and had indeed been pressured by his own father to enter the church against his inclinations. Beyond this, it is notable that Butler, a sensitive witness of men for all his filial biases, should depict complementary traits which add up to authoritarianism. Garnett, to be fair, realized much of the wider aspect. We should not, then, discount altogether the portrait of Pontifex as psychological evidence.

In compressing that portrait within a few pages, I have probably been rough with Butler's flashes on many matters, his nuances, his mastery of the oblique. This is inevitable if the portrait is to be given concisely but more than cursorily.

2. Ogilvy, 1963, p. 15.
3. Lasswell, 1960, pp. 127-35. (First published in 1930.)
4. Sartre, 1946, pp. 163-76.
5. Fromm, 1941.
6. Adorno *et al.*, 1950, especially pp. 759-62.

3. AN AUTHORITARIAN "SYNDROME"

1. Adorno *et al.*, 1950. A more recent study by Mark Chesler found that people showing marked intolerance of one minority group (i.e., Jews or blacks) tend to be intolerant not only of other ethnic minority groups but also of the physically disabled.

2. The interviews were supplemented by autobiographies and by Thematic Apperception Tests, in which the interviewed were asked to give explana-

tory stories about a series of ambiguous drawings. Much of the hypothesis came from earlier work by authors of *The Authoritarian Personality*.

3. The categories listed above are not quite the same as the nine cited in *The Authoritarian Personality*. The latter counts superstition and "black-and-white" stereotypes as one attribute; here they are two. On the other hand, hostility and cynicism here become a subcategory of aggression, whereas the original researchers made these two separate categories. There is no finding in the original F scale research to rule out such an arbitrary rearrangement.

4. Dicks, 1950: summarized on pp. 153-6 below. Dicks produced good quoted material but admittedly they held the same general psychoanalytic viewpoint as the authors of *The Authoritarian Personality*. Most samples used for the latter were middle-class, West Coast American.

5. See especially the research by Berkowitz (1959), Berkowitz and Holmes (1959) and Epstein (1965 and 1966), all summarized on p. 325-6 below. These studies, however, do not lend themselves to just one interpretation.

6. Recounted in conversation.

7. The original jargon for this category is "anti-intraception."

8. In addition to the findings of interviews, some of this is shown by correlations between F scores and scores on "Compulsiveness" items in a newer non-authoritarianism scale.

9. In other samples, admittedly, even non-authoritarians tended to score high on (agree very much with) these two particular statements, but the combination of *very* high scores on these and aggressive, "antisocial" behavior seems significant.

10. Referred to as "Projectivity" in the original F scale studies.

11. For an archteypical portrait this stands; however, a threat complex need not reflect projection.

12. Frenkel-Brunswik in Adorno et al., 1950, pp. 411-13.

4. THE INNER STRUCTURE

1. Robert Lifton, 1961, pp. 150-51 and elsewhere, especially the study of Father Simon, pp. 207-21. Lifton, however, does not use the terms "authoritarian" and "character structure" quite in the senses meant here.

2. In the brain, the physical basis of the ego would seem to be the roof brain, just as the physical seat of impulse seems to be the thalamus. The word "conscience" is used here to include both the child's primitive "super-ego" and the more mature conscience which has merged, more or less, with the ego (see text below).

3. I depart here from some earlier psychoanalytic writings; it is a debatable point.

4. This does not explain fully the way in which a child acquires morality, but it is supported by some research and with other studies it is compatible. See Kohlberg, 1964; Bloom, 1959; and Eysenck, 1964, chap. 5 ("Is Conscience a Conditioned Reflex?"), especially p. 118.

5. Certainly there are characters whose reason weakens their conscience and resolve, by mainly negative criticisms of moral values; there are likewise characters with an arid rationality which saps the drives born of impulse, but these are at least partly due to imperfections within the ego. The ego has many more facets than suggested here.

6. The following account of an authoritarian personality's inner organization is based on the interviews by Adorno *et al.* and further biographical studies.

7. In Western cultures, whose emphasis on guilt seems to be reflected in relatively high rates of depressive illness, authoritarian consciences may tend to be more internalized than, for example, in the authoritarian pattern described in the DuBois study of Alor, 1960 (first published 1944).

8. But displacement of hostility or of other feelings can be an effective way of managing them; it is not confined to ill-adjusted, insecure persons.

9. See *Officer Factory* by Kirst, 1962, the account, based on fact, of the Nazi cadet Hochbauer.

10. What actually happens in each individual case depends partly on the direct influence of outside circumstances, which can sometimes break the circle by gently pushing the ego into more self-exercise and self-reliance, or can do the reverse by cowing and frustrating the individual. The term "vicious circle" may be misleading, since the individual does not usually regress in absolute terms; rather, he stands still or develops very slowly compared with most non-authoritarians. Plunged into too new and uncertain a situation, however, the authoritarian may regress in absolute terms.

11. See Sanford's chapter in White, ed., 1966.

12. "Borderline cases" might include (1) people whose behavior is not so recurringly suggestive of authoritarianism that we can confidently label their dispositions as authoritarian; (2) people whose emotional expression seems very authoritarian at some times and over some concerns but who also persistently show traits which seem to go against the central qualities of authoritarianism and not just in the sense of being a "reaction formation." For example, they may confront their feelings of weakness to some extent and/or they may alternate between overt rebellion and suppression of rebellion (against their primary authorities). Again, they may recurringly attack targets which in a limited sense seem to represent weakness, inferiority, or "safe outlet," but also seem to represent authority.

Thus the "borderline" category may reflect our ignorance about a person as well as his real nature.

5. DEFINITION AND DETECTION: SOME PROBLEMS

1. And such behavior may be "situational authoritarian" rather than reflecting a specific authoritarian disposition. Even here, the suggestion of diverted aggression is less strong than in certain physical movements (biologically patterned?) among animals. See Lorenz, 1966.

2. Berkowitz, 1959, found that among girls at a university the most manifestly anti-Semitic were apt to register particularly high in hostility

toward their partners in a test exercise, when (and only when) frustrated and offended by the (presumably authoritative) test experimenter. Prior levels of hostility were allowed for. It seemed that the girls displaced hostility onto safe, or at least available, targets. Another part of the test suggested an authoritarian defensiveness and readiness to project in that the anti-Semitic girls, when angered by the experimenter, were especially likely to deny that their subsequent hostile behavior was true to their real selves. But another test, by Berkowitz and Holmes, 1959, showed that the person most likely to take out hostility on the partner was both predisposed to dislike the partner (prejudice) *and* to *express* hostility for the authoritative frustrator. This was expressed when solicited by a perhaps equally authoritative questionnaire, but we may also have here an unauthoritarian pattern in which hostility for the strong oppressor is not repressed but extended to a scapegoat (the partner) who may be seen as like the oppressor in at least some annoying attributes. The submissive are not the only scapegoaters; cf. the study of frustrated anti-Semites by Bettelheim and Janowitz, 1964, which appears to portray both authoritarians and anti-authoritarians.

In other tests, Epstein, 1965, found that people scoring high on the F scale tended, when frustrated by the experimenter, to be more aggressive than low scorers to manifestly high-class and low-class individuals, but particularly more so to the low-class. That this depended on frustration and displacement appears to be shown by another test of Epstein's (1966) in which experimenters encouraged individuals to show punitive aggressiveness against target persons (who, being secret accomplices of the experimenters. were in fact not hurt). In this test, frustration and oppression by the experimenters were not used, and the high F scores especially were *not* more likely to try to punish black than white targets, or low-class than high-class targets.

3. It may also be argued that "taking out one's aggression" on scapegoats may be an attempt to compensate for the humiliation of extreme submission, or even a displacement of self-contempt and general ire at submission, *without* involving rebellion displaced from the submitted-to figure itself. But in this case the scapegoat is at least an *alternative* to assertion against the authority, and in this sense receives a diversion of aggressiveness.

4. The narrow definition might thus read: (1) a submissive-aggressive tendency to align oneself with power against symbols of weakness and inferiority, in response to deep conflicts and anxieties; (2) in connection with the above, a marked ambivalence about authority involving the repression of rebelliousness and its diversion against scapegoats.

For the broad definition, one simply omits 2. Hostility to out-groups is not part of the definition, though this is often bound up with hostility to representatives of weakness and inferiority. Be it also noted that "submissive-aggressive" alone is a wider characterization than even the broad definition of authoritarianism: see the case study of "Fritz Muehlebach," pp. 161-2.

5. A study of Arab students by Melikian, 1959, illustrates some of these points, though the author does not explicitly make them.

NOTES 327

6. An alternative stability may be a more open division of feeling about the authority: the individual accepts that he likes or respects the authority on some counts but not on others. As already pointed out, a weak ego is not *invariably* a very repressive ego, and vice versa.

7. It may be wondered if the concentration-camp authoritarians described by Bettelheim (pp. 64-5 below) were more than "situational" authoritarians, since the accounts cited did not follow them after the camp. There is evidence that very harsh concentration-camp experiences disrupted personality in ways that were felt long afterward; the accounts suggest varying combinations of aggressiveness, submissiveness, depression, suspicion, guilt, and insistence on immediate gratification; but there is no clear evidence that authoritarianism was the predominant pattern among these legacies. Cf. Elkins, 1963, chap. 3; d'Harcourt, 1967.

8. This "breaking down" and "building up" pattern is not uncommon in military training but the personal techniques employed here seemed particularly harsh—a mixture of the brazen and subtle.

9. For more illustration of this and similar processes, see C. P. Snow's novel about public office and private feeling, *Corridors of Power*, 1964, p. 264; cf. pp. 54-61. But Gerard Lynn, who described the paratroop experience, has suggested that other motivations were at work as well.

10. At a health camp for poor children in upstate New York, the scores of counselors on a short authoritarianism scale increased during camp terms. But also, when the children were boys, the already-existing correlation between counselors' authoritarianism scores and their amount of autocratic behavior toward the children (as rated by the children) increased. The authors of the study suggested that boys, being more unruly than the girls, brought out "latent authoritarian trends" in counselors. The counselors were college girls. The authoritarianism-scale questionnaire had only seven statements but they were well chosen and virtually apolitical. See Eager and Smith, 1952.

11. In *The Authoritarian Personality*, T. W. Adorno described situational responses which he called "surface resentment," but this was a far-broader category than the one formulated here: it included several kinds of scapegoating and stereotyping reaction to social frustration. Adorno *et al.*, 1950, pp. 753-56.

6 CHILDHOOD PRESSURES

1. Neustatter, 1965. Case records of "overcontrolled" killers (cf. Megargee, 1965) may support more comprehensive studies of childhood and authoritarianism than attempted here.

2. Frenkel-Brunswik, 1951. Most of the interviewing was done by an independent observer, Claire Bradnor, who did not know the children's scores on a questionnaire about ethnic attitudes, and who, according to the writer, did not know the psychological hypothesis behind the study. Frenkel-Brunswik's writing in *The Authoritarian Personality* shows a strong anti-conservative bias; she, therefore, may have exaggerated the oppressiveness

of strict homes. Whether her interviewer had the same liability I do not know. Though Frenkel-Brunswik mentioned differences between middle- and working-class authoritarian children, it is not clear how much the study "controlled" for class. In the article, Frenkel-Brunswik said her findings would be more systematically reported in sequel articles, but she died before these were written and her files, which included statistical data, have either been lost or destroyed.

3. Like many social science reports, this one used the general word "prejudice" to mean mainly ethnic prejudice.

4. I do not count here studies which simply rely on F scores. A questionnaire study, comparing parents of anti-black children with parents of others, suggested that the former tended to be punitive and shaming without being evenly strict and without instilling self-discipline, but the researchers said little about *authoritarianism* among the children. Since the correlation between racial hostility and authoritarianism may vary in different groups, one doesn't know if the parental behavior mentioned above correlated with authoritarianism in children. The same thing might be said of Frenkel-Brunswik's piece, but in her archetype portrait she did show how authoritarianism and a certain kind of parent went together. See Harris et al., 1950.

5. Dicks, 1950. Hitler, too, exaggerated his father's unpleasantness yet at the time was cowed by him, according to contermporary observers.

6. The interview sample overwhelmingly contained high and low F scorers rather than "middle" scorers, so that, unfortunately, the high scorers were only compared with those individuals whose overt views were very liberal or otherwise anti-authoritarian. The sample consisted of forty men and forty women, fairly diverse in age, politics, and religion. Most—by no means all—were middle class, and the great majority lived in various parts of the West Coast. For more details on the sample, its scale scores and interviews, see Adorno et al., 1950, pp. 294 ff.

7. According to Adorno et al., authoritarians are too cramped in character to have a particular propensity for oral indulgence; but there are many exceptions, especially when food etc. offers a way of expressing material dependency.

Fantasies of aggression against parents were inferred by the authors from their subjects' responses to the TAT (Thematic Apperception Test), in which they had to invent stories about a series of ambiguous pictures. See Adorno et al., 1950, pp. 489-544. Among the interviewed *women* who scored high on the F scale, most of those who made up TAT stories with themes of aggression against parental figures (according to the authors' interpretation) turned out afterward to be the same ones who glorified their parents in the interviews. High-scoring *men*, however, did not show a particular propensity to tell stories of aggression against their parents. Perhaps more of them than of the women were simply tough-minded rather than "conflicted" authoritarians; perhaps also the male authoritarians found more social opportunity to find scapegoats for their resentments and thus mute their rebelliousness even on the level of TAT story telling.

8. In *The Second Sex,* Simone de Beauvoir observed that during a certain period of De Gaulle's career, the people who thronged the road to catch a glimpse of him were largely women and children. She believed there was a kind of woman who reacted to the subtly subordinated position of her sex by identifying with male authority.

9. This account does not pretend to cover all "anal" concerns. As already suggested, the anal tendencies of authoritarians are not clear cut because they also tend to show strong feelings of maternal dependence, classified by psychoanalysts as "oral."

10. Recounted by R. Nevitt Sanford.

11. In the original sample interviewed, a far larger proportion of high F scorers than of low scorers said they had lost their mothers in childhood. There was no significant difference in the numbers who had lost their fathers; in both groups the number was extremely small. Adorno *et al.*, 1950, p. 382.

12. Since writing this, I have seen the same point made by Benjamin Spock in describing his own childhood. He also says that he displaced resentment of his father onto his mother, and attacked "crybaby" behavior in his son as a reaction against his own childhood worries about "sissiness." His mother, on the other hand, was no great symbol of weakness. She was evidently a strict disciplinarian. See the remarks quoted by Spencer, 1968. The recognition of authoritarian trends in oneself, and the question of how it affects the authoritarianism, are explored later by further illustration, though none too conclusively. See pp. 135-6, and also the study of "Charles Lanlin," though not authoritarian, by M. Brewster Smith *et al.*, 1956.

13. Cf. Adorno *et al.*, 1950, pp. 763 ff., 823 ff. T. W. Adorno described a type with many aspects of this pattern; indeed, he appeared to assume that all rebel psychopaths are dogged by unconscious authoritarian desires to submit.

14. "Forever boys and burdens" is from Bales, 1946, but it applies here well. The second quotation is from the authors of the study themselves, M. K. Opler and J. L. Singer. See Singer, 1957, pp. 103-10. The term "schizophrenia" is a more general category of mental illness than the "split personality" often thought of by laymen. The Irish-American group consisted of forty patients at a Veterans Administration hospital. All were either immigrants or sons or grandsons of immigrants.

15. See Bales, 1946; Sperling, 1953. Bales made observations about both Irish peasant and Irish-American families. He and Sperling stress ambivalent dependency created by the mother more than does Opler, and Bales also mentions an uneven treatment of children by the parents.

16. The Irish homosexuality probably shared some causes with the homosexuality of other authoritarians—e.g., conflicts producing aversion to women—but not all.

17. The authors of the study did not use the concept of authoritarianism, and the inferences about rebelliousness are chiefly mine. The authors predicted that far more of the Irish than of the Italians would be alcoholics,

since the Irishmen's curbed impulses would seek an outlet in drinking and drunkenness.

Thirty of the Irish were matched for age, education, I.Q., and "generation" (number of generations' distance from the "old country") with thirty of the Italian Americans. The most systematic comparisons were made between these two groups, but the authoritarian tendencies described among the Irish are too strong to be counted a mere relative matter, evident only in comparison with spontaneous and rebellious Italians.

18. In general, neurological, glandular, and biochemical characteristics do seem to help determine how a person responds to external stress, but the relationship is two-way, since the age at which acute stress is felt may determine how glandular and other physical developments are affected. Even if physiological traits make some people relatively impervious to authoritarianism, we do not know how far it can make people susceptible specifically to authoritarianism, as opposed to other expressions of anxiety and conflict.

7 BEYOND THE FAMILY

1. *New York Times,* July 29, 1964.
2. It is well documented that different cultural milieus tend to produce different forms of psychopathology, in terms of mental state as well as behavior and idiom. Cf. Benedict and Jacks, 1954.
3. Bettelheim, 1943.
4. *Ibid.*
5. *Ibid.*
6. Bettelheim said that he himself escaped the worst effects by concentrating on an undetected and absorbing project—the study of other prisoners—which helped preserve self-respect and a sense of autonomy. In other camp situations it appears that some inmates were able to protect their egos through informal organization. Other accounts tell of emotional disturbance and aggressive outbreaks among ex-inmates. See the survey of reports by Elkins, 1959, pp. 103 ff. Elkins also reports cases of ultra-dependence on very cruel authority in Russia and elsewhere.

8 FLUX AND DISRUPTION

1. Golding, 1954.
2. "Preparatory schools" are upper-class boarding schools, for ages eight to thirteen.
3. It is symbolic that this boy, Simon, represents the old world of adult intelligence so much that he cannot adjust to the new. He finds the "beast," recognizes what he is physically (a dead parachutist) and what he means symbolically to the others. The knowledge crushes him; it brings on one of his nervous fainting spells; and in the eyes of the others he becomes subhuman.
4. Fromm, 1941.

5. One paragraph cannot summarize Fromm's work, which, despite a lack of evidence, is a milestone in the application of psychology to history. When Fromm wrote of "authoritarian character" and "sado-masochism" he did not do so in a primarily sexual sense. He meant a person who sought security both in trying to engulf others ("sadism") and in trying to be engulfed in strong authority ("masochism"). Fromm's "authoritarian" repressed his resentments of authorities who really humiliated him, and desiring to be aligned with strength, turned his hatreds on those who were goadingly weak. Despite these similarities with our own definition, Fromm's list of authoritarian variations departs from ours in some of the character types it includes and excludes (e.g., types of rebel and conforming democrat). See Fromm, 1941, chaps. 5, 7.

6. McCloskey and Schaar, 1965. "High scorers" on the anomie scale were counted as those who agreed with at least six of seven statements on the anomie scale devised by Leo Srole. Two samples were used: adult Minnesotans and a cross-section of the U.S. adult population.

7. These background categories were: education (eleventh grade and below versus twelfth grade and above, age (under 35, 35-54, 55 and over), type of community (rural versus urban), occupational class (three levels), region (North versus South), race (white versus nonwhite) and sex.

8. Several studies have shown this, including the one by McCloskey and Schaar. The latter did not measure authoritarianism as such, although some of the individual traits they tested for correlated very highly. Nor did they give direct evidence on relationships between social groups (widows and aged, etc.) and the character traits, although they found that "status frustration"—dissatisfaction with one's status and envious resentment of the better placed—accounted for only a little of the correlation between the character traits and anomic outlook. Other studies of anomie show explicit correlations with "authoritarianism," but rely too heavily on the F scale questionnaire, whose contents virtually duplicate much of the anomie scale's items. Cf. Roberts and Rokeach, 1956; McDill, 1961; Rhodes, 1956. It is true that the McCloskey-Schaar study also relied on questionnaires to gauge character traits, but these covered much more of behavior than any single scale which has been devised to measure authoritarianism.

9. In the interviews reported by *The Authoritarian Personality,* many of the high F scorers, but few of the low scorers, gave a description of their parents suggesting "status concern." This statistic does not, of course, prove that parents' status concern was a cause of high F scores, or of authoritarianism, and the finding is based on what the subjects themselves said. For the original report, see Adorno *et al.,* 1950, pp. 379, 382-84, and on points of method, see pp. 294 ff.

10. Luther's authoritarianism is described in Appendix B, 295 ff., where he is compared and contrasted with Cromwell.

11. There is no hard data showing disproportionate female suicides, but various impressions have pointed to this. Cf. Fei, 1946, Yang, 1959.

12. In her study of children, Frenkel-Brunswik, 1951, found an unusual amount of "geographic instability"—changing homes and moving around

—in the background of the more authoritarian and racially prejudiced group, as well as a relatively high proportion of foreign-born grandparents. But it is not clear if these backgrounds did correlate with authoritarianism and not simply with racial prejudice. Some individual cases of authoritarianism and geographic mobility are considered later, in the context of cultural conflict.

13. R. Benedict, 1946, chap. 7.

14. See Dubois *et al.*, 1960. (First published 1944.) These sparse examples are no substitute for systematic search through studies in anthropology; but very few of these studies give enough material on psychodynamic elements to make a judgment about authoritarianism. Even these tend to focus on central personality types rather than significant deviations which may also represent widespread types (however rough and ready the term "widespread" must be). Bernard Siegel, an anthropologist whose own thinking has touched on authoritarianism, suggested accounts of three societies which might indicate widespread authoritarianism; these included the Alorese study cited above. The other two were the Brazilian Kaingang, beautifully described by Henry (1941), who did not indicate authoritarianism; and the Dobuans of Melanesia, described by Fortune and Malinowski (1932), who did not give enough psychological information to afford a judgment. In all three societies, it turned out, social ties were loose and/or conflicting. In the absence of more numerous studies which would show whether social flux etc. and authoritarianism tend statistically to occur in the same communities, we must focus on individual studies showing whether social flux etc. can, in *any* circumstances, help to produce authoritarianism.

15. De Vos and Miner, 1958 and 1960. The authors did not use the authoritarian concept as such.

16. Incentives for leaving the oasis were very general. Water shortages prevented expansion of Sidi Khaled; two-thirds of its men between the ages of twenty and fifty had to seek a living elsewhere. Differences in economic background between those who left and those who remained were small. The psychological data came from interviews, and from Rorschach tests judged independently of the interviews. In the Rorschach test, the individual is shown ambiguously shaped inkblots and asked to say what they remind him of. In Western cultures certain responses have appeared to go with certain psychological tendencies, though the validity of Rorschach interpretations has remained controversial among psychologists. Prevailing ways of interpreting the test responses do not appear to work in all cultures, but in the Algerian study the Rorschach findings were strikingly consistent with the interview impressions.

17. Maruyamah, 1963, especially pp. 78-80, 108 ff., and 167-70.

18. Lifton, 1964.

19. *Ibid.* He also described two other types of response to the "sense of historical dislocations." One was a "mode of transformation," the path of leftist, radical reform. The other was an in-between path, a "mode of accommodation": adjustment to the most immediate changes, a blend of old and new, but maintenance of one's integrity and consistency by declaring the position to be very independent.

The transformationists, too, were concerned with purity: they attributed impurities to the past rather than the alien. In general Lifton's portraits of these two groups do not suggest authoritarianism as much as the restorationist picture does.

20. Western sinologists spell his name *Hung Hsiu-ch'uän*, but I have preferred the spelling used by the anthropologist Anthony Wallace in his study of Hung. Wallace analyzed several cults of "revitalization" as responses to phases of social disruption. He stressed a common pattern taken by messianic dreams and their significance as a response deep in the leader's personality. One of his other examples is the American-Indian leader, Handsome Lake, whose dreams seemed very sado-masochistic. But it is not clear whether authoritarianism really explained Handsome Lake's behavior; it is conceivable that his conversion to Quaker teaching led to a deeper humanity than Hung's conversion to the more wintry Baptist doctrines (see below). Wallace did not use the authoritarian concept and some of his examples may claim too much for the effect of social dislocation; but his speculations about a link between social stress and glandular and neurological processes are worth noting. See Wallace, 1956a, 1956b, 1952.

21. Not 1813, as many historians have it. Teng, 1950. p. 49.

22. Quoted by Wallace, 1956a.

23. Wallace also called this last phase the stage of "resyntheses" (*ibid.*). He argued that the conversion and dream experience often led to increased self-confidence due to a new sense of purpose. To some extent this may often have been so, but as we shall see, in Hung's case the resolution was not a firm one. Taiping propaganda seems to have elaborated Hung's dreams, but recent historical reviewers concede that Hung had at this time a number of visions and an intense emotional experience: Teng, 1950, pp. 53-54; de Bary, 1960, pp. 680-81. Even later elaborations would largely reflect the mind of Hung as author of Taiping doctrine. On the other hand, some details reported in many historical accounts are inaccurate—e.g., the statement that the last stage of Hung's illness lasted forty days. This appears to stem from Hung's later concern with the Gospel's "40 days." See Teng, 1950, p. 53.

24. A point made by Chien Yu-wen, *T'aip-ping chun Kwang-hsi shou-i-shih (A History of the Beginning of the Taiping Army's Revolution in Kwangsi)*, 1943, pp. 173-76, cited with other sources by Teng, 1950, p. 54.

25. Teng, 1950, p. 76.

26. From the Ten Heavenly Commandments.

27. Cf. Boardman, 1946.

28. De Bary, 1960, p. 685.

29. According to Anderson, 1958, a biographer of Hung, the story that Hung brutally kicked a pregnant concubine was the talk of enemies. She did not go further than to admit he was irritable with the stupid and slow-witted—but then Anderson's book is a most favoring account of Hung.

30. Teng, 1950, argues expressly and convincingly that Hung's personal example was a big factor in the lapses of other leaders (p. 71).

31. Anderson, 1958, claimed that Yang's medley of traits could only be

understood by concluding that the Northern King had a hypnotic hold over him (p. 229).

32. Marsh, 1961, p. 5.

33. Yuan Mei to Tang Shih-min, translated by Arthur Waley and quoted in *ibid.* p. 8.

34. In "conversion hysteria," the person responds to emotional stress by feeling or showing a physical symptom, but unlike psychosomatic illness, there is no underlying bodily disorder associated with the emotional trouble. A study of psychiatric patients reported in *The Authoritarian Personality* found that the more authoritarian ones tended to express their anxieties and maladjustments in unconsciously disguised form, owing to repression. Thus they tended to vague but strong anxiety, hypochondria, sudden attacks of rage or panic, and physical ailments like ulcers. (Adorno *et al.*, 1950, pp. 891-970, study by Maria Levinson.) But two studies found an *inverse* relationship between authoritarianism scores and "conversion hysteria": Jensen, 1954; Freedman *et al.*, 1956 (a study confined to Vassar girls).

35. The view of Chien Yu-Wen, a leading historian of the Taipings.

36. This interpretation of Hung's vision mentions only some of the themes which a lengthier analysis might offer.

37. Anderson, 1958, p. 338.

9. PURITAN CREEDS

1. Quoted from the New York *Herald*, February 24, 1924, by Sinclair, 1962, p. 26.

2. The quotation comes from Mather's "Bonifacius" (or "Essays to Do Good"). See Miller, ed., 1956, p. 218. Whether Cotton Mather himself could be called authoritarian is very much an open question. For conflicting portraits, see Parrington, 1930, vol. I, pp. 106-17, and Boas, 1923.

3. See Hofstadter, 1955, pp. 204-205, 205 n.

4. This is not to say that similar evidence might not be found elsewhere; it is simply that my own researches have concentrated on America.

5. This and the following account of Salem are drawn from Starkey, 1961, while also using the legal and broader historical perspective of Fox, 1968. Starkey used previous histories of the affair, including the work of Charles Upham, with its detailed research into Salem life. But she also found and used some primary sources which the previous historians seem to have missed.

6. It is not clear in Starkey's book, 1961, why Abigail was a charge of the Parrises. Her father appears to have died.

7. *Ibid.*, p. 32, 34.

8. In the case of Betty Sewell, we have no evidence that the early strain led to authoritarianism, which was only one response possible. See Sewell's *Diary* excerpted by Miller, 1956, p. 241. For a discussion of this and other puritan childhoods see Fleming, 1933, especially chaps. 13, 14.

9. Starkey, 1961, p. 47.

10. *Ibid.*, 32. Cf. pp. 42-43.

11. *Ibid.*, pp. 105, 107, 153-56, 171, 174.

12. For examples supporting this description, see Starkey, 1961, pp. 91, 215-16.

13. Quoted by Parkes, 1930, pp. 20-21.

14. *Ibid.*, 61, 79.

15. Winslow, 1940, pp. 126-29.

16. See, for example, *The Works of Jonathan Edwards*, ed. by Edward Hickman, Ball Arnold, London, 1840, vol. I, diary entries, December, 1722. We know very little of his childhood, and his memoirs make virtually no mention of his mother.

17. Parkes, 1930, p. 252.

18. Quoted by Barnes, 1933, p. 5.

19. Fleming, 1933, especially chaps. 13, 14.

20. A study of teenagers in North Carolina and Ohio found that, going by their own account, Catholic families tended more than Protestant ones to be autocratically run. Social class differences were allowed for. Elder, 1962.

21. See chap. 6, pp. 60-1 and 329-30 n., citing studies by Singer, 1957; Bales, 1962; and Sperling, 1953.

22. Cf. Degler, 1959, p. 293, and quoting Thomas Sugrue; Lolli *et al.*, 1958, p. 22.

23. There have been no modern studies showing a relationship between authoritarian psychodynamics and Catholic or fundamentalist Protestant religion. The closest is the study by Stern, 1962, but even this only shows a direct correlation between certain religious backgrounds and questionnaire responses (an expansion of the F scale), nor did it allow for urban-rural differences of background. More impressionistically, in later chapters, we will consider a religious influence in American Southern authoritarianism.

10. A GENERAL THEORY OF CAUSE

1. This argument implies a right-wing political propensity among authoritarians. There may be other kinds of cultural situations which just as characteristically produce left-wing authoritarians; if so, they have not come to my attention.

2. In America, at least, one study suggested that authoritarians were more reluctant than others to assume leadership positions. Another study, of naval cadets, found that authoritarian people tended not to be nominated as leaders by their peers. See F. H. Sanford, 1950; Hollander, 1953. These studies, however, relied on questionnaire scores as an index of authoritarianism.

3. This account of the Doukhobors is based chiefly on the report of Hawthorne *et al.*, 1955, which included historical and social description, and psychological observations and tests results (the TAT). In a letter to me in March, 1965, Hawthorne said that Sons of Freedom behavior had remained largely the same.

4. Holt, 1964, gives convincing descriptions both of this and of fire-

watching sexuality. But her book generally, for all its voluminous research, has a shrill, intrigued puritanism well in tune with the sect whose practices she attacks.

5. How the vicious circle began in the first place—the accidental coupling of doctrine, leadership, and personality—poses a fascinating problem which requires more research. But cf. the social history by Woodcock and Avakumovik, 1968.

6. The following account of Hutterites is based on information given by Kaplan and Plaut, 1956; Eaton et al., 1951; Eaton, 1952; Eaton with Weil, 1955; and Friedmann, 1961. Kaplan and Plaut used the TAT fantasy test and a sentence-completion test. I am grateful to Thomas Plaut for advice.

11. RIGID REBELS AND THE "LIBERAL" AUTHORITARIAN

1. Names in this account have been changed. The "we" and "us" here are myself and my wife.

2. Rokeach, 1960, reported fairly high correlation among college students between F scale scores and dogmatic, prejudiced outlooks and thinking. But, even assuming that high F scores usually reflect authoritarian character, this is not surprising, for only *some* of the low F scorers would be of the rigid, dogmatic type, and middle F scorers might well tend to be flexible and generally moderate people, less dogmatic than high scorers. A study of Houston, Texas, college students found that *both* the most racist and the least racist students tended to be most dogmatic and narrow-minded in a general sense. See Bay, 1965, pp. 208-209, reporting research by Irving Taylor.

3. Cf. the "protesting" type described by Adorno et al., 1950, pp. 774-76.

4. Merrill, 1963, p. 18 and elsewhere.

5. Epstein (1965) found that in experimental situations high F scorers were particularly apt to punish "badly-dressed" and lower-class-looking peoples; he classified these as simply a "low-status" target.

6. See also the life of the "racist-abolitionist" Hinton Rowan Helper by Bailey, 1965.

7. Blanchard, 1968.

8. For categories of scapegoating and hostility which cut across these, see the study of working-class elderly men by Reichard et al., 1962: especially the "Armored," "Angry," and self-hating types. See also the study of working-class anti-Semites by Bettelheim and Janowitz, 1964. The study of old men underestimated cultural family learning, but the authors recognized that in other subcultures the traits they looked for might form somewhat different archetype clusters.

9. In his modern typology of protesting liberals, T. W. Adorno describes both an impulsive kind of person and one more emotionally constricted, even inhibited—and very guilty. Adorno et al., 1950, pp.774 ff.

10. It is very difficult to say how "far out" for the time Comstock was in his selection of targets on grounds of obscenity. There were so many

opinion groups and standards. He did try to define his standards so as to leave a place for "real" art, and he was no vigilante; he mainly tried to get existing laws enforced to the hilt, though he also lobbied successfully for a Federal censorship law.

In their essay on Comstock, O'Higgins and Reede (1924) claim that his adolescent attack on the tavern was a reaction to a boyhood episode when he was whipped for getting tiddly on farm-made wine, supplied by a "bad influence" slightly older than he. According to this argument, he attacked the "bad self" represented by the tavern keeper. One might therefore see in the second episode an authoritarian identification with his punishing parents against his own "wild" ways. But so many years elapsed between the two episodes that the connection, if any, cannot even be guessed at.

11. Allegedly told to his friend and biographer Charles Trumbull; see Trumbull, 1913, pp. 42-43. He made other, similar statements at various times.

12. Quoted in Broun and Leech, 1927, p. 57. Comstock made his diary available to Broun and Leech, but never meant it for publication. At the beginning of it he scrawled, "No man's business but my own." In quoting it extensively, the biographers justified themselves archly by saying that this wasn't exactly a motto he followed himself. But their biography is sympathetic, while aware of psychological tensions.

13. Comstock, *Morals Versus Art*, 1881, p. 34.

14. *Ibid.*, 7.

15. Broun and Leech, 1927, circa p. 30.

16. Comstock, *Frauds Exposed*.

17. It is possibly connected that the Tammany boss was charitable to the poor—though largely with other people's dollars.

18. Manuscript journal 1, quoted by Woodward, 1963, pp. 17-18. Little is otherwise known about the relationship with his parents. Although the psychological categories are mine, the following account relies on Woodward's sensitive and detailed researches.

19. Woodward, 1963, pp. 341-42.

20. *Ibid.*, p. 433.

21. Quoted, *ibid.*, p. 395. Woodward believed that "with Watson, as with many men, a sense of misgivings and a need of reassurance were often expressed in reassuring someone else" (p. 395).

22. For various reasons, anti-Semitism had become a cultural attitude in Georgia and other parts of the Deep South.

23. *Watson's Jeffersonian Magazine*, April 14 and May 27, 1915.

24. *Ibid.*, June 14, 1915.

25. Emphasis Watson's. Letter to Dr. John Taylor, January 7, 1915, quoted by Woodward, 1963, p. 444.

26. Slaton's former law firm merged with the concern which defended Frank, but it was arranged that Slaton's partners should have nothing to do with the case and that Slaton should have no interest in the fees of the consolidated firm while he was governor. In his charges Watson frequently attacked Mrs. Slaton also, calling her "Chief Justice Sally."

27. A pseudonym.

28. See also the self-studies of "Novak" and "Trumbull," reported and discussed by Lane, 1969.

12. POLITICAL APPEALS

1. Several studies have shown a correlation between F scores and measures of political conservatism, but the research has not related political belief to psychodynamic tendencies. Some of this research is noted where we deal with American culture and character. The thought of a connection between fascism and submissive-aggressive character strains is not new, but to date these psychodynamic ideas have not been systematically extended to include other right-wing doctrines besides fascism.

2. For a somewhat different perspective shedding new light on these issues, see Rohter, 1968. The functions for personality served by political beliefs can be categorized in different ways: see the review by Lane, 1969. Refreshingly, Lane's own analysis does not confine itself to fanatics and "far-out" groups. See also Greenstein, 1969, and Katz, 1960, although the latter's categories overlap more than he seems to realize.

3. In deciding how much the political ideology reflects the basic disposition, one must avoid the pitfall of inferring a close connection simply because the ideology offers symbols and values that would seem sympathetic to the disposition. If we did this, we would automatically conclude that every authoritarian with a right-wing ideology expressed his authoritarianism very directly in that ideology. One must look to the *way* the person expresses his ideology—the emotional overtones.

To an extent, comparisons of political leanings can get round the difficulty by concentrating on statistical tendencies. That is to say, if authoritarians as a whole tend more than others to espouse certain ideologies, one may infer that their personalities are partly responsible. But really one can only make this inference if one has allowed for possible differences in social background between authoritarians and non-authoritarians. Otherwise, a correlation between authoritarianism and certain political views may simply mean that the same social and cultural circumstances tend to produce both.

4. German and Austrian Nazism, Mussolini's government, and the Japanese system which emerged in the 1930s would all fit this definition of fascism, though the Japanese fascists, more than the others, held power behind a traditional superstructure. (It has been much debated as to whether, and in what sense, the term "fascism" can be applied to militarist Japan.)

I am less confident about the term's application to Peronism in Argentina and the previous Vargas regime in Brazil, with their alliance between trade unions and military officers, and their emphasis on welfare legislation. Seymour Lipset puts these regimes under "left-wing fascism" as distinct from "classic fascism." Our definition of "fascism" essentially corresponds to the latter. Cf. Lipset, 1963, chap. 5.

5. Going by this definition, the national movements for George Wallace

have lacked somewhat the radicalism and elitism (despite their racial pique) which would make them fully radical right. The same could be said of McCarthyism, though both have had many right-wing values. On the question of attitudes to the past, it is true that German Nazism combined traditionalism with new political and moral forms. Some such combination is inevitable when a radical-right group wins office; simple restorations are unfeasible; the revolutionary element remains. The fact that political nostalgias tend to distort the imagined past makes it all the more impossible to draw a clear line between backward- and forward-looking movements. In this aspect particularly, the radical-right definition is a matter of more or less.

6. Like the "radical right" concept, the idea of "moderate or Burkian" conservatism is very much a generalization; individuals are *more* or *less* conservative in different areas. Nonetheless, McCloskey (1958) showed that a generally "conservative" outlook could be identified among various people, and the components of that outlook included the values listed above. McCloskey's list is summarized and explored cross-culturally by Wilkinson, 1964, pp. 110-112, 169-72. See also Tomkins, 1965.

7. Cf. Lipset, 1963, chap. 5. One exception is the Ku Klux Klan in the South, which has drawn from both small owners and manual working classes.

8. The slogan "National Essence" was actually used by Japanese militarists in the 1930s.

9. The symbolism and psychology of dirt and cleanliness has many more aspects than are mentioned here. The subject needs a literary as well as psychoanalytic treatment. At one point, for example, it involves the good-evil dichotomy between light and darkness: Hence the moral uses of the verbs "to sully" and "to tarnish."

10. In his study of Western communists, Almond (1965) found that communist affiliation offered a sense of identity, belonging, and purpose to those who felt, or indeed were, isolated or alienated from society (pp. 272-92). We have already noted Lifton's findings about Chinese thought reform and authoritarian susceptibilities, but it is difficult here to separate the emotional appeal of a specific ideology from the experience of a high-pressure conversion attempt by powerful figures. Actual evidence of an authoritarian attraction to communist doctrine per se is confined to the U.S. (see pp. 246-8 below).

13. THE FOLLOWERS

1. This portrait is based on a study by Dicks, 1950. More about the study is given later.

2. "Pseudo-remorse" is Dicks's term; the point about conflicting values is mine.

3. In a footnote Dicks (1950) said that he received a copy of *The Authoritarian Personality* after his report was written. "On first reading," he said, "[it] seems to embody nearly all the concepts of this present paper."

340 NOTES

One must add, however, that the time and circumstances of the research—the study of enemy prisoners by British psychiatrists—were not conducive to impartiality. It is true that the interviews by Dicks himself tried to focus on personal psychology, leaving political beliefs to other interviewers, whose results were only given to Dicks later. But it is conceivable that the investigators may have expressed anti-German and anti-Nazi feelings in psychiatric terms. We have little evidence that this is so, but the possibility should be raised.

4. See Kirst, 1962, for an account of various forms of martial and athletic homosexuality among German soldiers. Although a novel, *Officer Factory* is based on actual events at an officer training camp, and its material includes eye-witness accounts.

5. Here Dicks does not give enough nuance for me to judge this interpretation by itself. I presume that, like many intriguers of this sort, the officer talked of "the spirit of revolution" with a disapproving gusto.

6. Some of this is my own elaboration of Dicks's material, but the point about punishment through illness is Dicks's.

7. The number of pro-Nazis varied slightly according to the trait tested, since in some cases there was not enough information. "Tenderness taboo" was considered to be present in 37 out of 60 men. Homosexual trends, "gross or perceptibly heightened," 46 out of 64. Projection, "gross or perceptibly heightened," 45 out of 66. Anxiety, "gross or perceptible symptoms," 49 out of 65. "Antisocial" sadism, 42 out of 63. "Antisocial" was rather a misnomer, reflecting Dicks's British values as to what was "social" in a good sense. In practice, the classification seemed more sensible and largely a matter of degree—the extent to which a person overtly enjoyed or condoned infliction of suffering on others. On the question of identification with father, only 4 out of 62 took an anti-father, pro-mother or generally rebel position. Among the non-Nazis, 20 out of 72 took this position. On most of the other traits, numerical differences between pro-Nazi and non-Nazi groups were considerably less, though statistically significant.

8. Cf. Fromm, 1941; Erikson, 1950. The points made below are those which seemed to be corroborated in the POW study. Dicks said that his own explanation grew in part out of a first-hand experience of prewar Germany, and that on this basis he formed hypotheses for the POW study before he learned of Fromm's views.

9. Much less is known about authoritarianism among German girls, but a portrait of such a girl is given below.

10. See Erikson, 1950, for this and other aspects of "Wanderbird" groups.

11. An interpretation based in part on the POW material by Rees *et al.*, ed. 1947, pp. 198-99.

12. Dicks and Rees mention these aspects, but I have been more explicit about Oedipal processes and the split view of women. On the attack of Nazism *against* the (conservative) family, see Bendix, 1958.

13. Hagen, 1965.

14. A group of acquaintances is hardly a random sample, but the advantage was that Hagen could to some extent check what they said against

his first-hand impressions. He said he also checked with others who had known them. A flaw in Hagen's book is that in places the lengthy autobiographies and "quoted" material seem to be in his own words; they often have a standard, written quality which omits the finest nuances of individual character. They read, in short, as if he set down the gist of what was said after each interview.

15. "Trutz" and so on are pseudonyms, given by Hagen to protect identities.

16. The childhood accounts are based on what the individuals themselves reported. In most cases at least, Hagen did not know them until their late adolescence or early adulthood.

17. Hagen, 1965, pp. 15-16.

18. No information was given on Muehlebach's childhood and youth, except that his father was a market gardener.

14. THE EXECUTIVES

1. See p. 107 above.
2. See the study of Hung Siu-tshuen, pp. 76 ff.
3. Gilbert, 1950, chap. 3 and elsewhere. Gilbert was prison psychologist at Nuremberg, before becoming professor of psychology at Princeton.
4. Cf. the story of Cadet "Hochbauer" in *Officer Factory*, 1962, a novel based on fact by Hans Hellmut Kirst. The novel contains a very good triangular comparison between the fanatic but brittle Nazi, a young liberal, and a punctilious, severe, but humane Prussian commandant.
5. This and the following information about Himmler is drawn mainly from two biographies (Frischauer, 1953; Manvell and Fraenkel, 1965) and the diary of Himmler's doctor and confidante, Felix Kersten. Frischauer has a denigrating tone, but both biographies cite people who knew Himmler and his family at various points in his life. Kersten first met Himmler in 1939; his published notes on Himmler began in February, 1940. Reference has also been made to Angress and Smith, 1959.
6. Emphasis Himmler's.
7. Diary quoted by Manvell and Fraenkel, 1965, p. 6.
8. Reitlinger, 1956, argues, on negligible evidence, that Himmler was inwardly well adjusted and had no deep psychological need for anti-Semitism. Until the Final Solution, Himmler's race and purity concerns were not primarily and destructively focused on Jews, but that is not the same thing.
9. According to Kersten, 1956, Heydrich was extraordinarily obsequious to Himmler because Himmler knew that he had Jewish ancestry (or so Himmler told Kersten).
10. See Kersten, 1956. Kersten's influence over Himmler was jealously belittled by the Swedish statesman Count Bernadotte and his proponents; but Kersten's protagonists seem to have had the last word: see Trevor-Roper's introduction to Kersten's memoirs (1956) which also cites other books on Kersten.
11. Bullock, 1961, p. 632.

12. The bloodiest reprisal for Heydrich's death was the execution of all men in a Czech village where a suspect was found. The women and children were deported as prisoners, and the village was razed.

13. This is not to say that the policy, *taken by itself*, was unreasonable. It is well known that excessive drinking is often a military problem, and the promotion of soft drinks as a way of reducing the problem is not strange—it was consciously done by Switzerland in the late 1930s and still is today. In wartime France, the Germans instituted strict controls on the drink trade, and penalized the strongest beverages.

14. The Huns settled in what was to become Hungary in the late fourth century. Later the Avars, another nomadic group from central Asia, overran the same region. Reitlinger, 1956, argues that Himmler's Mongolian look was simply the result of short-sighted squinting behind glasses, and a flat nose.

15. For indication both of scruples and fear of Hitler, see Reitlinger, 1956, especially pp. 183, 278-79.

16. The reasons why people enjoy being frightened to a point (e.g., horror films) are too complex to be examined here.

17. See also Crichton, 1968, reviewing *Air War: Vietnam* by Frank Harvey.

18. Rolf Hochhuth's play *The Soldiers* brings together agonizingly many of the themes presented in the above pages; and in his book on the Dresden fire-bomb raid, Irving (1963) records some ritual expiations of guilt by a few RAF crews who sensed the horror of their mission.

19. Arendt, 1963.

20. Reported by Rudolph Hoess, Commandant of Auschwitz, to G. M. Gilbert, prison psychologist at Nuremberg, in what seems to have been a frank and relatively uninhibited interview. Hoess also said that when Himmler first told him of the Final Solution directive, he added an explanation (not usually given with directives), saying that human considerations had to be ignored, for it must be done to save Germany from the Jews. Gilbert, 1948, p. 150; 1950, p. 253.

21. See Frischauer, 1953.

22. Cf. Reitlinger, 1956, pp. 278-79.

23. The episode is described by Kersten, 1956. On Kersten's authenticity, see note 10, p. 341 above.

24. Kersten's phrase, 1956.

25. For a fuller, more orthodox psychoanalysis of Himmler, see Loewenberg, 1969. I think he "overinterprets" his material; for instance, he explains Himmler's early kindnesses as a defense against sadism and destructive impulses. This *may* be true, but it is surely not the whole truth about Himmler's humanity.

26. Not to be confused with Rudolph Hess.

27. Himmler's suicide is not dealt with at any length here because we have little information bearing on its psychological aspects.

28. This focus on authoritarianism does not cover all aspects of Gilbert's analysis; see Gilbert, 1950, pp. 240-61.

29. Hoess, 1959.

30. Told to Gilbert, 1950, p. 242. Although a wish to make himself look as little guilty as possible may conceivably have colored his prison testimony, he told Gilbert about his life willingly and at length.

31. This inference was not drawn by Gilbert, but when Hoess told about his childhood treatment, he said twice in a row that he would be punished for teasing his little sister or being unkind to her.

32. Quoted by Gilbert, 1950, p. 242.

33. It is not clear how guilty he was in fact made to feel in childhood. A traumatic incident in early adolescence, in which it appeared that his confessor had betrayed him to his father, may have encouraged his withdrawn attitude.

34. Hoess, 1959; Manvell and Fraenkel, 1967. Hoess told Gilbert (1950) that he became increasingly estranged from his wife at this time.

35. Quoted by Gilbert, 1950, p. 245.

36. The tests referred to were the Rorschach, in which almost all his responses were "whole-figure interpretations." When shown an inkblot image where such an interpretation was impossible, he rejected it, saying, "I always want to see the whole thing and not the details that don't belong together."
Gilbert said that the Rorschach tests showed "some residual signs of anxiety," but when Hoess saw images of corpses and withered bodies in the inkblots, Gilbert interpreted this mainly as a sign of Hoess's dehumanization. One might ask, however, if this did indicate a guilty and fearful preoccupation with his past killing and burning. Cf. *ibid.*, pp. 248-9.

37. This description was given me by Roger Manvell, who received it from a former camp inmate.

38. Hoess, 1959, pp. 92-96.

39. Manvell and Fraenkel, 1967.

40. See also *ibid.*

41. Cf. Kogon, 1946.

42. Manvell and Fraenkel, 1960, p. 2. The following information is drawn mainly from this book, though also from Reiss, 1949, and *The Goebbels Diaries* (Goebbels, 1960). Unlike their book on Himmler, Manvell and Fraenkel have a hostile tone, but they give much information. They draw extensively from Goebbels' diaries and letters and from many who knew him at different periods, including Maria, his sister.

43. Reiss, 1949, says that Goebbels as a boy was deeply attached to her, but the evidence for this is not clear and Manvell and Fraenkel, 1960, suggest that Reiss relied too heavily on official Nazi biographies. This matter is hard to judge; Reiss did interview relatives and family acquaintances.

44. Remarked to his aide, Wilfred von Oven, according to the latter in his book, *Mit Goebbels bis zum Ende,* and quoted by Manvell and Fraenkel, 1960, p. 4.

45. Entry for November 6, 1925.

46. For example, from his diary: "Strasser is quite a man! . . . What a wonderful Bavarian type he is. I am very fond of him."

47. The Strassers' political proposals were more anti-capitalist than Hitler's: they wanted to nationalize heavy industry and the big estates.

Correspondingly, Hitler was more adamant against international Bolshevism and in the speech to which Goebbels had objected he named Italy and Britain as good allies for Germany. Goebbels and the Strassers would have preferred an alignment with Russia.

48. A glimpse of maternal dependency was seen in the 1920s when overwork became an obsession with him. He wrote in his diary, "Mother, help me. I can't go on. I barely weigh a hundred pounds." On the other side of his relationship with women was the exhibitionism. When he and his wife, Magda, were newlyweds, they would exchange little public endearments in a theatrical way. Here, as in so many other spheres, Goebbels seemed to be striving for an impression.

Whether Goebbels' philandering was in part a defense against homosexual desires can only be speculated about. Psychoanalysts sometimes interpret his kind of behavior in this way.

49. Else's surname was not given.

50. In Hitler's bunker at the end, he destroyed his family before killing himself; but we should be cautious about interpreting this. Cf. West, 1965.

51. The symbolic ways in which fondness for animals can meet a variety of psychological needs would make a very interesting study.

52. The Old Catholics broke away from the Roman church when they refused to accept the decree of the Vatican Council, especially the dogma of papal infallibility, announced in 1870. They retained Roman ritual in German, but rejected some Roman doctrines and made confession optional.

53. The main source used on Frank is G. M. Gilbert's first-hand study at Nuremberg prison. See Gilbert, 1950, pp. 136-153; also Gilbert, 1947. There have been no full-scale biographies of Frank.

54. Reported by Gilbert, 1947 and 1950, but it is not clear how much Gilbert was generalizing from Frank's behavior in prison.

55. The cruelty of Nazi criminal law, and the arbitrary powers permitted by it, are well summarized by Ranulf, 1938, pp. 10-12. See also Friedmann, 1964, p. 55.

56. See Frischauer, 1953, p. 128; Gilbert, 1950, pp. 140-41.

57. Talk with Gilbert in his cell, *ibid.*, p. 150.

58. Frank turned his incriminating diary over to his captors, rather than destroying it, and in his extensive interviews with Gilbert he showed every sign of guilt. He both expressed and limited his self-castigation by seeing in himself two Franks, one good, the other evil. This image suggests both inner moral divisions and a shaky sense of identity, and again one may wonder if this is not related to a father whose image was flawed.

59. Frank described the German *Volk as* feminine, fickle, emotionally changeable, and much of this was exactly how he described himself. He spoke with great enjoyment of "the man," Hitler's seduction of the Volk; elsewhere he spoke of his own seduction by Hitler along with the rest. This summary does not do justice to the sequences and nuances reproduced at some length by Gilbert, 1950, p. 148. Frank's phallic imagery is described on p. 144, *ibid.* Gilbert argued that Frank's rage against Hitler included the resentment of a lover betrayed; but this is more speculative.

60. Psychiatrists examined Hess at length, both in Britain and at Nuremberg; see Rees *et al.*, 1947; Gilbert, 1950. Because the findings have already been published, I believe it is not wrong to cite some of them although the subject is identified and living.

61. See Kersten, 1956 (p. 89) for a wartime observation of his humane concern. Hess's dramatic flight to Scotland in search of a negotiated peace with the British Government was not overtly an act of revolt; apparently it was an attempt to restore a declining position of power near Hitler by obtaining what he thought Hitler wanted, against the advice of rivals.

62. See Gilbert, 1950, pp. 108-09, for Goering's Rorschach test responses at Nuremberg. Anthony Lanyi has described to me Goering's art collection, including the picture of a swan raping a maiden and a lushly grotesque painting of terrified water nymphs pursued by lust-ridden sea monsters with puffed red cheeks. Other pictures echoed this spirit of romanticized sadism.

63. In chap. 2, cynicism about people generally and their motives was mentioned as an authoritarian trait, but this is not a cynicism which plays near to one's primary authorities. Goering's cynicism was closer to the "subversive."

64. Cf. incidents recounted by Butler and Young, 1951, p. 22; see also p. 17.

65. Frischauer, 1951, p. 151; and Hagan, 1965, pp. 341-42 (observation by a non-Nazi friend). Gilbert, 1950, even maintained that Goering had a chivalrously aggressive attitude to all out-groups, while dividing them into "superior" and "inferior" categories.

66. See Gilbert, 1950, pp. 106, 113.

67. Adorno *et al.*, 1950, pp. 762-63.

68. Adorno, however, argued that some psychological nihilists, including Roehm, were rebels whose hatred of authority cloaked repressed feelings of dependency and a "secret readiness to 'capitulate' and to join hands with the 'hated' strong" (*ibid.*, pp. 762-63). But to strike at one's own submissiveness by both attacking authority and hating weakness does not necessarily entail the authoritarian pattern of repressed and diverted rebellion.

15. ADOLF HITLER

1. Reported by a one-time friend, Reinhold Hanisch: see Bullock, 1961, p. 12.

2. It has been said that some Nazi and military cliques privately engaged in overt homosexuality, but there is no evidence that this applied to the top circles nearest Hitler. The *unconscious* homosexuality emphasized in this account of German authoritarianism is compatible with the wish to punish overt homosexuals, given the surviving authority of traditional heterosexual values. We do not know to what extent overt homosexuals were also authoritarian; it is conceivable in some milieus if their beliefs opposed the notion that overt homosexuality was effeminate and decadent.

3. It might be said that the "euthanasia" program served a rational

purpose of eliminating a national waste by removing the need for hospital and caretaking facilities. But, apart from the immense effort, organization, and cost involved in the operation (transport, mass killing, and concealment), why should Hitler focus on this particular form of national "waste" when there were many others?

4. Schoenbaum, 1967, said that an "impressive number" of early Nazi leaders were *Auslandsdeutsche,* people who had spent their "impressionable years" in German communities abroad. He cited Karl Mannheim on this but gave no statistics.

The Czechs as a whole were among the peoples whom Hitler thought inferior and "not a nation," unlike the Hungarians. It has been argued, without definite proof either way, that Hitler's paternal grandfather was Jewish. Cf. Bullock, 1961, p. 2; Jetzinger, 1958.

5. See Jetzinger, 1958, pp. 43-44. The following assessment of Hitler's upbringing is based primarily on Jetzinger's study, which reappraises the evidence and uses first-hand witnesses. The chief witness used was August Kubizek, but Jetzinger persuasively criticized Kubizek's own book, *The Young Hitler.*

6. Bullock, 1961, p. 4. For basic information about Hitler throughout his life, I have drawn heavily on Bullock's book, which, at time of writing, is the most complete biography of the man, and contains much shrewd description.

7. The impression of Klara's piety is based on a remark made by Hitler to Goebbels. Explaining why he could not afford to strike hard at the Roman church directly because of public opinion, he said that if his mother had been alive she would still have been a devout churchgoer. As we shall see later, the adult Hitler tended to glorify his mother in contrast with his father; but in this case there are no great grounds for suspecting exaggeration.

8. Jetzinger, 1958, p. 51.

9. *Ibid.*, p. 71. Jetzinger denies the contention, made in earlier accounts of Hitler's youth, that his schoolmasters were an anti-Semitic influence.

10. *Mein Kampf (My Struggle)* was written after the 1923 *Putsch,* when Hitler was in his twenties. It was an effort to set forth his political position in intellectual form, but it also contained a little material about his own life and background.

11. Cf. Jetzinger, 1958, p. 51.

12. ". . . begging, cursing, until I could get him to budge. Then I would support him and finally get him home." As told to his relative Frank Hitler; see Gilbert, 1950.

13. The comparison of these two portraits in *Mein Kampf* is made by Gilbert, 1950, pp. 19-20. In general, however, Gilbert's interpretation suffers from taking at face value what Hitler said about his relationship with Alois. Writing before Jetzinger's work was published, Gilbert underestimated Hitler's childhood submission.

14. Noted to me by Joseph Katz.

15. Bullock, 1961, pp. 326-27. Independently arrived at, the ensuing

thoughts nonetheless develop Erich Fromm's ideas on Hitler (Fromm, 1942).

16. Speech at Munich, March 15, 1936.

17. For indications that this was not just romanticizing after the fact, see Bullock, 1961, pp. 27, 29-30. Cf. Gilbert, 1950, p. 34.

18. Bullock, 1961, p. 333.

19. *Mein Kampf* (trans. by James Murphy), Hurst and Blackett, London, 1939, pp. 46-47.

20. *Ibid.*, p. 55.

21. Another example of racist doctrine's influence on power was the brutal treatment of conquered populations in the Ukraine and the Baltic States. At first the local populace welcomed the Germans as liberators, but the brutal treatment they received—as Slavic "under-people"—prevented their initial response from being used to weaken Russia. This contrasts with Hitler's use of the Czechoslovakian Germans. Many Slavs were deported to Germany as slave labor, but here too an ideological aversion to using German mothers in the factories intensified the labor need.

22. In a speech at Munich, November 8, 1938, Hitler said typically: "Instinct is supreme and from instinct comes faith. . . . While the healthy common folk instinctively close their ranks to form a community of the people, the intellectuals run this way and that, like hens in a poultry-yard. With them it is impossible to make history; they cannot be used as elements supporting a community." This association of the disruptive with weakness is typical of Nazi authoritarianism.

16. CULTURE, CHARACTER, AND POLITICS

1. To be contrasted with other countries' neo-feudal traditions, where strong military discipline joins with greater attention to the humanity and "rights" of the weak. Cf. Christa Winslow's play, *Girls in Uniform*, written before Hitler became Chancellor.

Henry Dicks, 1950, also wrote of an increasing "ultra-Prussian" tendency, but he did not mention the obscurity of chivalric traditions, and he attributed the hardening of the culture more predominantly to the influence of authoritarian personalities than I would.

2. Cf. Bettelheim and Janowitz, 1964: a study of social mobility, frustration, and anti-Semitism among Americans, which refers to an earlier German study by one of the authors.

3. According to Dicks, 1950, the salient and authoritarian personality structure among the pro-Nazis he studied differed from the "norm of German national character in that they embodied this structure in more exaggerated or concentrated form." I argue that, on the level of personality organization, there was more variation than Dicks indicated, and that the variation was not so simply a matter of degree. I likewise question whether the formative childhood pattern described by Dicks, Erikson, and others was as predominate as they indicate. It has been suggested by others that the mother often did provide a strong counterweight to the father. Until

we know more about incidence rates, the terms "widespread" and "prevalent," must be used in a very rough and relative sense.

4. Quite aside from the fact that few Social Democrats had the education to pass the civil service exams, the sons of known Social Democrats were excluded for being just that. See Rohl, 1967.

5. Although the "professional class" proportion of Jews was larger than that of Protestants and Jews around the turn of the century, it was nowhere near large enough to cause a Jewish preponderance among the well educated. See Pulzer, 1964, p. 12 for some statistics.

6. Cf. *Der Hofmeister*, Brecht's development of the eighteenth-century play of the same name by Jakob Lenz, especially the little homily in verse at the end.

7. Erikson, 1950, *op. cit.* Cf. the unemployed white-collar worker quoted on the pangs of being "déclassé," as he himself put it: Schoenbaum, 1967, p. 9.

8. In general during the 1920s and '30s, the more religious or conservative the political party, the higher its feminine support.

9. Fromm, 1941, pp. 186-87; cf. Bettelheim and Janowitz, 1964, p. 109. David Schoenbaum, 1967, records that though the National Socialists began as a local small businessman's party, it also drew at the outset from unemployed ex-soldiers and workers.

10. According to Allen, this was "not unusual for the area and the times, as comparison with neighbouring towns shows." Allen, 1965, p. 17.

11. In 1930 the largest of the militarist and nationalist bodies had over 400 members; the smallest had 30. Twenty-three others ranged between. The town's population was 10,000, of whom but 120 were Jews. *Ibid.*

12. Observed to me by George T. Davies, who was a student in Munich at the time.

13. See the Nazi military rules and their effect cited by Barnett, 1969. But there were other factors too, as Barnett points out.

14. Wilkinson, 1964 (pp. 185-89) points out some of the continuities and breaks.

15. By and large the welfare and industrial legislation retained by the Nazis did not greatly develop that of the Weimar Republic. The main economic appeal of the Nazis to labor was "jobs." In their propaganda, the Nazis extolled the "dignity" of manual work and spoke against the social snobbery of employer and manager. But in the small town studied by Allen (1965), the Nazis opposed as "socialistic" a Social Democrat plan to give unemployed men a job project, building their own houses. This was the year before Hitler became Chancellor. In the same town, the Nazis did run soup kitchens during the depression, and later they endorsed and took credit for the building project. *Ibid.*, pp. 104-105, 107, and elsewhere. Cf. Schoenbaum, 1967; Vermeil, 1956.

16. The religion of *gottgläubig* ("God believer") looked to a primitive and vague deity, a Providence whose central subject was Germany. Although Hitler talked of Providence, Fate, etc., he did not himself care much for the elaborations of a state religion.

17. Dicks, 1950, implied that, among the pro-Nazi POWs whom he studied, the most tough-minded and nihilist tended to be atheists. Out of sixty-five pro-Nazis, thirty said they were either atheist or *gottgläubig* (see Note 16, above). As would be expected, fewer of the pro-Nazis than of the others were devout Protestants or Catholics. Dicks believed that if his sample had had a different social composition a relatively large proportion of the pro-Nazis would have been "low church" Protestants; but he gave no evidence for this, other than his own first-hand impressions of Germany. In the Weimar republic, voting preference for National Socialism did correlate with Protestant affiliation, allowing for social class, but we do not know how puritan the Nazi Protestants tended to be.

18. Lipset, 1963, p. 144, 144 n. The data on voting and community size surveyed by Lipset concentrated on the 1932 elections. In this year the Nazis became the largest party in the Reichstag (the national legislature's lower chamber), more than doubling their percentage of the popular vote gained in the previous, 1930, election.

19. *Ibid.*, p. 147 and elsewhere; Gerth, 1940. Bettelheim and Janowitz, 1964, observed that most S.S. guards below the rank of officer were the sons of farmers, small shopkeepers, and junior civil servants.

20. Cf. Allen, 1965, p. 17, referring to the 1920s and early '30s. In addition, the county Farmers' League and Artisans' League were unusually political among occupational clubs, and they sponsored right-wing speakers before eventually going Nazi. Among working classes, the Social Democrats (socialists) provided a counterweight through their influence in many working-class recreational clubs. In the country generally, Marxist internationalism provided some challenge to working-class nationalism, although there was still a great deal of the latter.

21. Cf. comments by Lasswell, 1933; Bullock, 1961, pp. 120-21.

22. See pp. 161-2 above.

23. Observed by Max Horkheimer *et al.*, *Studies in Philosophy and Social Science*, 1941, p. 135, and quoted by Adorno *et al.*, 1950, p. 763.

24. George T. Davies, a Briton who attended the University of Munich after World War I, said that his fellow students were the sort of people who would not only obey a "keep off the grass" sign (as would most Englishmen), but would insist everyone else do so too.

25. In Dicks's sample of POWs, the non-Nazi group, too, had a considerable number of submissive people, but their submissiveness tended to be more openly humble and gentle.

There are many ways of categorizing emotional susceptibility to Nazism. Our rough typology cuts across the more standard psychiatric categories, such as "schizoid," which Gilbert and others have used in Nazi case studies.

26. Quoted by Bullock, 1961, p. 357.

27. Arendt, 1963, has the lovely story of a minor civil servant who would knock at the *bottom* of his superior's door before entering.

28. Gerth, 1940, reported that 97 percent of German teachers belonged to the Nazi party "or its affiliates." A party census in 1935 reported that 33 percent of Nazi "political leaders" were teachers. Although the Nazi

regime purged the schoolteaching profession in the 1930s, Gerth claimed that teachers were attracted to Nazism anyway, because of a certain kind of middle-class moralism, a historic and unhappy subordination to the churches, and the inducements of a party which stressed education as an instrument of power. For a grass-roots account of Nazi influence on school education, and support from teachers before and after Hitler became Chancellor, see Allen, 1965, pp. 108-109, 249, ff.

29. Cf. Hoess, 1959, appendix. Of course modern technology made it easier to accomplish, but at the outset the killings still posed great technical problems.

17. THE WHITE SOUTH

1. McClean, 1946.

2. McClean referred particularly to the experiences of the Southern writer Lillian Smith, portrayed in her autobiographical novel, *Strange Fruit*.

3. Coles, 1967. This use of categories and definitions is far from the fluid way in which Coles reports on individuals and gives no impression of the many delicate points he makes. Coles stressed the unknown quality of human nature and the importance of accumulated experiences. My only general criticism is that sometimes he makes the factors influencing personality seem more mysterious than, I think, he means them to be.

4. *Ibid.*, chap. 7, section 1.

5. *Ibid.*, chap. 4, section 4. Elsewhere in the book, Coles records more open ways in which some Southerners dealt with their fondness for black family friends.

6. *Ibid.*, chap. 4. "Patterson," like other names, was a pseudonym. She did complain of her husband's lack of concern about the children's education and the black threat; it is possible that she may have criticized her husband to his face when Coles was not present.

7. From a long letter written to herself, as if to the local sheriff. *Ibid.*, chap. 7, section 2.

8. *Ibid.*, chap. 8, section 3. As Coles explains, the term "Daddy" is not unusual in the South.

9. These inferences are mine, but Coles did suggest that John's life had been a search for the freedom to speak his mind denied him as a boy. In this and elsewhere Coles also writes about the psychology and symbolism of color.

10. In recent years especially, some Baptist and other ministers have tried to oppose adamant racism.

11. According to various accounts, rural police brutality decreased in areas where the national press focused on it.

12. Cash, 1941, pp. 136-37 and elsewhere (Vintage ed.).

13. Percy, 1965, credits this observation to James Dabbs, *Who Speaks for the South?* Percy notes that Georgia too was poor and mainly rural, and had a large black minority, if not as large as Mississippi's. But in At-

lanta it had what Mississippi did not have: a big city which "shared . . . in the currents of American urban life."

14. Turner, p. 125.

15. Established by Raper (1933), and by Hovland and Sears (1940), who related their findings to a theory of displaced aggression. Statistically, their work has been much debated, and more recent studies have found that the correlation did not remain into later decades. As lynchings have become fewer, so perhaps they have become less dependent on levels of frustration in the general population, and more on catalyzing events in a few lines.

16. See Davis, 1968, pp. 75-76; also Woodward, 1963.

17. Silver, 1964; cf. Silver, 1963.

18. Coles, 1967, argued that, even in Mississippi, among "certain white people" whom he has observed for nearly a decade, "beliefs are often less important to them than the comfortable continuity of their lives." Elsewhere in the South he noticed new beliefs about right and wrong developing when social change was seen as inevitable and extreme segregationism disruptive, deluded, and eccentric.

19. Degler (1959, pp. 178-82) sums up very concisely the way in which the South shifted during the first half of the nineteenth century from mere acceptance of slavery and hospitality to freethinkers, to moral praise of slavery and suppression of dissent. He links this to a collective "inferiority complex," for in Western civilization only Russia retained a legal servitude approaching that of the American South.

20. I have witnessed first hand all the above reactions, but have also drawn on the experiences of another English traveler, Elizabeth Johnson.

21. Cf. Dollard, 1957, pp. 287-89 (first published 1937); Grier and Cobbs, 1968, pp. 184-85; also more recent incidents told by Griffin, 1964 (first published 1960). Dollard described many more emotional tendencies than are given here, but rather few of his assertions were supported by case examples.

22. Coles, 1967, p. 68. The author both talked with the children and did drawings with them. From what he reports I think he misinterprets the "rather unusual" drawing by "Allan," although Allan's case does show a connection between racial concerns and marked need for order and stereotypes (pp. 69-70). In some degree the children may have learned from their parents to associate the blacks with "bad" traits; Coles does not make this distinction, but he emphasizes an attributing of bad traits that seemed to go far beyond reality. Thus, learned values and attitudes seemed to be a vehicle for projection.

23. Griffin, 1964 (first published 1960).

24. Gant gave the following account in an undergraduate paper, elaborated in a seminar, at the University of Sussex, England. He said that his interpretations preceded psychoanalytic reading.

25. Cf. Dr. S. Stickney's first-hand account of homosexual tauntings and invitations on drunken Southern deer hunts, cited by Bakal, 1968. Sometimes the "sweaty fellowship" extends to black hunting companions who go officially as "help." Another perspective is given by the novels of Ellison

(1952) and Huie (1967), who describe Southern "games" in which male white groups force or foment sexual activity among trapped blacks.

26. Dollard described the Key-Ice ritual in which young university blades marched with flaming brands and ice, and the leader lifted a cup of water with the toast: "To Woman, lovely woman of the Southland, as pure and chaste as this sparkling water, as cold as this gleaming ice, we lift this cup and we pledge our hearts and our lives to the protection of her virtue and chastity." See Dollard, 1957, p. 136 n., quoting from Carl Carmer, *Stars Fell on Alabama*, 1934.

27. Cash, 1941, makes this point.

28. Sinclair, 1962, pp. 31-32. (New American Library paperback edition.)

29. Cash, 1941, p. 125 (Vintage ed.).

30. Cf. Ginzburg (no date given). In his report of lynching, Raper (1933) argued that the "manhunt tradition" attracted certain types of people on grounds both of disposition and availability (1963 edition, p. 9).

31. Griffin, 1964, pp. 99-102.

32. I would meet in the same way the claim by Rees, 1947, that many Nazi authoritarians showed pathology in politics but not in personal life, though his own evidence belied this for some.

33. Huie, 1967. This Southern novel is itself a paradigm of sadism pressed into liberal service.

34. Morris, 1961. Houston's strong radical-right movements seem to draw from the city's "get-rich-quick" qualities, but also from Southern evangelism.

18. OTHER SETTINGS

1. *Babbitt* was first published in 1922. A study of business pronouncements in that period (Jackson, 1970) shows that Babbitt's "boosterism" was not much exaggerated. Lewis well knew small-town and middle-town life, and he did not entirely scorn it. In his antagonisms, however, he may perhaps have exaggerated the pathologies of the middle-town mind, just as Samuel Butler may have exaggerated the neurosis of his father.

2. Babbitt was emotionally involved in labor troubles on both sides of the fence, and his affair with Tanis had him briefly mixed up with some festive bohemians.

3. See Hofstadter, 1955b, on the radical right; 1955a, especially chap. 4, on the Progressives. The concept of "pseudo-conservative" was taken from *The Authoritarian Personality*. In a later work (1965), Hofstadter applied the term "paranoid style in politics" to both left- and right-wing groups, but here he was careful to say that he did not necessarily mean "paranoid" in a psychiatric sense. Ginger, 1965, has effectively criticized the lack of proper comparisons in Hofstadter's study of Progressives (see Ginger's bibliographical essay). I must say, however, that Hofstadter's portrait of Theodore Roosevelt ("The Conservative as Progressive," 1948) is a superb description of middle-class energies and anxieties that seems to involve deep chords of character.

4. For some of the more relevant studies, see Barker, 1963; Hodges, 1956; Lipset, 1964; Milton, 1952; Sokol, 1960 and 1968; Williams and Wright, 1955. There is also an unpublished study by Robert Hodges (Sociology Department, San Jose State College) which compares McCarthyites and non-McCarthyites through interviews and Rorschach tests, without discussing authoritarian character as such.

5. Rohter, 1967; cf. Rohter, 1965 and 1969. His questionnaire tests controlled for "yea saying," the tendency of some people to answer questions in the affirmative.

6. Rohter's study gives some support to the Hofstadter thesis, except that it deals with a different decade and population of the radical right. Also, Rohter's report does not show what proportion of rightists *combined* in their individual characters and backgrounds a large number of the attributes he discusses. It is possible that only a minority of the rightists held their beliefs because of personal anxieties or psychodynamic need. Rohter himself denied that the psychological functions served by right-wing belief necessarily involved pathology, but his measure of psychopathology was simply their ability to perform conventional social roles (raising families, holding a job, etc.). See his letter in *Trans-Action,* July/August, 1967, p. 79.

7. Sanford, 1946.

8. This comment is not Sanford's. In talks with me during the early 1960s Sanford argued that an authoritarian "identification with the aggressor" was an important factor in much of America's pro-German isolationism before the war. I am not so sure. Certainly the "Quisling" portrayed here was unlike many right-wing isolationists in that he did not overtly fear a Japanese "Yellow Peril."

9. Krugman, 1953. Krugman also talked with the psychoanalysts for about two hours per case. His article does not specifically use the "authoritarian" concept.

10. Among neurotic people one would expect the most authoritarian to tend not to seek psychiatric treatment, because of self-censorship. On the other hand it has often been supposed that Jews, for various cultural reasons, are particularly ready to seek professional treatment for disorders. This is only relevant, of course, if the authoritarians were among the Jewish majority of Krugman's sample: twenty-nine out of thirty-five.

11. Almond, 1965, chap. 10.

12. No report was published on this. Although overt resentment of weak authority can be part of authoritarianism, it is not invariably so. I hope it is unnecessary to add that there are many emotional and intellectual reasons for Communist appeals in the West which cannot be categorized under "authoritarianism" or "anti-authoritarianism."

13. See Lane, 1969: the case studies of "Novak" and "Trumbull." Both were critical of their fathers, but it is not clear how long they had been critical or whether self-study was leading them away from authoritarianism. Lane had his students read about personality and politics, including material on authoritarianism; he then asked them to write an "ideological self-analysis," including personality needs but with a minimum of textbook

"psychologizing." This last injunction was not wholly kept, but Lane quoted and discussed useful chunks of their writings.

14. See pp. 295 ff.

15. The survey was of interview reports from the Student Development Study, Stanford.

16. *New York Times,* July 8, 1964. The anger was often leveled at the widespread editorial opposition to Goldwater. In Reston's view, the "torrent of vulgar and offensive personal abuse" exceeded any received by the *Times* since the latter days of Roosevelt's second administration.

17. Schiff, 1964a and 1964b. All but one campus, Ohio State, were in New England, but the students came from all over the country and a great range of class background.

18. Schiff, 1964a. "Anti-intraceptive" roughly corresponds to "self-censorship." Schiff referred explicitly to the authoritarian concept, and he elaborated on the point in a letter to me. He gave no concrete example of the authoritarian anti-Communist described above, but on most points he showed he was well aware of differences between authoritarianism and other patterns of submission-aggression, as well as the need to allow for sheer cultural learning of political attitudes.

19. Schiff, 1964b ("Obedient Rebels"). "Socially approved objects" meant "socially approved" as targets.

20. Schiff gave a certain amount of quoted material but not enough to show support for all his inferences, and for information on family background he relied on what the students themselves said. He compared the conservative group with ten campus liberals on a number of psychological questionnaire tests; but on several important points the contents of the questionnaire tests (kindly sent me by the author) do not yield as good a measure of authoritarian traits as the test titles suggest.

21. For studies of Birch disciples' behavior, see Broyles, 1966, and McEvoy, 1966.

22. The letters were published respectively in the January and February, 1965, issues. "Eleanors" presumably refers to liberal do-gooders epitomized by Eleanor Roosevelt. On Caldwell's own ambiguities about power and underdogs, see Barker, 1968. Even if the editors printed only the most favorable letters, and assuming they were genuine, the recurring admiration of the magazine's columnists from letters during this period (1964-65) was remarkable.

23. In what seems to have been a fairly sensitive study, Elms (1969) found no neurotic authoritarian tendencies or particular signs of social strain among Birch-type anti-Communists compared with other adults. Exposure to authoritative right-wing opinions at a formative time seems to have been the important factor. Elms's sample was from Dallas; elsewhere the sheer factor of exposure to opinion may not be quite so important. (The deception used by Elms in recruiting his anti-Communists raises ethical questions.)

24. See Wolfinger, 1963; Chesler and Schmuck, 1964; Rohter, 1967; and Lipset, 1963 and 1964.

25. For another perspective on right-wing subcultures and authoritarianism, see Riesman *et al.*, 1952, pp. 174 ff.: the study of "Parryville."

26. Lipset, 1969, has given an exceptionally useful summary of the "policeman's lot" in big cities.

27. Cf. the surveys of occupations' "standing" in public opinion, reported by Hodge *et al.*, 1966.

28. See the studies of police behavior in three Northern cities reported by Reiss, 1968; Westley, 1953.

29. On America's relatively low casualties in riots, see Gurr and Graham, 1969, chap. 17 (by Gurr). Research by Niederhoffer, 1969, showed an increase in "cynicism" and related attitudes among New York policemen after joining the force (see pp. 199 ff.). Elsewhere in the book Niederhoffer claimed to show that the police did not tend to recruit authoritarian personalities, but the claim rested on poor logic and method.

30. See Reiss, 1968. After the Chicago convention "police riot," a Yippie reported that, to his amazement, the police amazingly stopped beating him in the police station when he called out, "It's OK, I make girls too."

31. A sudden and striking occurrence of this—displacement from a threatening Hell's Angel to an intervening photographer—is recounted by Thompson, 1966 (1967 Penguin edition, pp. 211-12).

32. Jackson, 1967.

33. The quotations above are taken from speeches during a crime wave when he was trying to publicize law enforcement, but he spoke in this vein about penal policy and drug offenders, two subjects not in his jurisdiction. For all these points and more personal information on Hoover, see Baker, 1938; Alexander, 1938; Cook, 1964; McCrystal, 1969. Cook follows something of a muckraking tradition, but he is not a simple scapegoater of individuals and he and McCrystal draw on FBI and ex-FBI sources.

34. Karon, 1958, p. 172.

35. Pettigrew, 1964, pp. 11 ff.

36. Elkins, 1963.

37. Many combinations are possible here from the "humble-pie-eaters" in the liberal German group studied by Dicks, (1950, *op. cit.*), to the person who idealizes his parents, diverting deep criticism of them onto himself and identifying with underdog groups. See Reichard's "self-hating" type: Reichard *et al.*, 1962, chap. 12.

38. A nationwide sample of white college students was compared on many psychological tests with black students in the "Upper-South" and "Lower-South." Separate data were given for men and women in each category. See Brazziel, 1964, although questions of validity may be raised over possible differences in the way different cultural groups respond to the whole experience of psychological tests. For other questionnaire studies which at least raise issues about black authoritarianism, see Noel, 1964, and Steckler, 1957.

39. Kardiner, 1959.

40. See Kardiner and Ovesey, 1962 (first published 1951): especially pp. 214-23 on "A.T." Her account of her dreams is especially worth read-

ing. The sample was almost evenly divided between classes and between sexes, and about half were psychiatric out-patients. I presume that Kardiner's generalizations (referred to above) were largely based on these studies.

41. Among the many observations of this see Bayton *et al.*, 1965, and Rainwater, 1966. The evidence is mixed as to whether middle-class blacks held or expressed more anti-black attitudes than working-class blacks.

42. Several accounts of black upbringing, at least in the urban lower classes, have given an impression of these handicaps. High value on "fair" skin is found in many nations—we cannot here enlarge on the mythology and psychology of darkness and blackness versus lightness and whiteness. But among blacks the social, moral, and aesthetic connotations of darkness blended with special intensity: hence the "black is beautiful" reactions.

43. Cf. Pettigrew, 1964, p. 42.

44. *Ibid;* Dollard, 1957, chap. 13 first published 1937); Grier and Cobbs, 1968, p. 72. Also Silberman, 1964, pp. 115-18, including his discussion of the fight between Bigger Thomas and Gus in Richard Wright's novel *Notes of a Native Son.* I am grateful to Richard Rose for his account of black killings that he covered as a reporter in St. Louis.

45. Described by many people to Dollard, 1957, pp. 282-83. Dollard also quotes a case from Carl Carmer, *Stars Fell on Alabama*, 1934, p. 212. Dollard cited many witnesses of this before the war, pp. 282-83. See also the report of "pecking order" tyrannies in black colleges by Jencks and Riesman, 1968, pp. 425 ff.

46. *Invisible Man,* 1952.

47. Cf. the Harlem black "G.R.," described by Kardiner and Ovesey, 1962, p. 104 ff.; although Kardiner does not interpret his own description quite like this.

48. On the "vice versa" part, see Scheff, 1966. Cf. Elkins, 1963, pp. 86 n., 131-35.

49. Davis and Dollard, 1964 (first published 1940); Rohrer, Edmonsen *et al.*, 1960.

50. More recently published studies of black individuals give less information for our purposes. Cf. Grier and Cobbs, 1968; Coles, 1967. Coles drew from his intensive study of thirty-two black and white Southerners, but only six blacks were portrayed to an extent approaching a full personality study, and two of these were civil-rights protestors, unlikely to be authoritarian. For a very good discussion of Southern black resilience and Northern black pathology, by Coles and others, see the conference transcript in *Daedalus,* Winter, 1966, pp. 329 ff.

51. The names are pseudonyms. The case studies in both research reports (Davis *et al.;* Rohrer *et al.*) were taken from the same original sample of thirty individuals, covering virtually all social classes in black New Orleans. But none of the individuals portrayed here were described at length in both reports (not counting brief followup notes given in the second). The first report drew from extensive interviews with friends, parents, family friends, and teachers as well as the subjects; the second re-

port was based partly on interviews in the home and tests designed to tap fantasy. Black and white interviewers were used for both reports. Both were fairly psychoanalytic, and therefore stressed parental and family factors but they also paid attention to racial and social class factors, and the second report, especially, included material on relationships with authorities and social groups outside the family. The second report is more apt to jump to conclusions and even contradict the evidence (e.g., Rohrer *et al.*, 1964 pp. 254, 247) but I have tried to allow for this. My presentation, however, is not meant to be a full précis of the case studies as originally published.

52. Lower middle class, that is, by white standards. Davis and Dollard (1964) put them higher, arguing that a Pullman porter (the father's first job) was middle class by black standards, but today this is confusing. A colored Creole interviewed Jeanne; for the full case study see *ibid.*, chap. 6.

53. A relative distinction. Even those who express independence more by reaction *against* parents usually imitate the parents to some degree.

54. This last paragraph consists mainly of my own interpretation, since none of the case studies reviewed here used the authoritarian concept as such.

Jeanne's interviewer predicted that she would become a rather stern mother. The second New Orleans report (Rohrer and Edmonsen, 1964) gives but a few lines on Jeanne Manuel in the 1950s. She had married a Creole boy she had known since third grade, had done two years of college, and had settled comfortably in the West. She hoped to get her B.A., have a "lovely" home, and become more active in civic groups. They had two children.

55. Although interviewers and interviewed were not matched in the same way in all case studies reported by Davis and Dollard, the research showed some sensitivity on the selection of interviewers. For the full account of Ellen Hill, see Davis and Dollard, 1964, chap. 7.

56. Davis and Dollard stressed that Ellen Hill was undergoing virtual shock as a result of her family's economic decline. Her basic character may have changed considerably since their study. Two decades later, the brief followup notes stated that "her strong class feelings [seemed] to have mellowed." Her rage remained but it was "rigidly suppressed." Although she still showed "strong determination," her life was centered on her family: she was married to a policeman in the North (his race not given), and had six children. She was going through college part time and planned to teach. Rohrer and Edmonsen, 1964, pp. 297, 304.

57. Rohrer and Edmonsen, 1964, pp. 239-58.

58. The tests were the Machover Draw-a-Figure and the Rorschach ink blot tests.

59. Unlike the other case studies in the report, he and his family lived in Natchez, Mississippi, not New Orleans. See Davis and Dollard, 1964, chap. 9 and appendix. Judy came to adore his interviewer, an upper-middle-class man of the same town (not stated if black). It is not made clear what needs this reflected. Under the interviewer's influence, Judy behaved much

"better" at school, but the followup report in the 1950s stated briefly that he had spent the last twelve years in prison in the North, for reasons "we were unable to establish." Only two of the ten Tolliver children had married, and at least one was in a mental institution. Rohrer and Edmonsen, 1964, p. 297.

60. See *ibid.*, pp. 237-39, 258-73, for all the full case study. The authors referred back to earlier interview reports on Morgan as a teenager, though Davis and Dollard did not include him in their book. To protect his identity, his occupation was not given.

61. Rohrer *et al.*, 1960, pp. 136-57.

62. In 1966, 8 percent of black families with incomes of $7,000 or more, compared with 4 percent of white families were "female headed" (fathers absent). Below $3,000, the black proportion was 42 percent; whites 23 percent.

63. In 1960 the unemployment rate of black men was higher than that of black women (data based on work force populations). In the late 1950s and early '60s, the median income of black women increased much faster than that of men. In some areas more recently, estimated unemployment is generally less affected by economic fluctuations.

64. Grier and Cobbs (1968, p. 42 ff.) made the main points given above about hair straightening as well as other points about the pressures of sexual standards on black women. Writing in the late 1960s, they claimed that most black women had their hair "fixed" by some method, although a small number had turned to the "natural hairdo," and others seemed to have abandoned the whole area by permitting personal disarray, even physical deterioration—at earlier ages than equally poor whites. *Ibid.*, p. 47 ff.

65. Cf. *ibid.*, p. 57; Rainwater, 1966; Liebow, 1966.

66. Smith and Prothro, 1957.

67. "A.T.," the authoritarian black woman studied by Kardiner and Ovesey (1964, pp. 214-23) gives a vivid example of attitudes toward the despised free in this context. Her own account of her dreams about black and white neighborhoods are especially worth reading.

19. EPILOGUE: AUTHORITARIANISM AND THE FUTURE

1. Focus on the West is solely due to my relative ignorance of the non-West. It may be argued that developments in some Arab countries are highly conducive to authoritarianism.

2. On television early in the 1968 election year.

3. By and large it seems that punitive attitudes to deviants held most sway over public policy in the middle centuries of Christian Europe, when notions of individual responsibility were starkest. Cf. Biggs, 1955. One must, of course, distinguish between attitudes to moral deviants in the abstract and attitudes to personally known offenders, but I contend that on both levels, "understanding" vis-à-vis "blaming" is becoming more emphasized, even if the two are not in principle mutually exclusive.

4. The public flogging of women in England was not made illegal till 1817. See Gorer, 1955, pp. 13-15.

5. Cf. Lifton, 1968. Lifton himself recognizes, but does not much elaborate on, people who are superficially protean while basically being quite rigid. Lifton's own thesis is based on American observations, studies of Japanese and Chinese youth, and European and American literature.

6. As used in the following pages, "scientific" means "based on operations which draw, or seek to draw, general principles from observed, classified, and tested evidence." The term is used in a relative manner; no sharp line is drawn between pure and applied science, and with regard to evidence, it is recognized that provability varies; in this sense, social sciences are less "scientific" than physical sciences.

7. Consider also some of the experiments in learning and conditioning which inflict pain, stress, and starvation on animals, and occasionally have inflicted stress on a small child.

8. After seeing the switchblade scene from *Rebel Without a Cause*, male adults and adolescents gave more "shocks" to erring victims than they did before the film. See Walters *et al.*, 1962 and 1963, or the summary by Bandura, 1968. Milgram's experiments focused on situation rather than motive, but he acknowledged that different "cognitive and emotional defenses" might well be important.

9. Cf. Goffman, 1961.

10. See, for example, Braginsky *et al.*, 1969; Sarbin, 1969. I assume here that one can define mental disorder independently of its possible manifestation in social deviance; cf. p. 5 n. above

11. Great legal and philosophical dilemmas are raised by this: they involve issues of free will and of social equality. Cf. Hart, 1968.

12. Since writing this, I have seen that Szasz, 1963, makes much the same point, though he puts it differently and attributes it more to mental-health professionalism than to popular demand and values.

13. For example, Keniston, 1968; Szasz, 1963 and 1967. As the experiences of General Grigorenko and others show, the clearest political use of "mental health" as a state weapon has been in Soviet Russia.

14. I am grateful to Susan Wilkinson for giving some corroboration of this from her own professional experience and observations.

15. The opposing concepts "power elite" and "veto groups" are taken from the competing descriptions of American power structure given by Mills, 1956, and Riesman *et al.*, 1953.

16. I am grateful here for observations by Craig Comstock.

17. Some of this has already seemed to happen among jurors at criminal trials where psychiatrists have presented bad and conflicting arguments.

18. Fears catalyzed by immigration and crowding may build on biological instincts, however vestigial these may be: cf. Morris, 1967. But, in qualification to the above, it must be noted that a Boston area survey in the mid-1960s found no correlation between anxiety affirmed about crime in the streets and antipathy expressed against civil-rights movements.

19. This does not mean that children, if asked, even abused ones, would

ask to be removed from home—the idea might be inconceivable to them. But abuses are easier to conceal when the victims cannot easily communicate their distress to outsiders. The more so when polite behavior is the norm for both parents and children during social visits.

20. This is written before one can fully assess the plans for experimental early-learning centers and other programs announced by President Nixon.

21. Dennison, 1969.

22. See the case studies of Hung Siu-tshuen, Himmler, Goebbels, and Hitler, already given above.

23. Cf. the case studies by Madison, 1968.

24. A committee of enquiry into the British Civil Service has recommended that the elite Administrative Class should no longer require very high-grade undergraduate degrees in its selection of young officers from outside the service, and that eventually the university requirement should be done away with altogether. See Committee of Enquiry, 1969, pp. 43-44, 84. The chairman, J. G. W. Davies, assistant to the Governor of the Bank of England, is hardly a dis-Establishment figure.

25. On the decline of night law school and related issues, see Mayer, 1968, pp. 102-107. For a more sanguine and general view, see the *Economist*, October 14, 1967 ("Night School Story" in the American Survey section).

26. I believe that the terms "hawk" and "dove" were first used publicly in an article by Joseph Alsop on the Cuban missile crisis, trying to show opposite viewpoints among the President's advisers. The *tone* of Alsop's articles on Vietnam—indignantly gung-ho and fulsome in its tough-guy praise of the military—is to my mind quite odious.

27. At Yale, Robert Lane has pioneered in the use of "ideological self-analysis" among undergraduates, focusing on the psychological functions of political attitudes (see p. 248 above, and Lane, 1969). At the University of Sussex, England, graduate students in education have had to write an "educational autobiography"; its scope is left to them. But these innovations are rare. Jencks and Riesman, 1968, have noted that even psychology graduate programs practically never require students to do any kind of self-study. See, however, the classroom experiment in basic questioning described by Stern, 1962. It was designed with the problem of authoritarianism and dogmatism explicitly in mind.

28. Reviewing his autobiographical *Making It*, 1968.

29. Barnett, 1967, has described the relationship between industrial society and a packaging approach in American military education, even at staff-college level. The same applies, less strongly perhaps, to civilian education.

APPENDIX A

1. See Note 6, p. 361, below.

2. "Roger Stanton" and "Jerry White" are pseudonyms. The actual persons are not meant to be statistically representative of any precise social or politi-

cal group. To protect them, very little information is given here about the setting of the research and the groups studied, although I would be glad to give more information privately. A few details of life history and background have been changed, but nothing which would seem significant for the purposes of this inquiry. The original interviewing and testing were done upon the subjects' recognition that results might be published, provided identities were concealed.

My report and interpretation is mainly based on a study of interview tapes. The interviews and tests were conducted by other investigators who did not focus deliberately on the matter of authoritarianism but were generally informed by the F scale concepts. The interviews probed for many things, whereas the report given here concentrates on aspects that seem most relevant to the question of authoritarianism. By comparison, the case study reported by *The Authoritarian Personality* attempted a greater psychoanalytic depth and was aided in this by projective tests. The portraits here, on the other hand, say more about the interaction between character structure and social situation. Comparatively little is said about childhood factors since we only have the subjects' retrospective account to go upon.

I am indebted to Max Levin, whose work and advice largely made this study possible, and to the Danforth Foundation, which sponsored the original interview project and provided for some of my time.

3. See the self-portraits of "Novak" and, especially, "Trumbull," quoted and discussed by Lane, 1969. Briefly mentioned on p. 248 above.

4. Schiff, 1964, makes some fairly similar points in his study of right-wing students.

5. Cf. Whyte, 1956; Riesman *et al.*, 1953. One would expect many of the most authoritarian people to show extreme elements of both "inner-" and "other-direction." Elaine Soper has done an interesting F scale study which sheds light on this: see Lipset and Lowenthal, 1961, pp. 316 ff.

6. Of those surveyed in Stanton's class (about 850 students), 35 scored "high" on the F scale in their senior year—"high" being arbitrarily defined as 4.0 or above out of a maximum possible score of 7. Most of these seniors had already scored high in their freshman year, and 19 of the 35 showed an increase from their freshman year. Stanton's score was 4.47 in his freshman year and 4.69 as a senior. The corresponding scores of Jerry White were 5.06 and 3.84.

The second scale referred to is the newer "non-authoritarianism" scale sometimes called the Social Maturity Scale. Among college populations scores on it have shown a high, inverse correlation with F scores. See Webster, Sanford, and Freedman, 1955; cf. Katz *et al.*, 1968.

7. In his area at the time, the charge was true in a sense, but CORE argued that preferential employment was necessary to make up for past discrimination.

8. Some of this last paragraph's comments on parents were made in the previous two interviews. They were included here to avoid too much jumping back and forth between topics. I have done the same with other interviews in the case of a very few remarks; these have not distorted the

pattern of change and continuity portrayed between freshman and senior years.

9. The individual was given more categories than these three to choose from.

10. It may be objected that he was simply showing loyalty to his father in the presence of a relative stranger. But the question about disagreements only came after some neutral and favorable discussion of parents. There were other times, too, when he was quick and anxious to minimize and even suppress irked feelings—implied boredom, for example, on family holidays, and a rejected feeling when his brother and foster brother (see below) went off without him.

11. My original report included the study of an amiable right-wing girl from a big western city, who showed some ambivalence about male power and the Victorian morality in which she had been brought up. She longed for wild experiences but doubted whether she could handle them without the presence of a trusted, dominating male who would prevent her "going too far." She expressed a disapproving interest in the dating habits of others; but on the information we have, the concept of authoritarianism does not seem particularly applicable in her case.

APPENDIX B

1. The following account of Luther draws on the interpretations by Erikson, 1958, and Osborne, 1961, where these seem substantiated by events. To my knowledge there are no such psychological studies of Cromwell.

2. The part in parentheses is an approximate quotation, the precise words being unpreserved. See Grisar, 1914, II, pp. 217-18. It has been argued that much of this simply reflects Luther's robust way of expressing himself; but that in itself reflects character. Luther was a man of fierce temper, which he had had to bottle up in his youth.

3. Cf. Erikson, 1958. I have not used Erikson's analysis of an alleged fit by Luther in the church choir—a fit supposedly connected with an identity crisis of some kind—because the evidence for this event is highly unreliable.

4. Cf. Grisar, 1914, I, pp. 8-12. Johann Staupitz, Vicar-General of Luther's order, himself advised Luther on one of his visits to the monastery: "Why torment yourself with such thoughts and broodings? Look at the wounds of Christ and his Blood shed for you. There you will see your predestination to heaven shining forth to your comfort." *Ibid.*, 11.

5. *Ibid.*, 5.

6. Erikson, 1958, pp. 64-65. About Luther's mother very little is known. In the vast bulk of his recorded statements, Luther makes but fleeting reference to her, while saying a great deal about Hans. She possessed a strong mystic faith and seems to have been a person of character and interest but with a sad, submissive quality. "For me and you nobody cares. That is our common fault"—these are words of a song she is said to have sung little Martin. She used to beat him too, but childhood beatings were not uncommon for the time and place.

7. For a very clear and concise explanation of anal theories and their relation to the "Protestant ethic," see Lewis and Maude, 1950, pp. 119 n., 122 n. In deference to British sensibilities, Lewis and Maude banished their account to "the deep unconscious of the [foot]notes"—the notes practically take over two pages! According to the original F scale studies, authoritarians tend to exhibit those traits associated with extreme "anal" character: great concern with cleanliness and tidiness; rigid obstinacy; emphasis on getting, having, and controlling, both in money and personal relationships; and an emotional miserliness.

8. Of his tenderness, Cromwell's steward, John Maidstone, wrote, "He was naturally compassionate towards objects in distress even to an effeminate measure." *Thurloe State Papers, I,* p. 766, quoted by Ashley, 1962, p. 233. As Ashley says, "His letters are filled with concern for widows, bereaved parents, and the destitute" (*ibid.*). For examples of actual kindness, see Abbott, 1938, pp. 64, 82-83.

9. In fact Spenser described with some pain the "wretchedness" of Irish poverty; but he still urged the British commander in Ireland to harden his heart. For these and other attitudes to Ireland, including Cromwell's, see Buchan, 1934, pp. 337-42.

10. Trevelyan, 1960, p. 258.

11. This might be thought to resemble an authoritarian's dislike of introspection, but it was said in a different context and spirit, as a plea for tolerance.

12. Even after his subsequent religious and emotional crisis, Cromwell had lesser depressions when he feared he might not be saved.

13. As his letters suggest, he felt and expressed special warmth toward his younger daughters. Wedgwood, 1958, remarks on his marked tenderness to female relatives.

14. Of course there were many exceptions on both sides, e.g., Roger Williams, a very unauthoritarian puritan and the son of a London merchant tailor. As a boy, though, Williams received the knightly patronage of Sir Edward Coke.

15. It must also be remembered that the "merrie England" of Stuart times had a great deal of drunkenness, and that even by many modern standards sexual practices in royal circles and elsewhere were lax.

BIBLIOGRAPHY

NOTE: Italicized figures refer to journal volumes.

ABBOTT, WILBUR CORTEZ, ed., *Letters and Speeches of Oliver Comwell*, Harvard University Press, Cambridge, 1938.

ADORNO, T. W., "Scientific Experiences of a European Scholar in America," in Donald Fleming and Bernard Baileyn, eds., *The Intellectual Migration, Europe and America, 1930-1960*, Harvard University Press, Cambridge, 1969.

ADORNO, T. W., FRENKEL-BRUNSWIK, ELSE; LEVINSON, DANIEL; and SANFORD, R. NEVITT, with Betty Aron, Maria Levinson, and William Morrow, *The Authoritarian Personality*, Harper, New York, 1950.

ALEXANDER, JACK, "The Director" (3 articles), *The New Yorker*, September 25, October 2, and October 9, 1938.

ALLEN, WILLIAM SHERIDAN, *The Nazi Seizure of Power:* The Experience of a Single German Town, 1930-1935, Quadrangle, Chicago, 1965.

ALMOND, GABRIEL, *The Appeals of Communism*, Princeton University Press, 1965 (first published 1954).

ANDERSON, FLAVIA, *The Rebel Emperor*, Gollancz, London, 1958.

ANGRESS, WARNER T., and SMITH, BRADLEY, "Diaries of Himmler's Early Years," *Journal of Modern History*, 1959, *31*, pp. 206-24.

ARENDT, HANNAH, *Eichmann in Jerusalem*, Viking, New York, 1963.

ARMBRISTER, TREVOR, "Portrait of an Extremist," *Saturday Evening Post*, August 22-29, 1964.

ASHLEY, MAURICE, *The Greatness of Oliver Cromwell*, Collier, New York, 1962 (first published 1957).

BACON, M. K., et al., "A Cross-Cultural Study of Drinking," *Quarterly Journal of Studies on Alcohol*, 1965, Supplement 3.

BAILEY, HUGH, *Hinton Rowan Helper, Racist-Abolitionist,* University of Alabama Press, Tuscaloosa, 1965.
BAKAL, CARL, *No Right to Bear Arms,* Paperback Library, New York, 1968 (first published 1966).
BAKER, NEWMAN, "Editorial—J. Edgar Hoover," *Journal of Criminal Law and Criminology,* 1938, *28,* pp. 627-29.
BALAZS, *Chinese Civilization and Bureaucracy,* Yale University Press, New Haven, 1964.
BALES, R. F., "Attitudes Toward Drinking in the Irish Culture," in David J. Pittman and Charles R. Snyder, *Society, Culture and Drinking Patterns,* Wiley, New York, 1962.
——, "Cultural Differences in Rates of Alcoholism," *Quarterly Journal of Studies on Alcohol,* 1946, *6,* pp. 480-99.
BANDURA, ALBERT, "What TV Violence Can Do to Your Child," in *Violence and the Mass Media,* ed. by Otto Larsen, Harper, New York, 1968.
BANTON, MICHAEL, *Policeman in the Community,* Tavistock, London, 1964.
BARKER, EDWIN, "Authoritarianism of the Political Right, Center and Left," *Journal of Social Issues,* 1963, *19,* pp. 63-74.
BARKER, JUDITH, "Taylor Caldwell and Political Ideology," M.A. thesis University of Sussex, Falmer, 1968.
BARNES, GILBERT, *The Anti-Slavery Impulse,* Appleton, New York, 1933.
BARNETT, CORRELLI, "The Education of Military Elites," *Journal of Contemporary History,* 1967, *2,* pp. 15-36. Reprinted in *Governing Elites,* ed. by Rupert Wilkinson, Oxford University Press, New York, 1969.
BAY, CHRISTIAN, *The Structure of Freedom,* Atheneum, New York, 1965 (first published 1958).
BEARDSLEE, DAVID C., and O'DOWD, DONALD D., "Students and the Occupational World," in R. Nevitt Sanford, ed., *The American College,* Wiley, New York, 1962.
BELL, DANIEL, ed., *The Radical Right,* Doubleday Anchor, Garden City, 1964 (first published 1963).
BENDIX, REINHARD, "Compliant Behavior and Individual Personality," *American Journal of Sociology,* 1952, *58,* pp. 292-303.
BENEDICT, PAUL, and JACKS, I., "Mental Illness in Primitive Societies," *Psychiatry,* 1954, *17,* pp. 377-89.
BENEDICT, RUTH, *Patterns of Culture,* Houghton Mifflin, Boston, 1946.
BERKOWITZ, LEONARD, "Anti-semitism and the Displacement of Aggression," *Journal of Abnormal and Social Psychology,* 1959, *59,* pp. 182-88.
——, and HOLMES, DOUGLAS S., "The Generalization of Hostility to Disliked Objects," *Journal of Personality,* 1959, *27,* pp. 565-77.
BETTELHEIM, BRUNO, "The Individual and Mass Behavior in Extreme Situations," *Journal of Abnormal and Social Psychology,* 1943, *38,* pp. 424 ff.
——, and JANOWITZ, MORRIS, *Social Change and Prejudice,* Free Press, Glencoe, 1964.
BIGGS, JOHN, *The Guilty Mind,* Psychiatry and the Law of Homicide, Johns Hopkins Press, Baltimore, 1955.

BILLINGTON, RAY, *The Protestant Crusade, 1800-1860*, Quadrangle, Chicago, 1964 (first published 1938).
BISHOP, T. J. H., with Rupert Wilkinson, *Winchester and the Public School Elite*, Faber, London, 1967.
BLANCHARD, WILLIAM, *Rousseau and the Spirit of Revolt: A Psychological Study*, University of Michigan Press, Ann Arbor, 1968.
BLOOM, L., "Piaget's Theory of the Development of Moral Judgment," *Journal of Genetic Psychology*, 1959, 95, pp. 3-12. Reprinted in *Attitudes*, ed. by Marie Jahoda and Neil Warren, Penguin, Harmondsworth, 1966.
BOARDMAN, EUGENE, "The Biblical Influence Upon the Ideology of the Taiping Rebellion," doctoral dissertation, Department of History, Harvard, 1946.
BOAS, R., *Cotton Mather: Keeper of the Puritan Conscience*, Harper, New York, 1923.
BOHN, FRANK, "The Ku Klux Klan Interpreted," *American Journal of Sociology*, 1925, 30, pp. 385-407.
BRAGINSKY, BENJAMIN, et al., *Methods of Madness: The Mental Hospital as a Last Resort*, Holt, New York, 1969.
BRAZZIEL, WILLIAM F., "Correlates of Southern Negro Personality," *Journal of Social Issues*, 1964, 20, pp. 46 ff.
BROUN, HEYWOOD, and LEECH, MARGARET, *Anthony Comstock, Roundsman of the Lord*, Boni (Literary Guild edition), New York, 1927.
BROYLES, ALLEN, *The John Birch Society*, Beacon, Boston, 1964.
BUCHAN, JOHN, *Oliver Cromwell*, Hodder and Stoughton, London, 1934.
BULLOCK, ALAN, *Hitler*, Bantam, New York, 1961 (first published 1953).
BURKE, PETER, "The Cunning of Unreason," in D. May, ed., *Good Talk*, Gollancz, London, 1969.
BUTLER, EWAN, and YOUNG, GORDON, *Marshall Without Glory*, Hodder and Stoughton, London, 1951.
BUTLER, SAMUEL, *The Way of All Flesh*, Random House Modern Library (no date given: first published 1903).
BYRNE, DONN, "Parental Antecedents of Authoritarianism," *Journal of Personality and Social Psychology*, 1965, 1, pp. 569-75.

CALVERT, ROBERT, *Vocational Analysis of Male College Graduates in Liberal Arts*, Survey, Research Center, Berkeley, 1967.
CASH, W. J., *The Mind of the South*, Vintage, New York (first published 1941).
CHESLER, MARK, and SCHMUCK, RICHARD, "Participant Observation in a Super-Patriot Discussion Group," *Journal of Social Issues*, 1963, 19, no. 2.
CHRISTIE, RICHARD, "Eysenck's Treatment of the Personality of Communists," *Psychological Bulletin*, 1956, 53, pp. 411-30.
———, and COOK, P., "A Guide to Published Literature Relating to the Authoritarian Personality through 1956," *Journal of Psychology*, 1958, 45, pp. 171-99.

——, and GARCIA, JOHN, "Subcultural Variations in Authoritarian Personality," *Journal of Abnormal and Social Psychology*, 1951.

——, and JAHODA, MARIE, *Studies in the Scope and Method of the Authoritarian Personality*, Free Press, Glencoe, 1954.

CLARK, NORMAN, *The Dry Years: Prohibition and Social Change in Washington*, University of Washington, Seattle, 1965.

COBEN, STANLEY, "The American Red Scare of 1919-20," *Political Science Quarterly*, 1964, 79, pp. 52-75.

COHN, NORMAN, *Warrant for Genocide*, Eyre, London, 1967.

COLES, ROBERT, *Children of Crisis*, Little, Brown, Boston, 1967.

Committee of Enquiry, *Report of, The Method II System of Selection*, HMSO, London, 1969.

COMSTOCK, ANTHONY, *Morals Versus Art*, Ogilvie, New York, 1881.

COOK, FRED, *The FBI Nobody Knows*, Macmillan, New York, 1964.

CRICHTON, ROBERT, "The Air War in Vietnam," *New Society*, January 11, 1968.

CROMWELL, OLIVER, *Writings and Speeches of*, ed. by W. C. Abbott, Harvard University Press, Cambridge, 1938.

DAVIS, ALLISON, and DOLLARD, JOHN, *Children of Bondage*, Harper Torchbook, New York, 1964 (first published 1940).

DAVIS, DAVID, "Violence in American Literature," in Otto Larsen, ed., *Violence and the Mass Media*, Harper, New York, 1968.

DAVIS, KENNETH, *The Hero*, Doubleday, New York, 1950.

DE BARY, W. T., CHAN, W. T., and WATSON, B., eds. *Sources of Chinese Tradition*, Columbia University Press, New York, 1960.

DEGLER, CARL, *Out of Our Past*, Harper Colophon, New York, 1959.

DEMOS, JOHN, *A Little Commonwealth, Family Life in Plymouth Colony*, Oxford University Press, New York, 1970a.

——, "Underlying Themes in the Witchcraft of Seventeenth-Century New England," *American Historical Review*, 1970b, 75, pp. 1311-26.

DENNISON, GEORGE, *The Lives of Children, The Story of the First Street School*, Random House, New York, 1969.

DE VOS, GEORGE, and MINER, HORACE, "Algerian Culture and Personality in Change," *Sociometry*, 1958, *21*, pp. 255-68.

—— and ——, *Oasis and Casbah: Algerian Culture and Personality in Change*, University of Michigan, Ann Arbor, 1960.

D'HARCOURT, PIERRE, *The Real Enemy*, Longman, London, 1967.

DICKS, H. V., "Personality Traits and National Socialist Ideology," *Human Relations*, London, 1950, *3*, pp. 111-53.

DIXON, THOMAS, *The Clansman*, Grosset, New York, 1905.

DOLLARD, JOHN, *Caste and Class in a Southern Town*, Doubleday Anchor, Garden City, 1957 (first published 1937).

DORNBUSCH, SANFORD, and HICKMAN, LAUREN, "Other-Directedness in Consumer Goods Advertising," *Social Forces*, 1959, *38*, pp. 99-102.

DUBOIS, CORA, with KARDINER, ABRAM, and OBERHOLZER, EMIL, *People of Alor*, University of Minnesota, Minneapolis, 1944. (Harvard University Press edition, 1960.)

EATON, JOSEPH, "Controlled Acculturation: A Survival Technique of the Hutterites," *American Sociological Review*, 1952, *17*, pp. 331-40.
EATON, JOSEPH; WEIL, ROBERT; and KAPLAN, BERT, "The Hutterite Mental Health Study," *Mennonite Quarterly Review*, 1951, *25*, pp. 47-59.
EATON, JOSEPH, with ROBERT WEIL, *Culture and Mental Disorder: A Comparative Study of the Hutterites and Other Populations*, Free Press, Glencoe, 1955.
EDWARDS, JONATHAN, *The Works of*, ed. by Edward Hickman, Ball, London, 1840, vol. I.
ELDER, GLEN, "Structural Variations in the Child Rearing Relationship," *Sociometry*, 1962, *25*, pp. 241-62.
ELKINS, STANLEY, *Slavery*, Grosset Universal Library, New York, 1963 (first published 1959).
ELLISON, RALPH, *Invisible Man*, Random House, 1952.
ELMS, ALAN C., "Psychological Factors in Right-Wing Extremism," in R. A. Schoenberger, ed., q.v.
ENGLISH, HORACE and AVA, *A Comprehensive Dictionary of Psychological and Psychoanalytical Terms*, McKay, New York, 1958.
EPSTEIN, RALPH, "Authoritarianism, Displaced Aggression and Social Status of Target," *Journal of Personality and Social Psychology*, 1965, *2*, pp. 585-89.
———, "Aggression Towards Outgroups as a Function of Authoritarianism and Imitation of Aggressive Models," *Journal of Personality and Social Psychology*, 1966, *3*, pp. 574-79.
ERIKSON, ERIK, *Gandhi's Truth*, Norton, New York, 1969.
———, *Childhood and Society*, Norton, New York, 1950.
———, *Young Man Luther*, Norton, New York, 1958.
EVANS, HIRAM WESLEY, "The Klan's Fight for Americanism," *North American Review*, 1926, *223*, pp. 33-63.
EYSENCK, H. J., *Crime and Personality*, Routledge, London, 1964 (published by Houghton Mifflin in the United States).

FEI, HSIAO-TUNG, "Peasantry and Gentry," *American Journal of Sociology*, 1946, *3*, no. 1.
FLEMING, SANDFORD, *Children and Puritanism, The Place of Children in the Life and Thought of the New England Churches, 1620-1847*. Yale University Press, New Haven, 1933.
FORTUNE, REO, *Sorcerers of Dobu*, Routledge, London, 1932.
FOX, SANFORD J., *Science and Justice, The Massachusetts Witchcraft Trials*, Johns Hopkins Press, Baltimore, 1968.
FREEDMAN, MERVIN, WEBSTER, HAROLD, and SANFORD, NEVITT, "A Study of Authoritarianism," *Journal of Psychology*, 1956, *41*, pp. 315-22.
FRENKEL-BRUNSWIK, ELSE, "Further Explorations by a Contributor," in Richard Christie and Marie Jahoda, eds., *Studies in the Scope and Method of "The Authoritarian Personality,"* Free Press, Glencoe, 1954.
———, "Patterns of Social and Cognitive Outlook in Children and Parents," *American Journal of Orthopsychiatry*, 1951, *2*, pp. 543-48.

FREUD, SIGMUND, *A General Introduction to Psychoanalysis*, Permabook (Pocket Books), New York, 1964 (first published 1920).
FRIEDMANN, ROBERT, *Hutterite Studies*, Mennonite Historical Society, Goshen, 1961.
FRIEDMANN, WOLFGANG, *Law in a Changing Society*, Penguin, Harmondsworth, 1964 (first published 1959).
FRISCHAUER, WILLI, *The Rise and Fall of Hermann Goering*, Houghton Mifflin, Boston, 1951.
———, and MANVELL, ROGER, *Himmler*, Putnam, New York, 1965.
FROMM, ERICH, *Escape from Freedom*, Rinehart, New York, 1941. (London edition, *The Fear of Freedom*).

GALLAHER, ART, *Plainville Fifteen Years Later*, Columbia University Press, New York, 1961.
GANS, HERBERT, *The Levittowners*, Pantheon, New York, 1967.
GARNETT, R. S., *Samuel Butler and His Family Relations*, Dent, London, 1926.
GERTH, HANS, "The Nazi Party: Its Leadership and Composition," *American Journal of Sociology*, 1940, 45, pp. 517-41.
GILBERT, G. M., *Nuremberg Diary*, Farrar, Strauss, New York, 1947.
———, *The Psychology of Dictatorship*, Ronald, New York, 1950.
GINGER, RAY, *Age of Excess*, Macmillan, New York, 1965.
GINZBURG, RALPH, *100 Years of Lynching*, Lancer, New York (no date given).
GLAD, BETTY, *Charles Evans Hughes, The Illustrations of Innocence*, University of Illinois Press, Urbana, 1966.
GLAZER, NATHAN, and MOYNIHAN, DANIEL P., *Beyond the Melting Pot*, MIT, Cambridge, 1964.
GOEBBELS, JOSEPH, *The Goebbels Diaries*, ed. by Louis Lochner, Eagle, New York, 1960.
GOFFMAN, IRVING, *Asylums*, Doubleday Anchor, Garden City, 1961.
GOLDFRANK, ESTHER, "Socialization, Personality and the Structure of Pueblo Society," *American Anthropologist*, 1945, 47, pp. 516-39.
GOLDING, WILLIAM, *The Lord of the Flies*, Coward-McCann, New York, 1954.
GOLDSTEIN, ABRAHAM, *The Insanity Defense*, Yale University Press, New Haven, 1967.
GOOD, PAUL, "Klantown, USA," *The Nation*, February 1, 1965.
GORER, GEOFFREY, *Exploring English Character*, Criterion, New York, 1955.
GREENSTEIN, FRED I., *Children and Politics*, Yale University Press, New Haven, 1965a.
———, "Private Disorder and the Public Order: A Proposal for Collaboration between Psychoanalysts and Political Scientists," *Psychoanalytic Quarterly*, 1968, 37, pp. 261-80.
———, "Personality and Political Socialization: The Theories of Authoritarian and Democratic Character," *Annals of American Academy of Political and Social Science*, 1965b, 361, pp. 81-95.

——, *Personality and Politics*, Markham, Chicago, 1969.
——, "New Light on Changing American Values: A Forgotten Body of Survey Data," *Social Forces*, 1964, *42*, pp. 441-52.
GRIER, WILLIAM H., and COBBS, PRICE M., *Black Rage*, Basic Books, New York, 1968.
GRIFFIN, JOHN HOWARD, *Black Like Me*, Houghton Mifflin, 1964 (first published 1960).
GRISAR, HARTMAN, *Luther*, Kegan, London, 1914, vols. I & II.
GUSFIELD, JOSEPH, *Symbolic Crusade, Status Politics and the American Temperance Movement*, University of Illinois, Urbana, 1963.
——, *Symbolic Crusade*, University of Illinois, Urbana, 1963.
——, "Status Conflicts and Changing Ideologies of the American Temperance Movement," in David Pittman and Charles Snyder, eds., *Society, Culture, and Drinking Patterns*, Wiley, New York, 1962.
GUTTMACHER, MANFRED, "Normal and Sociopathic Murderers," in Marvin Wolfgang, ed., *Studies in Homicide*.

HAGEN, LOUIS, *The Mark of the Swastika*, Bantam, New York, 1965.
HARRIS, DALE H., GOUGH, HARRISON; and MARTIN, WILLIAM, "Children's Ethnic Attitudes: Relationship to Parental Beliefs Concerning Child Training," *Child Development*, 1950, *21*, pp. 169-82.
HARRIS, NATHANIEL, *Autobiography*, Macon, New York, 1925.
HART, H. L. A., *Punishment and Responsibility*, Oxford University Press, London, 1968.
HAWTHORNE, HARRY, ed., *The Doukhobors of British Columbia*, Dent and University of British Columbia, Vancouver, 1955.
HENRY, JULES, *Jungle People*, Augustin, Locust Valley, New York, 1941.
HERSEY, JOHN, *The Algiers Motel Incident*, Knopf, New York, 1968; also Bantam edition, 1968.
HICKS, GRANVILLE, *Small Town*, Macmillan, New York, 1947.
HIGHAM, JOHN, *Strangers in the Land*, Rutgers, New Brunswick, New Jersey, 1955.
HITLER, ADOLF, *Mein Kampf* (trans. by James Murphy), Stackpool, New York, 1939.
HODGES, HAROLD, *Social Stratification: Class in America*, Schenkman, Cambridge, Mass., 1964.
——, "A Sociological Analysis of McCarthy Supporters," unpublished paper, Sociology Department, San Jose State College, San Jose, California, 1956.
HOESS, RUDOLPH, *The Commandant of Auschwitz*, Weidenfeld, London, 1959 (first published 1951).
HOFSTADTER, RICHARD, *The American Political Tradition*, Vintage, New York, 1948. *The Age of Reform*, Vintage, New York, 1955a.
——, "The Pseudo-Conservative Revolt," in Daniel Bell, ed., *The New American Right*, Criterion, New York, 1955a. (Reprinted in Bell, ed., *The Radical Right*, Doubleday Anchor, Garden City, 1964.)
HOLLANDER, E. P., "Authoritarianism and Leadership Choice in a Military Setting," *American Psychologist*, 1953, *8*, p. 378 ff.

HOLLINGSHEAD, AUGUST, and REDLICH, FREDERICK, *Social Class and Mental Illness*, Wiley, New York, 1958.

HOLT, SIMMA, *Terror in the Name of God: The Story of the Sons of Freedom Doukhobors*, Crown, New York, 1964.

HORKHEIMER, MAX, ed., *Studies in Philosophy and Social Science*, Institute of Social Research, New York, 1941, vol. IX.

HOVLAND, C. I., *and* SEARS, R. R., "Minor Studies of Aggression: VI. Correlation of Lynchings with Economic Indices," *Journal of Psychology*, 1940, 9, pp. 301-10.

HUIE, WILLIAM B., *The Klansman*, Delacorte, New York, 1967.

IRVING, DAVID, *The Destruction of Dresden*, Kimber, London, 1963.

JACKSON, BRUCE, "Police on the Junkie Beat," *Atlantic*, January, 1967.

JACKSON, PETER, "Business—the Religion of the Twenties," undergraduate thesis, University of Sussex, 1970.

JACKSON, KENNETH, *The Ku Klux Klan in the City, 1915-30*, Oxford University Press, New York, 1967.

JAHODA, MARIE, "The Migration of Psychoanalysis: Its Impact on America," in Donald Fleming and Bernard Bailyn, eds., *The Intellectual Migration: Europe and America, 1930-1960*, Harvard University Press, Cambridge, 1969.

JENCKS, CHRISTOPHER, and RIESMAN, DAVID, *The Academic Revolution*, Doubleday, Garden City, 1968.

JENSEN, ARTHUR, "Authoritarian Attitudes and Personality Maladjustment," *Journal of Abnormal and Social Psychology*, 1957, 54, pp. 303-11.

JETZINGER, FRANZ, *Hitler's Youth*, Hutchinson, London, 1958.

KAPLAN, BERT, and PLAUT, THOMAS, *Personality in a Communal Society: An Analysis of the Mental Health of the Hutterites*, University of Kansas Press, Lawrence, 1956.

KARDINER, ABRAM, "Explorations in Negro Personality," in M. K. Opler, ed., *Culture and Mental Health*, Macmillan, New York, 1959.

——, and OVESEY, LIONEL, *The Mark of Oppression*, Meridian, Cleveland, 1964 (first published 1951).

KARON, BERTRAM, *The Negro Personality*, Springer, New York, 1958.

KATZ, DANIEL, "The Functional Approach to the Study of Attitudes," *Public Opinion Quarterly*, 1960, 24, pp. 164-204.

KATZ, IRWIN, et al., "The Influence of the Race of the Experimenter and Instructions upon the Expression of Hostility by Negro Boys," *Journal of Social Issues*, 1964, 20, pp. 54 ff.

KATZ, JOSEPH, and ASSOCIATES, *No Time for Youth*, Jossey-Bass, San Francisco, 1968.

KENISTON, KENNETH, *Young Radicals*, Harcourt, New York, 1968 (Harvest edition).

——, "How Community Mental Health Stamped out the Riots (1968-70)," *Trans-Action*, July/August, 1968.

KERSTEN, FELIX, *The Kersten Memoirs*, Hutchinson, London, 1956 (introduction by H. R. Trevor-Roper).

Kirscht, John P., and Dillehay, Ronald C., *Dimensions of Authoritarianism: A Review of Research and Theory,* University of Kentucky Press, Lexington, 1967.

Kirst, Hans Hellmut, *Officer Factory,* Collins, London, 1962.

Kogon, Eugene, *The Theory and Practice of Hell,* Farrar, Straus, New York, 1946.

Kohlberg, Laurence, "Development of Moral Character and Moral Ideology," in M. L. and L. W. Hoffman, eds., *Child Development Research,* Russell Sage, New York, 1964.

Krugman, Herbert, "The Role of Hostility in the Appeal of Communism," *Psychiatry,* 1953, *16,* pp. 253-61.

Lane, Robert E., "Fathers and Sons: Foundation of Political Belief," *American Sociological Review,* 1959, *24,* pp. 502-11.

——, *Political Thinking and Consciousness: The Private Life of the Political Mind,* Markham, Chicago, 1969.

——, *Political Ideology, Why the American Common Man Believes What He Does,* Free Press, Glencoe, 1962.

Lasswell, Harold, "The Psychology of Hitlerism," *Political Quarterly,* 1933, *4,* pp. 373-84.

——, *Psychopathology and Politics,* Viking, New York, 1960 (first published 1930).

Lewis, Roy, and Maude, Angus, *The English Middle Classes,* Knopf, New York, 1950.

Lewis, Sinclair, *Babbitt,* Harcourt, New York, 1922.

Liebow, Elliot, *Talley's Corner, A Study of Negro Streetcorner Men,* Little, Brown, Boston, 1966.

Lifton, Robert, *Thought Reform and the Psychology of Totalism,* Norton, New York, 1961.

——, "Protean Man," *Partisan Review,* 1968, *35,* pp. 13-27.

——, "Individual Patterns, in Historical Change: Imagery of Japanese Youth," *Comparative Studies in Society and History,* 1964, *6,* pp. 369-83.

Lindner, Robert, *The Fifty-Minute Hour,* Rinehart, New York, 1954.

Lipset, Seymour M., *Political Man,* Doubleday Anchor, Garden City, 1963 (first published 1960).

——, "The Wallace Whitelash," *Trans-Action,* December 1969.

——, "On the Politics of Conscience and Extreme Commitment," *Encounter,* August, 1968.

——, "The Politics of the Police," *New Society,* March 6, 1969.

——, "The Sources of the 'Radical Right'," in Daniel Bell, ed., *The Radical Right,* Doubleday Anchor, Garden City, 1964.

——, and Altbach, Philip, "U.S. Campus Alienation," *New Society,* September 8, 1966.

——, and Lowenthal, Leo, eds., *Culture and Social Character: The Work of David Riesman,* Free Press, Glencoe, 1961.

Lipsitz, Lewis, "Working Class Authoritarianism: a Re-evaluation," *American Sociological Review,* February, 1965.

LOEWENBERG, PETER, "The Adolescence of Heinrich Himmler," paper read before the American Historical Association, Pacific Coast branch, August, 1969.
LOLLI, GIORGIO, et al., *Alcohol in Italian Culture,* Free Press, Glencoe, 1958.
LORENZ, KONRAD, *On Aggression,* Harcourt, New York, 1966.
——, *King Solomon's Ring,* T. Y. Crowell, New York, 1952.
LYND, ROBERT and HELEN, *Middletown,* Harcourt, New York, 1929.
LYND, ROBERT and HELEN, *Middletown in Transition,* Harcourt (Harvest), New York, 1937.

MACKINNON, W. J., and CENTERS, R., "Authoritarianism and Urban Stratification," *American Journal of Sociology,* 1956, *61,* pp. 610-20.
MCCLEAN, HELEN, article in *The Annals,* American Political Science Association, 1946, *244,* p. 164 ff.
MCCLOSKEY, HERBERT, "Conservatism and Personality," *American Political Science Review,* March, 1958.
——, and SCHAAR, JOHN, "Psychological Dimensions of Anomy," *American Sociological Review,* 1965, *30,* pp. 14-40.
MCCORD, WILLIAM, *The Psychopath,* Van Nostrand, New York, 1964.
MCCORD, WILLIAM and JOAN, *Origins of Alcoholism,* Stanford University Press, Stanford, 1960.
MCCRYSTAL, CAL, "Profile [of J. Edgar Hoover]," *Sunday Times,* London, January 12, 1969.
MCDILL, E. L., "Anomie, Authoritarianism, Prejudice, and Socio-Economic Status: an Attempt at Clarification," *Social Forces,* 1961, *39,* pp. 239-45.
MCEVOY, JAMES, *Letters from the Right,* Institute for Social Research, Ann Arbor, 1966.
MADISON, PETER, "Dynamics of Development and Constraint: Two Case Studies" in Joseph Katz and Associates, *No Time for Youth,* Jossey-Bass, San Francisco, 1968.
MALIN, J. C., *John Brown and the Legend of '56.* American Philosophical Society, 1942.
MANVELL, ROGER, and FRAENKEL, HEINRICH, *Himmler,* Putnam, New York, 1965.
——, *The Incomparable Crime,* Heinemann, London, 1967.
——, *Doctor Goebbels,* Heinemann, London, 1960.
MARSH, ROBERT, *The Mandarins: The Circulation of Elites in China,* Free Press, Glencoe, 1961.
MARTIN, HAROLD, et al., "We Got Nothing to Hide," *Saturday Evening Post,* January 30, 1965.
MARUYAMAH, MASAO, "Patterns of Individuation and the Case of Japan," in Marius Jensen, ed., *Changing Japanese Attitudes Toward Modernization,* Princeton University Press, Princeton, 1965.
——, *Thought and Behavior in Modern Japanese Politics,* Oxford University Press, London, 1963.
MASLOW, A. H., "The Authoritarian Character Structure," *Journal of Social Psychology,* 1943, *18,* pp. 401-11.

MAYER, MARTIN, *The Lawyers*, Dell, New York, 1968 (first published 1966).
MEAD, G. H., "The Psychology of Punitive Justice," *American Journal of Sociology*, 1918, 23, pp. 577-602.
MECKLIN, JOHN, *The Ku Klux Klan, A Study of the American Mind*, Harcourt, New York, 1924.
MEGARGEE, EDWIN, "Assault with Intent to Kill," *Trans-Action*, September-October, 1965.
———, "Undercontrolled and Overcontrolled Personality Types in Extreme Antisocial Aggression," *Psychological Monographs; General and Applied*, 1966, 80, no. 3.
MELIKIAN, LEVON, "Authoritarianism and Its Correlates in Egyptian Culture and in the United States," *Journal of Social Issues*, 1959, 15, pp. 58-68.
MERRILL, WALTER, *Against Wind and Tide*, Harvard University Press, 1963.
MILGRAM, S., "Some Conditions of Obedience and Disobedience to Authority," *Human Relations*, 1965, 18, pp. 57-76.
MILLER, PERRY, ed., *The American Puritans: Their Prose and Poetry*, Doubleday Anchor, Garden City, New York, 1956.
MILLER, S. M., "The Credential Society," *Trans-Action*, December, 1967.
MILLS, C. WRIGHT, *The Power Elite*, Oxford University Press, New York, 1956.
MILOSZ, CZESLAW, *The Captive Mind*, Secker, London, 1953.
MILTON, O., "Presidential Choice and Performance on a Scale of Authoritarianism," *American Psychologist*, 1952, 7, pp. 597-98.
MONEY-KYRLE, ROGER E., *Psychoanalysis and Politics*, Duckworth, London, 1951.
MORRIS, DESMOND, *The Naked Ape*, McGraw Hill, New York, 1967.
MORRIS, WILLIE, "Houston's Superpatriots," *Harper's*, October, 1961.
MOTTRAM, V. H., *The Physical Basis of Personality*, Penguin, Harmondsworth, 1952.
MOWRY, GEORGE, *The Twenties*, Prentice-Hall, Englewood Cliffs, 1963.
MUIR, JOHN, *The Story of My Boyhood and Life*, University of Wisconsin Press, Madison, 1965.

NATION, CARRY, *The Use and Need of Carry A. Nation*, Steves, Topeka, 1905.
NEUSTATTER, W. LINDESAY, "The State of Mind in Murder," *The Lancet*, London, April 17, 1965, pp. 861-63.
NIEDERHOFFER, ARTHUR, *Behind the Shield: The Police in Urban Society*, Doubleday Anchor, Garden City, 1969 (first published 1967).
NOEL, DONALD L., "Group Identification Among Negroes: an Empirical Analysis," *Journal of Social Issues*, 1964, 20, pp. 71 ff.

O'CONNOR, EDWIN, *The Last Hurrah*, Little, Brown, Boston, 1956.
OGILVY, DAVID, *Confessions of an Advertising Man*, Longman, London, 1963 (published in United States by Atheneum).
O'HIGGINS, HARVEY, and REEDE, EDWARD, *American Mind in Action*, Harper, New York, 1924.

OSBORNE, JOHN, *Luther* (a play), 1961, Signet edition, New York, 1963.

PARKES, HENRY BAMFORD, *Jonathan Edwards*, Minton, New York, 1930.
PARRINGTON, VERNON, *Main Currents in American Thought*, Harcourt, New York, 1930, vol. I.
PEGLER, WESTBROOK, "Jimmy and the Chipmunk," *American Opinion*, Belmont, September, 1963.
PETTIGREW, THOMAS, "Personality and Sociocultural Factors in Intergroup Attitudes: a Cross-National Comparison," *Conflict Resolution*, 1958, 2, pp. 29-42.
——, *Profile of the Negro American*, Van Nostrand, Princeton, 1964.
PLOG, S. C., and EDGERTON, R. B., *Changing Perspective in Mental Illness*, Holt, New York, 1969.
PODHORETZ, NORMAN, *Making It*, Random House, New York, 1968.
POTTER, DAVID, "The Quest for National Character," in John Higham, ed., *The Reconstruction of American History*, Harper Torchbooks, New York, 1962.
PULZER, P. G., *The Rise of Political Anti-Semitism in Germany and Austria*, Wiley, New York, 1964.

RADIN, PAUL, *The World of Primitive Man*, Schumann, New York, 1953.
RAINWATER, LEE, "Crucible of Identity: The Negro Lower-Class Family," *Daedalus*, Winter, 1966.
RAND, AYN, *For the New Intellectual*, Random House, New York, 1963.
RANDEL, WILLIAM P., *The Ku Klux Klan*, Chilton, Philadelphia, 1965.
RANULF, SVEND, *Moral Indignation and Middle Class Morality*, Levin, Copenhagen, 1938.
RAPER, ARTHUR, *The Tragedy of Lynching*, University of North Carolina Press, Chapel Hill, 1963 (first published 1933).
REES, J. R., et al., *The Case of Rudolph Hess*, Heinemann, London, 1947.
REICHARD, SUZANNE, et al., *Aging and Personality*, Wiley, New York, 1962.
REISCHAUER, EDWIN, and FAIRBANK, JOHN K., *East Asia: The Great Tradition*, Houghton Mifflin, Boston, 1960.
REISS, ALBERT J., "Police Brutality," *Trans/Action*, July–August, 1968.
REISS, CURT, *Joseph Goebbels*, Hollis and Carter, London, 1949.
REITLINGER, GERALD, *The S.S.: Alibi of a Nation 1922-1945*, Viking, New York, 1968.
RHODES, A. L., "Authoritarianism and Alienation: the F Scale and the Srole Scale as Predictors of Prejudice," *Sociological Quarterly*, 1961, 2, pp. 193-202.
RIESMAN, DAVID, with NATHAN GLAZER and REUEL DENNEY, *The Lonely Crowd*, Yale University Press, Doubleday Anchor, 1953 (first published 1950).
——, with NATHAN GLAZER, *Faces in the Crowd*, Yale University Press, New Haven, 1952.
ROBERTS, A. H., and ROKEACH, M., "Anomie, Authoritarianism and Prejudice: a Replication," *American Journal of Sociology*, 1956, 61, pp. 355-58.

ROGIN, MICHAEL, *The Intellectuals and McCarthy*, M.I.T., Cambridge, Massachusetts, 1967.
ROGOW, ARNOLD A., *James Forrestal, A Study of Personality, Politics and Policy*, Macmillan, New York, 1963.
ROHL, J. C. G., "Higher Civil Servants in Germany, 1890-1900," *Journal of Contemporary History*, 1967, 2, pp. 101-21.
ROHRER, JOHN, and EDMONSEN, MUNRO S., *The Eighth Generation Grows Up*, Harper Torchbook, New York, 1964 (first published 1960).
ROHTER, IRA, "Attitudes about the Vietnam War: A Causal Theory and Empirical Model," Paper given to the American Political Science Association, Washington, D. C., September, 1968.
——, "The Righteous Rightists," *Trans-Action*, May, 1967.
——, "Some Personal Needs Met by Becoming a Radical Rightist," paper read before American Psychology Association, September 4, 1965.
ROKEACH, MILTON, *The Open and Closed Mind*, Basic Books, New York, 1960.
RUPP, GORDON, *Righteousness of God*, Philosophical Library, New York, 1953.

SABINE, GEORGE, *A History of Political Theory*, Holt, New York, 1950.
SANFORD, F. H., *Authoritarianism and Leadership*, Institute for Research in Human Relations, Philadelphia, 1950.
SANFORD, R. NEVITT, "The Approach of the Authoritarian Personality," in J. L. McCary, ed., *Psychology of Personality*, Logos, New York, 1956.
——, *The American College*, Wiley, New York, 1962.
——, "Identification with the Enemy: Case Study of an American Quisling," *Journal of Personality*, 1946, 15, pp. 53-58.
——, "A Psychoanalytic Study of Three Criminal Types," *Journal of Criminal Psychopathology*, 1943, 5, pp. 57-68.
SARTRE, JEAN-PAUL, "Portrait of the Antisemite," *Partisan Review*, 1946, 13, pp. 163-76.
SCHEFF, THOMAS, *Being Mentally Ill*, Aldine, Chicago, 1966.
SCHIFF, LAWRENCE, "Obedient Rebels," *Journal of Social Issues*, 1964, 20, 74 ff.
——, *The Conservative Movement on American College Campuses*, doctoral dissertation, Harvard, 1964.
SCHLESINGER, ARTHUR M., JR., *A Thousand Days*, Houghton Mifflin, New York, 1965.
SCHMUCK, RICHARD, and CHESLER, MARK, "On Super-Patriotism: A Definition and Analysis," *Journal of Social Issues*, 1963, 19, no. 2.
SCHOENBAUM, DAVID, *Hitler's Social Revolution*, Weidenfeld, London, 1967 (published in United States by Doubleday).
SCHOENBERGER, ROBERT A., ed., *The American Right Wing*, Holt, New York, 1969.
SCHUMPETER, JOSEPH, *Capitalism, Socialism and Democracy*, Harper, New York, 1950.
SEARS, R. R., "Experimental Studies of Projection: I. Attribution of Traits," *Journal of Social Psychology*, 1936, 7, pp. 151-63.

SEARS, R. R., "Experimental Studies of Projection: II. Ideas of Reference," *Journal of Social Psychology*, 1937, 8, pp. 389-400.
SEELEY, JOHN; SIM, R. A.; and LOOSLEY, ELIZABETH, *Crestwood Heights*, Basic Books, New York, 1956.
SELBY, HENRY, "*Elite* Selection and Social Integration," in Rupert Wilkinson, ed., *Governing Elites: Studies in Training and Selection*, Oxford University Press, New York, 1969.
SIDRAN, BEN, "Black Music and the Cultural Revolution," 1970 doctoral dissertation, University of Sussex, 1971.
SIEGEL, BERNARD, "High Anxiety Levels and Cultural Integration," *Social Forces*, October, 1955.
SIGAL, CLANCY, "A Short Talk with a Fascist Beast," *New Statesman*, October 4, 1958.
SILBERMAN, CHARLES E., *Crisis in Black and White*, Random House, New York, 1964.
SILVER, JAMES, "Mississippi Must Choose," *New York Times Magazine*, July 19, 1964.
———, *Mississippi the Closed Society*, Harcourt, New York, 1963.
SINCLAIR, ANDREW, *Prohibition*, Little, Brown, Boston, 1962.
SINGER, J. L., "Schizophrenia and Culture," *Scientific American*, 1957, *197*, pp. 103-10.
SMITH, ALLAN, "On the Inter-relation between the Prohibition Movement and the Drive for Restriction of Immigration," M.A. dissertation, University of Sussex, Falmer, 1967.
SMITH, C. U., and PROTHRO, J. W., "Ethnic Differences in Authoritarian Personality," *Social Forces*, 1957, 35, pp. 334-38.
SMITH, M. BREWSTER, et al., *Opinions and Personality*, Wiley, New York, 1956.
SNOW, C. P., *The Corridors of Power*, Macmillan, London, 1964 (published in United States by Scribner).
SOKOL, ROBERT, "Social Stratification, Power Orientations and Support for Senator McCarthy," paper read before American Sociological Association, August, 1960, New York.
———, "Power Orientation and McCarthyism," *American Journal of Sociology*, 1968, 73, pp. 443 ff.
SPENCER, HERBERT, "So This Is What Dr. Spock Is Like as a Father," *Nova*, London, March, 1968.
SPERLING, PETER, "A Study of the Psychotic Within Three Ethnic Groups," undergraduate honors thesis, Department of Social Relations, Harvard, 1953.
SPOCK, BENJAMIN, *Baby and Child Care*, Duell, Sloan and Pearce, New York, 1965.
SROLE, LEO, and LANGER, THOMAS, "Religious Origins," in Leo Srole *et al.*, eds., *Mental Health in the Metropolis, the Midtown Manhattan Study*, McGraw-Hill, New York, 1962.
STAFFORD-CLARK, DAVID, *Psychiatry Today*, Penguin, Harmondsworth, 1952, second edition, 1963.

STARKEY, MARION, *The Devil in Massachusetts, A Modern Enquiry into the Salem Witch Trials*, Doubleday Dolphin, Garden City, New York, 1961 (first published 1949).
STECKLER, G. A., "Authoritarian Ideology in Negro College Students," *Journal of Abnormal and Social Psychology*, 1957, *54*, pp. 396-99.
STERN, GEORGE, "Environments for Learning," in R. Nevitt Sanford, ed., *The American College*, Wiley, New York, 1962.
STEUART, JUSTIN, *Wayne Wheeler: Dry Boss*, Revell, Chicago, 1928.
STRASSBURGER, FRED, "The Measurement of Attitudes Towards Alcohol and Their Relation to Personality Variables," unpublished paper, Institute for the Study of Human Problems, Stanford, circa 1964.
SYKES, GRESHAM, *The Society of Captives*, A Study of a Maximum Security Prison, Atheneum, New York, 1966.
SZASZ, THOMAS, "Naming and the Myth of Mental Illness," *American Psychologist*, 1961, *16*, pp. 59-65.
——, *The Myth of Mental Illness*, Dell, New York, 1967 (first published 1961).
——, *Law, Liberty, and Psychiatry*, Macmillan, New York, 1963.

TENG, SAU-YU, *New Light on the Taiping Rebellion*, Harvard University Press, Cambridge, Massachusetts, 1950.
THOMPSON, HUNTER S., *Hell's Angels*, Random, New York, 1956. (Penguin edition, 1967).
THOMPSON, LAURA, *Culture in Crisis*, Harper, New York, 1950.
TOMKINS, SYLVAN, "The Psychology of Being Right—and Left," *Trans-Action*, November-December, 1965.
TREVELYAN, G. M., *England Under the Stuarts*, Penguin, Harmondsworth, 1960 (first published 1904).
TROW, MARTIN, *Right Wing Radicalism and Political Intolerance, A Study of Support for McCarthy in a New England Town*, doctoral dissertation, Columbia University, New York, 1957.
TRUMBULL, CHARLES, *Anthony Comstock*, Revell, New York, 1913.
TURNER, F. J., *The Frontier in American History*, Holt, New York, 1920.

VERMEIL, EDMOND, *The German Scene*, Harrap, London, 1956.
VIDICH, ARTHUR, and BENSMAN, JOSEPH, *Small Town in Mass Society*, Doubleday Anchor, Garden City, 1960 (first published 1958).

WALLACE, ANTHONY, "Handsome Lake and the Great Revival in the West," *American Quarterly*, 1952, *4*, pp. 149-65.
——, "Stress and Rapid Personality Change," *International Record of Medicine*, 1956a, *169*, pp. 761-63.
——, "Revitalization Movement," *American Anthropologist*, 1956b, *58*, pp. 264-79.
WALTERS, RICHARD, et al., "Enhancement of Punitive Behavior by Audiovisual Displays," *Science*, 1962, *136*, pp. 872-73.
WALTERS, RICHARD, and THOMAS, E. L., "Enhancement of Punitiveness by

Visual and Audiovisual Displays," *Canadian Journal of Psychology*, 1963, *16*, pp. 244-55.
WARNER, LLOYD, and SROLE, LEO, *The Social System of American Ethnic Groups*, Yale University Press, New Haven, 1945.
WEBSTER, H.; SANFORD, R. N.; and FREEDMAN, M., "A New Instrument for Studying Authoritarianism in Personality," *Journal of Psychology*, 1955, *40*, pp. 73-84.
WEDGWOOD, C. V., "The Cromwells at Whitehall," *History Today*, September, 1958.
WEST, D. J., *Murder Followed by Suicide*, Harvard University Press, Cambridge, Massachusetts, 1966.
WESTLEY, WILLIAM, A., "Violence and the Police," *American Journal of Sociology*, 1953, *59*, pp. 34-41.
WHALEN, RICHARD, *The Founding Father*, The Story of Joseph P. Kennedy, New American Library, New York, 1964.
WHITE, R. W., ed., *The Study of Lives*, Atherton, New York, 1966.
WHITE, THEODORE, *The Making of the President, 1964*, Atheneum, New York, 1965.
WHYTE, WILLIAM H., *The Organization Man*, Simon & Schuster, New York, 1956.
WILKINSON, RUPERT, *The Prevention of Drinking Problems, Alcohol Control and Cultural Influences*, Oxford University Press, New York, 1970.
———, *The Prefects*, Oxford University Press, 1964 (New York edition, *Gentlemanly Power*).
WILLIAMS, J. ALLEN, "Regional Differences in Authoritarianism," *Social Forces*, 1966, *45*, pp. 273-75.
WILLIAMS, ROBERT J., and WRIGHT, CHARLES, "Opinion Organization in a Heterogeneous Adult Population," *Journal of Abnormal and Social Psychology*, 1955, *51*, pp. 559-64.
WINSLOW, OLA, *Jonathan Edwards*, Macmillan, New York, 1940.
WOLFINGER, RAYMOND, "Clientele of the Christian Anti-Communism Crusade," paper read at American Political Science Association, meeting, New York, September, 1963.
WOODCOCK, GEORGE, and AVAKUMOVIK, IVAN, *The Doukhobors*, Faber, London, 1968.
WOODWARD, C. VANN, *Tom Watson: Agrarian Rebel*, Oxford University Press (Galaxy edition), New York, 1963 (first published, 1938).
WOOLF, LEONARD, *Sowing: An Autobiography of the Years 1880-1904*, Harcourt, New York, 1960.
WOOTTON, BARBARA, *Crime and the Criminal Law*, Stevens, London, 1963.

YANG, C. K., *The Chinese Family in the Communist Revolution*, Technology Press (M.I.T.), Cambridge, Massachusetts, 1959.

INDEX

abolitionism, 99-100, 121, 230, 232-3
activism, political, 18
addicts, police and, 255-6
Adorno, T. W., 1-6, 21, 122*n*, 195
affluence, authority and, 271-2
aggression, 21-2, 39-40
  communism, 147
  cynicism, 22
  displacement (*see also* Displacement), 34
  hostility, 22
  moralism, 9, 27
  Nazism, 154-5
  puritan curbs on, 96-7*n*
  ritual and, 69
alcoholism and drunkenness, Southern, 236-7*n*
Algeria, 74, 76
Allen, William Sheridan, 211, 216
Almond, Gabriel, 247
aloneness, 69-72
Alor, 73, 76
Altbach, Philip, 287*n*
American Opinion, 251
anarchism, concern with, 140-1
animals, fondness for, 188
anomie, 69-72
  Nazi, 209-10
anti-authoritarianism, 97*n*
  oversimplification of, rigid, 25
  rigid, 25, 115-36
anti-Catholicism, 131, 208, 212-13, 252

anti-Communism, 248-50, 252
  Nazi, 212, 218
anti-intellectualism, 24, 76, 204
  Nazi, 204, 213
anti-Semitism, 20, 28
  father hatred and, 222*n*
  Frank case, Watson and, 132-4
  German Nazi, 3, 160-2, 169-80, 184, 189, 192-4, 197, 203, 221-2
  German, pre-Nazi, 207, 208
  South, white American, 233
  United States, 2-3, 20, 233
Arendt, Hannah, 174-5
Aryanism, German (*see also* Anti-Semitism), 167-8, 178, 191
Atlanta (Ga.), Frank case, 132-4
Authoritarian Personality, The (Adorno *et al.*), 1-6, 12, 18, 20-1, 26, 28, 36, 52ff., 122*n*, 153, 243
authority, and attitudes toward, 1, 21-9, 44
  affluence and, 271
  diffusion, 271
  future, social change and, 270-5
  Nazi, 157-9, 188-9, 199-201
  parents, *see* Father relationships; Mother relationships; Parent relationships
  personality structure and, 31-7
  psychology (discipline) and, 271-80
  sexuality and, 27
  social sciences and, 271-80

authority (cont'd)
  traditional, 43-5
autonomy, drive for, 31

Baarova, Lida, 187
Babbitt (Lewis), 241-3, 269
Bacon, M. K., 237*n*
Bales, R. F., 111*n*
Banton, Michael, 236-7*n*
Barringer, Diana, 101*n*
Bay, Christian, 116*n*
behavior, 3-29
  degrees and dimensions of, 45-6
  disposition and, 39-40, 43-5
  police, under stress, 252-6
  science as authority and, 274-80
  situational authoritarianism, 46-8
  traditional, 43-5
Bettelheim, Bruno, 36, 40, 64-6, 257
bias, research, 243-4
bigness, opposition to, 142-3
biographies, historical, 11-12
Birch Society, 232, 243, 249-51, 305
Bishop, Bridget, 94
Bismarck, 187, 208, 213
black Americans, 111
  civil rights movement, 305
  hostility to blacks, 258-9
  oppression phobia, 256-7
  police behavior, 253-6
  regression, 257
  religion, 257
  "Sambo" character, 257
  Southern attitudes, *see* South, white American
  submissiveness, 259
Black Panthers, 258
Black Power, 243*n*, 258
Blanchard, William, 124
"boy scout" personality, 28
Brown, Joseph, 131
brutality
  investigations, scientific, of, 275-6
  Nazis, 155, 189, 194-5, 196
  rationalization, authoritative, 172
Bullock, Alan, 167, 198, 201
Butler, Samuel, 15-18, 71*n*

Caldwell, Taylor, 251
Calvinism, revival of (*see also* Protestantism; Puritanism), 97-9
Cash, W. J., 230, 232, 236, 237*n*, 237
caste culture, American Southern, 225, 230-2
Catholicism, 100
  anti-Catholicism, 131, 208, 212-13, 252
  confessional, 90
  German, 185-6, 192, 202, 208, 212-13
  Irish, 101-2, 103
  persecution of, 95
  puritanism of, 101
  purgatory, 95
censorship, political, 140, 142
characteristics, authoritarian, 1, 18-19, 21-9
Chesterton, G. K., 89
children (*see also* Youth)
  achievement pressures, 71, 286-7
  aggression, displaced, 51-2
  anal concerns, 57
  anti-authoritarian, 118-20
  attitudes toward, 118-19
  collectivized care, 282-4
  education, *see* Education
  father-dominated families, 54-8
  fathers and, *see* Father relationships
  gangs, criminal, 59
  German, rearing, 156-9, 206-10, 213
  heredity and susceptibility, 61, 103
  homosexuality, 57-8
  hostility, infantile, 36-7*n*
  kibbutz care, 283
  mobility values, parental, and, 70-1
  morality, development of, 32-3
  mother-dominated families, 59-61
  mothers and, *see* Mother relationships
  Oedipal relationships, *see* Oedipal relationships
  one-parent family, 58-9
  outside influences on, 61
  patterns of rearing, 5, 51-62
  pecking order, 43
  prejudiced, 52-3
  puritanism, 100
  rearing and care, reform of, 282-6
  repressive upbringing, 51-62
  self-confidence, lack of, 59
  sibling relationships, 61
  social disorganization and, 67-9
  Spock ethos, 285-6
  status concern, parental, 70-1
China
  Communism, 30, 212
  Imperial, 72
  puritanism, Red Guard, 147
  Taiping Rebellion, 76-88, 163
cleanliness, concern with, 26-7, 57, 145-6
  communism, 148
  elitism, 144
  Nazism, 148, 197-8
  radical right, 144-5, 148
Cohn, Norman, 222*n*
Coles, Robert, 10, 226-30, 234, 236-7*n*

colleges and universities
  conservatism, 248-50
  elitism and authoritarianism, 280-1
  psychiatric disorders, student, 287n
  restructuring, 286-9
  student character and cultural conflict, 295-312
command organizations, 253-4
communism, 147-8
  anti-communism, 248-50, 252
  China, 30, 147, 212
  cleanliness ethic, 148
  depersonalization of class struggle, 148
  Germany, 212, 218
  out-group scapegoats, 148
  susceptibility to conversion to, 30
  United States, 246-8
compensation and denial, 41-2
Comstock, Anthony, 124-9
concentration camps, 169, 176-80
  experimentation, 170
  prisoner behavior, 36, 40, 64-6
conflict, 44
  cultural, study of college students and, 295-312
  value, 73-4, 83-8, 103-11
conformism
  communism, 147
  orthodoxy, cultural, 89-102, 103-11
conscience, 31-8
conservatism
  campus, 248-50
  moderate, and radical right, 140-1
  radical right, backgrounds of, 244, 248-9
conspiracy theory, 142
  Hitler, 197
conventionalism, rigid, 26-7, 65
conversion hysteria, 84
Crafts, Rev. Wilbur, 237
criminals
  antagonism toward, 43, 44n
  conventionalism, 26
  gangs, youth, 59
  projection, 36
  punishment, changing attitudes toward, 272-3
Cromwell, Oliver, 313, 316-19
culture (*see also* Environment, social)
  conflicts, 73-4, 83-8, 103-11
  humaneness, 170-2
  industrialization and value systems, 69-71, 74-6
  initiative, 107
  invasion and social change, 74-6
  mass, 271
  orthodoxy, 89-102, 103-11
  pre-industrial, 71-4
cynicism, 22, 28, 274
  Nazis, 193-5

Daily People, 132
Darré, Walter, 167
Davis, Allison, 10, 260, 262-3
Day of Doom, The (Wigglesworth), 92, 95
definitions, 1, 42-3
degrees of authoritarianism, 45-6
De Leon, Daniel, 132
demography, 281
Demos, John, 96-7n
Denmark, child care, 283
Dennison, George, 286
dependency, drive for, 31
depersonalization, 148
detection of authoritarianism, 39-48
Dicks, Henry, 53-4, 153-9, 206, 213, 247
displacement, 34
  infantile, 37n
  Nazi, 154, 174-5
  puritanism, 89, 91, 97n
disposition, 30-1
  behavior and, 39-40
  and cultural conflict, college students, 295-312
  culture and, 73-4
  innate, 61, 103
  political beliefs and, 137-48
  situational behavior and, 48
dissociation, 41
Doenitz, Karl, 219
Dollard, John, 10, 236, 260, 262-3
Doukhobors, 108-11
drives, emotional, 31
DuBois, Cora, 73

economy
  anomie, 70
  China and Taiping rebellion, 79
  Germany and Nazism, 206-9, 212
Edmonsen, Munro S., 260
education, 61
  adult, 289
  child care, 283-5
  college and university, restructuring (*see also* Colleges and Universities), 286-9
  Germany, 208-9, 211, 220
  work-study programs, 288
Edwards, Jonathan, 97-9, 103, 241
ego, 31-8
Einstein, Albert, 75

384 INDEX

elitism, 143
  cleanliness ethic, 144
  of educated, 280-1
  fascist, 140
  Protestant, 90
  radical right, 140
Elkins, Stanley, 257-9
environment, social
  character and, 5-6
  childhood background and effect of, 64
  concentration camps, and inmate behavior, 36, 40, 64-6
  disorganization of, 67-71, 74-88, 103-11
  eliciting effect of, 63-4
  industrialized, 69-70, 75-6
  pre-industrial, 71-4
  social change, 74-6
  value conflicts, 73-4
Erikson, Erik, 158, 209
Escape from Freedom (Fromm), 69
ethics, 33
evangelicism, 89-90
  Southern, white American, 230, 236
evolutionism, social, 141

fantasy
  authoritarian expression in, 39
  as measure of authoritarianism, 45-6
  rejection of, 23-4
fascism, 139-40
fatalism, 24, 147
father, relationships with (*see also* Parent relationships)
  anti-Semitism and, 222*n*
  cruelty and hatred, 59
  death of mother, early, 58-9
  dominance of family, 54-8
  homosexuality and, 58
  identification, 54-5, 59, 122
  Nazis, 154, 157-9, 198-201
  prejudice and, 52-3, 222*n*
  repressive, 51-62
  resentment, 55
  threatening, psychically, 59
fear and shame, 31-2
films, dynamics of revenge in, 279*n*
Flagellants, 95
Fleming, Ian, 279*n*
Flisger, Richard, 183
France
  communists, 247-8
  radical right, 142
Frank, Hans, 8, 189-93, 214, 219
Frank, Leo, 132-4
Frederick the Great, 186-7, 213

Frenkel-Brunswick, Else, 52-3
Freud, Sigmund, 75
Fromm, Erich, 18, 69-71, 73, 74, 211
frontier culture, Southern American, 230-1
F scale studies, 5-6, 54, 57-8, 71, 268
fundamentalism, 89
  black Americans, 257
  radical right, 251-52

Gant, Patrick, 235-6
Garrison, William Lloyd, 121
generation gap, 270-1
genesis of authoritarianism
  aloneness (anomie), 69-72
  childhood, pressures of, 5, 51-62
  disorganization, social, 67-71, 74-88
  environment, social, 63-102
  mobility, social, 42-3, 70-1
  orthodoxies, cultural, 89-102
  pre-industrial societies, 71-4
  theory, general, 103-11
George, Stefan, 183
Georgia, 235-6
Germany (*see also* Nazis and Nazi Germany)
  anti-Semitism, 207, 208
  child rearing, 156-9, 206-10, 213
  class antagonisms, 208-9, 215-17
  communists, 212, 218
  economy, 206-9
  education, 208-9, 211, 220
  industrialization, 207-8
  intolerance, political, 208-9, 211
  Kulturkampf, 208, 213
  militarism, 209, 211, 216-17
  nationalism, 207-13
  violence, readiness for, 211-12
  ultra-Prussianism, 206
  Weimar Republic, 193
  World War I period, 206-7, 210-11
Gilbert, G. M., 163-4, 177, 192-4, 207*n*
Glazer, Nathan, 111*n*
Glover, Arthur, 131
Goebbels, Joseph, 8, 175, 180-90, 196, 214
  culture conflicts, 181-2
  examination failure, 182
  Hitler and, 184-6, 188-9
  hostility, 187-8
  influence, 220
  qualms, 189
  religion, 182-3, 185-6
  sexuality, 185-7
  submissiveness, 183-4, 219
  superstition, 188
Goering, Hermann, 193-4, 202, 208-9

Golding, William, 67-9, 71
Goldwater, Barry, 141-2, 232, 243
  campus followers, 248-9, 298, 300, 303
Great Awakening (Calvinist revival), 97-9, 103
Great Britain
  education, 286-9
Griffin, John Howard, 235, 238, 239n
guilt, 31-2
  puritanism, 89-95
Gundolph, Friedrich, 183

habit, 32
Hagen, Louis, 159-62
heredity, 61, 103
hero worship, 19
Hersey, John, 254n
Hess, Rudolph, 193
Heydrich, Reinhard, 166-7, 169
Himmler, Heinrich, 8, 164-70, 179, 180, 182, 191
  anti-Semitism, 221
  anxiety and insecurity, 166
  illnesses, 165-6, 176
  influence, 220
  nationalism, 208-9
  parent relationships, 164-5
  religion, 213
  sadism–tenderness conflict, 168-70, 172-6
  scientism, 167-9
  submissiveness, 166-7
  suicide, 177, 178
Hitler, Adolf (see also Nazis and Nazi Germany), 8-9, 196-205
  anti-intellectualism, 204, 213
  anti-Semitism and, 197, 203-4, 221-2
  attitudes toward, 160, 162, 166, 170, 175-6, 184-90, 192-4
  brutality, 213
  charisma, 218-19
  cleanliness, preoccupation with, 197-8
  conspiracy theory, 197
  domination, 196
  edginess, 196
  executive followers of (see also names), 8, 163-95
  as father figure, 154, 194
  father, relationships with, 199-201
  homosexuality, 200, 214-15
  hostility, 196-7
  nationalism, 208-9
  psychosomatic illnesses, 196
  Putsch, 190
  religicizing of, 210, 214
  religion, 201-3, 210
  Roehm purge, 190, 195
  sadism, 8
  self-pity, 204
  sexuality, 197-8, 214-15
  status concerns, appeal to, 216
  submissiveness, 198-203
  superstition and prejudice, 24
Hitler, Alois, 198-9
Hitler, Klara, 198-9
Hoess, Rudolph, 8, 176-80
Hofstadter, Richard, 243-4, 278
homosexuality, 57-8
  cultural conflict, 74
  Nazism, 154, 157, 169, 214-15
  South, white American, 235-6
Hoover, J. Edgar, 256
hostility, 22, 35
  anomie, 70
  blacks to blacks, 258-9
  infantile, 36-7n
  Nazis, 187-8, 196-7
  targets of, 39
Huie, William Bradford, 234n, 239
humaneness, 170-2
  increase of, 272-5
  Nazism, 169-70, 173-6, 178-80, 189-92, 194, 214
humanitarianism
  Protestant, 91, 99-100
Hung Siu-tshuen, and Taiping Rebellion, 76-88, 163, 182
Hutterites, 108, 110
hypochondria, 247

idealism, Jeffersonian, 248-9
ideologies (see also specific ideologies)
  interrelationships of, 143-4
  repressive, 89-102, 103-11
identification of authoritarianism, 39-48
identity, sense of, 33
imagination, impairment of, 25, 36
impulses, 31-8, 39, 106-7
individualism, frontier, 230-1
industrialization, 69-71
  elitism, intellectual, 280-1
  future, 270-1
  Germany, 208-9
  Japan, 75-6
  pre-industrial societies, 71-4
inferiority feelings, see Weakness, feelings of
in-group mystique, 139-40
initiative, cultural and moral, 107
intellectual ability, 25
introspection, 291-3
  compatibility with authoritarian processes, 135-6

introspection (*cont'd*)
  dangers of, 293n
  pre-emptive, 275
  proscription of, 24, 27
Irish and Irish Americans
  Catholicism, 101-2, 103
  family relationships, 60-1, 111n
Italian Americans, 60-1, 101
Italian Communists, 247-8

Jackson, Bruce, 255-6
Japan, 74-6, 141
Johnson, Andrew, 123

Kardiner, Abram, 258-267
Kaufman, Karl, 184
Keniston, Kenneth, 122n
Kersten, Felix, 166-7, 169, 174-6
King, Martin Luther, 234n
Klansman, The (Huie), 234n, 239
Krugman, Herbert, 246-8
Ku Klux Klan, 75, 143, 231

Lane, Robert, 248, 297
language, moralism and, 277-9
Lanier, Sidney, 126
Lasswell, Harold, 18
law-and-order concern, 63-4, 72, 141, 281
left-wing movements (*see also* Communism)
  mental health profession and, 277-8
Lenin, 190
Levin, Max, 254n
Lewis, Sinclair, 241-3
liberalism, authoritarian, 25, 115-36
Lifton, Robert, 4, 75-6, 273
Lindbergh, Charles, 246
Lipset, Seymour, 101, 287n
literature on authoritarianism, deficiencies of, 4-6
Lord of the Flies, The (Golding), 67-9
Lowenthal, Leo, 20
Lucier, Jim, 251
Luther, Martin, 71, 313-16

Making of the President, The (White), 234n
Martin, Suzanna, 94
martyr complex, 122n
Maruyamah, Masao, 74-6
Marx, Karl, 75
masochism, 154
Massachusetts witch hunts, 91-7, 103
mass media, influence of, 273-4
Mather, Cotton, 90

McClean, Helen, 225-6
McCloskey, Herbert, 69-70
McCord, William and Joan, 237n
Mead, George Herbert, 43
Mein Kampf (Hitler), 199-200, 203-4
mental health care, science as authority and, 276-80
Michael (Goebbels), 183-4
Milgram, S., 275n
militarism, 143-4
  admiration for, 142
  Germany, 209, 211, 216-17
Miller, Arthur, 269n
Mind of the South, The (Cash), 230
Mississippi, 18, 232, 238
mobility, social, 42-3, 70-1
  China, 81-2
  radical right, 244-5
  rebelliousness and, 84
Moonraker (Fleming), 279n
moralism, 9, 26-7
  communism, 147
  Hung and Taiping rebellion, 76-88 *passim*
  language, psychiatric, use of, 277-9
  police behavior and, 254-6
  puritanism, 85-7, 88-102
  science as authority and, 276-80
morality
  development of, 32-3
  humaneness, 170-2
  initiative, 107
  segregation code, 225-6
  value conflicts, 73
mother relationships (*see also* Parent relationships)
  death of mother, early, 58-9
  father-dominated family, 54-7
  mother-dominated family, 59-61
  Nazis, 152, 154, 157-9, 194, 199-200
  prejudice and, 52-3
Moynihan, Daniel P., 111n
Muir, John, 100

Napoleon, 130, 133
narcissism, 33, 35
Nation, Carry, 129n
nationalism, 139-40, 143
  radical right, 142-4
  German, 158-9, 193, 207-13
nativism, 250
Nazis and Nazi Germany (*see also* Germany; names), 8-9, 151-222
  aggression, 154-5
  anomie, 209-10
  anti-Semitism, 3, 160-2, 169-80, 184, 189, 192-4, 197, 203, 221-2

Nazis and Nazi Germany (cont'd)
  authority, attitude toward, 157-9, 188-9, 199-201, 212-13
  brutality, 155, 189, 194-5, 196, 213
  characteristics, pro-Nazi, 153-9
  cleanliness ethic, 148
  concentration camps, 36, 40, 64-6, 169, 170, 176-80
  corruption and profiteering, 164
  cynicism, 193-5
  economic program, 212
  Hitler (see also Hitler, Adolf), 8-9, 196-205
  homosexuality, 154, 157-8, 169, 193, 200, 214-15
  hostility, 187-8, 196-7
  humaneness and qualms, 169-70, 173-76, 178-80, 189-92, 194, 214
  influence, cultural, 219-22
  leadership (see also names), 8-9, 163-205, 217-22
  nationalism, 158-9, 193
  neurosis, 155-6
  nihilism, 195, 213
  Old Fighters, 163-4
  parents, relationships with, 152, 154, 157-9, 194, 198-201, 213
  Poland, 191, 213
  projection, 155
  psychosomatic illness, 155, 166-7, 176
  racism (see also Nazi and Nazi Germany, anti-Semitism), 167-8, 178, 191
  religion, 185-6, 192, 201-2, 210, 212-13
  restorationism, 141, 212-13, 217
  sadism, 154-5
  secondary rebellion, 156, 158-9, 213
  sexuality, 152, 154, 157-8, 185-7, 197-8, 200, 214-15
  tenderness taboo, 154, 206
  totalitarianism, 214, 220
  violence, legitimization of, 211-12
  woman, study of an authoritarian, 159-61
  women, attitudes toward, 152, 154, 157-9
  youth organizations, 158, 161, 220
neurosis, Nazism, 155-6
New England
  Calvinist revival, 97-9, 103
  Salem witch hunts, 91-7, 103
New Left, 243
New York City, 234n
New York Times, The, 248-9
nihilism, 195
North, American, 243n

Oedipal relationships, 42, 54-8, 62, 122, 158-9, 199-201, 239-40
  inverted, 58, 122, 156-7, 159
  South, white American, 239-40
Ogilvy, David, 18
oppression phobia, blacks, 256-7
organization, personality, 30-8
orthodoxy, cultural, 89-102, 103-11
oversimplification, 25
Ovesey, Lionel, 267

paranoia, white Americans, South, 239-40
parent relationships (see also Father relationships; Mother relationships)
  anti-authoritarian and authoritarian compared, 122-4
  de-emphasis of, 271
  one-parent family, 58-9
  re-education in child care, 282-6
Parris, Betty, 92-7
Parris, Rev. Samuel, 92
pecking order, 43
permissiveness, increase in, 271-4
Plymouth colony, 96-7n
Podhoretz, Norman, 291-2
Poland, Germany and, 191, 213
police behavior under stress, 252-6
political beliefs, character structure and (see also specific ideologies), 137-48
population explosion, 281
Populism, 129-34, 231
Poujadism, 142
power-mindedness, 22-3, 40-2
power, radical right attitude toward, 142-3
pre-industrial societies, 71-4
prejudice (see also Anti-Semitism), 9
  blacks against blacks, 258-9
  in children, 52-3
  superstition and, 24
prevention of authoritarianism, 281-93
  child care, reform of, 282-6
  education reform, 286-9
  strength, redefinition of, 289-91
Price, The (Miller), 269n
Progressives, 244
projection, 27-8, 34
  Nazism, 155
  puritanism, 89, 91, 97n
  threat complex, 28
  sexual, 27, 34
Protestantism, 69-71
  Calvinist revival, 97-9, 103
  elitism, 90
  fundamentalism, 89, 251-52, 257
  humanitarianism, 91, 99-100

Protestantism (*cont'd*)
  puritanism, 88-102, 313-19
  revivalism of 1830's, 99-100
Prothro, J. W., 257*n*
psychology (discipline), influence of, 270-80
psychism, 116
  Himmler, 167, 168
  Hitler, 201-2
  Hung and Taiping Rebellion, 77-8, 81, 84
psychosomatic illness, 84
  Nazis, 155, 166-7, 176, 196
puritanism
  aggression, curbs on, 96-7*n*
  anti-Catholicism, 252
  displacement, 89, 91, 97*n*
  humanitarianism, 91
  Luther and Cromwell, 313-19
  Hung and Taiping Rebellion, 5-7
  projection, 89, 91, 97*n*
  Southern, white American, 225-6, 230, 236
  state communism, 147
  witch hunts, Salem (Mass.), 91-7
Putnam, Ann, 92-7

racism (*see also* Anti-Semitism)
  Nazi, 167-8, 178, 191
  "scientific," 168, 230
  South, white American, 225-40
  stereotypes, 25
radical right, 137-43, 243-52
  campus, 248-50
  cleanliness ethic, 144-5
  conservatism of backgrounds, 244, 248-9
  conspiracy theory, 142
  elitism, 140
  fascism, 139-40
  fundamentalism, 251-52
  Japan, 75-6
  mental health professions and, 277-8
  mobility, social, 244-5
  Nazism, *see* Nazis and Nazi Germany
  power, attitudes toward, 142-3
  restorationism, 141-2
  South, white American, 232-3, 239
  status concern, 244-5
  status quo, 143
  terrorism, 75
Rand, Ayn, 141
Rasputin, 186-7
reaction formation, 121, 123, 193
reason, development of, 30
rebelliousness/rebellion
  conflict, 44
  diversion of, 44
  Oedipal, repression of (*see also* Oedipal relationships), 42, 54-6
  repression of, 1, 23, 34, 41
  secondary, 119-20, 123, 142, 156, 158-9, 213
  social disorganization and, 83-4
  underdog crusades as extension of, 120-21
  witchcraft delusion, 92-4
reform movement, 99-100
regression, 36
religion (*see also* Catholicism; Protestantism)
  Nazi, 185-6, 192, 201-2, 210, 212-13
  orthodoxies, 89-102
  Southern, white American, 225
  triangular model of authoritarian development, 108-11
repression, 29, 34-6
  conflict and, 44
  emotional, 26
Reston, James, 248-9
restorationism, 141-2
  Japan, 75-6, 141
  Nazi, 141, 212-13, 217
  South, white American, 232
Rhodesia, 233
right wing, *see* Radical right
ritual, aggression and, 69
Roberts, Rev. Issachar J., 79
Roehm, Ernst, 190, 195, 202
Rohrer, John, 260, 266
Rohter, Ira, 244-5
Rosenberg, Alfred, 167, 168, 178, 213
Rousseau, Jean-Jacques, 124

sadism, 9, 44
  Nazism, 154-5
  South, white American, 225, 237-9
sado-masochism, 69, 85, 98
Salem (Mass.) witch hunts, 91-7, 103
Sanford, Nevitt, 23, 36, 245-6
Sartre, Jean-Paul, 18
scapegoats, 19, 34, 121, 123
Schaar, John, 69-70
Schellenberg, Walter, 167
schizophrenics, Irish and Italian compared, 60-1, 101
schools, *see* Colleges and universities; Education
science and pseudo-science, 9
  authority and, 271-80
  moralism, 276-80
  Nazi, 167-9
  racism, 168, 230
  superstition as, 96

INDEX 389

Schiff, Lawrence, 249-50
self-analysis, *see* Introspection
self-censorship, 23-9
self-criticism, pre-emptive, 274-5
self-dislike, 35
   Oedipal repression and, 55
self-esteem, 33, 40
self-love, 33-5
self-pity, Nazis, 174-5, 204
Sewall, Samuel, 93, 97
sexuality, 9, 27, 34
   cultural conflicts, 74
   family relationships and, 51-62
   homosexuality, 57-8, 74, 154, 157-8, 169, 193, 200, 214-15, 235-6
   Irish Catholicism, 101
   Nazi, 152, 154, 157-8, 185-7, 197-8, 200, 214-215
   Oedipal, 42, 54-8, 62, 239-40
   South, white American, 225-6, 234-40
   witchcraft delusion, 93-4
   vote appeal, 214
siblings, influence of, 61
Sidi Khaled, Algeria, 74, 76
Sidran, Ben, 257*n*
Silver, James, 232
Sinclair, Andrew, 129*n*
situational authoritarianism, 46-8
Slaton, John, 133-4
Smith, C. U., 257*n*
Smith, Hoke, 131
social change, 74-6, 103-11
   future, authoritarianism and, 270-5
social revitalization movements, 78
social sciences, influence of, 271-80
Sons of Freedom, 108-11
South Africa, 233-4
South, white American, 9, 111, 225-40
   abolitionism, 230, 232-3
   alcoholism and drunkenness, 236-7*n*
   anti-Semitism, 233
   caste culture, 225, 230-2
   economy, 231-2
   frontier individualism, 230-1
   hedonism, 230
   homosexuality, 235-6
   Ku Klux Klan, 75, 143, 231
   paranoia, 239-40
   Populism, 129-34, 231
   puritanism, 225-6, 230, 236
   religion, 225
   restorationism, social, 232
   right-wing movements, 232-3, 239
   sadism, 225, 237-9
   sexuality, 225-6, 234-40
   status, concern with, 231
   violence, 230-1, 237-8
   women, attitudes toward, 236, 239-40
Spengler, Oswald, 190
spontaneity, 36
   distrust of, 23-4
Srole, Leo, 111*n*
Ssu-Yu Teng, 85
Starkey, Marion, 10, 93-4, 97
status concern, 53, 244
   cleanliness concern, 57
   failure to achieve, rebellion and, 84
   mobility, social, 70-1
   pre-industrial societies, 71-4
   prejudice in children and, 53
   radical right, 244-5
   South, white American, 231
status quo, appeal of, 141, 143
stereotypes, 25, 26, 28
   humaneness and, 171
Story of France, The (Watson), 129-31
Stoughton, William, 96
Strasser, Gregor, 184-5, 187
Strasser, Otto, 184-5
Straus, Oscar, 190
Strecher, Ivo, 215*n*
Streicher, Julius, 197
strength
   masculinity, 26
   redefinition, need for, 289-91
structure, personality, 30-8
submissiveness, 21, 34-5, 39-40
   father-dominated family, 54-7
   identification, 40-1
suicide, 35
superstition, 24, 28
   masked as science, 96
   Nazi, 188
suppression, 29
syndrome, authoritarian, 21-9

Taiping Rebellion, 76-88, 163
Tappan, Arthur, 99-100
tenderness, attitudes toward, 39
   approving, need for, 289-91
   authoritarian and rigid rebel compared, 122-4
   father-dominated family, 54-5
   Nazism, 154, 206, 214
tension, individual and social, 106-7
terrorism, Japan, 75
tests and testing authorities
   China, examination system, 72, 77, 81-5
   failure to satisfy, 71*n*, 77, 85, 182
Texas, 231

threat complex, 27-8
  homosexuality and, 58
  Nazi, 155
Tituba, 92
Tocqueville, Alexis de, 254n
toughness, 22-3
Truee, 157
Turner, Frederick Jackson, 231

United States (*see also* subjects), 9, 241-69
  Communists, 246-8
  rightist movements, *see* Radical right
  Salem (Mass.) witch hunts, 91-7
  South (*see also* South, white American), 225-40
universities, *see* Colleges and universities

value conflicts, 73-4, 83-8, 103-11
victimization, sense of, 27-8
violence
  Germany, readiness for, 211-12
  humaneness and, 170-72
  police behavior, 253
  South, white American, 230-1, 237-8
  vicarious enjoyment of, 44-5

Wallace, Anthony, 78
Wallace, George, 232, 250
Wallace, Henry, 246
Warner, Lloyd, 111n
Watson's Jeffersonian Magazine, 132-3
Watson, Tom, 129-34, 226, 231n, 241
Way of All Flesh, The (Butler), 15-18
weakness, feelings of, 1, 20-9, 34-5, 40

compensation and denial, 41-2
Nazism, 156
rebelliousness, repression of, 41-2
Welch, Robert, 305
Weld, Theodore, 99-100
White, Theodore, 234n
Whyte, William H., 302
Wigglesworth, Michael, 92, 95
Williams, Abigail, 92-7
witch hunts, Salem (Mass.), 91-7, 103
women, *see* Mothers; Women, attitudes toward; Women, authoritarian
women, attitudes toward, 117-18
  American, 231, 236
  father-dominated family, 54-7
  Nazi, 152, 154, 157-9, 186-7, 214
women, authoritarian
  China, Imperial, 72
  father-dominated family, 55-7
  homosexuality, 58
  Nazi, 159-61
  Oedipal feelings, 55-6
  power urge, 23
Woodward, C. Vann, 130-31, 134, 231n
work ethic, 27

Yang Hsiu-ching, 81, 87
Young Americans for Freedom, 249
youth (*see also* Children)
  achievement pressures, 71, 286-9
  conservatism, 248-50
  education, *see* Education
  examinations, failure at, 71n, 77, 85, 182, 287
  Nazi organizations, 158, 161, 220
  psychiatric disorders, 287n
  social disorganization and, 69-76